The HOW-TO *Book of*
HEALTHY COOKING

READER'S DIGEST

The **HOW-TO** *Book of*

HEALTHY COOKING

Reader's
Digest

The Reader's Digest Association, Inc.
Pleasantville, New York/Montreal

THE HOW-TO BOOK OF HEALTHY COOKING
was created and produced by Carroll & Brown Limited.

Project Editor	*Madeline Weston*
Editors	*Anne Hildyard, Patricia Shine*
Art Editor	*Lisa V. Webb*
Designers	*André-Scott Bamforth, Simon Daley*
Recipe Developer	*Anna Brandenburger*
Recipe Testers	*Marthajean White, Jean Galton*
Photographers	*David Murray, Jules Selmes*
Photographer's Assistants	*Nick Allen, Sid Sideris*
Food for Photography	*Eric Treuillé*
Home Economist	*Maddalena Bastianelli*
Production Consultant	*Lorraine Baird*
Production	*Wendy Rogers, Amanda Mackie*
Colour reproduction	*Colourscan, Singapore*

FOR READER'S DIGEST

Project Editor	*Lee Fowler*
Senior Art Editors	*Joan Mazzeo, Henrietta Stern*
Copy Editor	*Virginia Croft*
Prepress Manager	*Garry Hansen*
Quality Control Manager	*Ann Kennedy Harris*

Printed in the United States of America

Library of Congress Cataloging in Publication Data
The how-to book of healthy cooking
  p.   cm.
  Includes index
  ISBN 0-89577-789-4 (hard cover)
  1. Cookery.   2. Low-fat diet – Recipes.   3. Low-cholesterol diet –
Recipes.   4 Salt-free diet – Recipes.   5. Sugar-free diet – Recipes.
I. Reader's Digest Association.   II. Reader's digest.
TX714.H687   1995
641.5'63 – dc20   *95-5940*

ABOUT THIS BOOK

The How-To Book of Healthy Cooking
*shows you how to cook food that is low in fat,
cholesterol, sugar, and sodium yet high in taste.
You'll find 98 superb master recipes, each one
designed to teach a healthy cooking technique and
illustrated with easy-to-follow step-by-step photos. Every
master recipe is accompanied by two or three delicious
variations using the same basic cooking technique with
different meats, grains, fruits, and vegetables — more than
400 recipes in all. There are also beautiful color photographs
of each master recipe and many of the variations, so you can
see what these delicious dishes look like. You will discover a
wide range of recipes, from old favorites like Chicken Pot Pie
to hearty meatless main dishes and exciting Tex-Mex and
Oriental specialities. All the recipes have been tested by a
home economist to ensure perfect results, and each one is
accompanied by a complete nutritional breakdown so that
you can eat balanced meals throughout the day. In
addition, you'll find a wealth of information on diet
and good health, from helpful hints on selecting,
storing, and cooking food to important tips about
food safety. With the help of* **The How-To Book
of Healthy Cooking**, *you can enjoy good
food and good health.*

CONTENTS

◆

Eat well, stay well 8

◆

SOUPS

◆

POULTRY

◆

FISH

◆

MEAT

◆

VEGETABLES

◆

EAT WELL, STAY WELL

I n recent years, research has shown that food has a profound effect on our health. High blood cholesterol is a risk factor in the development of heart disease, while low dietary fiber has been linked to colon cancer. However, you'll find more good news than bad, because studies show that eating the right foods can help prevent disease.

One recent study showed that people with heart disease could reduce clogging of the arteries by eating less saturated fat, more fruits, vegetables, and whole grains, and by exercising daily. Vitamin E appears to reduce the risk of cataracts, while vitamin C has been linked to lower rates of lung and colon cancer.

Of course, diet is only one factor. Getting enough exercise is very important; so are regular medical checkups. However, by eating the right foods you can increase your chances of living a long, healthy life.

The U.S. Department of Agriculture advises following the Food Guide Pyramid, eating small amounts of foods at the top of the pyramid – sugars and fats. Make the foods at the base – grains, fruits, and vegetables – the foundation of your diet. Eat the foods in the middle – milk, eggs, cheese, meat, and poultry – in moderation.

The U.S. Food Guide Pyramid has been criticized by the Harvard School of Public Health and the World Health Organization. These bodies recommend a diet similar to that eaten in Mediterranean countries, where people live longer than Americans and have fewer diet-related ill-nesses. The Mediterranean Diet Pyramid allows up to 40% of your calories from fat, so long as most of it comes from monounsaturates like canola oil or olive oil. It includes moderate amounts of dairy products and fish, and wine in moderation. But it restricts red meat to just a few servings a month.

Until new research resolves the contro-versial issues, the following guidelines reflect a consensus of current opinion.

1 REDUCE INTAKE OF FATS AND OILS

Fat, especially saturated fat, is a major factor in the development of heart disease and obesity. Nutritionists recommend that you limit consumption of saturated cooking fats, such as butter, and replace them with monounsaturates, such as olive or canola oil. Margarine contains trans-fatty acids, which act like saturated fat in the body and may increase your risk of heart disease, so eat it in limited amounts. Choose low-fat meats, poultry, and dairy products, and consume them in moderation. You should reduce your consumption of all fats to 30% of your daily calories – or better yet 20–25% – and saturated fat to 10% or less.

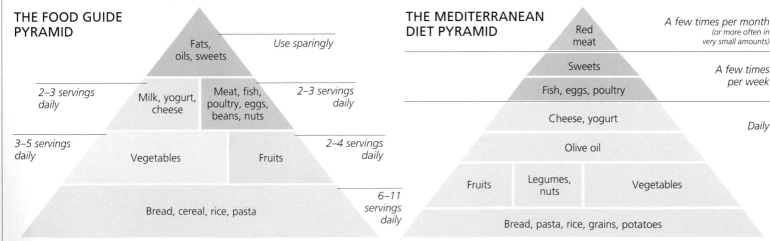

THE FOOD GUIDE PYRAMID

- Fats, oils, sweets — *Use sparingly*
- Milk, yogurt, cheese — *2–3 servings daily*
- Meat, fish, poultry, eggs, beans, nuts — *2–3 servings daily*
- Vegetables — *3–5 servings daily*
- Fruits — *2–4 servings daily*
- Bread, cereal, rice, pasta — *6–11 servings daily*

Source: U.S. Department of Agriculture U.S. Department of Health and Human Services.

A serving is: 1 slice bread or ½ cup cooked cereal, pasta, or rice; ½ cup cooked vegetables; 1 piece fruit; 1 cup milk or 1½ ounces natural cheese; 2 to 3 ounces cooked lean beef, poultry, or fish.

THE MEDITERRANEAN DIET PYRAMID

- Red meat — *A few times per month (or more often in very small amounts)*
- Sweets — *A few times per week*
- Fish, eggs, poultry
- Cheese, yogurt — *Daily*
- Olive oil
- Fruits / Legumes, nuts / Vegetables
- Bread, pasta, rice, grains, potatoes

Source: Oldways Preservation & Exchange Trust and Harvard School of Public Health.

The Mediterranean Diet Pyramid recommends regular physical excercise and permits moderate consumption of wine. Other monounsaturated fats such as canola oil can be substituted for olive oil.

2 EAT MORE FISH, LESS RED MEAT

You need 50 to 60 grams of protein a day. However, most Americans consume more than that, most of it coming from red meat and poultry, which even when lean still contain a fair amount of fat. Experts now advise eating less animal protein and increasing protein intake from whole grains and legumes, which are low in fat. Many nutritionists recommend 2 to 3 meatless meals a week. Fish is a good alternative because it is low in fat and calories, and high in protein. Fish also contains a large amount of omega-3s, fatty acids that appear to lower risk of heart disease and stroke. Although shellfish contain cholesterol, they are lower in saturated fat than red meat. And it is saturated fat, combined with low fiber intake, that is thought to raise blood cholesterol levels. It is now thought that dietary cholesterol is a secondary factor. So you can eat shellfish in moderation.

3 LOAD UP ON FRUITS AND VEGETABLES

Fruits and vegetables appear to offset the damaging effects of saturated fat. Studies have shown that people who eat large amounts of fruits and vegetables produce more "good" cholesterol (HDL), which reduces the risk of heart attack. Fruits and vegetables – especially cruciferous vegetables – also appear to lower the risk of lung, gastrointestinal, and other cancers. Nutritionists now recommend that you make sure you eat 5 servings of fruits and vegetables every day.

YOUR DAILY NUTRITIONAL REQUIREMENTS

The recipes in this book are all accompanied by nutritional breakdowns to help you plan what you eat. The guidelines below are for healthy men and women. If you have heart disease, high blood pressure, or other serious health disorders, check with your doctor.

	Men	Women
Calories	2,500–3,000	2,000
Protein	63g	50g
Total fat	60–75g	50–60g
Saturated fat	20–25g	15–20g
Cholesterol	300g	300g
Fiber	20–30g	20–30g
Carbohydrate	340mg	275mg
Sodium	2,400mg	2,400mg

4 PILE ON THE PASTA, GRAINS, AND BEANS

Many foods that we used to think of as fattening, such as pasta, bread, rice, and beans, are now thought to be good for us. They are high in complex carbohydrates, which the body turns into sugars to produce energy. Bread, cereals, whole grains, and beans are also high in dietary fiber and a good source of low-fat protein, when served together. (See page 11 for tips on protein combining.) Nutritionists now recommend eating 7 or more servings of grain, pasta, cereal, and bread a day.

5 EAT EGGS, CHEESE, AND MILK IN MODERATION

Dairy foods are a good source of calcium, which is important for older women because it combats osteoporosis. However, dairy products can also be high in saturated fat and cholesterol, so choose low-fat milk, cheese, and yogurt. Egg yolks are high in cholesterol, but they are also rich in nutrients, so you shouldn't avoid them altogether. Nutritionists recommend 4 whole eggs per week for a healthy person, just 1 yolk plus a few whites for anyone with heart disease.

6 GO EASY ON SUGAR

Refined sugar is not harmful, except for causing tooth cavities, but it has no nutritional value. Experts advise cutting back on your sugar intake. This includes honey, brown sugar, fruit sugars, and corn syrup, which are pure sugar with flavoring.

7 WATCH THE SALT AND ALCOHOL

For people who are salt sensitive, excess sodium can cause high blood pressure. If you have high blood pressure, check with your doctor and reduce sodium to 1,000mg per day or less. Eat more potassium and calcium, which appear to lower blood pressure. If your blood pressure is normal, you can enjoy salt in moderation. Drinking excessive amounts of alcohol can be addictive and cause liver damage. But several studies have shown that moderate drinkers are less likely to suffer heart attacks than non-drinkers. If you do drink, do so in moderation. Men should limit drinks to two 5-ounce glasses of wine or 2 ounces of hard liquor; women to one 5-ounce glass of wine or 1 ounce hard liquor daily.

A New Way to Cook

Eating a healthy diet doesn't mean rabbit food. You can still enjoy all of your favorite foods, like beef, pasta, pork, rice, and desserts. However, you must change the way you cook and serve them to keep your fat consumption low and increase your intake of vitamins, minerals, and fiber. It's quite easy, if you keep these five basic guidelines in mind:

Start by selecting low-fat ingredients

Choose leaner cuts of meat and poultry, and trim off the fat before cooking. When you buy ground beef, make sure that it is 90 percent lean. Most of the fat in poultry lies just under the skin, so remove the skin before eating the meat. Switch to lower-fat dairy products, and select from part-skim, nonfat, or reduced-fat cheeses. Yogurt is a good alternative to cream and is available in nonfat varieties. Use reduced-fat sour cream and evaporated skim milk in place of heavy cream. Oily fish contain more of the omega-3 fatty acids, which have a protective effect on the heart, so you can eat any fish you like. However, you should buy water-pack tuna – it contains just a trace of fat compared to 7 grams of fat in oil-packed.

Plan less meat, more vegetables, fruits, and grains

Change the emphasis of your menus, and make meat just one part of the meal instead of the centerpiece. When you cook a steak, for example, serve potato, one or two vegetables, salad, and bread. Keep the servings of meat small – about 4 ounces per person. This reduces your intake of saturated fat and cholesterol and increases intake of vitamins and fiber.

Cook with less fat

Instead of frying foods in fat, rely on methods that require little or no oil, such as grilling, broiling, roasting, and oven-frying. Drain off any fat after cooking and skim it off the top of stews. Cook fish and poultry in parchment paper, which requires just a touch of oil for flavor. If you prefer to fry food, invest in a non-stick skillet so you can cook either without fat or with a very small amount. When stir-frying, use the minimum amount of oil and heat until very hot. The oil spreads farther, so that you'll need less. Instead of using oil when sautéeing, cook onions or garlic in a little reduced-sodium stock over low heat.

Add herbs, spices, and fruit juice for flavor

Add herbs and spices to savory dishes so that you don't need salt or sugar. Use vinegar, fruit, or shredded citrus peel to accent the flavor of fish and meat recipes. Serve grilled meats and poultry with simple homemade salsas instead of salt, prepared sauces, or gravy. Replace the flavor lost when you cut down on fat by adding more fruits and vegetables to casseroles and stews. They will boost the vitamin and fiber content as well as reducing the need for seasoning. Spice up pasta dishes with a dash of Parmesan cheese. Cut back on the sugar in baked goods by mixing in fruit juice, nuts, and seeds instead. They add texture as well as flavor.

Serve more meatless meals

Cut down on saturated fat and cholesterol by getting more protein from plant sources, such as grains and legumes (dried beans, lentils, and peas). They are much lower in fat than meat and an excellent source of dietary fiber. However, grains and legumes must be properly combined. Unlike the protein in meat, which contains all 20 of the amino acids needed for good health, the protein in plant foods is incomplete. Grains, for example, are low in lysine and high in methionine, while legumes are typically high in lysine but low in methionine.

The solution is simple. Serve grain and legumes together, so that the strength of one makes up for the deficiency in the other. You'll find many delicious meatless dishes in the chapters that follow. (They are listed in the index on page 348.) In some, the protein has already been combined, as in Fettuccine with Tomato Sauce and Ricotta Dumplings (page 252), which pairs pasta with cheese. In others, you need to mix and match the protein yourself.

Fettuccine with Tomato Sauce and Ricotta Dumplings

How to combine protein

However, as the chart below shows, protein combining is easy. Just pair a grain with a legume or with a small amount of complete protein. For example, you could serve a bean recipe, like Pinto Bean and Tomato Casserole (page 238) with a grain, like Home-style Corn Bread (page 310). There are many possible combinations, all of which add up to delicious high protein, low-fat eating.

Rice	+	Red beans		
Pasta	+	Cheese		
Bread	+	Peanut butter	+	Milk
Rice	+	Lentils	+	Yogurt
Bread	+	Walnuts	+	Seeds
Tortilla	+	Black beans		
Cereal	+	Nuts		
Split peas	+	Ham		
Pasta	+	White beans		
Corn	+	Lima beans		

Key:
- Grains
- Legumes
- Nuts/Seeds
- Complete Protein

FOODS THAT PROTECT YOUR HEALTH

Vitamins, minerals, and other nutrients do more than build a strong, healthy body – they also help prevent disease. According to new medical research, the nutrients listed below are especially promising and may help reduce your risk of developing cancer, heart disease, or other serious illnesses.

Nutrient	Effect	Best Sources
Calcium *2–3 servings daily*	• Fights osteoporosis	Milk, yogurt, cheese, arugula, kale, broccoli, dandelion leaves, sardines.
Cruciferous vegetables *3–4 servings weekly*	• Fights lung and gastro-intestinal cancers • Stabilizes free radicals	Cabbage, kale, arugula, broccoli, Brussels sprouts, mustard greens, turnips, collard greens.
Dietary fiber *3 servings daily*	**Insoluble** • Cuts risk of colon cancer and diverticulosis **Soluble** • Helps lower cholesterol • Cuts risk of heart disease	Barley, brown rice, wheat bran, raspberries, apples, pears. Lima beans, pinto beans, lentils, oat bran, rice bran, sunflower seeds, almonds, peanuts.
Omega-3 fatty acids *2 servings weekly*	• Reduces blood clotting • Reduces risk of heart disease • May help lower blood pressure and cholesterol	Salmon, tuna, halibut, sardines, mackerel, orange roughy, tilefish.
Beta carotene *3–4 servings weekly*	• Lowers risk of lung, mouth, and stomach cancers • Combats heart disease and macular degeneration • Stabilizes free radicals	Carrots, sweet potatoes, spinach, kale, butternut squash, turnip greens, dandelion greens, beet greens.
Vitamin C *1 serving daily*	• Reduces risk of cancers of mouth, esophagus, and stomach • Helps lower blood pressure • Linked with longevity	*$3^1/_2$-ounce servings:* Broccoli 93mg, fennel 93mg, Brussels sprouts 85mg, asparagus 33mg, red peppers 190mg, green peppers 243mg, peas 40mg, oranges 53mg, grapefruit 37mg, strawberries 57mg, cantaloupe 42mg.
Vitamin E *1 serving daily*	• Free-radical inhibitor • Reduces blood clotting – reducing risk of heart disease • Strengthens immune system in elderly	Almonds, walnuts, peanuts, sesame seeds, sunflower seeds, wheat germ, oatmeal, brown rice.

Stocking the Pantry

Most of the ingredients needed for healthy cooking are probably on your shelves right now, like fresh fruits and vegetables, rice, pasta, lean meats, and poultry. Some other foods that are called for may be unfamiliar but are worth stocking because they make food tastier and more healthful. The list below introduces these new ingredients and tells you how to use them. All are available in most large supermarkets. For information about herbs and spices, see page 14.

Apricots, when dried, add flavor to sweet or savory dishes. They are rich in fiber, beta carotene, iron, niacin, and minerals.

Balsamic vinegar is aged until it becomes dark and mellow, with a sweet-sour flavor. It is so intense in flavor that you need very little oil for salad dressings.

Barley adds interesting flavor and texture to soups and stews, as well as soluble fiber.

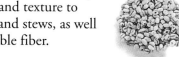

Basmati rice is a long-grained rice with a nutty flavor and fragrance.

Brown rice is the whole grain, with only the outer tough husk removed, and so takes longer to cook than white rice. It is rich in B vitamins, as well as calcium and iron.

Buttermilk is smooth and quite thick, with a sour, tangy taste. It is low in fat and used as a substitute for cream in baked goods, pancakes, and soups.

Canola oil contains more monounsaturated fat than any other oil except olive. It is best for stir-frying because the flavor is bland and it can withstand high heat.

Coarse-grained mustard has a grainy texture and a medium-hot fruity taste. Good with bacon and salads.

Cornmeal is made from dried corn kernel and is used for corn bread, corn cakes, and corn sticks. Yellow cornmeal has slightly more vitamin A than white.

Cornstarch is made from the endosperm of the corn kernel. It is used to thicken sauces and stews in place of flour and fat.

Couscous is a granular semolina that is soaked until soft. It is served like rice.

Dijon mustard is medium hot, with a clean, sharp taste and a pale color. Use for meats, dressings, and sauces.

Dried mushrooms add an intense flavor to stews and soups but must be soaked before use. The best variety is *cèpes*, known in Italy as *porcini*. The rich flavor means you need only about 1 ounce for a dish for four.

Filo dough comes in fresh or frozen paper-thin layers and is similar to strudel pastry.

Nuts come in varied forms and are a nutritious cooking ingredient: *Almonds* are high in calcium, minerals, and dietary fiber. *Cashews* are a good source of iron and folic acid. *Hazelnuts* are rich in minerals and folic acid. *Pecans* are high in fat and low in protein compared to other nuts and so should be eaten sparingly. *Walnuts* are a fairly good source of iron and vitamin B6.

Olive oil is low in saturated fats and high in monounsaturated fat. It's ideal for salad dressings and marinades and can be used for low- to medium-heat cooking.

Parmesan cheese is a robust-flavored Italian cheese ideal for those cutting down on fat because it is made with skim or part-skim milk. It is often used grated, so not much is needed. Use in pasta dishes and salads.

Prunes are dried plums. They are high in fiber, half of which is cholesterol-lowering soluble fiber. They are also rich in beta carotene, B vitamins, and minerals.

Pumpkin seeds are dark green seeds also known as pepitas. They are a good source of iron and fairly low in fat.

Rolled oats or "old-fashioned" are steamed and flattened oats. They are high in soluble and insoluble fiber and are rich in vitamins and minerals.

Sun-dried tomatoes are intensely flavored and can be added to sauces, salads, or soups. Available dried or in oil.

Sunflower seeds are rich in iron and low in saturated fat. They are good for snacks or in salads, cooked recipes, and breads.

Tacos are corn tortillas that are fried until crisp, then filled with spicy meat and topped with shredded lettuce, chopped tomatoes, salsa, sour cream, and cheese.

Tomato paste is made of concentrated tomatoes, and only a small amount is needed to give a rich tomato flavor. It's conveniently packaged in cans or tubes. If you use it occasionally, it helps to buy it in tubes so that you can use a tablespoon at a time with no waste.

Tortillas are made from finely ground corn or flour. Corn tortillas have a coarser texture than those made from wheat flour. Both are used for Mexican dishes and, when eaten with beans, form a complete protein.

Vegetable oil cooking spray can be used in place of oil or other fat for baking, frying, or browning. It prevents food from sticking and works best when used with a nonstick pan.

Wheat germ is the heart of the wheat kernel and is a source of vitamin E, thiamine, riboflavin, iron, and fiber. It's good added to breads, casseroles, and baked goods.

Whole-wheat flour contains the bran and the germ and so is high in fiber. It is also rich in B vitamins and E.

Wild rice is actually a grass that is often cooked with brown rice to add a nutty taste and more texture.

Yogurt is a tart, thickened milk product. It can be used in place of sour cream, but do not boil because it tends to separate. Look for low-fat varieties. Yogurt is rich in calcium, protein, and vitamin B12.

Oriental ingredients

Many of the Chinese recipes in this book call for authentic Oriental ingredients. Although some are a little high in sodium, they're worth using because they add delicious flavor to your dish. Look for them in the Oriental section of your supermarket. You can remove some of the sodium from canned vegetables by rinsing them.

Baby corn is tiny cobs of corn that are eaten whole or halved in Oriental or Thai dishes. Tender and sweet when lightly cooked, they can be white or yellow.

Rice vinegar is made from soured, fermented rice. It has a clear, straw color and a mild flavor that adds a piquancy to Oriental dishes.

Sesame oil has a distinctive aroma and nutty taste. Usually small amounts are added to dishes and marinades as flavoring.

Sesame seeds are sprinkled in stir-fries and salads to add a slightly sweet, nutty flavor and crunchy texture. They are a good source of calcium and iron.

Soy sauce is a brown, salty sauce made from fermenting soy beans with wheat or barley. A reduced-sodium soy sauce is also available that has about half the amount of sodium as regular soy sauce.

Water chestnuts are the edible tubers of a water plant. They add crunch to stir-fries and other Asian dishes.

Left to right: Baby corn, sesame oil, water chestnuts, rice vinegar, soy sauce, sesame seeds

Cooking with Herbs & Spices

Taste is lost when you cut back on fat and sodium. So herbs and spices are especially important in healthful cooking, adding flavor to both savory and sweet dishes. Fresh herbs, if available, are especially delicious. For tips on storing herbs, see page 283, and on grinding spices, see page 217.

Allspice tastes like a mixture of cinnamon, cloves, nutmeg, ginger, and pepper. It adds a spiciness to all dishes.

Basil has a distinctive warm, minty flavor and is used for pesto sauce and tomato dishes.

Bay has a pungent woodsy flavor and aroma. Good with meats, soups, and stews.

Black peppercorns are sharp and aromatic. They are ground into a powder or small flakes and used in savory dishes.

Caraway seeds are small and aromatic, with an anise flavor. They add a nutty flavor and texture to breads, cakes, cheese, vegetables, and meat dishes.

Cayenne is hot and peppery. It is made from dried red chili peppers, including the seeds which are the hottest part.

Celery seeds have an intense celery flavor. Use them sparingly.

Chervil is aromatic, with a spicy aniseed flavor. Good with eggs, fish, and salads.

Chili powder comes hot or mild and is a mixture of dried chilies, garlic, oregano, cumin, coriander, and cloves. *Red pepper flakes* are made from dried and crushed chili peppers. They are fiery hot.

Chives can be purchased fresh, frozen, or freeze-dried. They add sweet onion flavor to salads and sauces.

Cilantro/Coriander has an intensely aromatic flavor. The leaves and seeds are best in spicy dishes, such as curries.

Cinnamon comes in stick form or ground. It has an aromatic flavor ideal for cakes and puddings.

Cloves are used to stud hams before baking or spike apples for punch. Use ground cloves for sweet or savory dishes.

Cumin seeds and ground cumin have a distinctive earthy flavor that is good in Mexican, bean, and shellfish dishes.

Dill has an aniseed flavor. Use seeds and leaves in fish, chicken, egg, and potato recipes.

Fennel seeds have an anise flavor. Good with fish or pork.

Ginger root is lemony and sharp. Fresh ginger is grated and added to stir-fries or spicy dishes. Ground ginger is used in cakes, cookies, and curry powder.

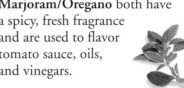

Marjoram/Oregano both have a spicy, fresh fragrance and are used to flavor tomato sauce, oils, and vinegars.

Mint has a very light, fresh taste. It's good with lamb, fish, bulgur, or salads.

Nutmeg has a warm, sweet, nutty flavor that complements spinach, pumpkin, or cheese dishes.

Paprika is made from a mixture of mild and hot ground red peppers but is milder than cayenne. It is used with fish dishes or as a garnish on pale-colored dishes.

Parsley comes in two varieties: curly and flat leaved. It adds fresh taste to any savory dish and is a good source of vitamin C, iron, and beta carotene.

Rosemary has a powerful flavor and should be used sparingly. It lends an intense flavor to pork, lamb, or game.

Sage has a woodsy aromatic flavor that is often used in Italian cooking, blending well with garlic and tomatoes.

Tarragon has a slight aniseed taste and adds flavor to chicken and green salads.

Thyme has a light, spicy flavor that marries well with beef, pork, lamb, and some oil-rich fish.

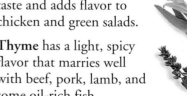

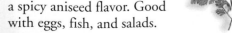

Equipping the Kitchen

The right equipment helps you prepare food more efficiently, cook in less fat, preserve nutrients in vegetables, and drain off any excess fat. Here's what you need to get started.

Butcher's knife is a large heavy knife for chopping vegetables and slicing meat. The small **paring knife** is used for peeling and slicing fruits and vegetables, and for trimming meat. Choose good quality knives and keep them sharpened.

Dutch oven has a thick bottom that conducts heat evenly, and a lid to retain heat. It is ideal for long slow cooking, such as braising, or for dishes that begin on top of the stove and finish in the oven.

Nonstick skillet requires very little or no oil. It is used for browning, stir-frying, sautéeing, and simmering.

Parchment is a grease resistant paper that is wrapped around fish, poultry, and vegetables before baking. The food steams in its own juices with little added oil. It is also used to line cake pans.

Processor or blender is used to purée vegetables for low-fat gravies and soups. The processor quickly chops or shreds vegetables for casseroles and stews.

Roasting pan with wire rack lets the fat drain away from roasting meat or poultry.

Sieve is a fine wire mesh bowl – perfect for straining soups for smooth finish.

Slotted spoons and spatulas allow any fat or liquid to run off while you remove food from the pan.

Rubber spatula is a flexible tool used to scrape down the sides of the food processor bowl.

Stovetop grill pan allows grilling without fat. Use as an alternative to an outdoor barbecue.

Vegetable steamer cooks food in vapor. Place the basket in a pan above 1 inch boiling water. Cover pan to retain steam.

Wok is a bowl-shaped pan which allows rapid stir-frying with very little oil over high heat. This retains texture, color, and nutrients of the food.

MEASURING INGREDIENTS

Tin measuring cups are best for dry ingredients. Fill with ingredient, then level off with a knife. Pack butter or margarine firmly.

A glass measure is best for liquids. Measure on a level surface and check at eye level. For less than $^1/_4$ cup, use measuring spoons.

SOUPS

The beauty of soups is their versatility. They can be smooth and creamy, thin and clear, full of healthful vegetables, or thickened with pasta and rice. This chapter shows you how to make a wide variety of soups – from cream of vegetable to fish chowder – all with less fat and sodium than traditional recipes. Whatever the occasion, you're sure to find the right soup. On a cold day Beef and Root Vegetable makes a satisfying and nutritious lunch, while on hot summer days Red Gazpacho is a refreshing starter. Kids will love the fruit soups. They come in four luscious flavors: Peach, Black Cherry, Cantaloupe, and Summer Pudding.

Cream of Carrot
and Parsnip Soup,
page 24

S oup should be brimming with good nutrition as well as flavor. Unfortunately, canned soups, in addition to being high in sodium and fat, lose many of their vitamins in the canning process. So it pays healthwise to make your soups from scratch with vitamin-rich fruits and vegetables; low-fat meat, fish, or poultry; and grains or beans for fiber. You will also discover that the extra effort is well worth it – the taste of homemade soup is far superior to canned.

Soup and your health

You can also choose soups to suit different nutritional needs. If you're looking for a high-protein soup to serve as a main course, try a milk-based chowder made with fish or corn. If you want to increase the fiber in your diet, nothing beats a bean soup. For the highest vitamin content, choose a fresh fruit soup or gazpacho, which is made with raw vegetables.

The way you cook soups will affect the nutritional content. Slow-cooking is a poor way to cook fresh vegetables because vitamins are lost in the cooking water, but it is a good method for making soups because most of the vitamins leach into the stock. Therefore many of the soups in this chapter are slow-cooked to condense the flavors and retain the vitamins.

Taking stock

A delicious soup begins with the very best foundation, and that means a robust stock. This chapter goes back to basics and shows you how to make a low-fat stock that is rich in vitamins and minerals as well as good flavor. If you don't have much time, use canned low-sodium broth; the following chart gives you nutritional information on different options.

WHEN YOUR RECIPE CALLS FOR STOCK…

You have three choices. You can use homemade stock, canned low-sodium stock, or mix regular canned stock with half water. Do not use regular canned stock at full strength or bouillon cubes – they are both very high in sodium.

1 cup	Sodium mg	Fat g	Calories
Beef stock			
Homemade, page 26	84	1	29
Canned reduced-sodium	620	0	20
Canned, full strength	782	1	17
Chicken stock			
Homemade, page 20	65	0	23
Canned reduced-sodium	640	1	21
Canned, full strength	985	1	28
Fish stock			
Homemade, page 32	75	0	28
Canned clam broth			
Half canned/water	258	0.5	3
Canned, full strength	516	1	6
Vegetable stock			
Homemade, page 34	53	0	15
Half canned/water	506	0.5	11
Canned, full strength	1012	1	22

Reducing fat and sodium

The soup recipes in this chapter show you how to add flavor with herbs, lemon juice, and citrus zest instead of salt. You can also create flavor by combining fruits and vegetables in interesting ways. For example, curry powder and spices are sautéed with onion and garlic to add fragrance to Curried Cauliflower Soup with Lime. In White Gazpacho, cucumbers, green grapes, garlic, vinegar, and oil are processed to blend the flavors, then allowed to stand for 1 hour to intensify them. Cutting back on fat is also top priority. In addition to using less meat than called for in standard recipes, you can sauté onions and vegetables in olive oil instead of butter. Instead of thickening soups with fat and flour, you'll find it's more healthful to use puréed vegetable or potato – they add vitamins and fiber as well as bulk. You can enrich soups with buttermilk and low-fat sour cream in place of heavy cream. Finally, you can make meat soups ahead, refrigerate them until the fat congeals, then scrape it off the top before reheating.

Serving soups

A light soup will stimulate the appetite before a filling main course, while a hearty soup makes a satisfying main dish rounded out with a crisp salad and whole-wheat bread. When soup is the first course, plan about 1 cup per person. If it is the entrée, you will need 2 cups or even 3 for hearty eaters. Serve clear and light cream soups in a cup, chowders and hearty meat or vegetable soups in a bowl. Bring main course soups to the table in a tureen or an attractive oven-to-table Dutch oven. They will keep the soup hot and ready for second helpings. If soup is to be served as a starter, it should harmonize with the main course that follows it and offer different flavor, color, texture, and richness.

Great garnishes

The way a soup is presented can transform its taste and appearance. Any garnish should be appropriate both to the soup and the occasion.

Shredded low-fat Cheddar, Monterey Jack, or Parmesan cheese makes a nourishing topping for bean or vegetable soups.

Chopped chives and minced fresh herbs add piquant flavor to mild cream soups.

Herb-filled ice cubes add refreshing flavor to cold soups.

Carrot curls, chopped sweet pepper, and celery tops add color and crunch to cream soups.

A feathered swirl of low-fat sour cream is pretty in colorful cream soups.

The bread basket

Bread is always good with soup, but try to match flavors and textures. Serve a hearty Italian or French loaf with chunky meat or vegetable soups, delicate bread sticks with light cream soups. Bland crackers or biscuits are the perfect foil for rich chowders, while garlic bread stands up well to spicy fish stews. Corn bread goes especially well with bean or Mexican-style soups. Serve fruit soups with a baking-powder biscuit or pumpernickel or sourdough bread, which offsets the sweetness.

Storing and freezing

Most soups can be covered and refrigerated for 3 or 4 days. Some soups can be frozen, but herbs and spices can change flavor after freezing, so it is best to adjust the seasonings after thawing. Ingredients such as potatoes, yogurt, eggs, or low-fat sour cream do not freeze well and should be added afterward. For example, with Sweet Corn and Seafood Chowder, it is better to add freshly cooked potato just before serving. In Cuban Black Bean Soup, the garlic, thyme, and sour cream should be added once the soup is thawed.

To freeze, chill the soup, then transfer to a large freezer container, leaving $1/2$-inch headspace for expansion. Frozen soup can be stored for 3 months. Let the soup thaw overnight in the refrigerator, then reheat gently and thoroughly.

MAKING LOW-FAT CROUTONS

1 *Remove the crusts from the bread and cut into cubes or shapes using a small cutter.*

2 *Place the bread shapes on a broiler rack, brush with a little olive oil, and broil until golden on both sides.*

MAKING HERB ICE CUBES

1 *Add small sprigs of the herbs of your choice to the ice cube tray. Chop the leaves of larger herbs like basil.*

2 *Add water to half fill the tray. The herbs will float to the top. Freeze, fill the tray with water, and freeze again.*

Basic Chicken Stock

Reduce sodium ▪ *Flavor the stock with garlic, herbs, and vegetables instead of salt.*
Add flavor ▪ *For an especially rich stock, use a whole chicken instead of the trimmings.*

● Makes **9 cups** ● Preparation Time **15 minutes** ● Cooking Time **1½–2 hours**

PER CUP
Calories **21**, Saturated Fat **0g**,
Total Fat **0g**, Sodium **60mg**,
Cholesterol **0mg**, Protein **4g**,
Carbohydrate **1g**, Fiber **0g**.

3 pounds chicken wings, necks, and gizzards	1 clove garlic, left whole
3 quarts water, more as necessary	Parsley sprigs
2 stalks celery, cut into 2-inch pieces	2 bay leaves
1 large onion, quartered but not peeled	2 large carrots, cut into 2-inch pieces
	10 black peppercorns

1 Cut off all fat and skin from the chicken pieces. Rinse the chicken, place in a large stockpot, and cover with the water. Bring to a boil over moderate heat.

2 Using a large spoon, skim off and discard the gray scum that rises to the surface.

3 Add the celery, onion, garlic, herbs, carrots, and peppercorns to the stockpot. Return the mixture to a boil.

Basic Chicken Stock will enhance your soup and main-dish recipes with its delicate herbed flavor.

4 Partially cover and simmer the stock, skimming the fat from the surface occasionally, 1½ to 2 hours.

5 Remove from the heat and strain the stock through a cheesecloth-lined or very fine mesh sieve. Discard the chicken and vegetables in the sieve.

6 Remove the fat from the stock by drawing a sheet of paper towel across the surface. Or allow to cool, chill, then remove the hardened fat with a spoon.

Home-style Chicken and Rice Soup

- Makes **9 cups**
- Preparation Time **10 minutes**
- Cooking Time **30 minutes**

³/₄ **cup long-grain white rice**

2 quarts chicken stock, page 18

2 boneless, skinless chicken breast halves (8 ounces), cut into ¹/₄-inch slices

12 ounces fresh spinach leaves or 1 small head escarole, washed and shredded

1 tablespoon lemon juice

¹/₈ **teaspoon each salt and pepper**

1 Place the rice in a sieve and rinse under cold running water until the water runs clear.

2 Place the rice in a 4-quart saucepan with the chicken stock and bring to a boil. Simmer about 10 minutes.

3 Add the sliced chicken to the rice mixture and simmer, partially covered, about 5 minutes longer. Stir in the spinach and simmer about 5 minutes longer, until the rice is tender and the chicken and spinach are cooked.

4 Season with the lemon juice, salt, and pepper.

PER CUP
Calories **125**, Saturated Fat **1g**, Total Fat **1g**, Sodium **137mg**, Cholesterol **22mg**, Protein **13g**, Carbohydrate **15g**, Fiber **1g**.

Chunky Chicken Soup with Pasta

- Makes **9 cups**
- Preparation Time **10 minutes**
- Cooking Time **25–30 minutes**

2 quarts chicken stock, page 18

1 cup small pasta shells or bows

1 large carrot, diced

2 stalks celery, diced

¹/₄ **teaspoon each dried oregano and basil**

4 ounces green beans, cut across into ¹/₄-inch slices

1 cup canned crushed tomatoes

¹/₈ **teaspoon each salt and pepper**

2 tablespoons chopped fresh basil

1 Pour the stock into a 4-quart saucepan and bring to a boil over high heat. Add the pasta, reduce the heat, and simmer about 5 minutes, stirring occasionally.

2 Add the carrot, celery, and dried herbs to the stock. Simmer, stirring occasionally, about 5 minutes or until the pasta and vegetables are almost cooked through.

3 Add the green beans, crushed tomatoes, salt, and pepper and simmer, stirring occasionally, about 5 minutes longer.

4 Stir the fresh basil into the soup and serve at once.

PER CUP
Calories **116**, Saturated Fat **0g**, Total Fat **1g**, Sodium **145mg**, Cholesterol **0mg**, Protein **5g**, Carbohydrate **21g**, Fiber **2g**.

Chicken Soup with Kale

- Makes **7½ cups**
- Preparation Time **15 minutes**
- Cooking Time **40 minutes**

1 pound all-purpose potatoes, peeled and thinly sliced

6 cups chicken stock, page 18

4 ounces chorizo sausages or turkey sausage, thinly sliced

1 clove garlic, finely chopped

12 ounces kale leaves or collard greens, washed and shredded

¹/₄ **cup water**

¹/₈ **teaspoon pepper**

1 Combine potatoes and stock in a saucepan. Simmer 10 to 15 minutes or until the potatoes are very soft. With a fork, mash about half of the potatoes against the side of pan. Remove from heat.

2 Add chorizo to a nonstick skillet and cook over moderate heat, stirring, about 5 minutes or until crisp and fat is rendered. Spoon off almost all fat.

3 Add garlic to skillet and cook, stirring, about 3 minutes, until softened. Add kale and stir to combine; then add measured water, cover skillet, and cook 5 minutes or until kale is wilted.

4 Stir kale and chorizo into potatoes. Simmer the soup about 5 minutes. Season with pepper.

PER CUP
Calories **112**, Saturated Fat **1g**, Total Fat **3g**, Sodium **190mg**, Cholesterol **10mg**, Protein **7g**, Carbohydrate **15g**, Fiber **3g**.

Cream of Leek and Potato Soup

Reduce cholesterol ▪ *Instead of the traditional heavy cream, thicken the soup with puréed potatoes and low-fat sour cream.*

Cooking technique ▪ *To give the soup a smooth consistency, be sure to cook the leeks and potatoes until they are quite soft.*

Increase fiber ▪ *The leeks not only give this soup fresh flavor, but also add fiber.*

● Makes 7½ cups ● Preparation Time **15 minutes** ● Cooking Time **45 minutes**

PER CUP
Calories **111**, Saturated Fat **1g**,
Total Fat **3g**, Sodium **105mg**,
Cholesterol **2mg**, Protein **4g**,
Carbohydrate **17g**, Fiber **2g**.

1 tablespoon olive or canola oil

8 ounces leeks, white part only, thickly sliced

1 large onion, coarsely chopped

6 cups chicken or vegetable stock, page 18

1 pound all-purpose potatoes, peeled and diced

⅛ teaspoon each salt and ground white pepper

⅓ cup low-fat sour cream

Chopped chives, for garnish (optional)

1 In a 4-quart saucepan, heat the oil over moderate heat. Stir in leeks and onion, then ¾ cup of the stock. Cover and cook, stirring frequently, about 10 minutes, until soft but not browned.

2 Add the potatoes to the saucepan and stir to coat with the leek and onion mixture.

3 Pour in half of the remaining stock and bring to a boil. Simmer, partially covered, 15 to 20 minutes, until potatoes are very soft.

4 Remove from the heat. Using a ladle, transfer the contents of the pan to a blender or food processor and purée until very smooth.

5 Pour the remaining stock into the pan. Add the vegetable purée and bring the soup to a simmer, stirring constantly, 2 to 3 minutes. Season with the salt and pepper.

6 Remove from the heat and stir in the sour cream. Ladle into soup bowls and garnish with the chives, if using.

The whole family will enjoy **Cream of Leek and Potato Soup**, *a low-fat version of* vichyssoise, *a classic French soup.*

Cream of Celery Root and Potato Soup with Watercress

Celery root has a slightly stronger flavor than regular celery. If it is not available, sliced celery works just fine, but use only the pale-green stalks because the dark green ones are too stringy.

- Makes 9½ cups
- Preparation Time 20 minutes
- Cooking Time 50 minutes

1 tablespoon olive or canola oil

2 large onions, coarsely chopped

2 quarts chicken or vegetable stock, page 18

12 ounces celery root, diced, or celery, thickly sliced

1 large all-purpose potato, peeled and diced

¼ teaspoon dried thyme

1 bay leaf

½ cup buttermilk or 1% low-fat milk

⅛ teaspoon each salt and pepper

½ cup watercress or torn spinach leaves

1 In a 4-quart saucepan, heat the oil over moderate heat. Add the onions, then ¾ cup of the stock, and sauté until softened but not browned.

2 Stir in the celery root and potato. Pour in the remaining stock, add the herbs, and bring to a boil. Simmer the soup, partially covered, stirring occasionally, for 20 to 25 minutes, until all the vegetables are very soft.

3 Remove the bay leaf and, using a slotted spoon, transfer the vegetables to a blender or food processor. Purée until very smooth.

4 Add the vegetable purée to the saucepan and return to a simmer. Add the buttermilk, salt, and pepper and simmer the soup about 5 minutes longer.

5 Stir in the watercress leaves. Remove the pan from the heat and let the leaves wilt in the soup.

PER CUP
Calories 81, Saturated Fat 1g, Total Fat 2g, Sodium 121mg, Cholesterol 0mg, Protein 4g, Carbohydrate 12g, Fiber 3g.

Bay leaves can be dried and stored, but will not have the same amount of flavor as fresh.

Cream of Carrot and Parsnip Soup

This tasty soup comes very close to being fat-free. If you'd like to reduce the fat even more, use skim milk. Although it's made with winter vegetables, this soup tastes just as delicious in summer served chilled.

- Makes 9½ cups
- Preparation Time 20 minutes
- Cooking Time 50 minutes

1 tablespoon olive or canola oil

1 large onion, coarsely chopped

1 tablespoon chopped fresh ginger or ½ teaspoon ground ginger

1 pound carrots, coarsely chopped

8 ounces parsnips, coarsely chopped

2 quarts chicken or vegetable stock, page 18

½ cup 1% low-fat milk

⅛ teaspoon each salt and pepper

1 In a 4-quart saucepan, heat the oil over moderate heat. Add the onion and ginger to the pan and sauté about 5 minutes or until softened.

2 Add the carrots and parsnips and sauté about 5 minutes longer, stirring constantly, until they are slightly softened.

3 Pour in the stock, bring to a boil, and simmer, partially covered, 20 to 25 minutes, until the carrots and parsnips are very soft.

4 Using a slotted spoon, transfer the vegetables to a blender or food processor and purée until very smooth. Add the vegetable purée to the saucepan and return to a simmer.

5 Add the milk, salt, and pepper to the pan. Simmer the soup about 5 minutes, until the flavors are blended.

PER CUP
Calories 35, Saturated Fat 1g, Total Fat 2g, Sodium 109mg, Cholesterol 1mg, Protein 3g, Carbohydrate 13g, Fiber 3g.

CHOPPING GINGER

1 *Using a sharp vegetable peeler, thinly peel the skin from a piece of fresh ginger root.*

2 *Using a sharp kitchen knife, cut the ginger across into slices. Then finely chop into very small dice.*

Pumpkin and Sweet Potato Soup with Bacon Bits

Pumpkin flesh has a mild, sweet flavor – the smaller the pumpkin, the sweeter and more subtle it will be. For this recipe you can use either fresh or canned pumpkin. Like all orange vegetables, pumpkin and sweet potatoes are very high in beta carotene. This luscious soup gives you a double helping of this vital nutrient.

- Makes 9½ cups
- Preparation Time **15 minutes**
- Cooking Time **35 minutes**

2 ounces reduced-sodium bacon or turkey bacon, coarsely chopped

2 shallots or small onions, finely chopped

2 quarts chicken or vegetable stock, page 18

12 ounces sweet potatoes, peeled and cut into ½-inch pieces

1 can (16 ounces) solid-pack pumpkin or 2 cups cooked winter squash (see box)

⅛ teaspoon each salt and pepper

Pinch of ground nutmeg

2 tablespoons chopped parsley

1 In a 4-quart saucepan, cook the bacon over moderate heat about 3 minutes, until the fat is rendered and the bacon is crisp. Using a slotted spoon, transfer the bacon to paper towels and reserve.

2 Add the shallots to the saucepan, then ¼ cup of the stock, and sauté, stirring constantly, about 3 minutes, until softened.

3 Add the sweet potatoes and cook, stirring, about 3 minutes. Pour in the remaining stock and bring to a boil. Simmer, partially covered, about 10 minutes, until the sweet potatoes are very soft.

4 Using a slotted spoon, transfer the vegetables to a blender or food processor and purée until smooth. Add the pumpkin and process to combine.

5 Add the vegetable purée to the saucepan and return to a simmer. Stir the salt, pepper, and nutmeg into the soup. Serve sprinkled with the crumbled bacon and parsley.

PER CUP
Calories **96**, Saturated Fat **0g**, Total Fat **4g**, Sodium **128mg**, Cholesterol **6mg**, Protein **3g**, Carbohydrate **12g**, Fiber **2g**.

Pumpkin and Sweet Potato Soup with Bacon Bits is garnished with chopped parsley to add more color and flavor.

COOKING AND PUREEING WINTER SQUASH

1 *Halve the squash lengthwise. With a spoon, scoop out the seeds and fibrous threads and discard them. Cut the squash into large chunks.*

2 *Place the squash in a saucepan, cover with water, and cook 25 to 30 minutes, or until tender. Drain the squash and remove and discard the skin. Place the flesh in a bowl.*

3 *Purée the squash in a food processor until smooth. Or purée the squash in batches in a blender.*

Basic Beef Stock

Cooking technique ▪ *For richer color and flavor, roast the bones 30 minutes at 400° F before beginning the stock.*

Reduce cholesterol ▪ *Skim as much fat as possible from the surface of the stock after cooling.*

● Makes **9 cups** ● Preparation Time **7 minutes** ● Cooking Time **1 hour 50 minutes**

PER CUP
Calories **20**, Saturated Fat **0g**,
Total Fat **0g**, Sodium **43mg**,
Cholesterol **0mg**, Protein **4g**,
Carbohydrate **1g**, Fiber **0g**.

3 pounds beef or veal bones, cut into 2-inch pieces	2 bay leaves
	Parsley sprigs
3 quarts water, more as necessary	2 large carrots, cut into 2-inch pieces
2 large onions, halved but not peeled	2 stalks celery, cut into 2-inch pieces
2 cloves garlic, left whole	1 cup canned crushed tomatoes
10 black peppercorns	

1 Rinse the meat bones under cold water. Place in a large stockpot and cover with the water. Bring to a boil over moderate heat.

2 Using a large slotted spoon, skim off and discard the gray scum that rises to the surface.

3 Add the onions, garlic, peppercorns, herbs, carrots, and celery. Return the mixture to a boil.

*Made from meaty bones and fresh vegetables, **Basic Beef Stock** is rich with flavor and goodness.*

4 Simmer the stock, partially covered, skimming the fat occasionally, about 1 hour. Add tomatoes and simmer about 30 minutes.

5 Remove from the heat and strain the stock through a cheesecloth-lined sieve. Discard the contents of the sieve.

6 Remove fat from the stock by drawing a sheet of paper towel across the surface. Or allow to cool, chill, then remove the hardened fat with a spoon.

Old-Fashioned Beef Vegetable

- Makes **10 cups**
- Preparation Time **15 minutes**
- Cooking Time **55 minutes**

1 ounce reduced-sodium bacon, coarsely chopped

8 ounces lean beef stew meat, cut into thin strips

1 large onion, coarsely chopped

1 clove garlic, finely chopped

2 large carrots, cubed

8 ounces parsnips, diced

8 ounces all-purpose potatoes, peeled and diced

2 teaspoons tomato paste

2 quarts beef stock, page 18

1 teaspoon dried sage

1 bay leaf

1/8 teaspoon each salt and pepper

1 In a 4-quart saucepan, cook the bacon, stirring, about 3 minutes, until it is quite crisp and the fat is rendered. Discard bacon.

2 Add beef, onion, and garlic and sauté until browned. Stir in carrots, parsnips, and potatoes, and cook about 7 minutes, until lightly browned.

3 Stir in tomato paste, stock, and herbs. Simmer, partially covered, stirring occasionally, 30 to 45 minutes, until beef and vegetables are tender and broth is rich. Discard bay leaf and season with salt and pepper.

PER CUP
Calories **123**, Saturated Fat **1g**, Total Fat **3g**, Sodium **142mg**, Cholesterol **15mg**, Protein **8g**, Carbohydrate **16g**, Fiber **3g**.

Beef, Barley, and Mushroom Soup

- Makes **8½ cups**
- Preparation Time **15 minutes**
- Cooking Time **65 minutes**

2 tablespoons olive or canola oil

8 ounces lean beef stew meat, cut into thin 1/2-inch strips

2 leeks or onions, trimmed and sliced

8 ounces mushrooms, sliced

1/2 cup pearl barley

7 cups beef stock, page 18

1 cup red wine or beef stock

2 teaspoons lemon juice

1/8 teaspoon each salt and pepper

1 In a 4-quart saucepan, heat 1 tablespoon of the oil over moderate heat. Add beef and sauté, stirring, until browned. Using a slotted spoon, transfer the beef to a plate lined with paper towels and reserve.

2 Add the remaining oil to the saucepan, then stir in the leeks and sauté until softened. Add the mushrooms and cook, stirring, until softened.

3 Return beef to saucepan with barley, stock, and red wine. Bring to a boil, then simmer, partially covered, about 45 minutes, until beef and barley are very tender. Season with lemon juice, salt, and pepper.

PER CUP
Calories **167**, Saturated Fat **1g**, Total Fat **6g**, Sodium **125mg**, Cholesterol **16mg**, Protein **10g**, Carbohydrate **15g**, Fiber **3g**.

Jamaican Pepperpot Soup

- Makes **10 cups**
- Preparation Time **15 minutes**
- Cooking Time **1¼ hours**

8 ounces lean beef stew meat, cut into thick slices

2 quarts beef stock, page 18

4 scallions, coarsely chopped

2 cloves garlic, finely chopped

1–2 fresh hot red or green chili peppers, finely chopped

8 ounces sweet potatoes, peeled and cut into 1/2-inch cubes

1/8 teaspoon ground allspice

4 ounces okra, cut into 1/2-inch slices, or 1/2 package (10 ounces) frozen cut okra, thawed

1/8 teaspoon each salt and pepper

1 In a 4-quart saucepan, bring the beef and stock to a boil over moderate heat. Simmer for 2 minutes. Strain the liquid, then return the beef and stock to the saucepan.

2 Add the scallions, garlic, and chili pepper to the saucepan and return to a boil. Simmer the mixture, partially covered, 30 to 45 minutes, until the beef is very tender.

3 Add the sweet potatoes and allspice, and simmer for 10 minutes. Stir in the okra, salt, and pepper; simmer about 10 minutes longer.

PER CUP
Calories **86**, Saturated Fat **1g**, Total Fat **2g**, Sodium **114mg**, Cholesterol **14mg**, Protein **8g**, Carbohydrate **9g**, Fiber **2g**.

Lentil Soup with Root Vegetables

Cooking technique ■ *Lentils and dried peas are a good source of low-fat protein. For an easy nutritious soup, simmer them with stock, vegetables, and herbs. Serve with bread or a little yogurt to complete the protein.*
Reduce sodium ■ *Instead of adding salt at table, serve lentil soup Mediterranean style – with a squeeze of lemon juice.*

● Makes **9 cups** ● Preparation Time **15 minutes** ● Cooking Time **1 hour**

PER CUP
Calories **217**, Saturated Fat **1g**,
Total Fat **3g**, Sodium **160mg**,
Cholesterol **0mg**, Protein **15g**,
Carbohydrate **35g**, Fiber **8g**.

2 cups brown lentils

1 tablespoon olive oil

1 large onion, diced

2 stalks celery, diced

2 cloves garlic, finely chopped

8 ounces turnip or parsnip, diced

2 large carrots, diced

2 quarts beef or vegetable stock, page 18

1 tablespoon tomato paste

¹/₄ teaspoon dried thyme

1 bay leaf

¹/₈ teaspoon each salt and pepper

1 Place the lentils in a sieve and rinse under cold water. Pick over the lentils, discarding any small stones.

2 In a 4-quart saucepan, heat the oil over moderate heat. Add the onion, celery, and garlic and sauté, stirring constantly, about 6 minutes, until softened and golden brown.

3 Add the turnip and carrots, then about ¹/₄ cup of the stock and cook, stirring frequently, until slightly soft.

4 Add the lentils, tomato paste, thyme, remaining stock, and bay leaf to the pan and stir to combine.

5 Bring to a boil and simmer the soup, partially covered and stirring occasionally, about 50 minutes, until the lentils and vegetables are very tender.

6 Season the soup with salt and pepper. Remove and discard the bay leaf before serving.

Lentil Soup with Root Vegetables *makes a warm and satisfying meal.*
For extra color, sprinkle a little chopped parsley on top.

Split Pea Soup with Smoked Ham

A small ham hock adds rich, smoky flavor to soup, and if you cut off any visible fat before cooking, it won't add too much cholesterol.

- Makes **8 cups**
- Preparation Time **20 minutes**
- Cooking Time **1 hour 10 minutes**

---

1 tablespoon olive or canola oil

4 ounces shallots or small white onions, finely chopped

2 stalks celery, coarsely chopped

¹/₄ teaspoon caraway seeds

7 cups water or chicken stock, page 18

1 small ham hock (8 ounces)

2¹/₂ cups yellow or green split peas

2 carrots, diced

1 bouquet garni, made with parsley stems and 1 bay leaf (see page 31)

1 tablespoon chopped parsley

¹/₈ teaspoon pepper

1 In a 4-quart saucepan, heat the oil over moderate heat. Add the shallots, celery, and caraway seeds, then about 2 tablespoons of the water, and sauté, stirring frequently, about 5 minutes, until softened and slightly browned.

2 Meanwhile, cut off as much fat from the ham hock as possible. Stir the split peas into the saucepan, then add the ham hock with the remaining water, the carrots, and bouquet garni. Bring to a boil and simmer the soup, partially covered and stirring occasionally, about 1 hour, until the split peas are very tender and the ham comes easily off the bone.

3 Remove the soup from the heat and discard bouquet garni. Lift out the ham and cut the meat from the bone, reserving the juices.

4 Add the ham and juices to the soup, return to the heat, and simmer about 5 minutes longer. Stir in the parsley and pepper.

PER CUP
Calories **262**, Saturated Fat **1g**, Total Fat **3g**, Sodium **146mg**, Cholesterol **4mg**, Protein **18g**, Carbohydrate **42g**, Fiber **10g**.

TRIMMING A HAM HOCK

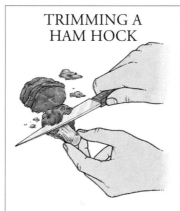

Hold the ham hock steady with one hand and, with a sharp knife, carefully cut off all the meat. Discard any fat.

Spicy Lentil Soup with Spinach

If you're using fresh spinach, it's very important to wash it thoroughly before cooking to get rid of any grit.

- Makes **8 cups**
- Preparation Time **15 minutes**
- Cooking Time **about 1 hour**

---

1 tablespoon olive or canola oil

2 stalks celery, coarsely chopped

2 cloves garlic, finely chopped

1 large onion, coarsely chopped

¹/₄ teaspoon curry powder

Pinch each of ground coriander and cumin (optional)

Pinch of cayenne pepper

2 cups brown lentils, washed and picked over

2 quarts vegetable stock, page 18

2 cups packed fresh spinach leaves, washed and stems removed, or 5 ounces (¹/₂ package) frozen, thawed

¹/₈ teaspoon salt

¹/₂ cup nonfat plain yogurt

1 In a 4-quart saucepan, heat the oil over moderate heat. Add the celery, garlic, onion, and spices. Sauté, stirring frequently, about 5 minutes, until softened.

Lentils are a good source of iron, phosphorous, and fiber.

2 Add the lentils with the stock and bring to a boil. Simmer the soup, partially covered and stirring occasionally, 50 to 60 minutes, until the lentils and vegetables are tender.

COOKING TIP
Brown lentils are the most flavorful and readily available, but you can use yellow or red lentils if you prefer.

3 Stir in the spinach leaves and salt and simmer about 5 minutes longer, until very soft.

4 Serve each portion of soup topped with a spoonful of yogurt.

PER CUP
Calories **222**, Saturated Fat **0g**, Total Fat **3g**, Sodium **131mg**, Cholesterol **0mg**, Protein **17g**, Carbohydrate **36g**, Fiber **8g**.

Purée of Yellow Split Peas

Green split peas may be used if yellow ones are not available. This soup freezes well if you want to prepare it ahead of time. Defrost it in the refrigerator overnight before reheating.

- Makes **8 cups**
- Preparation Time **15 minutes**
- Cooking Time **1 hour 10 minutes**

---

1 ounce reduced-sodium bacon, coarsely chopped

1 onion, coarsely chopped

2 large carrots, coarsely chopped

4 stalks celery, coarsely chopped, with leaves reserved

1 clove garlic, finely chopped

2 cups yellow or green split peas

1 bouquet garni, made with parsley stems, 1 bay leaf, and a few thyme sprigs (see box, right)

2 quarts vegetable or chicken stock, page 18

1/8 teaspoon pepper

---

1 In a 4-quart saucepan, cook the bacon over moderate heat about 3 minutes, until crisp and the fat is rendered. Remove the bacon with a slotted spoon and drain on paper towels.

2 Add the onion, carrots, celery, and garlic to the saucepan and sauté until softened and the onions are lightly golden. Stir in the split peas, bouquet garni, and the stock and bring to a boil. Simmer the soup, partially covered and stirring occasionally, about 45 minutes, until the split peas and vegetables are very tender.

3 Remove the saucepan from the heat and discard the bouquet garni. Purée the soup in a blender or food processor until smooth.

4 Return the soup to the saucepan and return to the heat. Stir in the reserved bacon and simmer about 3 minutes longer. Season with the pepper and garnish with the reserved celery leaves.

PER CUP
Calories **216**, Saturated Fat **1g**, Total Fat **3g**, Sodium **120mg**, Cholesterol **4mg**, Protein **14g**, Carbohydrate **36g**, Fiber **8g**.

GETTING AHEAD

Use bacon bits as garnishes for soups and salads; they can be made ahead of time and stored. Cook chopped bacon as in Step 1, then store the bacon bits in an airtight container in the refrigerator for up to 1 week.

MAKING A BOUQUET GARNI

1 *Hold together parsley stems, thyme sprigs, and 1 to 2 bay leaves in a small bunch.*

2 *Wind a piece of kitchen string around the herbs a few times, then tie the two ends together. Leave one length of string long in order to tie it to the pan handle.*

*Garnish **Purée of Yellow Split Peas** with green celery tops and serve as a warming starter or light meal.*

Basic Fish Stock

Cooking technique ▪ *Simmer 2 pounds of fish trimmings to extract and condense all of the flavor. For best results, use lean fish, such as cod or flounder.*

Reduce sodium ▪ *You can forgo adding salt to the stock, especially since the citrus adds the necessary zip.*

• Makes **10 cups** • Preparation Time **10 minutes** • Cooking Time **55 minutes**

PER CUP
Calories **25**, Saturated Fat **0g**,
Total Fat **0g**, Sodium **60mg**,
Cholesterol **0mg**, Protein **5g**,
Carbohydrate **1g**, Fiber **0g**.

2 pounds fish heads, bones, and trimmings from fish, such as cod, flounder, or salmon	2-inch piece of pared lemon zest
	2-inch piece of pared orange zest
3 quarts water	8 black peppercorns
2 carrots, cut into 2-inch pieces	1 bay leaf
1 large onion, quartered but not peeled	Parsley stems

1 Rinse the fish bones and trimmings under cold water and cut them into 3-inch pieces. Place them in a large stockpot and cover with the water. Bring to a boil over moderate heat. With a large slotted spoon, skim off and discard the gray scum that rises to the surface.

2 Add the carrots, onion, lemon and orange zest, peppercorns, and herbs to the stockpot. Return the mixture to a boil.

Basic Fish Stock is rich-tasting, yet light. Freeze some in an ice-cube tray so you can add small quantities to fish soups and stews when needed.

3 Reduce the heat to low and simmer the stock, partially covered, skimming the fat and scum from the surface occasionally, about 30 minutes.

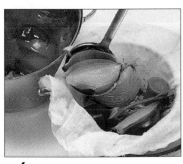

4 Strain the stock through a cheesecloth-lined sieve and discard the contents of the sieve.

COOKING TIP

For a richer stock, return the strained stock to a clean pan and continue simmering for another 20 minutes.

Hot and Sour Shrimp Soup

- Makes **7 cups**
- Preparation Time **15 minutes**
- Cooking Time **25 minutes**

---

6 cups fish stock, page 18

1 tablespoon finely chopped lemongrass or ¹/₂ teaspoon finely grated lime zest

1 clove garlic, finely chopped

1 fresh hot red or green chili pepper, finely chopped

8 ounces mushrooms, sliced

4 ounces medium shrimp, peeled and deveined

2 tablespoons rice vinegar or white vinegar

1 tablespoon reduced-sodium soy sauce

1 tablespoon cornstarch

2 scallions, thinly sliced

---

1 Combine fish stock, lemongrass, garlic, and chili pepper in a saucepan. Simmer, partially covered, about 5 minutes.

2 Stir in mushrooms and shrimp; simmer, partially covered, about 3 minutes longer, until mushrooms are soft and shrimp turn pink.

3 In a small bowl, combine rice vinegar and soy sauce with cornstarch until smooth. Stir mixture into simmering soup, and allow to return to a boil. Remove from heat and stir in sliced scallions.

PER CUP
Calories **58**, Saturated Fat **0g**, Total Fat **0g**, Sodium **176mg**, Cholesterol **25mg**, Protein **8g**, Carbohydrate **5g**, Fiber **0.5g**.

Caribbean Fish Soup

- Makes **11 cups**
- Preparation Time **15 minutes**
- Cooking Time **35 minutes**

---

2 onions, coarsely chopped

1 large sweet red or green pepper, coarsely chopped

2 cups canned crushed tomatoes

Dash hot red pepper sauce

¹/₂ teaspoon dried thyme

1 bay leaf

5 cups fish stock, page 18

1 cup white wine or fish stock

8 ounces all-purpose potatoes, peeled and thinly sliced

Finely grated zest and juice of 1 lime

1 pound firm white fish fillets, cut into 2-inch pieces

¹/₈ teaspoon pepper

---

1 In a 4-quart saucepan, combine onions with sweet pepper, tomatoes, hot red pepper sauce, herbs, stock, and white wine. Bring to a boil over moderate heat.

2 Stir in potatoes and simmer, partially covered, about 15 minutes, stirring occasionally.

3 Stir in lime zest and juice and simmer about 5 minutes. Add pieces of fish, cover, and gently simmer about 5 minutes longer or until potatoes are tender and fish flakes easily. Remove and discard bay leaf. Season with pepper.

PER CUP
Calories **108**, Saturated Fat **0g**, Total Fat **1g**, Sodium **108mg**, Cholesterol **20mg**, Protein **11g**, Carbohydrate **10g**, Fiber **2g**.

Mediterranean Fish Soup

- Makes **12 cups**
- Preparation Time **15 minutes**
- Cooking Time **45 minutes**

---

1 tablespoon olive or canola oil

2 cloves garlic, finely chopped

1 large onion, coarsely chopped

6 ounces fennel bulb or celery, coarsely chopped

1 large sweet red pepper, diced

6 cups fish stock, page 18

2 cups canned crushed tomatoes

1 bay leaf

1 pound firm white fish, such as flounder, cod, grouper, or perch, cut into 2-inch pieces

8 ounces medium shrimp, peeled and deveined

¹/₈ teaspoon each salt and pepper

---

1 Heat oil in a 4-quart saucepan over moderate heat. Add garlic, onion, fennel, and sweet pepper to the pan. Sauté about 5 minutes or until softened.

2 Add stock, crushed tomatoes, and bay leaf. Bring to a boil and simmer about 25 minutes.

3 Add fish and shrimp, cover the pan, and cook about 4 minutes or until fish flakes easily and shrimp are cooked through. Remove and discard bay leaf. Season with salt and pepper.

PER CUP
Calories **104**, Saturated Fat **0g**, Total Fat **2g**, Sodium **165mg**, Cholesterol **40mg**, Protein **13g**, Carbohydrate **8g**, Fiber **2g**.

Basic Vegetable Stock

Cooking technique ▪ *Use the freshest vegetables possible and slowly simmer so that all the flavors blend together to give a rich stock.*

● Makes 8½ cups ● Preparation Time **10 minutes** ● Cooking Time **1 hour 10 minutes**

PER CUP
Calories **15**, Saturated Fat **0g**, Total Fat **0g**, Sodium **53mg**, Cholesterol **0mg**, Protein **0g**, Carbohydrate **0g**, Fiber **0g**.

4 stalks celery, cut across into ½-inch slices, with leaves

2 leeks or onions, trimmed and cut into 1-inch chunks

2 large carrots, unpeeled, cut into ½-inch chunks

2 small parsnips, unpeeled, cut into ½-inch chunks

2 shallots or 1 small onion, peeled and quartered

½ head cabbage (about 12 ounces), coarsely shredded

Sprigs of fresh herbs, such as parsley, thyme, and bay leaves

10 black peppercorns

3 quarts cold water

1 Place all the vegetables, herbs, and peppercorns in a large stockpot and cover with the water.

2 Bring to a boil over moderate heat and simmer, partially covered and occasionally skimming off any scum that rises to the surface, about 45 minutes.

Basic Vegetable Stock is brimming with good taste and great nutrition.

3 Remove from the heat and strain the stock through a cheesecloth-lined sieve. Discard the solids.

4 Simmer the strained stock, uncovered, until it is reduced to about 8½ cups.

COOKING TIP
For an even richer vegetable stock, sauté the vegetables until they are brown before placing them in the stockpot with the water.

Mushroom and Chive Soup

- Makes 9 cups
- Preparation Time 15 minutes
- Cooking Time 25 minutes

5 cups vegetable stock, page 18

½ ounce dried porcini mushrooms (optional)

2 teaspoons olive or canola oil

1 shallot or small onion, finely chopped

1 stalk celery, coarsely chopped

8 ounces mushrooms, trimmed and sliced

1 tablespoon chopped fresh or frozen chives

⅛ teaspoon each salt and pepper

2 tablespoons low-fat sour cream

1 In a small saucepan, bring 1 cup stock to a boil. Remove from the heat and add porcini mushrooms if using. Allow to soften at least 10 minutes. Drain, reserving liquid, and chop mushrooms.

2 In a 4-quart saucepan, heat oil over moderate heat. Add shallot and celery and cook about 4 minutes, until softened and golden.

3 Stir in all mushrooms; cook about 5 minutes. Add remaining stock and soaking liquid; simmer, partially covered, for 10 minutes or until mushrooms are very soft.

4 Stir in chives, salt, and pepper; simmer 3 minutes. Serve with a little sour cream on each portion.

PER CUP
Calories **34**, Saturated Fat **0g**,
Total Fat **2g**, Sodium **68mg**,
Cholesterol **0mg**, Protein **1g**,
Carbohydrate **4g**, Fiber **0g**.

Chunky Vegetable Soup with Pasta

- Makes 11 cups
- Preparation Time 15 minutes
- Cooking Time 35 minutes

2 tablespoons olive or canola oil

2 leeks or onions, trimmed and thinly sliced

2 large carrots, cut into ½-inch dice

8 ounces rutabaga, cut into ½-inch dice

8 ounces fennel or celery, cut into ½-inch dice

6 cups vegetable stock, page 18

2 cups canned crushed tomatoes

4 ounces orzo or any small pasta

⅛ teaspoon each salt and pepper

¼ cup shredded fresh basil or 2 teaspoons dried

2 tablespoons grated Parmesan cheese

1 In a large saucepan, heat oil over moderate heat. Sauté leeks until softened but not browned.

2 Sauté remaining vegetables until softened. Stir in stock. Simmer, partially covered, about 5 minutes or until vegetables are almost soft.

3 Stir in tomatoes and return to a boil. Add orzo and simmer about 8 minutes. Add salt, pepper, and basil. Serve with a little cheese sprinkled on each portion.

PER CUP
Calories **113**, Saturated Fat **1g**,
Total Fat **3g**, Sodium **178mg**,
Cholesterol **1mg**, Protein **3g**,
Carbohydrate **19g**, Fiber **2g**.

Texas Vegetable Soup

- Makes 7½ cups
- Preparation Time 15 minutes
- Cooking Time 30 minutes

1 tablespoon olive or canola oil

1–2 jalapeño peppers, finely chopped, or canned and rinsed

1 large onion, coarsely chopped

1 sweet red pepper, diced

2 carrots, diced

1 tablespoons all-purpose flour

½ teaspoon dry mustard

2 quarts vegetable stock, page 18

2 cups fresh or frozen corn kernels

⅛ teaspoon each salt and pepper

2 ounces reduced-fat Cheddar cheese, shredded

1 In a large saucepan, heat oil over moderate heat. Add jalapeño pepper, onion, sweet red pepper, and carrots. Sauté the vegetables until softened.

2 Stir in flour and dry mustard and cook until vegetables are coated with mixture.

3 Add stock and bring to a boil. Simmer about 8 minutes, until vegetables are tender.

4 Add corn and return to a boil. Simmer about 5 minutes, until corn is tender. Add salt and pepper. Serve with a little cheese sprinkled on each portion.

PER CUP
Calories **118**, Saturated Fat **0g**,
Total Fat **3g**, Sodium **121mg**,
Cholesterol **4mg**, Protein **5g**,
Carbohydrate **20g**, Fiber **2g**.

White Bean Soup with Carrots

Cooking technique ▪ *Simmer dried beans and vegetables in broth to make a protein-rich soup that has very little fat.*
Reduce sodium ▪ *Use homemade stock or a low-sodium canned broth. It's always a good idea to cook with dried beans. They are much lower in sodium than canned.*

● Makes **8 cups** ● Preparation Time **10 minutes plus soaking time** ● Cooking Time **1³/₄ hours**

PER CUP
Calories **136**, Saturated Fat **0g**,
Total Fat **2g**, Sodium **87mg**,
Cholesterol **0mg**, Protein **6g**,
Carbohydrate **24g**, Fiber **5g**.

2 cups dried white beans such as
Great Northern or navy beans,
washed and picked over

1 tablespoon olive oil

1 large onion, sliced

6 cloves garlic, coarsely chopped

6 cups vegetable stock, page 18

2 large carrots, sliced

1 tablespoon chopped fresh sage
or ¹/₂ teaspoon dried sage,
crumbled

¹/₈ teaspoon each salt and pepper

1 Place the beans in a large saucepan and generously cover with water. Bring to a boil, boil about 2 minutes, then remove from the heat. Allow to soak at least 1 hour or overnight.

2 Drain the beans, rinse thoroughly under cold water, and drain the beans again.

3 In a 4-quart saucepan, heat the oil over moderate heat. Add onion and garlic and about 2 tablespoons of stock, and sauté about 5 minutes, until softened but not browned. Add carrots and sage and sauté, stirring, about 2 minutes longer.

4 Add the soaked beans and the remaining stock and bring to a boil. Simmer the soup, partially covered and stirring occasionally, about 1¹/₂ hours, until the beans are quite tender.

5 Remove the soup from the heat. Transfer about 1¹/₂ cups of the beans and vegetables to a blender or food processor and purée until quite smooth. Add about ¹/₂ cup of the liquid and process to combine.

6 Return the purée to the soup and season with salt and pepper. Return the soup to the heat and simmer about 3 minutes longer.

*Sage adds magnificent flavor to **White Bean Soup with Carrots**, which is served here with bread rolls and a sprinkling of fresh basil.*

White Bean and Pasta Soup with Basil

Small shell-shaped pasta work very well in this Italian-influenced variation. For the best flavor, use fresh basil for garnish.

- Makes **9 cups**
- Preparation Time **20 minutes** plus soaking time
- Cooking Time **2 hours**

---

2 cups dried white kidney beans

1 tablespoon olive or canola oil

2 carrots, sliced

4 cloves garlic, coarsely chopped

8 cups vegetable stock, page 18

1 tablespoon chopped fresh basil or 1 teaspoon dried

1 can (16 ounces) sliced plum tomatoes

1 zucchini, sliced

1/2 cup small pasta shapes or pieces of broken spaghetti

1 tablespoon grated Parmesan cheese

1/8 teaspoon pepper

1 teaspoon chopped fresh basil or parsley for garnish

---

1 Place the beans in a large saucepan and cover generously with water. Bring to a boil, boil about 2 minutes, then remove from the heat. Cover and allow to soak at least 1 hour or overnight.

2 Drain the beans, rinse under cold water, and drain again.

3 In a 4-quart saucepan, heat the oil over moderate heat. Add the carrots and garlic, then about 2 tablespoons of the stock, and sauté about 5 minutes, until softened but not browned.

4 Add the basil and sauté, stirring constantly, about 2 minutes longer. Add the soaked beans with the remaining stock and bring to a boil. Simmer, partially covered and stirring occasionally, about 1 hour 20 minutes, until the beans and vegetables are very tender.

5 Add the tomatoes, zucchini, and pasta, and return to a boil. Simmer the soup about 10 minutes longer, until the zucchini and pasta are tender.

6 Add the Parmesan cheese and season with pepper. Serve garnished with chopped basil or parsley leaves.

PER CUP
Calories **199**, Saturated Fat **0g**, Total Fat **2g**, Sodium **152mg**, Cholesterol **1mg**, Protein **11g**, Carbohydrate **36g**, Fiber **6g**.

There is a wide variety of small pasta shapes to choose from. Fresh basil makes a colorful garnish.

Cuban Black Bean Soup

Take great care when puréeing hot soup: Never fill the blender or food processor to the top, or the hot liquid may be forced out when the machine is turned on. Blend for short periods — don't leave running for longer than a few seconds at a time.

- Makes **9 cups**
- Preparation Time **15 minutes** plus soaking time
- Cooking Time **1 1/2 hours**

---

2 cups dried black beans, such as turtle beans, rinsed and picked over

1 ounce lean salt pork or turkey bacon, coarsely chopped

2 cloves garlic, coarsely chopped

1 large onion, coarsely chopped

1 large sweet green pepper, coarsely chopped

1/4 teaspoon ground cumin

1/4 teaspoon dried thyme leaves

4 cups vegetable stock, page 18

1 cup water

1 can (28 ounces) crushed tomatoes

1 tablespoon lime juice

1/8 teaspoon pepper

Dash hot red pepper sauce

1/3 cup low-fat sour cream

Chopped fresh thyme or parsley for garnish

---

1 Place the black beans in a large saucepan and cover generously with water. Bring to a boil, boil about 2 minutes, then remove from the heat. Cover and allow to soak at least 1 hour or overnight.

2 Drain the beans, rinse under cold water, and drain again.

3 In a 4-quart saucepan, heat the salt pork over moderate heat and cook, stirring frequently, until crisp and the fat is rendered. Using a slotted spoon, remove the salt pork and discard.

4 Add the garlic, onion, and green pepper and sauté, stirring constantly, about 5 minutes, until softened and slightly browned. Stir in the cumin and thyme and sauté about 2 minutes longer.

5 Stir in the stock with the water, tomatoes, and the soaked beans, and bring to a boil. Simmer the soup, partially covered and stirring occasionally, about 1 hour, until the beans and vegetables are very tender.

6 Remove from the heat, transfer about 2 cups of the beans and vegetables to a blender or food processor, and purée until very smooth. Add about half of the liquid and process to combine. Return the mixture to the soup and return to the heat. Stir in the lime juice, pepper, and a dash of hot red pepper sauce. Serve garnished with a spoonful of sour cream and a little chopped thyme or parsley.

PER CUP
Calories **215**, Saturated Fat **0g**, Total Fat **4g**, Sodium **235mg**, Cholesterol **0mg**, Protein **12g**, Carbohydrate **36g**, Fiber **6g**.

Tuscan Red Bean Soup

You can bring out the flavor even more by using fresh oregano and basil – use 1 teaspoon of each and freeze the surplus in parcels wrapped in foil.

- Makes **9 cups**
- Preparation Time **15 minutes** plus soaking time
- Cooking Time **1¼ hours**

---

2 cups dried red kidney beans, washed and picked over

1 tablespoon olive or canola oil

2 leeks or small onions, cleaned and coarsely chopped

2 stalks celery, coarsely chopped

2 carrots, coarsely chopped

6 cups vegetable stock, page 18

1 can (28 ounces) crushed tomatoes

¼ teaspoon each dried oregano and dried basil

1 bay leaf

1 cup shredded cabbage leaves

4 ounces green beans, cut across into 1-inch pieces

⅛ teaspoon each salt and pepper

2 tablespoons grated Parmesan cheese

---

1 Place the beans in a large saucepan and cover generously with water. Bring to a boil, boil about 2 minutes, then remove from the heat. Cover and allow to soak at least 1 hour or overnight.

2 Drain the beans, rinse under cold water, and drain again.

3 In a 4-quart saucepan, heat the oil over moderate heat. Add the leeks, celery, and carrots and sauté about 5 minutes, until softened but not browned.

4 Add the stock with the tomatoes, herbs, and soaked beans. Bring to a boil and boil 10 minutes, then reduce the heat and simmer the soup, partially covered and stirring occasionally, about 45 minutes, until the beans and vegetables are tender.

5 Add the cabbage and green beans, and simmer about 10 minutes longer, until tender.

6 Season with the salt and pepper. Serve sprinkled with the grated Parmesan cheese.

PER CUP
Calories **203**, Saturated Fat **1g**, Total Fat **3g**, Sodium **259mg**, Cholesterol **1mg**, Protein **111g**, Carbohydrate **36g**, Fiber **7g**.

BOILING KIDNEY BEANS

To get rid of the toxins from the skin of red kidney beans, it is essential to boil them rapidly for 10 minutes.

A dusting of grated Parmesan cheese adds the finishing touch to this hearty Mediterranean soup.

GETTING AHEAD

Make the soup a day ahead. The beans will absorb more flavor from the oregano and basil if the soup is allowed to stand longer. Cover and chill in the refrigerator until you need it, then make sure you reheat thoroughly.

Cream of Broccoli Soup

Cooking technique ▪ *Thicken the soup with puréed potato instead of cream.*
Add nutrients ▪ *Substitute thin-skinned new potatoes with no green patches*
and leave them unpeeled to retain more of the nutrients.

● Makes **10 cups** ● Preparation Time **25 minutes** ● Cooking Time **30 minutes**

PER CUP
Calories **82**, Saturated Fat **1g**,
Total Fat **2g**, Sodium **90mg**,
Cholesterol **1mg**, Protein **4g**,
Carbohydrate **12g**, Fiber **2g**.

1 pound broccoli	1 pound all-purpose potatoes, peeled and diced
1 tablespoon olive or canola oil	6 cups chicken stock, page 18
3 leeks or 1 onion, trimmed and sliced	1 cup 1% low-fat milk
2 cloves garlic, finely chopped	1/8 teaspoon each salt and pepper
1/2 cup water	

1 Cut the broccoli florets from the stems. Using a vegetable peeler, peel the broccoli stems, then slice them.

2 In a 4-quart saucepan, heat oil over moderate heat. Sauté leeks and garlic until softened. Add the water and cook about 5 minutes, until soft.

3 Add broccoli stems to the saucepan with potatoes, stock, and milk. Simmer, partially covered, about 8 minutes, until broccoli and potatoes are tender.

Cream of Broccoli Soup *appeals to the eye as well as to the taste buds; serve it with bread rolls on the side.*

4 Stir in the broccoli florets and simmer the soup about 5 minutes longer, until the florets are very tender.

5 Remove from the heat. With a skimmer or slotted spoon, transfer the vegetables to a blender or food processor. Purée until very smooth.

6 Return the purée to the liquid in the saucepan. Return the pan to the heat until the soup is warmed through. Season with the salt and pepper.

Summer Squash Soup

- Makes **9 cups**
- Preparation Time **20 minutes**
- Cooking Time **30–35 minutes**

1 tablespoon olive or canola oil

1 large onion, coarsely chopped

2 cloves garlic, fincly chopped

2 quarts chicken stock, page 18

8 ounces all-purpose potatoes, peeled and coarsely chopped

8 ounces zucchini, sliced

8 ounces yellow squash, sliced

$^1/_2$ cup packed basil leaves, finely shredded

$^1/_8$ teaspoon each salt and pepper

1 In a 4-quart saucepan, heat oil over moderate heat. Add onion, garlic, and 2 tablespoons of stock. Sauté until softened but not browned.

2 Stir in potatoes and remaining stock; simmer, partially covered, about 5 minutes, until tender.

3 Stir in zucchini and yellow squash and return to a boil. Simmer 10 to 15 minutes, until potatoes and squash are tender.

4 Remove from the heat. Using a slotted spoon, transfer vegetables to a blender or food processor and purée. Return purée to liquid in pan and return to the heat.

5 Stir in basil and season with salt and pepper.

PER CUP
Calories **78**, Saturated Fat **1g**, Total Fat **2g**, Sodium **92mg**, Cholesterol **0mg**, Protein **3g**, Carbohydrate **11g**, Fiber **2g**.

Red Pepper and Tomato Soup

- Makes **8 cups**
- Preparation Time **20 minutes**
- Cooking Time **about 1 hour**

2 tablespoons olive or canola oil

2 large sweet red peppers, coarsely chopped

1 pound fresh plum tomatoes, cored and halved

2 cloves garlic, sliced

1 large onion, coarsely chopped

4 cups chicken stock, page 18

2 cups water

$^1/_4$ cup packed cilantro or parsley, coarsely chopped

$^1/_8$ teaspoon each salt and pepper

1 Preheat oven to 375°F. Coat bottom of a roasting pan with half the oil. Add peppers, tomatoes, and garlic, and toss to coat. Roast, stirring once, 25 to 30 minutes.

2 In a 4-quart saucepan, heat remaining oil over moderate heat. Add onion; sauté about 3 minutes, until softened. Add pepper mixture with stock and water; simmer, partially covered, 20 to 25 minutes, until soft.

3 Remove from the heat. Using a slotted spoon, transfer vegetables to a blender or food processor. Strain liquid into a clean pan, and purée vegetables with 1 cup liquid. Strain purée into liquid and simmer 5 minutes. Stir in cilantro, salt, and pepper.

PER CUP
Calories **77**, Saturated Fat **1g**, Total Fat **4g**, Sodium **75mg**, Cholesterol **0mg**, Protein **2g**, Carbohydrate **9g**, Fiber **2g**.

Curried Cauliflower Soup with Lime

- Makes **11 cups**
- Preparation Time **20 minutes**
- Cooking Time **40 minutes**

$1^1/_2$ tablespoons olive or canola oil

2 large onions, coarsely chopped

2 cloves garlic, finely chopped

2 teaspoons curry powder

Pinch each of ground ginger and turmeric (optional)

$1^1/_2$ pounds cauliflower florets

8 ounces all-purpose potatoes, pceled and diced

2 quarts chicken stock, page 18

1 tablespoon fresh lime juice

$^1/_8$ teaspoon each salt and pepper

1 In a 4-quart saucepan, heat oil over moderate heat. Add onions and garlic; sauté about 3 minutes, until softened. Stir in curry powder and spices, if using, and sauté about 3 minutes longer.

2 Coarsely chop the cauliflower florets. Add the florets, potatoes, and stock to pan; simmer, partially covered, 20 to 25 minutes, until soft.

3 Remove pan from the heat. Using a slotted spoon, transfer vegetables to a blender or food processor and purée; add to pan and return to the heat. Stir in lime juice, salt, and pepper.

PER CUP
Calories **85**, Saturated Fat **1g**, Total Fat **3g**, Sodium **84mg**, Cholesterol **0mg**, Protein **4g**, Carbohydrate **12g**, Fiber **3g**.

Sweet Corn Chowder

Cooking technique ■ *For a rich home-style taste, use 2 ounces of bacon — it will render just enough fat to cook the vegetables and flavor the chowder.*

Reduce fat ■ *Instead of the whole milk called for in traditional recipes, use a combination of low-fat milk and chicken stock.*

Reduce sodium ■ *Use low-sodium bacon. Season with pepper and just a touch of salt.*

Increase fiber ■ *Sweet corn, whether fresh or frozen, offers plenty of fiber; celery and potato add even more.*

● Makes **11 cups** ● Preparation Time **20 minutes** ● Cooking Time **45 minutes**

PER CUP
Calories **88**, Saturated Fat **1g**,
Total Fat **3g**, Sodium **87mg**,
Cholesterol **4mg**, Protein **4g**,
Carbohydrate **14g**, Fiber **3g**.

---

2 ounces reduced-sodium bacon or lean salt pork, coarsely chopped

2 large onions, diced

2 large carrots, diced

2 stalks celery, diced

12 ounces all-purpose potatoes, peeled and diced

6 cups chicken stock, page 18

2 cups fresh or frozen corn kernels

2 cups 1% low-fat milk

¹/₈ teaspoon each salt and pepper

Cayenne pepper

1 In a 4-quart saucepan, cook the bacon over moderate heat about 4 minutes, until it is browned and the fat is rendered. Remove the bacon with a slotted spoon and reserve for garnish. (If using salt pork, discard.)

2 Add the onions, carrots, and celery to the saucepan and sauté about 5 minutes, until softened.

3 Stir in the potatoes with the chicken stock and bring to a boil. Simmer the soup, partially covered, stirring occasionally, about 10 minutes or until the vegetables are tender.

4 Add the corn kernels and return the soup to a boil. Simmer, uncovered, about 5 minutes longer.

5 Remove from the heat and, using a ladle or slotted spoon, transfer about 2½ cups of the vegetables to a blender or food processor. Purée until smooth.

6 Add the purée and milk to the saucepan, and simmer about 3 minutes. Season with salt, pepper, and a pinch of cayenne. Serve garnished with the bacon.

*Served with bread on the side, **Sweet Corn Chowder** makes a light but filling meal.
If you have time, it's worth making it with fresh corn.*

New England Clam Chowder

The work preparing fresh clams is worth it – not only do they taste better, but they are much lower in sodium than canned.

- Makes 8½ cups
- Preparation Time **25 minutes**
- Cooking Time **50 minutes**

---

1 dozen littleneck or cherrystone clams or 1 can (10 ounces) whole baby clams, drained and rinsed

6 cups fish stock, page 18

1 ounce lean salt pork or reduced-sodium bacon, coarsely chopped

2 large onions, coarsely chopped

1 pound all-purpose potatoes, peeled and diced

2 cups 1% low-fat milk

⅛ teaspoon each salt and pepper

2 tablespoons chopped parsley

1 Prepare clams (see box, right) in ¼ cup fish stock. When cool enough, remove the clams from their shells and coarsely chop.

2 Cook salt pork in a 4-quart saucepan over moderate heat about 3 minutes, until crisp and fat is rendered. With a slotted spoon, remove pork and discard. If using bacon, reserve for garnish.

3 Add the onions to the pan with ¼ cup of the stock. Sauté about 5 minutes or until softened but not browned.

4 Stir in potatoes and remaining fish stock and bring to a boil. Simmer, partially covered, stirring occasionally, about 10 minutes or until the potatoes are very tender.

5 Remove from the heat and purée about 2 cups of the vegetables in a blender or food processor until smooth. Add the purée to the soup and return to the heat.

6 Add the milk and the chopped clams and simmer about 5 minutes to blend the flavors. Season with the salt and pepper and stir in parsley. Garnish with the bacon, if using.

PER CUP
Calories **126**, Saturated Fat **1g**, Total Fat **3g**, Sodium **138mg**, Cholesterol **11mg**, Protein **8g**, Carbohydrate **17g**, Fiber **2g**.

*A touch of salt pork gives this low-fat version of **New England Clam Chowder** hearty old-fashioned flavor.*

PREPARING CLAMS

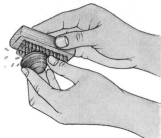

1 *Scrub the clam shells well under cold water to remove any sand and grit.*

2 *Place in a large saucepan with the amount of stock specified in the recipe. Cover and bring to a boil. Simmer about 5 minutes, until the shells open. Remove the clams with a slotted spoon and cool.*

3 *Open the shells and remove the clams. Discard any shells that have not opened.*

Sweet Corn and Seafood Chowder

For a richer chowder, you can add 8 ounces fresh mussels or clams. Simply stir them into the soup in Step 3 along with the shrimp and simmer until they have opened.

- Makes **10 cups**
- Preparation Time **20 minutes**
- Cooking Time **35 minutes**

1¹/₂ tablespoons olive or canola oil

2 large onions, diced

2 large carrots, diced

2 stalks celery, diced

1 pound all-purpose potatoes, peeled and diced

5 cups fish stock, page 18

8 ounces medium shrimp, peeled and deveined

2 cups fresh or frozen corn kernels

2 cups 1% low-fat milk

¹/₈ teaspoon each salt and pepper

Pinch of paprika

1 In a 4-quart saucepan, heat oil over moderate heat. Add the onions, carrots, and celery and sauté, stirring, about 5 minutes, until softened but not browned.

2 Stir in the potatoes with the fish stock and bring to a boil. Simmer the soup, partially covered, stirring occasionally, 10 to 15 minutes, until the vegetables are tender.

3 Purée about 2 cups of the vegetables in a blender or food processor until smooth. Add the purée to the saucepan with the shrimp, corn, and milk. Return to a boil and simmer about 3 minutes. Season with salt, pepper, and paprika.

PER CUP
Calories **144**, Saturated Fat **1g**, Total Fat **3g**, Sodium **132mg**, Cholesterol **25mg**, Protein **8g**, Carbohydrate **21g**, Fiber **3g**.

PEELING AND DEVEINING SHRIMP

1 *Using the tips of your fingers, carefully peel off the shells from the shrimp and discard the shells.*

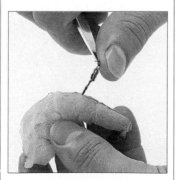

2 *Make a shallow cut along the back of the shrimp with a small knife. Gently pull out and discard the dark intestinal vein.*

Succotash Chowder

The combination of corn, lima beans, and milk gives this chowder lots of protein with very little fat and cholesterol. Serve it with sliced tomatoes and whole-wheat rolls.

- Makes **11 cups**
- Preparation Time **15 minutes**
- Cooking Time **35 minutes**

1¹/₂ tablespoons olive or canola oil

2 large onions, diced

2 carrots, diced

2 stalks celery, diced

6 cups chicken or vegetable stock, page 18

2 cups fresh or frozen corn kernels

2 cups fresh or frozen baby lima beans

2 cups 1% low-fat milk

1 tablespoon cornstarch

¹/₂ teaspoon dry mustard

¹/₂ teaspoon finely grated lemon zest

¹/₈ teaspoon each salt and pepper

1 In a 4-quart saucepan, heat oil over moderate heat. Add the onions, carrots, celery, and ¹/₄ cup of the stock, and sauté about 5 minutes, until softened.

2 Stir the corn kernels and lima beans into the onion, carrot, and celery. Add the remaining stock and bring the mixture to a boil.

3 Simmer the soup, partially covered, stirring occasionally, about 10 minutes, until the vegetables are tender.

4 Combine ¹/₂ cup of the milk with the cornstarch and dry mustard until smooth. Stir into the soup with the remaining milk and the lemon zest. Return the soup to a boil and simmer about 3 minutes. Season with the salt and pepper.

PER CUP
Calories **132**, Saturated Fat **1g**, Total Fat **3g**, Sodium **108mg**, Cholesterol **2mg**, Protein **7g**, Carbohydrate **21g**, Fiber **5g**.

COOKING TIP
If you are using frozen corn or lima beans, rinse them quickly under running water. This washes off any ice, so that you are not adding more liquid to your chowder .

Fresh lima beans are available from June to September; they are also available frozen.

Chilled Cream of Zucchini

Cooking technique ■ *For soup that's creamy yet low in fat, use potato or puréed vegetables as a thickener. Then stir in low-fat milk, yogurt, or sour cream.*

● Makes **8** cups ● Preparation Time **20–25** minutes plus chilling time ● Cooking Time **25–30** minutes

PER CUP
Calories **94**, Saturated Fat **0g**,
Total Fat **2g**, Sodium **123mg**,
Cholesterol **2mg**, Protein **5g**,
Carbohydrate **15g**, Fiber **2g**.

1 tablespoon olive or canola oil
1 large onion, coarsely chopped
2 cloves garlic, finely chopped
6 cups vegetable stock, page 18
8 ounces all-purpose potatoes, peeled and diced

1 pound zucchini, trimmed and thinly sliced
1½ cups flat-leaf parsley leaves
1 cup 1% low-fat milk
⅛ teaspoon each salt and pepper
1 cup nonfat plain yogurt

1 In a 4-quart saucepan, heat oil over moderate heat. Add the onion and garlic, then about ¼ cup of the stock. Sauté until softened but not browned.

2 Add the potatoes to the saucepan and stir to coat with the onion and garlic mixture. Pour in the remaining stock and bring to a boil.

3 Add the zucchini to the saucepan and simmer the soup, partially covered, about 10 minutes, until all the vegetables are very tender.

*It tastes as good as it looks – **Chilled Cream of Zucchini** soup, decorated with a pretty swirl of yogurt.*

4 Remove from the heat and stir in the parsley. Strain the soup into a large bowl; purée the vegetables in a blender or food processor until very smooth.

5 Stir the purée into the stock and allow to cool. Stir in the milk, salt, and pepper, and chill the soup until ready to serve.

6 Before serving, spoon a large spoonful of yogurt into each bowl of soup. With the tip of the spoon, gently draw the yogurt out in a circle to make a swirl.

Chilled Cream of Watercress Soup

- Makes **8 cups**
- Preparation Time **20 minutes** plus chilling time
- Cooking Time **25 minutes**

1 tablespoon olive or canola oil
2 large onions, coarsely chopped
6 cups vegetable stock, page 18
1 pound all-purpose potatoes, peeled and diced
2 cups watercress leaves, stems removed
1 cup 1% low-fat milk
¹/₈ teaspoon each salt and pepper
Grated nutmeg

1 In a 4-quart saucepan, heat oil over moderate heat. Add onions, then about 2 tablespoons of stock, and sauté about 5 minutes, until softened but not browned.

2 Add potatoes with remaining stock and bring to a boil. Simmer soup, partially covered, stirring occasionally, about 10 minutes or until potatoes are very tender.

3 Remove from the heat and stir in the watercress leaves. Strain soup into a large bowl and purée vegetables in a blender or food processor until very smooth.

4 Stir purée into stock and allow to cool. Stir in milk, salt, pepper, and a pinch of nutmeg, and chill the soup until ready to serve.

PER CUP
Calories **109**, Saturated Fat **1g**, Total Fat **3g**, Sodium **116mg**, Cholesterol **2mg**, Protein **5g**, Carbohydrate **18g**, Fiber **2g**.

Chilled Yellow Squash and Pepper Soup

- Makes **8¹/₂ cups**
- Preparation Time **15 minutes** plus chilling time
- Cooking Time **30 minutes**

2 large sweet yellow peppers, coarsely chopped
2 cloves garlic, finely chopped
1 teaspoon tomato paste
6 cups vegetable stock, page 18
1 pound yellow squash, sliced
1 cup 1% low-fat milk
1 tablespoon chopped chives or parsley
¹/₈ teaspoon each salt and pepper

1 In a 4-quart saucepan, combine yellow peppers, garlic, and tomato paste. Add stock; simmer, partially covered, about 8 minutes, stirring occasionally, until pepper is tender.

2 Add squash and continue simmering, partially covered, 10 to 15 minutes, until squash and pepper are soft.

3 Remove from the heat and strain into a large bowl. Purée vegetables in a blender or food processor until very smooth.

4 Stir purée into stock and allow to cool. Stir in milk, chives, salt, and pepper, and chill soup until ready to serve.

PER CUP
Calories **44**, Saturated Fat **0g**, Total Fat **1g**, Sodium **95mg**, Cholesterol **1mg**, Protein **3g**, Carbohydrate **9g**, Fiber **1g**.

Chilled Tomato and Fennel Soup

- Makes **9¹/₂ cups**
- Preparation Time **20 minutes** plus chilling time
- Cooking Time **30 minutes**

1¹/₂ tablespoons olive or canola oil
1¹/₄ pounds fennel, coarsely chopped, with fronds reserved
3 cups vegetable stock, page 18
1 can (28 ounces) crushed tomatoes
1 cup low-sodium tomato juice
¹/₂ cup dry white wine or vegetable stock
1 bay leaf
¹/₃ cup low-fat sour cream
¹/₈ teaspoon each salt and pepper

1 Using method given in Step 1 of master recipe, sauté fennel in oil and ¹/₄ cup stock.

2 Stir in tomatoes, tomato juice, wine, and remaining stock. Add bay leaf and bring to a boil. Simmer, partially covered, about 25 minutes, until fennel is very soft and mixture has thickened slightly.

3 Remove from the heat and discard bay leaf. Purée soup and allow to cool as in master recipe.

4 Stir in sour cream, salt, and pepper, and chill soup until ready to serve. Serve garnished with reserved fennel fronds.

PER CUP
Calories **86**, Saturated Fat **1g**, Total Fat **3g**, Sodium **216mg**, Cholesterol **1mg**, Protein **3g**, Carbohydrate **12g**, Fiber **3g**.

Red Gazpacho

Cooking technique ■ *Marinate finely chopped vegetables in oil and spices – serve chilled.*
You'll enjoy the vitamin benefit of raw vegetables plus great fresh taste.

● Makes 6½ cups ● Preparation Time **20 minutes** plus chilling time

PER CUP
Calories **129**, Saturated Fat **1g**,
Total Fat **5g**, Sodium **167mg**,
Cholesterol **0mg**, Protein **3g**,
Carbohydrate **19g**, Fiber **3g**.

3 ounces French or Italian bread

1 large sweet red or green
   pepper, coarsely chopped

1 red onion, coarsely chopped

1 small cucumber, peeled,
   seeded, and sliced

8 ounces plum tomatoes,
   cored and quartered

¼ cup packed basil or parsley

1 clove garlic, finely chopped

2 tablespoons olive oil

2 tablespoons red or white
   wine vinegar

3 cups reduced-sodium tomato
   juice

⅛ teaspoon pepper

1 Remove the crusts from the
bread and tear the bread into
pieces. Place in a bowl and cover
with water. Allow to stand at
least 5 minutes.

2 Drain some of the water
from the bowl and, with your
hands, squeeze out most of the
remaining water from the bread.
Reserve the soaked bread.

3 Place the sweet pepper,
red onion, and cucumber in
a food processor and process
until very finely chopped. Pour
the mixture into a large bowl.

*The perfect start to a hot summer night's meal – **Red Gazpacho** served with pita-bread fingers.*

4 Add the tomatoes and basil to the food processor and process until very finely chopped but not totally puréed. Add to the pepper mixture in the bowl.

5 Add garlic, oil, wine vinegar, soaked bread, and tomato juice to the food processor and process until blended. Stir into the soup until thoroughly combined.

6 Add the pepper. Cover the bowl and refrigerate the soup for at least 1 hour before serving.

Green Gazpacho

- Makes **6 cups**
- Preparation Time **20 minutes plus chilling time**

3 ounces French or Italian bread

1 cucumber, peeled, seeded, and sliced

1/2 cup packed watercress leaves

1/4 cup packed parsley leaves

2 sweet green peppers, coarsely chopped

2 stalks celery, sliced

2 scallions, white and green parts, sliced

3 cups vegetable stock, page 18

2 tablespoons olive oil

2 tablespoons white or red wine vinegar

1/8 teaspoon each salt and pepper

1 Remove the crusts from the bread and tear the bread into pieces. Place in a bowl and cover with water. Allow to stand at least 5 minutes.

2 Drain off the water from the bowl and, with your hands, squeeze out most of the remaining water from the bread. Reserve the bread.

3 Place the cucumber in a food processor with the watercress and parsley and process until very finely chopped but not totally puréed. Pour the mixture into a large bowl.

4 Place the sweet peppers, celery, and scallions in the food processor and process until very finely chopped. Add to the cucumber mixture in the bowl.

5 Place the soaked bread in the food processor with the vegetable stock, olive oil, and wine vinegar and process until blended. Add the salt and pepper and then stir into the contents of the bowl.

6 Cover the bowl and refrigerate the soup for at least 1 hour or until ready to serve.

PER CUP
Calories **110**, Saturated Fat **1g**, Total Fat **5g**, Sodium **178mg**, Cholesterol **0mg**, Protein **3g**, Carbohydrate **15g**, Fiber **2g**.

White Gazpacho

- Makes **5 cups**
- Preparation Time **20 minutes plus chilling time**

3 ounces French or Italian bread

1 cup 1% low-fat milk

1 cup coarsely chopped blanched almonds

1 cucumber, peeled, seeded, and sliced

1 1/2 cups seedless green grapes, halved

1 clove garlic

2 cups vegetable or chicken stock, page 18

2 tablespoons white or red wine vinegar

1/8 teaspoon each salt and pepper

Fresh mint sprigs for serving

1 Remove the crusts from the bread and tear the bread into pieces. Place in a bowl and cover with the milk. Allow to stand at least 5 minutes.

2 Place the bread and milk in a food processor with the chopped almonds and process until very finely chopped and almost puréed. Transfer to a large bowl.

3 Place the cucumber, grapes, and garlic in the food processor and process until very finely chopped. Add to the almond mixture in the bowl. Stir in the vegetable stock, vinegar, salt, and pepper.

4 Cover the bowl and refrigerate the soup for at least 1 hour or until ready to serve. Serve the soup garnished with the mint leaves.

PER CUP
Calories **278**, Saturated Fat **2g**, Total Fat **16g**, Sodium **224mg**, Cholesterol **2mg**, Protein **10g**, Carbohydrate **27g**, Fiber **4g**.

Peach Soup with Almonds

Cooking technique ■ *Poach fresh fruit until tender, then purée it in the processor. Although these thick creamy soups taste like dessert, they are rich in fiber and vitamins and contain 4 to 7 grams of protein per serving.*

Reduce cholesterol ■ *Use buttermilk in place of heavy or sour cream.*

● Makes **4 cups** ● Preparation Time **20 minutes plus chilling time** ● Cooking Time **20 minutes**

PER CUP
Calories **216**, Saturated Fat **1g**, Total Fat **4g**, Sodium **135mg**, Cholesterol **4mg**, Protein **7g**, Carbohydrate **41g**, Fiber **4g**.

1¹/₂ **pounds fresh peaches or 20 ounces, frozen and thawed**
1 **cup water**
2 **tablespoons sugar**
Pared zest of 1 lemon

2 **cups buttermilk or 1% low-fat milk**
Pinch of ground nutmeg
1 **cup peach nectar**
¹/₄ **cup sliced almonds**

1 Bring a large saucepan of water to a boil. Add a few peaches to the pan and return to a boil. Transfer the peaches to a bowl of cold water.

2 When cool enough, peel the peaches with a small knife and cut into chunks; discard the pits. Poach and peel the remaining peaches, working in batches.

3 Bring 1 cup water, the sugar, and lemon zest to a boil and add the peaches. Cover, and simmer, stirring occasionally, 5 to 8 minutes, until very soft.

Peach Soup with Almonds – a refreshing way to enjoy your daily serving of fruit.

4 Remove pan from the heat; discard lemon zest. Pour 1 cup buttermilk into a food processor or blender. Reserving peach syrup, add peaches, and purée.

5 Transfer purée to a bowl. Add remaining buttermilk, the nutmeg, and peach nectar. Stir in reserved syrup. Cover and refrigerate at least 1 hour.

6 Preheat oven to 350°F. Spread almonds on a cookie sheet; toast until golden, about 10 minutes. Cool almonds and sprinkle on soup before serving.

Black Cherry Soup

- Makes **4½ cups**
- Preparation Time **10 minutes** plus chilling time
- Cooking Time **25 minutes**

1 cup water

3 whole cloves

Finely grated zest and juice of 1 lemon

1 cinnamon stick

2 cans (1 pound each) black cherries in heavy syrup

1 cup low-fat sour cream

Fresh mint leaves for garnish

1 In a saucepan, combine water with cloves, lemon zest and juice, and cinnamon. Bring to a boil over moderate heat. Stir in cherries with syrup and return to a boil.

2 Simmer cherries, stirring occasionally, 10 to 15 minutes, until they are very soft and almost falling apart. Remove from the heat. Discard the spices.

3 Strain the contents of the saucepan into a bowl and transfer cherries to a food processor or blender and purée until smooth. Stir the purée into the bowl, mix together, and strain into another large bowl.

4 Stir in sour cream until combined. Cover bowl and refrigerate at least 1 hour. Serve garnished with mint leaves.

PER CUP
Calories **242**, Saturated Fat **2g**, Total Fat **4g**, Sodium **70mg**, Cholesterol **9mg**, Protein **5g**, Carbohydrate **51g**, Fiber **1g**.

Summer Pudding Soup

- Makes **4 cups**
- Preparation Time **20 minutes** plus chilling time
- Cooking Time **5 minutes**

1 cup fresh blueberries or frozen and thawed

1 cup water

2 tablespoons sugar

Pared zest of 1 lemon

1 cup fresh strawberries or frozen and thawed

1 cup fresh raspberries or frozen and thawed

½ cup low-fat sour cream

½ cup 1% low-fat milk

1 Rinse fresh blueberries and drain. Bring 1 cup water to a boil in a saucepan with sugar and lemon zest. Simmer blueberries about 2 minutes, until they begin to split.

2 Remove from the heat, discard lemon zest, and add strawberries and raspberries. Purée fruit and juices in a food processor or blender.

3 Strain purée into a large bowl, pressing fruit through sieve with back of a wooden spoon.

4 Add sour cream and milk to blender, and process until smooth. Add about 2 cups of purée, and blend. Stir mixture back into remaining purée. Cover bowl and refrigerate at least 1 hour.

PER CUP
Calories **124**, Saturated Fat **1g**, Total Fat **3g**, Sodium **55mg**, Cholesterol **6mg**, Protein **4g**, Carbohydrate **23g**, Fiber **4g**.

Cantaloupe and Orange Soup

- Makes **6 cups**
- Preparation Time **25 minutes** plus chilling time

3 large oranges

1 large cantaloupe melon, halved and seeded

2 cups orange juice

Juice of 1 lime

1 tablespoon honey

1 cup plain nonfat yogurt

1 cup fresh raspberries

1 Finely grate zest from 1 or 2 oranges, according to taste, and reserve. With a sharp knife, peel melon. Cut melon flesh into chunks and place in a food processor or blender. Peel and section oranges; cut sections into pieces and add to melon. Purée fruit until smooth.

2 Strain purée through medium-gauge sieve into a large bowl, pressing fruit through sieve with back of a wooden spoon.

3 Stir in orange and lime juice, honey, and yogurt until blended. Cover bowl and refrigerate at least 1 hour.

4 Serve soup garnished with orange zest and fresh raspberries.

PER CUP
Calories **149**, Saturated Fat **0g**, Total Fat **1g**, Sodium **41mg**, Cholesterol **1mg**, Protein **5g**, Carbohydrate **34g**, Fiber **3g**.

POULTRY

Imagine a platter of succulent fried chicken, crisply egged and crumbed. Can you still enjoy this family favorite on a low-fat diet? The answer is yes. This chapter shows you how simple it is to make healthful poultry dishes without sacrificing flavor. Begin by removing the skin, use a low-fat cooking method such as grilling, oven-frying, or poaching, then season to perfection with herbs, mustard, or garlic instead of salt. On the following pages you'll find a wealth of new recipes, from low-fat versions of down-home dishes like fried chicken and chicken pot pie to Mexican specialities — all healthful, all delicious.

Asian Chicken Parcels, page 77

Poultry is an excellent source of low-fat protein. For example, 3¹/₂ ounces of white meat chicken contains 4 grams of fat, compared to 18 grams in 3¹/₂ ounces of lean ground meat. Poultry is also an excellent source of minerals and some B vitamins.

Buying chicken

Check for freshness: look for unbroken skin with no dark patches, plump breast, pliable breastbone, and fresh smell. Check the sell-by date and keep poultry refrigerated for up to 2 days after that. Freeze any poultry that you don't use. See box (next page) for safe freezing tips.

SELECTING LOW-FAT POULTRY

Removing the skin reduces your intake of fat and calories. White meat is leaner than dark.

3¹/₂ ounces cooked	Calories	Fat g	Saturated Fat g	Cholesterol mg
Turkey				
Breast w/o skin	135	1	1	83
Breast with skin	153	3	1	90
Leg w/o skin	159	4	1	119
Leg with skin	170	5	2	70
Wing w/o skin	163	3	1	102
Wing with skin	207	10	3	115
Ground	123	7	2	37
Chicken (broilers)				
Breast w/o skin	165	4	1	85
Breast with skin	197	8	2	84
Leg w/o skin	191	8	2	94
Leg with skin	232	13	4	92
Wing w/o skin	203	8	2	85
Wing with skin	290	20	5	84
Ground	176	7	2	82
Duck				
w/o skin	201	11	4	89
with skin	334	28	10	83
Cornish hen				
White meat	190	18	4	117
Dark meat	245	22	6	152

Most supermarkets now carry boneless, skinless chicken and turkey parts, ground chicken and turkey, and some even have duck breasts and thighs.

There are two advantages to buying poultry parts. The first is convenience – the butcher has done most of the work for you, although you may pay more for it. The second is health. The skinless cuts are lower in fat, because most of the fat lies just under the bird's skin. Also, white meat has less fat and therefore fewer calories than dark. So if you're trying to cut back on fat, you may prefer breast meat.

The dark meat, however, is more flavorful and, because it doesn't dry out as fast, works better in stews and other recipes that require long cooking. Either way, the availability of poultry parts makes it easier to eat healthfully.

Is natural better?

Recently there has been concern that poultry may contain residues of the hormones injected into chickens to make them grow and the antibiotics that are used in chicken feed. The FDA insists that any remaining residues are so small as to be harmless. Animal rights activists also object to what they consider the inhumane overcrowding of factory-farmed chickens. In response, a number of producers have changed the way they raise and process poultry. As a result, you now have four options to choose from:

Free-range chickens have enough space to move freely. They eat a natural diet of insects and grain that contains no antibiotics. They are not given any hormones or growth enhancers. Although free-range chickens are more expensive, they usually have better flavor. This is because they exercise more than confined birds, which gives them more muscle.

Natural chickens and turkeys are fed a special diet of whole-grain organic food with no antibiotics. They are not injected with hormones or growth enhancers. However, they are raised in confined areas and do not move freely.

Kosher birds are processed according to the strict requirements for cleanliness demanded by the orthodox Jewish religion and under the supervision of a rabbi.

REMOVING THE SKIN FROM CHICKEN

1 To remove the skin from a chicken breast, start by peeling it back from one end.

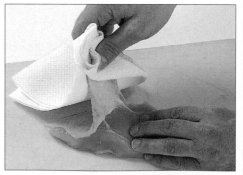

2 Holding the skin with a piece of paper towel, pull it away from the meat.

The term *kosher*, however, applies only to the processing. It does not indicate whether the birds have been injected with hormones or allowed to move freely. They are sometimes processed with salt, so they have a slightly higher sodium content.

Factory-farmed poultry, which includes most name brands on the supermarket counter, must be processed according to USDA regulations. Antibiotics and hormones are permitted, and most of this poultry is not allowed to move freely. It is usually the least expensive.

In taste tests conducted by panels of expert cooks, free-range, natural, and kosher chickens were almost always preferred over factory-farmed birds. If price is an issue, however, choose factory-farmed poultry, which costs about 30 to 40 percent less than the others. If you're concerned about hormones and antibiotics, then purchase natural chickens.

Reducing fat

Always remove any visible fat before cooking poultry. For some dishes, such as roast chicken, you may want to leave the skin on while the bird is cooking because it keeps the meat moist, then remove the skin before serving. Instead of sautéing or deep-frying poultry, choose a cooking method that requires little or no added fat, such as poaching, grilling, roasting, stir-frying, or baking in parchment.

SAFETY FIRST

No matter what brand you buy, most poultry is contaminated with bacteria, including the more expensive free-range, kosher, and natural birds. Therefore you must be very careful in the way that you store, defrost, and cook poultry to prevent salmonella and food poisoning.

◆ Refrigerate poultry at 40°F as soon as you bring it home from the supermarket. Do not let it sit at room temperature for more than 30 minutes.

◆ To freeze poultry at home, rinse and dry carefully; wrap poultry and giblets separately in freezer bags and seal.

◆ To freeze poultry pieces, spread on a tray and freeze until hard. Transfer to freezer bags and seal tightly.

◆ Wash your hands before and after handling raw poultry, and keep poultry separate from other foods.

◆ Wash the counter or chopping board after preparing poultry. Wood or butcher block is preferable to synthetic boards because bacteria don't live as long on the surface. Wash utensils as well.

◆ Cook chicken completely through to destroy bacteria. There must be no trace of pinkness in the meat, and the juices should run clear. The safest way is to use a meat thermometer. See page 59 for the right temperature.

◆ Thaw frozen poultry completely before cooking. Don't defrost frozen poultry by letting it sit at room temperature. It should either be defrosted in the refrigerator or microwave. If you defrost it in the refrigerator, make sure that the liquid does not drip on other foods.

CARVING A CHICKEN OR TURKEY

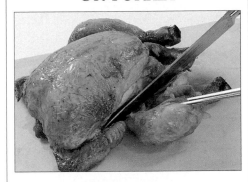

1 *With a sharp knife, cut each drumstick and thigh from the body. Separate the thigh from the drumstick.*

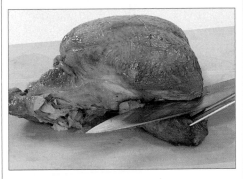

2 *Make a deep horizontal cut just above wing through the breast until the knife touches the breastbone.*

3 *Make a series of vertical cuts through the breast meat, going all the way down to the first horizontal cut. This makes thin slices at the point where the cuts meet.*

Perfect Roast Chicken

Cooking technique ■ *For tender, juicy meat, start roasting the bird breast side down, which forces the juices into the breast.*
Reduce fat ■ *Cut off excess fat before cooking. Instead of gravy, skim fat from the pan after roasting and make a rich-tasting sauce with the pan juices, herbs, and stock. Remove the skin from the bird before serving.*
Add flavor ■ *Season with herbs and onions. Baste with reduced-sodium chicken stock.*

● Serves **4** ● Preparation Time **20 minutes** ● Cooking Time **1 hour 35 minutes**

PER SERVING
Calories **267**, Saturated Fat **2g**,
Total Fat **7g**, Sodium **241mg**,
Cholesterol **136mg**, Protein **44g**,
Carbohydrate **3g**, Fiber **0g**.

1 roasting chicken (about
3¹/₂ pounds)

10 sprigs parsley

1 bay leaf

2 tablespoons snipped chives,
fresh or frozen

1 yellow onion, quartered

1 tablespoon olive or canola oil

¹/₈ teaspoon each salt and pepper

1¹/₂ tablespoons all-purpose
flour

1¹/₂ cups chicken stock,
page 18

1 Preheat the oven to 375°F. Cut off the fat from the neck and tail ends of the chicken and wipe the inside with paper towels. Stuff the parsley, bay leaf, chives, and onion pieces inside the body cavity.

2 Tuck the neck skin and wings under the bird. Fold the skin over the body cavity opening. Close the cavity by tying the legs together securely with string.

3 Brush the oil all over the chicken and sprinkle with the salt and pepper. Place breast side down on a rack in a roasting pan. Roast in the oven 30 minutes.

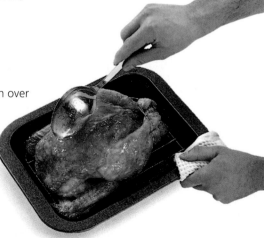

4 Turn the chicken over and baste all over with the pan juices. Roast the chicken about 55 minutes longer or until cooked through, basting every 10 to 15 minutes.

5 Transfer the chicken to a platter, cover with aluminum foil, and keep it warm. Spoon off all the clear fat from the pan, leaving the brown juices. Add the flour and cook over moderate heat, stirring, 3 to 4 minutes.

6 Gradually pour in the chicken stock and bring the mixture to a boil, stirring constantly. Keep the sauce warm. Skin the chicken and carve the bird into serving pieces. Pass the sauce on the side.

Perfect Roast Chicken *is our healthful new version of an old family favorite, offering succulent flavor with only a fraction of the fat.*
After carving the bird, remove the skin, pour the sauce over, and serve with potatoes and garden vegetables.

Roast Cornish Hens with Orange Sauce

Stuff the Cornish hens with orange halves and onion quarters, then roast breast side down for the first 15 minutes. The fat will run off into the pan and can be removed before serving. Then glaze the hens with a tangy orange mixture that penetrates the skin to add more flavor. To reduce the fat even further, remove the skin before serving.

- Serves 4
- Preparation Time 15 minutes
- Cooking Time 1 hour 10 minutes

---

2 Rock Cornish hens (about 1³/₄ pounds each), thawed if frozen

2 small oranges, halved

1 small onion, quartered

¹/₄ cup orange marmalade

2 teaspoons Worcestershire sauce

¹/₂ teaspoon garlic powder

¹/₈ teaspoon each salt and pepper

---

1 Preheat the oven to 375°F. Cut off the excess fat from the neck and tail ends of each Cornish hen and wipe the insides with paper towels. Stuff each body cavity with 1 orange half and 2 onion quarters.

2 Tuck the neck skin and wings under each bird. Fold the skin over the body cavity opening. Close the cavity by tying the legs together securely with string.

3 Place the hens, breast side down, on a rack in a roasting pan. Roast the hens in the oven about 15 minutes.

4 For the glaze: Combine the marmalade with Worcestershire sauce and garlic powder. Make shallow slashes in the birds' skin.

5 Turn the hens over and brush with about half of the glaze. Continue roasting the hens about 55 minutes longer or until cooked through. Brush them with the remaining marmalade mixture after 30 minutes.

6 Tilt the hens to drain the cavity juices into the pan. Using a sharp knife or poultry shears, cut each hen lengthwise in half. Scoop out and discard the onion quarters and orange halves. Transfer the hens to a platter, cover with aluminum foil, and keep them warm.

7 Spoon off all the fat from the pan, leaving the pan juices. Squeeze the juice from the remaining orange halves into the pan juices. Place the pan over moderate heat, stir to combine, and heat until bubbling. Add salt and pepper. Remove skin from the hens and serve them with the orange pan juices poured over.

PER SERVING
Calories 262, Saturated Fat 1g, Total Fat 6g, Sodium 214mg, Cholesterol 155mg, Protein 35g, Carbohydrate 17g, Fiber 0g.

Roast Turkey Breast with Garlic Sauce

The white breast meat of turkey is exceptionally low in fat and cholesterol. To add flavor without extra fat, roast garlic cloves in the pan with the turkey, then purée them with the pan juices to make a delicious creamy sauce.

- Serves 10
- Preparation Time 20 minutes
- Cooking Time 2 hours

---

1 turkey breast (about 5 pounds), thawed if frozen

3 tablespoons olive or canola oil

¹/₄ teaspoon each salt and pepper

15 cloves garlic, unpeeled

1¹/₂ cups chicken stock, page 18

2 teaspoons lemon juice

Garlic cloves

1 Preheat the oven to 350°F. Cut off any fat from the turkey breast. Place the turkey, skin side up, in a shallow roasting pan. Brush the oil all over the breast and sprinkle with half of the salt and pepper. Cover loosely with aluminum foil and roast in the oven about 45 minutes.

2 Using a knife handle, lightly crush the garlic cloves to break their skins. Remove the foil and scatter the garlic cloves around the turkey, coating them with the pan juices. Roast the turkey about 1¹/₄ hours longer or until a meat thermometer inserted into the thickest part reads 180°F.

3 Remove the skin and transfer the turkey to a platter. Cover it with aluminum foil and keep warm. Spoon off all the fat from the pan, leaving the pan juices. With a spoon, squeeze the garlic cloves from their skins into the pan. Discard the skins.

4 Place the roasting pan over moderate heat, stir in ¹/₂ cup of the chicken stock, and heat until bubbling. Transfer the mixture to a blender or processor and purée until smooth. Return the mixture to the roasting pan and bring to a boil over moderate heat. Stir in the remaining chicken stock, the lemon juice, and remaining salt and pepper, and simmer about 3 minutes. Slice the turkey breast and serve with the garlic sauce.

> **COOKING TIP**
> *A meat thermometer is best for cooking a whole turkey breast. Other tests for doneness aren't reliable on large cuts of poultry.*

PER SERVING
Calories 139, Saturated Fat 1g, Total Fat 2g, Sodium 111mg, Cholesterol 73mg, Protein 26g, Carbohydrate 2g, Fiber 0g.

Poultry Roasting Timetable

Check the weight of the bird before roasting so that you can calculate the cooking and serving times. Dark meat takes longer to cook than white, so you must baste the bird to keep the breast moist while the legs are cooking. If you use a roasting rack, you will find it is easier to get to the juices. Once cooked, the bird will stay moist and be easier to cut if it stands before carving — about 10 minutes for small birds, 20 minutes for large.

	Pounds	°F	Hours	Internal °F
Chicken, unstuffed*	2½–3	375	1¼–1½	175–180
	3½–4	375	1½–1¾	175–180
	4½–5	375	1½–2	175–180
Capon, unstuffed*	5–7	350	2¼–3	180–185
	7–9	350	3–4	180–185
Rock Cornish hen	1–1½	375	1¼–1½	180–185
Turkey, unstuffed*	6–8	325	3–3½	180–185
	8–12	325	3½–4	180–185
	12–16	325	4–4½	180–185
	16–20	325	4½–5	180–185
Duckling	4–5	375	1¾–2½	180

* *add 30–45 minutes extra for stuffed birds*

TESTING POULTRY FOR DONENESS

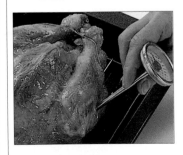 

The most reliable way to test for doneness is to use a meat thermometer. Toward the end of cooking, insert the thermometer at the thickest part of the leg, making sure that the tip does not touch the bone.

Or, using the tip of a sharp knife or skewer, pierce the flesh at the thickest part of the leg or between one thigh and the breast. The juices that run out of the bird should be clear, with no trace of pink.

Roast Cornish Hens with Tarragon Sauce

This elegant dish is easy to prepare. Roast the hens as in the master recipe, with onions, garlic, and tarragon. For the savory sauce, just purée the vegetables, stock, and tarragon with low-fat sour cream.

- Serves **4**
- Preparation Time **20 minutes**
- Cooking Time **1 hour 10 minutes**

2 Rock Cornish hens (about 1¾ pounds each), thawed if frozen
2 onions, quartered
2 cloves garlic, coarsely chopped
¼ cup fresh tarragon leaves or 2 tablespoons dried
1 cup chicken stock, page 18
⅛ teaspoon each salt and pepper
½ cup low-fat sour cream

1 Preheat the oven to 375°F. Cut off the excess fat from the neck and tail ends of each Cornish hen and wipe the insides with paper towels.

2 Tuck the neck skin and wings under each bird. Fold the skin over the body cavity opening. Close the cavity by tying the ends of the legs together securely with string. Place the hens, breast side down, in a roasting pan and roast in the oven, about 20 minutes.

3 Turn the hens over and baste them with the pan juices. Add the onions, garlic, and about three-quarters of the tarragon to the pan and toss to coat well with the pan juices. Continue roasting the hens, basting them every 15 minutes, about 55 minutes longer or until cooked through

4 Tilt the hens to drain the cavity juices into the pan. Cut each one lengthwise in half, transfer to a platter, cover with aluminum foil, and keep them warm. With a slotted spoon, transfer the onions, garlic, and tarragon to a blender or processor.

5 Spoon off all the fat from the roasting pan, leaving the pan juices. Stir the chicken stock into the pan juices until well combined.

6 Add the stock mixture, the remaining tarragon, salt, and pepper to the blender or processor and purée until smooth, then return to the pan. Bring to a boil over moderate heat, and simmer about 2 minutes. Turn off the heat and stir in the sour cream to combine. Skin the hens and serve with the tarragon sauce.

PER SERVING
Calories **275**, Saturated Fat **3g**,
Total Fat **8g**, Sodium **236mg**,
Cholesterol **160mg**, Protein **38g**,
Carbohydrate **11g**, Fiber **1g**.

Tarragon flavors the low-fat sauce.

Poached Chicken

Cooking technique ■ *Poaching requires no added fat. Just cook the chicken in simmering stock until tender. Don't let the water boil – it will toughen the meat.*
Reduce fat ■ *Purée the pan vegetables to make a velvety-smooth low-fat sauce.*
Reduce sodium ■ *Enhance the natural flavors with lemon juice – keep salt to a minimum.*

● Serves 4 ● Preparation Time 25–30 minutes ● Cooking Time 1¼–1½ hours, mostly unattended

PER SERVING
Calories **299**, Saturated Fat **2g**,
Total Fat **7g**, Sodium **354mg**,
Cholesterol **134mg**, Protein **47g**,
Carbohydrate **30g**, Fiber **5g**.

1 whole chicken (3½ pounds)
6 cups chicken stock, page 18
5 cups water
4 carrots, cut into 1-inch pieces
2 leeks, white part only, or onions, sliced

2 large potatoes, peeled and cut into cubes
6 cloves garlic, peeled
1 bouquet garni, made with 8 sprigs parsley and 2 bay leaves
1 tablespoon lemon juice
⅛ teaspoon each salt and pepper

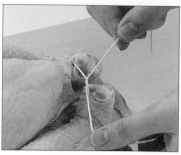

1 Cut fat from both ends of bird and wipe inside with paper towels. Tuck wings under bird. Fold skin over body cavity opening; tie legs together with string.

2 Place chicken in a 4-quart Dutch oven. Add stock and water to cover. Bring to a boil over moderate heat and, using a large spoon, skim off any scum.

3 Add vegetables, garlic, and herbs to the Dutch oven and simmer, partially covered, about 1¼ hours or until chicken and vegetables are cooked through.

Poached Chicken is served with carrots and potatoes cooked in its broth, and a creamy sauce of puréed vegetables.

4 Transfer chicken to a platter, cover with aluminum foil, and keep warm. Strain stock into a bowl and skim off fat. Reserve vegetables and discard herbs.

5 Purée half of the vegetables and 1½ cups stock in a blender or food processor; pour into a pan. Add lemon juice, salt, and pepper.

6 Remove skin from chicken and carve meat. Meanwhile, warm sauce gently. Place chicken and remaining vegetables on a platter and pour sauce over.

Greek Poached Chicken and Lemon Stew

- Serves **4**
- Preparation Time **20 minutes**
- Cooking Time **1 hour 40 minutes**, mostly unattended

1 chicken (3½ pounds), cut into serving pieces
6 cups chicken stock, page 18
3 cups water
2 carrots, cut into 1-inch pieces
2 leeks, white part only, or small onions, sliced
6 cloves garlic, peeled
1 bouquet garni, made with 8 sprigs parsley and 2 bay leaves
Grated zest and juice of 1 lemon
1 teaspoon dried oregano
⅓ cup orzo pasta or long-grain rice
2 teaspoons cornstarch
1 cup nonfat plain yogurt
⅛ teaspoon pepper

1 Cook chicken pieces, vegetables, garlic, and herbs as in Steps 2 to 4 of the master recipe, reducing time to 40 minutes. Skim off fat and pour stock into a large saucepan. Add zest of lemon to stock. Add oregano and bring to a boil. Simmer stock about 40 minutes or until reduced to 5 to 6 cups.

2 Meanwhile, remove the skin from the chicken and cut the meat into about 1-inch pieces. Add the orzo or rice to the stock, cover, and simmer 15 to 20 minutes or until tender.

3 In a small bowl, combine cornstarch with ¼ cup of stock until smooth. Stir mixture back into stock. Simmer about 1 minute or until thickened.

4 Add chicken, vegetables, and lemon juice to stock and return to a boil. Remove from heat, stir in yogurt, and season with pepper.

PER SERVING
Calories **291**, Saturated Fat **2g**, Total Fat **7g**, Sodium **313mg**, Cholesterol **135mg**, Protein **50g**, Carbohydrate **25g**, Fiber **2g**.

Poached Chicken Breasts with Tomato Sauce

- Serves **4**
- Preparation Time **30–35 minutes**
- Cooking Time **55 minutes**

4 boneless, skinless chicken breast halves (1½ pounds)
3 cups chicken stock, page 18
1 cup water
8 ounces plum tomatoes, skinned and chopped
4 large carrots, diced
2 parsnips, diced
3 cloves garlic, finely chopped
1 bay leaf
1 tablespoon lemon juice
⅛ teaspoon salt and pepper

1 Cut off any fat from chicken breasts. Combine the stock and water in a deep skillet or wide flameproof casserole. Bring to a boil over moderate heat.

2 Add tomatoes with carrots, parsnips, garlic, and bay leaf. Return to a boil, cover the pan, and simmer about 10 minutes or until vegetables are tender.

3 Add chicken breasts to the pan so they are covered with vegetables and stock. Cover the pan and simmer the chicken about 10 minutes or until cooked through.

4 With a slotted spoon, transfer the chicken breasts to a plate, cover, and keep warm. Transfer the vegetables to a blender or food processor and purée until smooth. Add about 1 cup of the stock mixture and process to combine.

5 Discard bay leaf and simmer remaining stock, uncovered, until reduced to about 1½ cups. Stir in vegetable purée with lemon juice, salt, and pepper. Return sauce to a boil, add chicken, and simmer together about 3 minutes or until heated through.

PER SERVING
Calories **312**, Saturated Fat **1g**, Total Fat **3g**, Sodium **374mg**, Cholesterol **97mg**, Protein **44g**, Carbohydrate **27g**, Fiber **7g**.

Grilled Chicken with Herbs

Cooking technique ■ *Grilling allows fat to drip off the chicken into the fire, so less winds up on your plate. You can also make these recipes in the broiler.*

Reduce cholesterol ■ *Remove the skin. Use monounsaturated olive oil for the marinade.*

Reduce sodium ■ *Heighten the flavor with fresh herbs instead of extra salt. If you can't find fresh basil or mint, substitute Italian parsley.*

● Serves 4 ● Preparation Time 15 minutes plus marinating time ● Cooking Time 30 minutes

PER SERVING
Calories **306**, Saturated Fat **3g**,
Total Fat **15g**, Sodium **208mg**,
Cholesterol **126mg**, Protein **40g**,
Carbohydrate **2g**, Fiber **0g**.

1 chicken (about 3¹/₂ pounds),
cut into serving pieces, wings
reserved for another use

3 cloves garlic, finely chopped

3 tablespoons chopped parsley

2 tablespoons chopped basil

2 tablespoons chopped mint

¹/₃ cup olive or canola oil

¹/₂ teaspoon pepper

¹/₈ teaspoon salt

1 Remove the skin from the chicken pieces by loosening it with the tip of a sharp knife. Then use your fingers to pull off the skin. With the knife, cut off any fat and make 2 to 3 slashes in each piece of chicken.

2 Make the marinade: In a small bowl, combine the garlic with the parsley, basil, mint, oil, pepper, and salt.

Grilled Chicken with Herbs
is served with fresh corn and baked potatoes. Cut the potatoes open and top with a spoonful of yogurt mixed with chopped chives.

3 Place the chicken pieces in a large dish, add the marinade, and turn the chicken in the mixture so that it is well coated. Cover the dish and marinate in the refrigerator at least 4 hours, turning the chicken occasionally.

4 Prepare the grill or preheat the broiler, setting the rack 4 inches from the heat. Arrange the chicken pieces bone side down on the grill or broiler rack, reserving the marinade. Grill the chicken about 20 minutes or until browned on one side, brushing once with the reserved marinade. Turn the pieces over, brush with the remaining marinade, and grill 10 minutes longer or until cooked through and the juices run clear.

> COOKING TIP
> *For safe and healthy grilling tips, see page 125.*

Grilled Chicken Barbecue-Style

- Serves **6**
- Preparation Time **10 minutes**
- Cooking Time **20 minutes**

12 chicken drumsticks (about 3 pounds)

$^{1}/_{4}$ cup tomato paste

$^{1}/_{4}$ cup apple juice

2 cloves garlic, finely chopped

2 tablespoons dark molasses

2 tablespoons cider vinegar

1 teaspoon dry mustard

$^{1}/_{4}$ teaspoon each salt and pepper

1 Prepare the grill or broiler. Remove the skin from the chicken drumsticks and slash the meat as in Step 1 of the master recipe.

2 Make the barbecue sauce: In a small bowl, combine the tomato paste with the apple juice, garlic, molasses, vinegar, mustard, salt, and pepper.

3 Arrange the drumsticks on the grill or broiler rack. Brush with about half of the barbecue sauce and grill 10 minutes.

4 Turn drumsticks over and brush with the remaining barbecue sauce. Continue grilling about 10 minutes longer or until cooked through and the juices run clear.

PER SERVING
Calories **181**, Saturated Fat **1g**, Total Fat **5g**, Sodium **247mg**, Cholesterol **95mg**, Protein **26g**, Carbohydrate **8g**, Fiber **1g**.

Honey-Mustard Grilled Hens

- Serves **4**
- Preparation Time **15 minutes**
- Cooking Time **40 minutes**

2 Rock Cornish hens (about 1$^{3}/_{4}$ pounds each)

Finely grated zest and juice of 1 lime

$^{1}/_{2}$ cup coarse-grained prepared mustard

$^{1}/_{4}$ cup honey

$^{1}/_{8}$ teaspoon pepper

1 Prepare grill or broiler. Using a sharp knife or poultry shears, cut the hens lengthwise in half. Remove skin and excess fat; wipe the insides with paper towels.

2 In a small bowl, mix the lime zest and juice. Add the mustard, honey, and pepper and blend together.

3 Arrange the hens, cut side down, on the grill or broiler rack. Brush them with half the honey-mustard mixture. Grill about 20 minutes or until browned and almost tender.

4 Turn the hens and brush with the remaining honey-mustard mixture. Continue grilling about 20 minutes longer or until cooked through and the juices run clear.

PER SERVING
Calories **275**, Saturated Fat **1g**, Total Fat **6g**, Sodium **357mg**, Cholesterol **155mg**, Protein **34g**, Carbohydrate **18g**, Fiber **0g**.

Turkey Kabobs

- Serves **6**
- Preparation Time **20 minutes** plus marinating time
- Cooking Time **10–12 minutes**

1$^{1}/_{2}$ pounds boneless, skinless turkey or chicken breast

$^{1}/_{4}$ cup reduced-sodium soy sauce

2 tablespoons olive or canola oil

2 cloves garlic, finely chopped

$^{3}/_{4}$ teaspoon ground ginger

$^{1}/_{4}$ teaspoon crushed red pepper

2 sweet red peppers, cubed

2 sweet green peppers, cubed

3 zucchini, cut into thick slices

For the yogurt sauce

1$^{1}/_{4}$ cups low-fat plain yogurt

$^{1}/_{4}$ teaspoon ground cumin

$^{1}/_{4}$ cup chopped mint

1 Remove fat from the turkey; cut meat into 1-inch cubes.

2 In a bowl, combine soy sauce, oil, garlic, ginger, and crushed red pepper. Add turkey and mix. Cover and marinate for 1 hour.

3 Prepare the grill or broiler. On 6 long metal skewers, thread the turkey, peppers, and zucchini. Brush with marinade.

4 Grill kabobs 5 to 6 minutes. Turn once and grill 5 to 6 minutes or until turkey is cooked through.

5 In a bowl, mix the yogurt, cumin, and mint. Serve.

PER SERVING
Calories **250**, Saturated Fat **1g**, Total Fat **7g**, Sodium **522mg**, Cholesterol **71mg**, Protein **33g**, Carbohydrate **16g**, Fiber **3g**.

Oven-Fried Chicken

Cooking technique ■ *For deep-fried flavor with just a fraction of the fat, coat the chicken pieces in a crumb mixture, then brown them in just a little oil. This produces a crispy crust that keeps the chicken moist and tender.*
Reduce fat ■ *Remove the skin before cooking. Coat the chicken with egg whites instead of whole eggs.*
Increase fiber ■ *Use whole-wheat bread crumbs instead of white.*

● Serves **4** ● Preparation Time **15 minutes** ● Cooking Time **40–45 minutes**

PER SERVING
Calories **398**, Saturated Fat **2g**,
Total Fat **14g**, Sodium **345mg**,
Cholesterol **135mg**, Protein **48g**,
Carbohydrate **13g**, Fiber **0g**.

1 chicken (about 3¹/₂ pounds), cut into serving pieces

3 egg whites

1¹/₂ cups fresh bread crumbs

1 tablespoon chopped parsley or 1 teaspoon dried

1 tablespoon chopped chives or 1 teaspoon dried

¹/₈ teaspoon paprika

¹/₈ teaspoon each salt and pepper

¹/₄ cup all-purpose flour

3 tablespoons olive or canola oil

1 Preheat the oven to 350°F. Remove the skin from each piece of chicken by loosening it from one edge with the tip of a sharp knife. Then use your fingers to pull the skin off the chicken.

2 Lightly whisk the egg whites together in a shallow dish until just foamy. In another shallow dish, combine the bread crumbs with the chopped parsley and chives, paprika, salt, and pepper and spread out evenly.

3 Dredge the skinned chicken pieces very lightly with the flour. Dip the floured chicken pieces in the egg whites until completely covered.

4 Coat the chicken pieces with the seasoned bread crumbs in the dish, pressing the bread crumbs onto the flesh with your fingers to form an even layer.

5 In a large oven-safe skillet, heat the oil over moderate heat until it sizzles when a few bread crumbs are added. Add half of the chicken pieces and cook about 3 minutes, until they are well browned on one side.

6 Turn the pieces and brown the other side. Transfer the chicken to a plate and brown the remaining chicken pieces in the same way. Return all the pieces to the skillet and bake about 30 minutes, until cooked through.

*A quick twist of fresh lemon is delicious on **Oven-Fried Chicken**, which is served here with a simple rice salad and dilled cucumbers.*

Herbed Oven-Fried Chicken

These crispy drumsticks are delicious for summer picnics. If you like, you can substitute chicken breast cutlets and bake for only 20 minutes.

- Serves **4**
- Preparation Time **15 minutes**
- Cooking Time **45 minutes**

8 chicken drumsticks (about 2 pounds)

3 egg whites

1 cup fresh bread crumbs

1 clove garlic, finely chopped

1 tablespoon chopped fresh herbs, such as parsley, chives, or dill

1 tablespoon finely grated lemon zest

$^{1}/_{8}$ teaspoon each salt and pepper

$^{1}/_{4}$ cup all-purpose flour

2 tablespoons olive or canola oil

1 Preheat the oven to 350°F. Remove the skin from the chicken drumsticks by loosening it from the thick end with the tip of a sharp knife, then use your fingers to pull the skin off the drumsticks.

2 Lightly whisk the egg whites together in a shallow dish until just foamy. In another shallow dish, combine the bread crumbs with the garlic, herbs, lemon zest, salt, and pepper, and spread out evenly.

3 Dredge the chicken drumsticks very lightly with the flour. Dip the floured drumsticks in the egg whites to cover completely. Roll the drumsticks in the seasoned bread crumbs, pressing the bread crumbs onto the meat with your fingers to form an even layer.

4 In a large oven-safe skillet, heat the oil over moderate heat. Add half of the drumsticks and cook about 3 minutes or until they are well browned on one side.

> ### COOKING TIP
> *Make the bread crumbs in a food processor. They should be very fine so that they form an even coating for the chicken.*

5 Turn drumsticks and brown the other side. Transfer to a plate and brown remaining pieces in the same way. Return all the drumsticks to the skillet and bake 30 minutes or until cooked through.

PER SERVING
Calories **281**, Saturated Fat **2g**, Total Fat **12g**, Sodium **275mg**, Cholesterol **95mg**, Protein **30g**, Carbohydrate **12g**, Fiber **1g**.

Fresh herbs increase the flavor without adding sodium.

Turkey Bites with Tomato-Fruit Salsa

These spicy bite-size turkey morsels make a terrific hors d'oeuvre or main course. You can also use this coating to make Oven-Fried Chicken, as in the master recipe.

- Serves **6**
- Preparation Time **15 minutes**
- Cooking Time **30 minutes**

2 pounds turkey breast (in 1 piece)

3 egg whites

$1^{1}/_{2}$ cups fresh bread crumbs

$^{1}/_{2}$ teaspoon garlic salt

$^{1}/_{2}$ teaspoon ground celery seeds

$^{1}/_{2}$ teaspoon paprika

$^{1}/_{4}$ teaspoon chili powder

$^{1}/_{4}$ teaspoon pepper

$^{1}/_{4}$ cup all-purpose flour

2 tablespoons olive or canola oil

2 large tomatoes, diced

1 mango, diced (see box) or 2 peaches, peeled and diced

$^{1}/_{8}$ teaspoon salt

1 Preheat the oven to 350°F. Pull the skin from the turkey breast with your fingers. Cut the meat from the bone, then cut across into 1-inch slices. Cut the slices crosswise into 1-inch strips.

2 Lightly whisk the egg whites together in a shallow dish until just foamy. In another shallow dish, combine the bread crumbs with the garlic salt, celery seeds, paprika, chili powder, and half of the pepper, and spread out evenly.

3 Dredge the turkey very lightly with the flour. Dip in the egg whites to cover completely. Coat with the seasoned bread crumbs. Place on a sheet of wax paper.

4 In a large nonstick skillet, heat $1^{1}/_{2}$ teaspoons of the oil over moderate heat. Cook a quarter of the turkey strips 2 to 3 minutes or until browned on all sides. Transfer to a large baking sheet.

5 Brown remainder in remaining oil, working in 3 batches. Bake turkey about 15 minutes or until tender and cooked through.

6 Meanwhile, make the tomato-fruit salsa. In a bowl, combine the diced tomatoes, mango, salt, and remaining pepper. Serve with the turkey bites.

PER SERVING
Calories **321**, Saturated Fat **1g**, Total Fat **8g**, Sodium **399mg**, Cholesterol **94mg**, Protein **40g**, Carbohydrate **22g**, Fiber **3g**.

DICING A MANGO

Cut mango lengthwise on both sides of pit. Cut each piece of mango in a lattice without cutting through peel. Push peel to turn each piece inside out, then cut cubes from peel.

Southern-Style Turkey Scallops

Slices of turkey breast are pounded thin to make them tender, then coated with a crunchy mix of pecans, cornmeal, and bread crumbs. If pressed for time, use turkey cutlets and omit the pounding.

- Serves **6**
- Preparation Time **20 minutes**
- Cooking Time **20 minutes**

1¹/₂ pounds boneless, skinless turkey breast (2 breast halves)

3 egg whites

1 cup fresh bread crumbs

¹/₂ cup yellow cornmeal

¹/₄ cup finely chopped pecans

Finely grated zest of 1 orange

1 clove garlic, finely chopped

¹/₈ teaspoon each salt and pepper

¹/₄ cup all-purpose flour

3 tablespoons olive or canola oil

1 Preheat the oven to 350°F. Trim, slice, and pound the turkey breast halves between sheets of wax paper (see box below).

2 Lightly whisk the egg whites together in a shallow dish until just foamy. In another shallow dish, combine the bread crumbs with the cornmeal, pecans, orange zest, garlic, salt, and pepper, and spread out evenly.

3 Dredge the turkey scallops lightly with the flour. Dip them in the egg whites until completely covered. Coat the scallops with the bread crumb mixture, pressing it onto the flesh.

4 In a large nonstick skillet, heat a quarter of the oil over moderate heat. Add a quarter of the turkey and cook about 2 minutes on each side or until golden; transfer to a baking sheet. Brown the remaining turkey in the remaining oil, working in 3 more batches.

5 Transfer the scallops to the oven and bake until they are cooked through, about 5 minutes.

PER SERVING
Calories **176**, Saturated Fat **1g**, Total Fat **7g**, Sodium **105mg**, Cholesterol **40mg**, Protein **17g**, Carbohydrate **10g**, Fiber **1g**.

Southern-Style Turkey Scallops are served with boiled new potatoes in their skins and a medley of steamed broccoli, cauliflower, and carrot sticks.

SLICING AND POUNDING TURKEY SCALLOPS

1 *With a small sharp knife, cut off all the fat from each of the turkey breast halves and trim ends.*

2 *Hold each breast half steady with one hand. Starting at the plump end, with a long knife held at a 45° angle, cut the flesh crosswise into ¹/₂-inch-thick slices. You should have about 12 slices.*

3 *Place 2 of the turkey slices between 2 large sheets of wax paper. With a rolling pin, lightly pound them to about ¹/₄-inch thickness. Repeat with the remaining slices.*

GETTING AHEAD

All of the oven-fried poultry recipes can be prepared ahead of time. In fact, they are even better when chilled because the coating firms up, making a crisper crust. As in the master recipe, skin the chicken pieces, dredge in flour, dip in egg whites, and coat with bread crumbs. Refrigerate the coated chicken pieces, uncovered, for up to 4 hours. About 15 minutes before cooking, let the chicken come to room temperature. Cook as directed.

Sautéed Turkey Cutlets in Mushroom Sauce

Cooking technique ■ *Pound the cutlets to tenderize, then dredge in flour to seal in the juices.*
Reduce cholesterol ■ *Get the sauce off to a low-fat start by removing most of the oil from the skillet. Use low-fat sour cream and cornstarch to thicken it.*

● Serves 4 ● Preparation Time **15 minutes** ● Cooking Time **about 10 minutes**

PER SERVING
Calories **251**, Saturated Fat **2g**,
Total Fat **9g**, Sodium **168mg**,
Cholesterol **72mg**, Protein **29g**,
Carbohydrate **8g**, Fiber **1g**.

4 turkey breast cutlets (1 pound)	³/₄ cup chicken stock, page 18
2 tablespoons all-purpose flour	¹/₄ cup vermouth or chicken stock
Salt and white pepper	1 tablespoon cornstarch
2 tablespoons olive or canola oil	2 tablespoons low-fat sour cream
4 ounces mushrooms, sliced	2 tablespoons minced parsley

1 Place 1 turkey cutlet between 2 sheets of wax paper. With a rolling pin, pound the cutlet lightly to flatten it; repeat with the others.

2 Spread flour on a plate and season with a pinch each of salt and pepper. Dredge the cutlets with the flour, patting the flour into both sides of the cutlets.

3 In a nonstick skillet, heat the oil. Over moderate heat, sauté 2 cutlets at a time about 2 minutes on each side, until golden and cooked through.

Sautéed Turkey Cutlets in Mushroom Sauce are tender and juicy – serve them with rice or noodles.

4 Transfer the cutlets to a platter, cover with aluminum foil, and keep warm. Remove the skillet from the heat and spoon off all but 1 tablespoon of the oil.

5 Sauté the mushrooms about 1 minute. Add the stock and simmer 2 to 3 minutes. In a bowl, blend vermouth with cornstarch; add to skillet and simmer, stirring.

6 When thickened, remove the skillet from the heat and stir in the sour cream and parsley until blended. Season with pepper. Pour the sauce over the cutlets.

Turkey Cutlets with Lemon and Chives

- Serves **4**
- Preparation Time **15 minutes**
- Cooking Time **18 minutes**

4 turkey breast cutlets (1 pound)

1 lemon

2 tablespoons all-purpose flour

Salt and white or black pepper

2 teaspoons cornstarch

1/4 cup dry white wine or chicken stock

2 tablespoons olive or canola oil

1/2 cup chicken stock, page 18

2 tablespoons chopped chives

1 Pound turkey cutlets between wax paper as in master recipe. Finely grate zest of lemon onto a plate and combine with flour and a pinch each of salt and pepper. Squeeze lemon juice into a small bowl. In another bowl, blend cornstarch with wine.

2 Dredge cutlets with seasoned flour and sauté until cooked through as in master recipe.

3 Transfer cutlets to a platter, cover with aluminum foil, and keep warm. Spoon off all but 1 tablespoon of oil, and heat stock and lemon juice in skillet. Stir in cornstarch mixture; simmer until thickened, stirring constantly. Stir in chives and season with a pinch of pepper. Pour over cutlets.

PER SERVING
Calories **225**, Saturated Fat **2g**,
Total Fat **9g**, Sodium **152mg**,
Cholesterol **70mg**, Protein **27g**,
Carbohydrate **6g**, Fiber **0g**.

Chicken Cutlets with Fresh Cranberry Sauce

- Serves **4**
- Preparation Time **15 minutes**
- Cooking Time **15 minutes**

4 boneless, skinless chicken breast halves (1 pound)

2 tablespoons all-purpose flour

Salt and pepper

2 tablespoons olive or canola oil

1 1/2 cups chicken stock, page 18

6 ounces cranberries

1 tablespoon red wine vinegar

1 tablespoon dark brown sugar

1 Cut off fat from chicken. Season flour with a pinch each of salt and pepper. Cut each breast half across into 3 cutlets. Pound cutlets and dredge with flour as in Steps 1 and 2 of the master recipe

2 Sauté cutlets until cooked through as in master recipe; transfer to a platter, cover with aluminum foil, and keep warm.

3 Spoon off all but 1 tablespoon of oil from the skillet. Pour in stock and bring to a boil as in master recipe. Stir in cranberries, vinegar, and sugar, and simmer about 3 minutes, until cranberries become soft.

4 Season sauce with salt and pepper; pour over cutlets.

PER SERVING
Calories **241**, Saturated Fat **1g**,
Total Fat **9g**, Sodium **166mg**,
Cholesterol **66mg**, Protein **28g**,
Carbohydrate **12g**, Fiber **2g**.

Chicken Cutlets Paprikash

- Serves **4**
- Preparation Time **15 minutes**
- Cooking Time **25 minutes**

4 boneless, skinless chicken breast halves (1 pound)

2 tablespoons all-purpose flour

1/8 teaspoon each salt and pepper

2 tablespoons olive or canola oil

4 large onions, thinly sliced

1 tablespoon sweet paprika

1/4 teaspoon cayenne pepper

1 1/2 cups chicken stock, page 18

1/4 cup low-fat sour cream

1 Cut off fat from chicken. With a sharp knife, cut each breast across into 1/2-inch strips. Spread flour out on a plate and season with salt and pepper. Dredge chicken strips lightly with flour.

2 Sauté strips until cooked through as in master recipe, 5 to 6 minutes. Transfer to a plate, cover with aluminum foil, and keep warm. Spoon off all but 1 tablespoon of oil. Add sliced onions to skillet with paprika and cayenne pepper, and cook over moderate heat about 6 minutes, stirring frequently, until onions are very soft and golden.

3 Stir in stock, bring to a boil, and simmer about 5 minutes. Stir in sour cream, then return chicken strips to skillet and simmer about 4 minutes, until heated through.

PER SERVING
Calories **319**, Saturated Fat **2g**,
Total Fat **10g**, Sodium **190mg**,
Cholesterol **68mg**, Protein **31g**,
Carbohydrate **26g**, Fiber **4g**.

Chicken and Vegetable Stir-Fry

Cooking technique ▪ *Fry the food quickly over high heat, stirring constantly so it doesn't burn.*
Reduce fat ▪ *Make sure the oil is very hot so that the food doesn't absorb it.*
Add nutrients ▪ *Cook vegetables just until tender to preserve fragile vitamins.*

● Serves 4 ● Preparation Time **20 minutes** ● Cooking Time **12 minutes**

PER SERVING
Calories **200**, Saturated Fat **1g**,
Total Fat **7g**, Sodium **397mg**,
Cholesterol **49mg**, Protein **23g**,
Carbohydrate **13g**, Fiber **3g**.

2 boneless, skinless chicken breast halves (about ³/₄ pound)

2 teaspoons cornstarch

¹/₂ cup chicken stock, page 18

2 tablespoons reduced-sodium soy sauce

1¹/₂ tablespoons canola oil

2 cloves garlic, finely chopped

1 tablespoon finely chopped fresh ginger

2 sweet red or green peppers, thinly sliced

2 carrots, thinly sliced

2 stalks celery, thinly sliced

4 ounces mushrooms, sliced

¹/₈ teaspoon pepper

1 Dry the chicken breasts with paper towels, and cut off any fat. Holding a sharp knife at an angle, cut each chicken breast half across into very thin slices.

2 In a bowl, blend cornstarch, stock, and soy sauce. Heat oil in a wok or nonstick skillet over high heat until a piece of pepper sizzles when added to the oil.

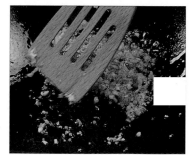

3 Add the garlic and ginger; cook, stirring constantly with a wooden spatula or stirrer, 1 to 2 minutes or until lightly browned and fragrant.

*For even more color, sprinkle **Chicken and Vegetable Stir-fry** with chopped green onions.*

4 Add the chicken slices and cook, stirring constantly, 3 to 4 minutes or until browned and cooked through. Transfer chicken to a bowl.

5 Allow the oil in the wok to reheat, then add the vegetables and cook, stirring constantly, about 4 minutes, until softened and lightly browned.

6 Return chicken and juices to wok and stir in the cornstarch mixture. Cook, stirring, until liquid comes to a boil and thickens slightly. Season with pepper.

Chicken Stir-Fry with Baby Corn

- Serves **4**
- Preparation Time **15 minutes**
- Cooking Time **12 minutes**

---

2 boneless, skinless chicken breast halves ($^3/_4$ pound)

2 teaspoons cornstarch

$^1/_3$ cup chicken stock, page 18

3 tablespoons reduced-sodium soy sauce

$1^1/_2$ tablespoons canola oil

2 cloves garlic, finely chopped

2 tablespoons finely chopped fresh ginger

8 ounces bok choy, shredded

1 can (14 ounces) baby corn, drained

$^1/_8$ teaspoon pepper

---

1 Thinly slice the chicken. In a small bowl, combine cornstarch with stock and soy sauce.

2 Heat oil in a wok or nonstick skillet; stir-fry garlic and ginger until golden. Add chicken and stir-fry as in Step 4 of master recipe; transfer to a bowl.

3 Reheat oil; add bok choy and baby corn. Stir-fry for about 4 minutes, until the bok choy is slightly softened and the corn is lightly browned.

4 Return chicken to pan with cornstarch mixture and pepper; cook, stirring, to thicken slightly.

PER SERVING
Calories **205**, Saturated Fat **1g**,
Total Fat **7g**, Sodium **708mg**,
Cholesterol **49mg**, Protein **24g**,
Carbohydrate **14g**, Fiber **1g**.

Duck Stir-Fry

- Serves **4**
- Preparation Time **15 minutes**
- Cooking Time **15 minutes**

---

2 boneless, skinless duck breast halves ($^3/_4$ pound)

2 tablespoons reduced-sodium soy sauce

1 tablespoon cornstarch

$^3/_4$ cup chicken stock, page 18

$1^1/_2$ tablespoons canola oil

8 ounces Napa cabbage, shredded

1 can (8 ounces) sliced water chestnuts, drained

$^1/_4$ cup toasted sliced almonds or chopped walnuts

---

1 Thinly slice the duck. In a bowl, toss duck slices with soy sauce to coat well.

2 In a small bowl, combine cornstarch with $^1/_4$ cup of stock.

3 Heat 1 tablespoon oil in a wok or nonstick skillet; stir-fry duck as in master recipe, about 3 minutes. Transfer to a plate. Heat remaining oil and stir-fry cabbage and water chestnuts about 3 minutes.

4 Stir in remaining stock, cover, and cook about 3 minutes. Return duck to wok and simmer about 3 minutes longer.

5 Stir in cornstarch mixture and cook, stirring, about 2 minutes, until slightly thickened. Sprinkle with the toasted almonds.

PER SERVING
Calories **255**, Saturated Fat **3g**,
Total Fat **16g**, Sodium **363mg**,
Cholesterol **57mg**, Protein **19g**,
Carbohydrate **11g**, Fiber **2g**.

Turkey and Citrus Stir-Fry

- Serves **4**
- Preparation Time **15 minutes**
- Cooking Time **15 minutes**

Finely grated zest and juice of 1 large orange and 1 lime

1 tablespoon cornstarch

$^1/_2$ teaspoon dry mustard

2 cloves garlic, finely chopped

2 tablespoons finely chopped fresh ginger

$^1/_8$ teaspoon salt

1 pound boneless, skinless turkey breast

2 tablespoons canola oil

4 onions, thinly sliced

4 ounces snow peas, trimmed

---

1 Reserving $^1/_2$ cup orange juice, blend cornstarch, mustard, garlic, ginger, and salt with remaining fruit juices and zest.

2 Thinly slice turkey. Add slices to fruit juice mixture and toss. Cover and marinate about 10 minutes.

3 Heat 1 tablespoon oil in a wok or nonstick skillet; stir-fry onions about 4 minutes or until soft. Add snow peas and stir-fry 3 minutes.

4 Transfer vegetables to a bowl. Heat remaining oil; stir-fry turkey about 3 minutes or until cooked through. Return vegetables to wok with reserved orange juice. Simmer about 3 minutes.

PER SERVING
Calories **291**, Saturated Fat **1g**,
Total Fat **9g**, Sodium **149mg**,
Cholesterol **70mg**, Protein **30g**,
Carbohydrate **23g**, Fiber **3g**.

Herb-Stuffed Chicken Breasts

Cooking technique ▪ *Begin with skinless chicken breasts, then cut a pocket in each and fill it with a tasty, nutritious stuffing. The flavors have been carefully balanced to enhance the chicken without overpowering it.*

Reduce cholesterol ▪ *To make a rich-tasting stuffing with very little fat, use low-fat cream cheese.*

Reduce sodium ▪ *Garlic and herbs add a burst of flavor to the stuffing, so you'll need very little added salt.*

● Serves **4** ● Preparation Time **15–20 minutes** ● Cooking Time **25 minutes**

PER SERVING
Calories **212**, Saturated Fat **4g**,
Total Fat **10g**, Sodium **226mg**,
Cholesterol **82mg**, Protein **28g**,
Carbohydrate **1g**, Fiber **0g**.

---

3 ounces low-fat cream cheese, at room temperature

1 clove garlic, finely chopped

2 tablespoons finely chopped parsley

1 tablespoon finely chopped mint or ³/₄ teaspoon dried

¹/₈ teaspoon salt and pepper

4 boneless, skinless chicken breast halves (about 1¹/₂ pounds)

1 tablespoon olive or canola oil

2 cups prepared marinara sauce (optional)

1 Preheat the oven to 350°F. Make the stuffing: In a medium bowl, combine the cream cheese with the garlic, parsley, mint, salt, and pepper.

2 Cut off any fat from the chicken breasts. Remove the long fillet from each chicken breast and reserve for another use.

3 With a sharp knife, cut a deep horizontal slit, about 2 inches long, in each chicken breast, starting at the rounded end. Take care not to cut through the sides of the chicken breast.

4 Using a teaspoon, insert about a quarter of the stuffing into each pocket so that it fills the pocket completely but does not spill out of the opening.

5 Fasten the opening of each chicken breast with a wooden toothpick, weaving the toothpick through the edges of the meat a few times.

6 Place chicken on a rack over a roasting pan; brush with oil. Roast about 20 minutes, until cooked through. Transfer to hot broiler; brush with remaining oil and broil about 5 minutes. Serve with marinara sauce, if you like.

Herb-Stuffed Chicken Breasts *are infused with the sweet
fresh flavor of garlic and parsley.*

Spinach- and Walnut-Stuffed Chicken Breasts

Serve with rice or orzo for a substantial meal. Leave out the walnuts if you're concerned about reducing fat.

- Serves **4**
- Preparation Time **20 minutes**
- Cooking Time **40 minutes**

2 tablespoons olive or canola oil
1 clove garlic, finely chopped
2 shallots or small onions, finely chopped
1 package (10 ounces) frozen spinach, thawed and drained
1/2 cup finely chopped walnuts
1 ounce low-fat cream cheese, at room temperature
1/8 teaspoon each salt and pepper
Pinch of grated nutmeg
4 boneless, skinless chicken breast halves (about 1 1/2 pounds)

1 Preheat the oven to 350°F. Heat 1 tablespoon of oil in a skillet over moderate heat. Add garlic and shallots and sauté about 5 minutes, until softened and golden.

COOKING TIP
Use shallots in place of regular onions to add greater depth of flavor.

---

2 Remove from the heat and stir in the spinach, walnuts, cream cheese, salt, pepper, and grated nutmeg.

3 Cut off any fat from chicken breasts; remove the long fillet from each and reserve for another use. With a sharp knife, cut a deep slit in each chicken breast from the rounded end, as in Step 3 of the master recipe.

4 Using a teaspoon, insert about a quarter of the stuffing into each pocket so that it fills the pocket but does not spill out. Fasten the opening of each chicken breast with a wooden toothpick, weaving the toothpick through the edges of the flesh a few times.

5 Place the chicken on a rack over a roasting pan; brush lightly with the remaining oil. Roast about 15 minutes or until tender and cooked through. Transfer to the hot broiler and broil about 5 minutes, until browned.

PER SERVING
Calories **392**, Saturated Fat **3g**, Total Fat **20g**, Sodium **270mg**, Cholesterol **104mg**, Protein **45g**, Carbohydrate **9g**, Fiber **3g**.

DRAINING SPINACH

Drain the thawed spinach in a sieve and then press it firmly with the back of a wooden spoon to remove as much of the excess water as possible.

Mushroom-Stuffed Chicken Breasts

Also known as cèpes, *porcini mushrooms lend a deep, smoky flavor to any dish. However, they are not essential here. If you are unable to find them, you can simply omit them from the recipe.*

- Serves **4**
- Preparation Time **35 minutes**
- Cooking Time **45 minutes**

1/2 ounce dried porcini mushrooms (optional)
2 tablespoons olive or canola oil
2 shallots or small onions, finely chopped
1 pound mushrooms, finely chopped
1/4 teaspoon dried thyme
1 tablespoon finely grated Parmesan cheese
1/8 teaspoon each salt and pepper
4 boneless, skinless chicken breast halves (about 1 1/2 pounds)

1 Preheat the oven to 350°F. Place the porcini mushrooms, if using, in a bowl and cover with boiling water. Soak about 10 minutes, then drain the mushrooms and chop finely.

2 Heat 1 tablespoon of oil in a skillet over moderate heat. Add the shallots and sauté about 3 minutes, until softened and golden.

3 Stir in soaked and fresh mushrooms and cook, stirring frequently, about 10 minutes, until very soft. Stir in thyme and continue cooking, stirring occasionally, 5 to 10 minutes longer, until mixture becomes quite dry. Remove from the heat; stir in Parmesan, salt, and pepper.

4 Cut off any fat from chicken breasts. Remove the long fillet from each chicken breast and reserve for another use. With a sharp knife, cut a deep horizontal slit in each chicken breast from the rounded end, as in Step 3 of the master recipe.

5 Using a teaspoon, insert about a quarter of the stuffing into each pocket so that it fills the pocket completely but does not spill out. Fasten the opening of each chicken breast with a wooden toothpick, weaving the toothpick through the edges of the flesh a few times.

6 Place the chicken on a rack over a roasting pan and brush lightly with the remaining oil. Roast about 15 minutes or until the chicken is tender and cooked through. Transfer to hot broiler and broil about 5 minutes, until browned.

PER SERVING
Calories **303**, Saturated Fat **2g**, Total Fat **10g**, Sodium **212mg**, Cholesterol **100mg**, Protein **43g**, Carbohydrate **10g**, Fiber **3g**.

Orange-Stuffed Duck Breasts

Many supermarkets and butchers now carry duck breasts. If you prefer, chicken breasts can be substituted for the duck.

- Serves **4**
- Preparation Time **20 minutes**
- Cooking Time **45 minutes**

$^1/_4$ **cup chicken stock, page 18**

$^1/_4$ **cup orange juice**

$^1/_3$ **cup couscous**

---

2 tablespoons olive or canola oil

---

1 small red or yellow onion, finely chopped

---

1 stalk celery, finely chopped

---

1 teaspoon finely grated orange zest

$^1/_2$ **teaspoon dried tarragon**

$^1/_8$ **teaspoon each salt and pepper**

---

4 boneless, skinless duck breast halves (about $1^1/_2$ pounds)

For the orange sauce

$^2/_3$ **cup orange juice**

Juice of 1 lemon

---

1 tablespoon honey

---

1 tablespoon red wine vinegar

---

1 tablespoon cornstarch

---

1 orange, sectioned

---

1 Preheat the oven to 350°F. Bring the chicken stock and orange juice to a boil in a small saucepan. Stir in the couscous, and prepare as in box (right).

2 Meanwhile, heat 1 tablespoon of oil in a skillet over moderate heat. Sauté the onion and celery about 5 minutes, until softened. Stir in the orange zest and tarragon and cook, stirring frequently, about 3 minutes longer. Remove from heat, stir in couscous, salt, and pepper. Transfer to a bowl and let cool.

3 Cut off any fat from the duck breasts. Remove the long fillet from each duck breast and reserve for another use. With a sharp knife, cut a deep horizontal slit in each duck breast from the rounded end, as in Step 3 of the master recipe.

4 Using a teaspoon, insert about a quarter of the stuffing into each pocket so that it fills the pocket completely but does not spill out. Fasten the opening of each duck breast with a wooden toothpick, weaving the toothpick through the edges of the flesh a few times.

5 Place the duck breasts on a rack over a roasting pan and brush lightly with the remaining oil. Roast in the oven about 20 minutes or until the duck is cooked through. Transfer to hot broiler and broil about 5 minutes, until lightly browned.

6 Meanwhile, make the orange sauce: In a pan, heat the orange juice, lemon juice, honey, and vinegar. Mix the cornstarch with 1 tablespoon water and add to the pan. Cook about 4 minutes, stirring, until thickened. Add the orange sections and serve.

PER SERVING
Calories **401**, Saturated Fat **3g**, Total Fat **14g**, Sodium **182mg**, Cholesterol **131mg**, Protein **37g**, Carbohydrate **30g**, Fiber **2g**.

Orange-Stuffed Duck Breasts are served with couscous, green beans, and orange sauce.

HOW TO PREPARE COUSCOUS

1 *In a saucepan, bring the liquid to a boil, add the couscous, and stir to combine. Remove the pan from the heat and cover with a plate.*

2 *Allow the couscous to stand about 5 minutes, until the grains are soft and the liquid is absorbed. Gently stir with a fork to fluff up the grains.*

Savory Chicken Parcels

Cooking technique ▪ *Bake poultry, herbs, and vegetables in sealed aluminum packets. The food will cook in its own juices, creating exquisite flavor with little fat.*

Reduce cholesterol ▪ *Use monounsaturated olive oil in the seasoning mixture. For an even more rewarding taste, try extra-virgin olive oil.*

● Serves **4** ● Preparation Time **15 minutes** ● Cooking Time **30–35 minutes**

PER SERVING
Calories **287**, Saturated Fat **2g**,
Total Fat **9g**, Sodium **195mg**,
Cholesterol **99mg**, Protein **42g**,
Carbohydrate **9g**, Fiber **3g**.

4 boneless, skinless chicken breast halves (1¹/₂ pounds)

4 ounces mushrooms, sliced

2 carrots, cut into 1¹/₂-inch matchsticks

2 zucchini, cut into 1¹/₂-inch matchsticks

2 tablespoons olive or canola oil

1 tablespoon chopped basil or 1 teaspoon dried

2 tablespoons lemon juice

¹/₈ teaspoon each salt and pepper

1 Preheat the oven to 375°F. Cut 4 sheets of aluminum foil, about 12 inches square. Place 1 chicken breast on each; arrange a quarter of the vegetables on top.

2 Prepare the seasoning mixture: In a small bowl, whisk together the oil, chopped basil, lemon juice, salt, and pepper until combined.

3 Spoon about a quarter of the seasoning mixture evenly over each chicken and vegetable mound.

*The delicate flavor of **Savory Chicken Parcels** is complemented by sugar snap peas and a medley of wild and white rice.*

4 With the chicken and vegetable mound crosswise on the foil, fold the 2 sides over both ends of the chicken breast.

5 Fold the nearest edge over the chicken; then fold the farthest edge toward you over the whole parcel so that the end folds underneath the parcel.

6 Bake the parcels in a baking dish for 30 to 35 minutes. Unwrap each parcel and transfer the chicken and vegetables to a serving platter with the juices.

Tex-Mex Turkey Parcels

- Serves **4**
- Preparation Time **15 minutes**
- Cooking Time **25 minutes**

4 boneless, skinless turkey breast cutlets (1 pound)

4 tomatoes, diced

1¹/₂ cups fresh or frozen corn kernels

1 small red onion, finely chopped

1 fresh or canned jalapeño pepper, drained and rinsed if canned, finely chopped

2 tablespoons lime juice

¹/₄ teaspoon chili powder

¹/₈ teaspoon each salt and pepper

1 Preheat the oven to 375°F. With a small knife, remove any fat from the turkey cutlets.

2 In a medium bowl, combine the tomatoes with the corn, red onion, jalapeño pepper, lime juice, chili powder, salt, and pepper.

3 Prepare the foil as in Step 1 of the master recipe. Arrange the turkey cutlets and vegetables on the foil as in Step 3 of the master recipe.

4 Seal the parcels, place in a baking dish, and bake in the oven about 25 minutes. Serve as in Step 6 of the master recipe.

PER SERVING
Calories **218**, Saturated Fat **1g**, Total Fat **3g**, Sodium **227mg**, Cholesterol **70mg**, Protein **30g**, Carbohydrate **20g**, Fiber **5g**.

Spinach and Turkey Parcels

- Serves **4**
- Preparation Time **15 minutes**
- Cooking Time **35 minutes**

4 boneless, skinless turkey breast cutlets (1 pound)

1 package (10 ounces) frozen spinach, thawed and drained

1¹/₂ tablespoons olive oil

2 shallots or small onions, finely chopped

2 cloves garlic, finely chopped

Finely grated zest of ¹/₂ lemon

¹/₈ teaspoon each salt and pepper

Pinch of ground nutmeg

¹/₂ cup low-fat ricotta cheese

1 Preheat the oven to 375°F. With a small knife, remove any fat from turkey cutlets. Drain spinach (see page 74).

2 In a skillet, heat oil. Add shallots and garlic, and cook, stirring, about 3 minutes or until softened but not browned. Remove from the heat and stir in spinach, lemon zest, salt, pepper, and nutmeg. Stir in ricotta cheese.

3 Prepare foil as in the master recipe. Place 1 cutlet on each, then spoon about a quarter of spinach mixture on top of each cutlet.

4 Seal parcels, place in a baking dish, and bake about 25 minutes. Serve as in the master recipe.

PER SERVING
Calories **249**, Saturated Fat **3g**, Total Fat **9g**, Sodium **244mg**, Cholesterol **80mg**, Protein **33g**, Carbohydrate **8g**, Fiber **2g**.

Asian Chicken Parcels

- Serves **4**
- Preparation Time **20 minutes**
- Cooking Time **30–35 minutes**

2 tablespoons chopped cilantro or parsley leaves

1 tablespoon finely chopped fresh ginger

1¹/₂ teaspoons reduced-sodium soy sauce

1 teaspoon Oriental sesame oil

¹/₈ teaspoon pepper

4 boneless, skinless chicken breast halves (1¹/₂ pounds)

2 scallions, thinly sliced diagonally

1 each large sweet red and green peppers, diced

1 Preheat the oven to 375°F. Prepare the seasoning mixture: In a small bowl, combine the cilantro with the ginger, soy sauce, sesame oil, and pepper until well mixed.

2 Prepare foil as in Step 1 of the master recipe. Arrange chicken breasts and vegetables on the foil as in Step 3 of the master recipe, then spoon over the seasoning mixture.

3 Seal the foil parcels, place in a baking dish, and bake in the oven 30 to 35 minutes. Serve as in Step 6 of the master recipe.

PER SERVING
Calories **232**, Saturated Fat **1g**, Total Fat **4g**, Sodium **189mg**, Cholesterol **97mg**, Protein **41g**, Carbohydrate **8g**, Fiber **2g**.

Braised Duckling with Oranges

Cooking technique ■ *Skin the duckling before cooking – or have your butcher do it – to cut the fat by a third. Braise the bird in fruit juice to keep it moist.*
Add flavor ■ *Make a light sauce with fresh oranges, honey, and herbs.*

● Serves **4** ● Preparation Time **35 minutes** ● Cooking Time **1¼ hours**

PER SERVING
Calories **588**, Saturated Fat **10g**, Total Fat **26g**, Sodium **252mg**, Cholesterol **201mg**, Protein **56g**, Carbohydrate **31g**, Fiber **3g**.

1 duckling (4–5 pounds), cut into 8 serving pieces

3 oranges

2 tablespoons honey

2 tablespoons cider vinegar

1 teaspoon Dijon mustard

1 tablespoon chopped fresh rosemary leaves or 1 teaspoon dried

2 large onions, diced

1½ cups chicken stock, page 18

⅛ teaspoon each salt and pepper

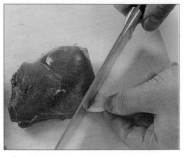

1 With your fingers, remove all the skin from the duckling pieces. Using a sharp knife, cut off all the excess fat.

2 Finely grate the zest from 2 of the oranges, squeeze the juice, and add to a bowl with the honey, vinegar, mustard, and rosemary.

3 Heat a flameproof casserole over moderate heat. Cook half of the duckling pieces about 10 minutes, turning once, until well browned. Transfer to a plate and cook remaining duckling.

*For a nice finishing touch, sprinkle a little chopped fresh rosemary over **Braised Duckling with Oranges**.*

4 Remove all but 1 tablespoon fat from casserole. Add the onions and sauté, stirring, about 5 minutes, until golden.

5 Stir the orange mixture into the sautéed onions so that they are well coated. Add the chicken stock, salt, and pepper, and bring to a boil.

6 Return the duckling pieces to the pan and coat with the onion mixture. Cover the pan and braise the duckling about 50 minutes, until cooked through. Stir in the third orange, cut into sections.

Braised Autumn Duckling

- Serves **4**
- Preparation Time **25 minutes**
- Cooking Time **1¼ hours**

1 duckling (4–5 pounds), cut into 8 serving pieces
⅛ teaspoon each salt, pepper, and ground nutmeg
2 onions, cut into quarters
4 stalks celery, cut diagonally into ½-inch slices
1½ cups chicken stock, page 18
2 tablespoons red currant jelly (optional)
8 ounces mushrooms, trimmed and halved

1 Preheat the oven to 350°F. Remove all the skin from the duckling pieces and cut off all the excess fat. Sprinkle the duckling with the salt, pepper, and nutmeg.

2 Heat a large flameproof casserole over moderate heat. Working in batches, add the duckling pieces and cook about 10 minutes, until well browned on all sides. Transfer to a plate.

3 Remove all but 1 tablespoon of the fat from the skillet and add the onions and celery. Cook, stirring frequently, about 5 minutes, until softened. Stir in the chicken stock and red currant jelly and bring to a boil.

4 Return the the duckling pieces to the casserole and stir gently. Cover the casserole and bake in the oven about 50 minutes, until the duckling is cooked through. Stir in the mushrooms and cook about 10 minutes longer, until the mushrooms are tender.

> ### COOKING TIP
> *No oil is needed for browning since fat is released from the duckling while it cooks.*

PER SERVING
Calories **534**, Saturated Fat **10g**, Total Fat **26g**, Sodium **271mg**, Cholesterol **201mg**, Protein **56g**, Carbohydrate **17g**, Fiber **3g**.

Braised Duckling with Red Cabbage and Apples

- Serves **4**
- Preparation Time **30 minutes**
- Cooking Time **1½ hours**

1 duckling (4–5 pounds), cut into 8 serving pieces
1 large onion, diced
1 pound cooking apples, peeled and diced
1 cup unsweetened apple juice
¼ cup balsamic or red wine vinegar
2 tablespoons sugar
2 pounds red cabbage, cored and coarsely shredded
¼ cup raisins
⅛ teaspoon each salt and pepper

1 Remove all the skin from the duckling pieces and cut off all the excess fat. Heat a flameproof casserole over moderate heat. Working in batches, add the duckling pieces and cook about 10 minutes, until well browned on all sides. Transfer to a plate and reserve.

2 Add the onion and apples to the casserole and sauté about 10 minutes, stirring frequently, until lightly browned. Remove from the heat.

3 Combine the apple juice, vinegar, and sugar in the casserole. Stir in the onion-apple mixture and cabbage and bring to a boil over moderate heat.

4 Place the duckling pieces on top of the cabbage, cover, and simmer about 1 hour, until the duckling is cooked through and cabbage is tender. Stir in the raisins, salt, and pepper, cover, and cook about 5 minutes longer.

PER SERVING
Calories **676**, Saturated Fat **10g**, Total Fat **27g**, Sodium **270mg**, Cholesterol **201mg**, Protein **57g**, Carbohydrate **54g**, Fiber **7g**.

Chicken Pot Pie

Reduce fat ▪ *In this slimmed-down version of a winter favorite, the crust is made with low-fat cream cheese – the gravy with stock, cornstarch, and milk.*

Save time ▪ *You can use packaged pie crust, but it will increase the fat slightly.*

- Serves 6 ● Preparation Time **30 minutes plus chilling time**
- Cooking Time **1 hour 10 minutes**

PER SERVING
Calories **350**, Saturated Fat **3g**, Total Fat **8g**, Sodium **301mg**, Cholesterol **74mg**, Protein **34g**, Carbohydrate **34g**, Fiber **5g**.

---

¹/₄ **cup low-fat cream cheese**

2 **tablespoons margarine or butter**

1 **cup all-purpose flour**

Salt and pepper

2–3 **tablespoons cold water**

4 **boneless, skinless chicken breast halves (about 1¹/₂ pounds)**

2 **cups chicken stock, page 18**

3 **carrots, diced**

2 **zucchini, diced**

2 **stalks celery, diced**

1 **onion, diced**

8 **ounces frozen peas**

6 **tablespoons 1% low-fat milk**

2 **tablespoons cornstarch**

¹/₄ **cup chopped parsley or 1 tablespoon dried**

CUTTING LEAF SHAPES FROM DOUGH

1 *Roll out dough thinly. With a sharp knife, cut several strips of dough 1-inch wide. Make diagonal cuts along each strip to make diamond-shaped pieces.*

2 *With the knife, very gently score lines on each diamond to make the veins of the leaf.*

1 Place the cream cheese and margarine in a large bowl. Using a wooden spoon, beat until blended.

2 Add the flour to the bowl with ¹/₈ teaspoon salt. Using a pastry cutter or 2 knives, cut the mixture until it resembles coarse crumbs.

3 Add the water 1 tablespoon at a time, lightly mixing until the dough holds together. Cover and refrigerate at least 1 hour.

4 Meanwhile, trim fat from chicken and halve lengthwise. Bring stock to a boil. Add chicken and simmer about 5 minutes or until tender; transfer to a plate.

5 Return stock to a boil; add the vegetables and simmer about 5 minutes. With a slotted spoon, transfer the vegetables to a bowl. Shred chicken; add to vegetables.

6 Simmer stock about 8 minutes, until reduced to 1¹/₂ cups. In a bowl, blend ¹/₄ cup of the milk with the cornstarch. Stir into the stock to thicken slightly.

7 Remove stock from the heat; combine with the chicken and vegetables. Add parsley, and season with pepper. Spoon into a 13" x 9" x 2" baking dish.

8 Preheat the oven to 350°F. On a lightly floured board, roll out dough to fit dish. Lay the dough over dish, press to seal the edges, and trim the overhang.

9 Make pastry leaves from trimmings and brush pie with remaining milk. Bake 45 to 60 minutes, until crust is golden and the chicken is hot.

Chicken Pot Pie *is a meal in itself, but if you want an accompaniment, choose a fresh green vegetable like broccoli or beans.*

Mexican Chicken Pot Pie

Take your dinner south of the border with this enticing variation. The amount of chili powder called for here is on the mild side, so add a little more if you really like to spice things up.

- Serves 6
- Preparation Time 30 minutes plus chilling time
- Cooking Time 1 hour 10 minutes

---

¹/₄ cup low-fat cream cheese

2 tablespoons margarine or butter

1 cup all-purpose flour

Salt and pepper

4–5 tablespoons water

4 boneless, skinless chicken breast halves (about 1¹/₂ pounds)

1 cup chicken stock, page 18

1 can (14 ounces) plum tomatoes, drained, with liquid reserved

1¹/₂ tablespoons cornstarch

1 tablespoon olive or canola oil

1 onion, chopped

1 clove garlic, chopped

1 sweet green pepper, diced

2 teaspoons chili powder

1 can (1 pound) red kidney beans, rinsed and drained

1 cup fresh or frozen corn kernels

2 tablespoons 1% low-fat milk

1 Make the cream cheese pastry dough with 2 to 3 tablespoons of the water as in the master recipe; cover and refrigerate 1 hour.

2 Meanwhile, cook the chicken breasts in the stock and the liquid from the tomatoes. Then shred into bite-size pieces as in Steps 4 and 5 of the master recipe. Simmer stock 10 to 12 minutes or until reduced to about 1 cup.

3 Blend cornstarch with remaining 2 tablespoons water until smooth. Stir into hot stock mixture. Remove from the heat.

4 In a large skillet, heat the oil over moderate heat; sauté onion with garlic, sweet pepper, and chili powder. Stir in the tomatoes and reduced chicken stock mixture; simmer together about 5 minutes.

5 Remove from the heat and stir in chicken, kidney beans, and corn. Season with ¹/₈ teaspoon each salt and pepper and spoon into a 13" x 9" x 2" baking dish as in the master recipe.

6 Preheat the oven to 350°F. Roll out the dough and cover the pie as in the master recipe. Brush with milk and bake in the oven 45 to 60 minutes, until crust is golden and chicken is hot.

COOKING TIP
Instead of placing the dough in the refrigerator for 1 hour, save precious time and put it in the freezer for only 25 minutes. This prevents the pastry from shrinking during cooking.

PER SERVING
Calories **388**, Saturated Fat **3g**, Total Fat **10g**, Sodium **468mg**, Cholesterol **73mg**, Protein **36g**, Carbohydrate **39g**, Fiber **6g**.

Chicken and Potato Pie

To prevent the paper-thin layers of filo dough from drying out, cover with a moist clean towel until you're ready to use them.

- Serves 6
- Preparation Time 40 minutes
- Cooking Time 1 hour

---

2 cups chicken stock, page 18

1 cup water

1 pound small red potatoes, quartered

1 package (10 ounces) frozen carrots

1 jar (15 ounces) baby onions

4 boneless, skinless chicken breast halves (about 1¹/₂ pounds)

2 tablespoons olive or canola oil

1¹/₂ tablespoons cornstarch

¹/₄ cup 1% low-fat milk

1 teaspoon dried tarragon

¹/₈ teaspoon each salt and pepper

1 package (10 ounces) frozen peas, thawed

6 sheets filo dough (18 x 14 inches), thawed if frozen

1 In a saucepan, bring the chicken stock and water to a boil. Simmer the potatoes in the stock mixture 8 to 10 minutes, until almost tender. Using a slotted spoon, transfer potatoes to a large bowl. Cook the carrots for 4 minutes, drain and transfer to the bowl. Drain the onions and add to the bowl.

2 Cut the chicken into ¹/₂-inch pieces and simmer in the stock 2 to 4 minutes or until tender. Using a slotted spoon, transfer the chicken to the same bowl. Continue simmering the stock about 10 minutes, until reduced by about half.

3 Meanwhile, preheat oven to 400°F. Lay 1 sheet of filo on a lightly floured board and brush with a little oil. Cover with a second sheet and brush again with oil. Repeat layering the filo, reserving a little oil.

4 In a small bowl, blend the cornstarch with the milk until smooth. Stir into stock with tarragon, salt, and pepper until it thickens slightly. Combine with potatoes, onions, chicken, and peas and spoon into baking dish as in Step 7 of the master recipe.

5 Place sheets of dough loosely over pie. Trim dough edge, leaving about ¹/₄ inch extra around dish. Seal edge by pressing gently with your fingers. Cut slits in dough and brush with remaining oil. Bake in the oven 30 to 35 minutes, until crust is golden and chicken is hot.

COOKING TIP
To make a deep dish pie as shown on the book cover, omit the filo dough. Using master recipe for dough (page 80) or packaged pie crust mix, roll out a 10-inch crust and pastry leaves. Prepare filling as above and pour into a 9-inch soufflé dish. Cover the pie as in master recipe and bake 30 to 35 minutes in a 400° F oven.

PER SERVING
Calories **440**, Saturated Fat **1g**, Total Fat **7g**, Sodium **418mg**, Cholesterol **66mg**, Protein **37g**, Carbohydrate **56g**, Fiber **4g**.

Home-style Turkey Pot Pies with Buttermilk Crust

It's just a myth that buttermilk is fattening. It's not made from butter but from the liquid left after the butter has been churned from the milk. The amount of buttermilk here accounts for only about 25 calories and a trace of fat per serving.

- Serves **6**
- Preparation Time **20 minutes**
- Cooking Time **35–40 minutes**

1¹/₂ pounds turkey breast cutlets

2 cups chicken stock, page 18

1 tablespoon olive or canola oil

1 sweet red pepper, diced

4 ounces mushrooms, sliced

2 cups fresh or frozen corn kernels

1 cup buttermilk

1¹/₂ tablespoons cornstarch

Salt and pepper

2 cups all-purpose flour

2 teaspoons baking powder

¹/₄ teaspoon baking soda

4 tablespoons margarine or butter

1 Cook the turkey breast in the chicken stock as in the master recipe. Remove from the stock and cut into ¹/₂-inch cubes. Simmer the stock about 8 minutes, until reduced to 1¹/₂ cups.

2 Meanwhile, in a large non-stick skillet, heat the oil; sauté red pepper and mushrooms 3 to 4 minutes, until slightly soft. Remove from the heat and stir in the corn kernels and the turkey.

3 In a small bowl, blend ¹/₄ cup of the buttermilk with the cornstarch until smooth. Stir into the chicken stock until it thickens slightly. Add the sauce to the turkey and vegetables. Add ¹/₈ teaspoon each salt and pepper, and spoon into eight 4-inch round baking dishes.

4 Preheat the oven to 400°F. Make the buttermilk biscuit dough (see box, below). On a lightly floured board, roll out the dough to about ¹/₂ inch thick. Using a 3-inch cookie cutter, cut out 8 rounds from the dough.

5 Place a round of dough on each baking dish. Bake in the oven 15 to 20 minutes, until the biscuits are browned and the turkey mixture is hot.

Sprinkle a little parsley over Home-style Turkey Pot Pies with Buttermilk Crust.

PER SERVING
Calories **457**, Saturated Fat **3g**, Total Fat **13g**, Sodium **504mg**, Cholesterol **72mg**, Protein **35g**, Carbohydrate **48g**, Fiber **4g**.

MAKING BUTTERMILK BISCUIT DOUGH

1 *Sift the flour into a large bowl with the baking powder, baking soda, and ¹/₄ teaspoon salt.*

2 *Rub in the margarine with your fingers until coarse crumbs form.*

3 *Stir in ³/₄ cup of buttermilk and blend just until the mixture forms a soft dough.*

GETTING AHEAD

Make a batch of pastry dough ahead of time – it will keep in the freezer for about 6 months or in the refrigerator for up to 3 days. Defrost frozen dough in the refrigerator the day before you need it.

French Chicken Ragout

Cooking technique ■ *To defat this classic French dish (pronounced "rah-goo"), skin the chicken first. Make the sauce with cornstarch and low-fat sour cream.*

● Serves **4** ● Preparation Time **15 minutes** ● Cooking Time **30 minutes**

PER SERVING
Calories **368**, Saturated Fat **3g**, Total Fat **15g**, Sodium **303mg**, Cholesterol **124mg**, Protein **34g**, Carbohydrate **19g**, Fiber **3g**.

1¹⁄₄ **pounds boneless chicken thighs**

2 **tablespoons olive or canola oil**

2 **cloves garlic, finely chopped**

1 **onion, coarsely chopped**

8 **ounces mushrooms, halved**

3 **carrots, cut into 1-inch strips**

2 **stalks celery, thickly sliced**

1¹⁄₂ **cups chicken stock, page 18**

¹⁄₂ **cup white wine or chicken stock**

1 **tablespoon cornstarch**

¹⁄₂ **cup 1% low-fat milk**

¹⁄₂ **cup low-fat sour cream**

¹⁄₈ **teaspoon each salt and pepper**

1 **tablespoon chopped parsley**

1 Remove the skin from the chicken thighs by pulling it off with your fingers. Cut off any fat from the thighs and cut them into quarters.

2 In a large saucepan, heat oil over moderate heat. Brown the thighs about 4 minutes; drain on paper towels. Spoon off all but 1 tablespoon fat from pan.

3 In pan, sauté garlic and onion, stirring, 3 minutes. Stir in mushrooms, carrots, and celery; cook 3 minutes longer, until mushrooms brown.

Spoon the creamy sauce over noodles and enjoy **French Chicken Ragout.**

4 Return chicken to pan, stir in stock and wine, and bring to a boil. Reduce heat, cover, and simmer 15 to 20 minutes, until chicken and vegetables are cooked.

5 In a small bowl, combine the cornstarch with the milk until smooth. Stir in the sour cream.

6 Stir cornstarch mixture into ragout and simmer about 2 minutes, until thickened. Season with salt and pepper. Sprinkle chopped parsley on top.

Mustard Chicken Ragout

- Serves **4**
- Preparation Time **20 minutes**
- Cooking Time **30 minutes**

4 skinless chicken breast halves (2 pounds)

¹/₄ cup coarse-grained mustard

2 tablespoons olive or canola oil

2 large onions, chopped

4 carrots, cut into ¹/₂-inch cubes

2 parsnips, cut into ¹/₂-inch cubes

2 cups chicken stock, page 18

2 tablespoons low-fat sour cream

2 tablespoons chopped parsley

¹/₈ teaspoon each salt and pepper

1 Cut fat from chicken breasts. Spread both sides of each breast with the mustard.

2 In a deep skillet, heat oil over moderate heat. Brown chicken about 5 minutes; transfer to a plate, cover, and keep warm.

3 Brown the onions, carrots, and parsnips, stirring, 5 to 7 minutes. Add stock and bring to a boil, scraping bottom of skillet.

4 Return chicken to skillet, cover, and simmer vegetables and chicken about 15 minutes, until cooked.

5 Transfer chicken to a serving platter. Stir sour cream, parsley, salt, and pepper into sauce. Pour sauce over chicken.

PER SERVING
Calories **377**, Saturated Fat **2g**, Total Fat **10g**, Sodium **372mg**, Cholesterol **100mg**, Protein **43g**, Carbohydrate **26g**, Fiber **6g**.

Creole Ragout

- Serves **4**
- Preparation Time **15 minutes**
- Cooking Time **25–30 minutes**

4 boneless, skinless chicken breast halves (1¹/₂ pounds)

2 tablespoons olive or canola oil

2 onions, coarsely chopped

2 cloves garlic, finely chopped

3 stalks celery, sliced

1 sweet green pepper, coarsely chopped

¹/₂ teaspoon dried thyme

¹/₄ teaspoon cayenne pepper

1 cup chicken stock, page 18

1 cup canned crushed tomatoes

1 package (10 ounces) frozen corn kernels, thawed

¹/₈ teaspoon each salt and pepper

1 Cut fat from chicken breasts; cut the chicken into 1-inch pieces.

2 In a large skillet, heat the oil over moderate heat. Brown the chicken lightly about 3 minutes. Drain on paper towels.

3 Brown onions and garlic in the skillet, stirring, 3 to 4 minutes. Add celery, green pepper, thyme, and cayenne, and cook 3 to 4 minutes, until slightly softened.

4 Return chicken to skillet; add stock and tomatoes. Cover and simmer 10 to 15 minutes, until chicken is cooked through. Stir in the corn, salt, and pepper, and cook about 2 minutes longer.

PER SERVING
Calories **366**, Saturated Fat **1g**, Total Fat **10g**, Sodium **324mg**, Cholesterol **97mg**, Protein **44g**, Carbohydrate **28g**, Fiber **6g**.

Mediterranean Turkey Ragout

- Serves **4**
- Preparation Time **10 minutes**
- Cooking Time **about 1 hour**

3 turkey drumsticks (2 pounds)

3 tablespoons all-purpose flour

4 teaspoons olive or canola oil

1 onion, diced

4 cloves garlic, finely chopped

³/₄ cup chicken stock, page 18

1 sweet red pepper, diced

3 strips orange zest

¹/₂ cup orange juice

¹/₄ teaspoon dried rosemary

Pinch of dried thyme

1 can (14 ounces) crushed tomatoes

¹/₄ cup sliced black olives

1 Remove skin and dredge turkey lightly with flour. In a large skillet, heat oil over moderate heat; sauté turkey about 5 minutes, until browned.

2 Transfer turkey to a plate. Sauté onion and garlic, stirring, about 2 minutes, until softened. Stir in ¹/₂ cup of stock and cook about 5 minutes longer.

3 Stir in red pepper, orange zest and juice, and herbs. Simmer 5 minutes. Add tomatoes, remaining stock, and turkey. Cover and simmer about 40 minutes, until turkey is cooked. Add olives. Cut meat off the bone before serving.

PER SERVING
Calories **394**, Saturated Fat **4g**, Total Fat **15g**, Sodium **271mg**, Cholesterol **137mg**, Protein **43g**, Carbohydrate **21g**, Fiber **3g**.

Herbed Turkey Burgers

Reduce fat ▪ *Grind the turkey in your own food processor to get meat that is lower in fat than store-bought. If you are short of time, use 1 pound packaged ground turkey. Vegetables add vitamins and keep the burgers moist.*

Reduce cholesterol ▪ *On a fat-restricted diet, use breast meat instead of thigh.*

● Serves **4** ● Preparation Time **15** minutes ● Cooking Time **12–15** minutes

PER SERVING
Calories **178**, Saturated Fat **2g**,
Total Fat **5g**, Sodium **139mg**,
Cholesterol **78mg**, Protein **25g**,
Carbohydrate **6g**, Fiber **1g**.

1¼ **pounds boneless turkey thighs**	½ **cup fresh bread crumbs**
1 **small yellow onion**	2 **teaspoons Dijon mustard**
2 **cloves garlic, finely chopped**	2 **tablespoons chopped parsley**
1 **small sweet green pepper, finely chopped**	1 **egg white**
	⅛ **teaspoon each salt and pepper**

1 Using your fingers, remove the skin from the turkey thighs. Cut off any visible fat and cut the meat into small pieces.

2 Either place the turkey in the work bowl of a food processor and finely chop, scraping down the sides occasionally, or finely chop the turkey by hand.

3 Chop the onion in the food processor or by hand. Transfer to a bowl. Add the garlic and pepper, and toss to combine.

*Kids will love them – **Herbed Turkey Burgers** topped with sliced tomatoes and sesame buns. Serve them with coleslaw or a salad on the side.*

4 Add the bread crumbs, mustard, parsley, egg white, salt, and pepper. Add the turkey and stir to combine.

5 Preheat the broiler, setting the rack 5 inches from the heat. Divide the mixture into quarters and form each into a round, compact patty.

6 Arrange the turkey patties on the broiler rack and cook them 6 to 7 minutes on each side or until cooked through.

Chicken and Spinach Burgers

- Serves **4**
- Preparation Time **15 minutes**
- Cooking Time **12–15 minutes**

1 pound boneless chicken thighs
1 package (10 ounces) frozen chopped spinach, thawed
1 yellow onion, finely chopped
$^1/_2$ cup fresh bread crumbs
2 tablespoons finely chopped chives or 2 teaspoons dried
1 egg white
$^1/_8$ teaspoon ground nutmeg
$^1/_8$ teaspoon each salt and pepper

1 Remove skin from the chicken and finely chop as in Steps 1 and 2 of the master recipe.

2 Squeeze out all the water from the spinach, then combine with the onion in a large bowl. Stir in the chicken with the bread crumbs, chives, egg white, nutmeg, salt, and pepper.

3 Preheat the broiler, form the patties, and broil the burgers as in Step 6 of the master recipe, 6 to 7 minutes on each side or until cooked through.

PER SERVING
Calories **179**, Saturated Fat **1g**,
Total Fat **5g**, Sodium **241mg**,
Cholesterol **94mg**, Protein **25g**,
Carbohydrate **8g**, Fiber **2g**.

Savory Turkey Nuggets

- Serves **4**
- Preparation Time **20 minutes**
- Cooking Time **8–10 minutes**

1$^1/_4$ pounds boneless turkey thighs
1 small yellow onion
1 small sweet red or green pepper, finely chopped
2 cloves garlic, finely chopped
$^1/_2$ cup fresh bread crumbs
2 teaspoons Dijon mustard
1 egg white
$^1/_8$ teaspoon dried sage or thyme
$^1/_8$ teaspoon each salt and pepper
Sweet Pepper and Corn Salsa, page 183, or prepared salsa

1 Remove the skin and fat from the turkey thighs, cut into pieces, and finely chop as in Steps 1 and 2 of the master recipe.

2 Finely chop the onion and mix with the sweet pepper and garlic. Stir in the turkey with the bread crumbs, mustard, egg white, sage, salt, and pepper until combined.

3 Preheat the broiler. Form the turkey mixture into balls about the size of large marbles, and roll them between your palms. Place the nuggets on the broiler rack and cook 5 inches from the heat, turning them occasionally, 8 to 10 minutes or until cooked through. Serve with salsa.

PER SERVING
Calories **327**, Saturated Fat **3g**,
Total Fat **14g**, Sodium **215mg**,
Cholesterol **98mg**, Protein **32g**,
Carbohydrate **19g**, Fiber **4g**.

Cajun Chicken Loaf

- Serves **4**
- Preparation Time **20 minutes**
- Cooking Time **45–60 minutes**

1 tablespoon olive or canola oil
1 onion, finely chopped
2 stalks celery, finely chopped
2 cloves garlic, finely chopped
1 sweet green pepper, finely chopped
1 pound boneless chicken thighs
1 egg white
$^1/_2$ cup fresh bread crumbs
$^1/_8$ teaspoon dried thyme
$^1/_8$ teaspoon hot red pepper sauce
$^1/_8$ teaspoon each salt and pepper

1 In a nonstick frying pan, heat the oil over moderate heat. Sauté the onion, celery, garlic, and pepper about 4 minutes or until softened. Transfer to a bowl.

2 Preheat the oven to 350°F. Remove skin from the chicken and finely chop the meat as in the master recipe. Stir into vegetables. Add the remaining ingredients.

3 Cover a wire rack with foil and set in a roasting pan. Pierce the foil to allow juices to drain. Form the chicken mixture into an 8" x 4" x 2" loaf on the rack.

4 Bake 45 to 60 minutes or until firm and cooked through.

PER SERVING
Calories **208**, Saturated Fat **2g**,
Total Fat **8g**, Sodium **226mg**,
Cholesterol **94mg**, Protein **25g**,
Carbohydrate **8g**, Fiber **1g**.

FISH

*Making fish part of your diet is good
sense – it's low in fat and calories and
an excellent source of protein and minerals.
Cooking fish is easy too, as it is equally at home
on the broiler, grill, or in the skillet. Just take care
not to overcook or the texture and flavor will be
lost. This chapter offers a myriad of low-fat cooking
techniques featuring an exciting assortment of fish,
from salmon to snapper, catfish to cod. If you can't find
the fish suggested in a recipe, turn to the substitution
chart on page 90. You'll also find lots of new recipes.
The colorful fish loaves make an impressive company
dish, while the spicy low-fat jambalayas are
sure to please hearty appetites.*

Shrimp and Broccoli Stir-Fry with Peppers, page 109

For those of us intent on improving our diet and health, fish is the ideal food. It is a rich source of protein, vitamins, and minerals but has very little fat. The small amount it does contain is unsaturated. In addition, fish is low in calories, and oily fish such as herring and mackerel are rich in vitamins A and D.

Good for your heart

At one time it was thought that shellfish were dangerously high in cholesterol. Recent research, however, has shown that shellfish are lower in cholesterol than meat and eggs. For example, $3\frac{1}{2}$ ounces of clams contain just 67mg of cholesterol, compared to 84mg for filet mignon. So shellfish can definitely be part of a healthy diet.

Another important discovery is that fish appears to help prevent heart attacks. Doctors and nutritionists attribute this to a form of polyunsaturated fat called omega-3 fatty acids, which are found in fish fat and appear to reduce blood clotting and therefore protect against heart disease. For this reason, nutritionists recommend eating fish two or three times a week, and that includes canned fish because the omega-3 fatty acids are not destroyed in the canning process. As a general rule, fish that comes from the coldest salt water have the most fat and therefore the most omega-3's.

Whole drawn fish

Fish steak

Fish fillets

Cuts of fish

Fish is available in three different forms:

Fillets are cut lengthwise from each side of the fish, away from the backbone. Fillets are usually boneless.

Steaks are crosswise slices cut from the fish and will contain bones.

Whole drawn is a whole fish with internal organs removed. Sometimes it will be scaled. If the head, fins, tail, and internal organs are removed, it is known as drawn.

Choosing fresh fish

When buying fish, look for shiny, bright skin and eyes and pinkish red gills. When the flesh is pressed, it should spring back. Pick moist, firm steaks and fillets that look freshly cut; avoid any that look dry or opaque. Fresh fish has a clean odor and should not smell strong. When buying in a supermarket, check the sell-by date.

Fish and shellfish safety

Lake fish may be polluted with methyl mercury (a neurological poison), which is extremely toxic to humans. Variety is the key. Do not eat the same lake fish on a regular basis. Alternate with other types of freshwater fish or with ocean fish. Or buy frozen fish, which is likely to have been "flash-frozen" in super-cold commercial freezers. This ensures that any parasites are killed.

Shellfish (such as oysters, mussels, and clams) that live in polluted waters can pick up bacteria that cause hepatitis. Always purchase shellfish from a reputable market to make sure it comes from clean water. Your risk is lower with farmed mussels. It is also dangerous to cook dead shellfish. Live shellfish have closed shells. If the shell is open, drop it on the counter or squeeze – the shell should close. If it doesn't, discard. After cooking, the reverse is true – the shells should open. Discard any cooked shellfish with closed shells. To be extra safe, you can cook shellfish an extra 4 to 5 minutes after they have opened.

Thawing fish

If quick-frozen within a few hours of being caught, frozen fish will equal fresh in quality. Always thaw frozen fish before cooking, either in the refrigerator or in the microwave oven. Microwave on medium-low, covered with a lid or microwave wrap, for 6 to 8 minutes per pound. Let stand a few minutes before cooking.

Storing and freezing

Refrigerate fresh fish as soon as possible after purchase, as it spoils quickly. Cook on the same day or at least within 2 days. If you refrigerate, wrap well and place on a low shelf where any drips will not affect other food. Store frozen fish at 0°F.

Cooking fish

Fish cooks very quickly and is naturally tender, so it should never be overdone. To test for doneness, look for flesh that is white all through, flakes easily, or comes off the bone. It should not be translucent. Remove from heat at once as fish will continue cooking. Add salt after cooking to avoid drying out.

Dark fish, such as mackerel and bluefish, contain more oil and are best broiled or grilled. Because they may have a strong flavor, avoid steaming or poaching. Light fish, such as trout, suit any cooking method. Cod, whiting, and mahi mahi need basting because they cook quickly and tend to dry out. Baking and braising are better because they keep the fish moist.

SELECTING AND SUBSTITUTING FISH

Fish is a healthful choice. It is an excellent source of protein, it's low in calories, saturated fat, and cholesterol.

Per 3½-ounce serving	Color	Calories	Protein g	Fat g	Cholesterol	Level of omega-3's	Suggested alternatives
Bluefish	Dark	123	20	6	79	medium	Mackerel, Pike
Brook trout	Light	147	21	7	58	medium	Sea trout, Pollock
Catfish	White	116	18	6	58	low	Red snapper, Sea trout
Cod	White	82	23	1	55	low	Haddock, Pollock
Flounder	White	91	19	2	68	low	Whiting, Sole
Grouper	White	91	19	1	37	low	Bass, Snapper
Haddock	White	86	24	1	74	low	Cod, Whitefish
Halibut	White	109	27	3	41	medium	Cod, Flounder
Mahi mahi	Light	85	19	1	73	low	Bass, Snapper
Orange roughy	White	125	15	9	27	low	Ocean perch, Pompano
Perch	White	90	25	1	115	low	Sea Bass, Rainbow trout
Rainbow trout	Light	117	26	4	73	medium	Pike, Sea trout
Red snapper	White	99	26	2	47	low	Rockfish, Whitefish
Rockfish	Light	93	24	2	44	low	Perch, Red snapper
Salmon, sockeye	Dark	167	27	11	87	high	Swordfish, Mahi mahi
Scrod	White	82	23	1	55	low	Haddock, Pollock
Sea bass	Light to dark	96	24	4	53	medium	Sea trout, Orange roughy
Sea trout	White	103	20	10	66	low	Cod, Haddock
Snapper	White	82	21	2	47	low	Rockfish, Lake trout
Sole	White	91	18	1	43	low	Flounder, Pike
Solid white tuna	Dark	155	30	6	49	high	Mackerel, Swordfish
Striped bass	Light to dark	96	18	2	80	medium	Snapper, Grouper
Swordfish	Light	120	25	5	50	medium	Tuna, Sea bass
Tilefish	Pinkish white	95	18	5	64	medium	Bass, Mahi mahi

Grilled Citrus Trout

Cooking technique ■ *Grilling allows you to cook with little or no fat. Marinate the fish first in herbs and fruit juice, then brush frequently with the extra marinade to keep it moist. It's essential to cover the grill with foil or use a hinged basket so the fish doesn't fall through the wires. You can also make these recipes on the broiler.*

● Serves **4** ● Preparation Time **15 minutes plus marinating time** ● Cooking Time **20 minutes**

PER SERVING
Calories **196**, Saturated Fat **1g**,
Total Fat **4g**, Sodium **147mg**,
Cholesterol **121mg**, Protein **33g**,
Carbohydrate **5g**, Fiber **0g**.

---

1 lemon, thinly sliced

1 lime, thinly sliced

1 small red onion, sliced

¹/₄ cup chopped parsley

¹/₂ cup orange juice

2 teaspoons olive or canola oil

2 cloves garlic, finely chopped

¹/₄ teaspoon dry mustard

¹/₄ teaspoon dried rosemary, crumbled

¹/₈ teaspoon pepper

4 pan-dressed rainbow trout or pollock (about 8 ounces each)

Vegetable oil cooking spray

1 In a 13" x 9" x 2" baking dish, place the lemon, lime, and onion slices. Add the parsley, orange juice, oil, garlic, mustard, rosemary, and pepper, and stir until well mixed.

2 Add the fish to the dish, and turn the fish to cover with the marinade mixture. Cover the dish and refrigerate about 1 hour.

3 Preheat grill or broiler, with rack about 5 inches from the heat. Cover the rack with foil, perforate it, and coat foil with vegetable oil spray. *Do not use spray near hot grill.* Or coat a hinged fish grill basket with vegetable oil spray or canola oil.

4 Using a slotted spatula, transfer the fish to the foil-covered broiler rack. Strain the remaining marinade mixture into a small saucepan, reserving the lemon, lime, and onion slices. Warm marinade over low heat.

5 Broil or grill the fish on one side, brushing them frequently with the marinade, 6 to 8 minutes. Using a metal spatula, carefully turn the fish over.

6 Brush the fish again with the marinade. Add the lemon, lime, and onion slices in an even layer on top of the fish, and continue broiling 6 to 8 minutes longer.

*Hearty and healthy – **Grilled Citrus Trout** served with steamed spinach and the family favorite, Oven Fries, page 185.*

Grilled Fish Steaks in Balsamic Vinegar Marinade

Fish is often overcooked, making the meat dry and tasteless. It's far better to remove the fish from the heat just a moment before it's done because it will continue cooking for a short while after.

- Serves **4**
- Preparation Time **10 minutes** plus marinating time
- Cooking Time **20 minutes**

1 small onion, finely chopped

2 cloves garlic, finely chopped

4 tablespoons olive or canola oil

$^1/_2$ cup balsamic or red wine vinegar

$^1/_2$ cup chicken stock, page 18

$^1/_4$ cup dry white wine or water

$^1/_3$ cup brown sugar

Pinch of ground cloves

4 tuna, swordfish, or halibut steaks (about 6 ounces each)

Vegetable oil cooking spray

1 In a small saucepan, simmer the onion, garlic, olive oil, vinegar, chicken stock, wine, sugar, and cloves over moderate heat, stirring constantly, 5 minutes, until the brown sugar is dissolved. Remove the saucepan from the heat and allow the mixture to cool slightly.

2 Place the fish in a large baking dish and pour the marinade over. Gently turn the fish to coat both sides. Cover and refrigerate up to 2 hours, turning the fish occasionally.

3 Preheat the grill or broiler, with the rack about 5 inches from the heat. Cover the rack with aluminum foil, perforate it, and coat foil with vegetable oil spray. *Do not use spray near hot grill.* You can also coat a hinged fish grill basket with vegetable oil spray or canola oil.

4 Grill the fish, basting frequently with the marinade, about 4 minutes on each side, until the fish flakes easily when tested with a fork.

PER SERVING
Calories **389**, Saturated Fat **3g**, Total Fat **16g**, Sodium **86mg**, Cholesterol **71mg**, Protein **43g**, Carbohydrate **15g**, Fiber **0g**.

> **COOKING TIP**
> *Do not marinate fish for more than 2 hours, as the acid will make the flesh too soft and fragile.*

PERFORATING FOIL

Place the aluminum foil over the broiler rack and turn the edges of the foil underneath to secure. With a fork, make a series of perforations in the foil to allow the fat to drain through.

Grilled Fish, Barbecue Style

There's no high-calorie barbecue sauce weighing these fillets down. They're dipped in a light and zesty blend of vinegar, oil, and spices that you can make as spicy as you wish.

- Serves **4**
- Preparation Time **10 minutes**
- Cooking Time **35 minutes**

Vegetable oil cooking spray

$1^1/_4$ cups vegetable stock, page 18, or water

$^1/_2$ cup red wine vinegar

2 tablespoons olive or canola oil

2 tablespoons Dijon mustard

2 cloves garlic, finely chopped

1 red onion, finely chopped

2 teaspoons brown sugar

$1^1/_2$ teaspoons chili powder

$^1/_4$ teaspoon each black pepper, cayenne pepper, paprika, and ground ginger or to taste

4 fish fillets, such as catfish, bluefish, or striped bass (about 6 ounces each)

> **COOKING TIP**
> *Catfish, bluefish, and striped bass are all relatively fatty and are perfect for broiling or grilling as they remain moist.*

1 Preheat the grill or broiler, with the rack about 5 inches from the heat. Cover the rack with aluminum foil, perforate it, and coat foil with vegetable oil spray. *Do not use spray near hot grill.* You can also coat a hinged fish grill basket with vegetable oil spray or canola oil.

2 In a large saucepan, combine the vegetable stock, vinegar, olive oil, mustard, garlic, onion, sugar, chili, black and cayenne peppers, paprika, and ginger.

3 Bring to a boil and simmer 10 to 15 minutes. Remove the sauce from the heat and allow to cool slightly.

4 Using tongs, dip the fish fillets in the sauce, allowing any excess sauce to drip back into the pan.

5 Arrange the fish on the rack and cook, basting every few minutes with the sauce, about 4 minutes on each side, until the fish flakes easily when tested with a fork. Heat any remaining sauce and serve with the fish.

PER SERVING
Calories **315**, Saturated Fat **3g**, Total Fat **15g**, Sodium **320mg**, Cholesterol **100mg**, Protein **35g**, Carbohydrate **11g**, Fiber **1g**.

Red wine vinegar adds its distinctive flavor to this sauce.

Grilled Shrimp and Scallop Skewers with Pineapple

If you like, you can use frozen shrimp and scallops and thaw them in a colander under cool running water; do not let thawing seafood sit in its own liquid or it will lose its firmness.

- Serves **4**
- Preparation Time **20 minutes** plus marinating time
- Cooking Time **20 minutes**

1 can (16 ounces) crushed pineapple

1 tablespoon olive or canola oil

1/4 cup reduced-sodium soy sauce

1 tablespoon honey

1/8 teaspoon white or black pepper

12 ounces sea scallops (about 16 large scallops) (see box, right)

2 scallions, sliced

1 tablespoon toasted sesame seeds

12 ounces large shrimp, peeled and deveined (about 12 large shrimp)

1 cup pineapple or orange juice

1/2 teaspoon cornstarch

2 1/2 ounces snow peas (about 32 snow peas)

Vegetable oil cooking spray

1 In a food processor or blender, purée the pineapple until smooth. Add the olive oil, soy sauce, honey, and pepper, and process until well blended.

2 In a bowl, combine 1 cup of the marinade with the scallops. Stir in half of the scallions and half of the sesame seeds. In a small bowl, combine 1 cup of the marinade with the shrimp and the remaining scallions and sesame seeds. Cover both bowls and marinate at room temperature about 1 hour.

> **COOKING TIP**
> *You can marinate the shrimp and scallops for up to 4 hours in the refrigerator. However, before cooking, allow them to come to room temperature, about 30 minutes.*

3 In a small saucepan, combine remaining marinade with fruit juice and cornstarch. Bring to a boil, reduce heat, and continue to cook for 1 minute. Remove from heat and keep the pan warm.

4 Meanwhile, bring a medium saucepan of water to a boil. Add the snow peas and cook about 30 seconds, until just crisp-tender. Drain and rinse under cold running water, drain again, and gently pat dry.

5 Fill four 10-inch metal skewers as follows: Starting with a snow pea pod, then a scallop, a snow pea, a shrimp, continue threading in this order until they are all used.

---

6 Preheat the grill or broiler, setting the rack about 4 inches from the heat. Cover the rack with aluminum foil, perforate it, and coat foil with vegetable oil spray. *Do not use spray near hot grill.* You can also coat a hinged fish grill basket with vegetable oil spray or canola oil.

7 Grill the kebabs about 1 minute each side, until the shrimp and scallops are opaque.

PER SERVING
Calories **325**, Saturated Fat **1g**, Total Fat **7g**, Sodium **836mg**, Cholesterol **125mg**, Protein **31g**, Carbohydrate **38g**, Fiber **2g**.

*Serve **Grilled Shrimp and Scallop Skewers with Pineapple** on a bed of white rice with diced carrots.*

PREPARING SCALLOPS

1 *If necessary, remove and discard the tough muscle at the side of each scallop.*

2 *Rinse the scallops with cold water, drain, and pat dry with paper towels. Using a small knife, cut large scallops crosswise in half.*

Fish Stuffed with Corn Salsa

Cooking Technique ▪ *Stuff whole fish with a zesty vegetable or fruit salsa in place of the traditional high-fat bread stuffing. Bake with no added oil.*

● Serves **4** ● Preparation Time **20 minutes** ● Cooking Time **1 hour 5 minutes**

PER SERVING
Calories **268**, Saturated Fat **1g**, Total Fat **6g**, Sodium **202mg**, Cholesterol **63mg**, Protein **37g**, Carbohydrate **17g**, Fiber **3g**.

1 tablespoon olive or canola oil

1 onion, finely chopped

1 clove garlic, finely chopped

2 stalks celery, thickly sliced

¹/₂ teaspoon chili powder

1 cup fresh or frozen corn kernels, thawed

1 small cucumber, peeled, seeded, and diced

1 fresh or canned jalapeño pepper, chopped

3 tablespoons chopped fresh parsley or 1 tablespoon dried

2 tablespoons lime juice

¹/₈ teaspoon each salt and pepper

1 or 2 pan-dressed mild fish, such as snapper, perch, or trout (2 pounds total)

1 Preheat the oven to 450°F. In a nonstick skillet, heat the oil over moderate heat. Sauté the onion and garlic, stirring, about 5 minutes or until soft but not browned. Add the celery and chili powder; cook 3 to 4 minutes longer.

2 Transfer the onion mixture to a large bowl. Add the corn, cucumber, jalapeño pepper, parsley, lime juice, salt, and pepper, and toss gently to combine.

Fish Stuffed with Salsa
is delicious served hot or at room temperature. Garnish with cilantro or parsley sprigs.

3 Coat a baking sheet with vegetable oil cooking spray. Using a spoon, stuff the fish cavity with salsa mixture and transfer to the baking sheet.

4 Bake 40 to 55 minutes or until fish flakes easily when tested with a fork.

COOKING TIP
Make extra corn salsa and use as a tasty relish for burgers or grilled chicken. It can be stored 2 days in the refrigerator.

Oriental Stuffed Fish

- Serves **4**
- Preparation Time **20 minutes**
- Cooking Time **1 hour 5 minutes**

1 tablespoon olive or canola oil
2 teaspoons sesame oil (optional)
1 tablespoon finely chopped ginger or $1/4$ teaspoon ground
2 cloves garlic, finely chopped
2 tablespoons reduced-sodium soy sauce
2 carrots, julienned
$1/2$ small zucchini, julienned
$1/2$ yellow squash, julienned
2 stalks celery, julienned
4 scallions, julienned
$1/8$ teaspoon each black pepper and cayenne pepper
1 or 2 pan-dressed light fish such as mullet or bass (2 pounds total)

1 Preheat oven to 450°F. In a nonstick skillet, heat the oils over moderate heat. Sauté the ginger and garlic 30 seconds. Stir in soy sauce and remove from heat.

2 Stir in the carrots, zucchini, squash, celery, scallions, and black and cayenne peppers.

3 Coat 1 or 2 baking sheets with vegetable oil cooking spray. Stuff fish with vegetable mixture and bake for 40 to 55 minutes as in Step 4 of the master recipe.

PER SERVING
Calories **269**, Saturated Fat **2g**, Total Fat **10g**, Sodium **407mg**, Cholesterol **84mg**, Protein **35g**, Carbohydrate **9g**, Fiber **3g**.

Fish Stuffed with Cranberries and Pears

- Serves **4**
- Preparation Time **15 minutes**
- Cooking Time **about 1 hour**

1 tablespoon olive or canola oil
1 onion, finely chopped
1 clove garlic, finely chopped
2 stalks celery, thickly sliced
1 tablespoon chopped fresh sage or 1 teaspoon dried
6 ounces fresh or frozen cranberries, thawed
2 pears, halved, cored, and diced
$1/4$ cup soft brown sugar
2 tablespoons honey
1 tablespoon lemon juice
1 or 2 pan-dressed light fish such as mullet or bass (2 pounds total)

1 Preheat oven to 450°F. In a nonstick skillet, heat oil over moderate heat. Sauté onion and garlic, stirring, about 5 minutes or until soft. Add celery and sage and cook for 3 to 4 minutes longer.

2 Transfer mixture to a bowl. Stir in cranberries, pears, brown sugar, honey, and lemon juice.

3 Coat 1 or 2 baking sheets with vegetable oil cooking spray. Stuff fish with cranberry mixture and bake for 40 to 55 minutes as in Step 4 of master recipe.

PER SERVING
Calories **402**, Saturated Fat **2g**, Total Fat **10g**, Sodium **134mg**, Cholesterol **84mg**, Protein **34g**, Carbohydrate **45g**, Fiber **3g**

Trout Stuffed with Raisins

- Serves **4**
- Preparation Time **15 minutes**
- Cooking Time **33 minutes**

2 tablespoons olive or canola oil
2 onions, finely chopped
2 stalks celery, thinly sliced
$3/4$ cup golden or dark raisins
$1/4$ cup chopped walnuts
2 tablespoons chopped parsley or 1 teaspoon dried
$1/4$ teaspoon each ground cinnamon and cumin
$1/8$ teaspoon each salt and pepper
4 pan-dressed brook trout (8–10 ounces each), boned

1 Preheat oven to 450°F. In a large nonstick skillet, heat $1^{1}/2$ tablespoons oil over moderate heat. Sauté onions and celery, stirring, about 7 minutes or until soft.

2 Remove from heat and stir in raisins, walnuts, parsley, cinnamon, cumin, salt, and pepper.

3 Coat large baking dish with vegetable oil cooking spray. Stuff each fish with $1/4$ cup stuffing and arrange in a single layer in the dish; brush with remaining oil.

4 Surround the fish with the remaining stuffing. Bake 5 minutes, lower heat to 400°F, and bake 15 to 20 minutes as in Step 4 of the master recipe.

PER SERVING
Calories **424**, Saturated Fat **3g**, Total Fat **17g**, Sodium **137mg**, Cholesterol **96mg**, Protein **38g**, Carbohydrate **31g**, Fiber **4g**.

Oven-Fried Fish with Orange-Mustard Sauce

Reduce fat ■ *Instead of frying, coat the fish with bread crumbs and bake or broil.*
Add nutrients ■ *Top with a light sauce or fresh fruit relish for extra flavor and vitamins.*

● Serves **4** ● Preparation Time **20 minutes** ● Cooking Time **10–12 minutes**

PER SERVING
Calories **427**, Saturated Fat **3g**,
Total Fat **12g**, Sodium **532mg**,
Cholesterol **233mg**, Protein **46g**,
Carbohydrate **32g**, Fiber **1g**.

1 egg

2 tablespoons Dijon mustard

1¹/₂ cups fine, dry whole-wheat
bread crumbs

1 tablespoon brown sugar

3 tablespoons minced parsley
or 1 teaspoon dried

1 tablespoon minced fresh
thyme or 1 teaspoon dried

1¹/₂ teaspoons minced fresh
rosemary or ¹/₂ teaspoon dried

¹/₂ teaspoon dry mustard

¹/₄ teaspoon salt (optional)

¹/₄ teaspoon pepper

Finely grated zest of 1 large
orange

4 pan-dressed trout, sea trout, or
pollock (10–12 ounces each)

For the sauce

1¹/₂ cups 1% low-fat milk

4 teaspoons cornstarch

1 tablespoon coarse-grained
mustard

Juice of 1 large orange

1 Preheat oven to 500°F. Place a wire rack, large enough to hold all the fish without overlapping them, on a baking sheet. Lightly oil the rack.

2 Whisk together the egg and Dijon mustard until evenly combined.

3 In a shallow dish, mix the bread crumbs, brown sugar, parsley, thyme, rosemary, dry mustard, salt, and pepper. Add orange zest and stir to combine.

4 Dip each fish in the egg mixture, turning it over in the mixture so that it is completely covered.

5 Gently roll the fish in the seasoned bread crumb mixture, pressing the mixture onto the skin with your fingers to form an even layer.

6 Place fish on rack and bake 10 to 12 minutes, until the crumb mixture is golden and fish flakes easily when tested with a fork. Make the sauce: In a small saucepan, mix milk and cornstarch to a smooth paste; add coarse mustard and orange juice. Whisk over heat until thickened.

*Oven-Fried Fish with Orange-Mustard Sauce is garnished with sprigs of fresh thyme and rosemary.
The piquant sauce provides the perfect foil for the delicate fish.*

Pesto Fillets with Tomato Relish

The crisp and colorful tomato and zucchini relish will quickly convince you that a fat- and cholesterol-laden sauce is a thing of the past. To reduce the number of calories in the fish coating, replace some of the chopped walnuts with more bread crumbs.

- Serves **4**
- Preparation Time **20 minutes**
- Cooking Time **6–8 minutes**

1 large tomato, diced

1 zucchini, diced

3 tablespoons minced fresh basil or 1 tablespoon dried

1 teaspoon olive or canola oil

1 tablespoon lemon juice

$^1/_8$ teaspoon pepper

$^1/_2$ cup nonfat plain yogurt

1 large egg white

1 tablespoon Dijon mustard

1 cup dry bread crumbs

$^1/_4$ cup walnuts, toasted and finely chopped

1 tablespoon grated Parmesan cheese

$^1/_4$ teaspoon garlic powder

4 flounder, sole, red snapper, or orange roughy fillets (5–6 ounces each)

1 Preheat the broiler, setting the rack about 4 inches from the heat. Place a wire rack, large enough to hold the fish without overlapping them, on a baking sheet. Lightly oil the rack.

2 In a small bowl, toss the diced tomato and zucchini, 1 tablespoon of the basil, the olive oil, and lemon juice. Season with half the pepper. Cover and set aside.

3 In a medium bowl, whisk together the yogurt with the egg white and mustard until blended.

4 On a sheet of wax paper, combine bread crumbs with the walnuts, Parmesan cheese, garlic powder, the remaining basil, and pepper.

5 Dip fillets in the yogurt mixture and then in the bread crumb mixture, pressing the mixture onto the flesh with your fingers to form an even layer.

6 Place coated fillets on the rack, making certain they do not touch. Broil the fish about 4 minutes on each side or until the flesh flakes easily when tested with a fork. Spoon about a quarter of the tomato-zucchini mixture over each fish fillet and serve.

PER SERVING
Calories **255**, Saturated Fat **2g**, Total Fat **9g**, Sodium **317mg**, Cholesterol **73mg**, Protein **16g**, Carbohydrate **28g**, Fiber **3g**.

Nuts are a source of protein.

Spicy Broiled Snapper

Broiling these Louisiana-style fillets brings out the intense flavors of the spicy coating, and it requires no oil.

- Serves **4**
- Preparation Time **20 minutes**
- Cooking Time **10 minutes**

$^1/_4$ cup 1% low-fat milk

1 tablespoon Dijon mustard

$^1/_2$ cup cornmeal

1 tablespoon paprika

$^1/_2$ teaspoon salt

1 teaspoon onion powder

1 teaspoon garlic powder

$^3/_4$ teaspoon black pepper

$^1/_2$ teaspoon cayenne pepper

$^1/_2$ teaspoon each dried thyme and oregano, crumbled

4 snapper, grouper, or catfish fillets (5–6 ounces each)

4 lime or lemon coronets (see box, right)

1 Preheat the broiler, setting the rack about 4 inches from the heat. Place a wire rack, large enough to hold the fish without overlapping them, on a baking sheet. Lightly oil the rack.

2 In a medium bowl, whisk together the milk and mustard until blended. On a sheet of wax paper, combine the cornmeal, paprika, salt, onion powder, garlic powder, black and cayenne peppers, thyme, and oregano.

3 Dip the fillets in the milk mixture, then into the cornmeal mixture, pressing the mixture onto the flesh with your fingers to form an even layer.

4 Place coated fillets on the rack, making certain they do not touch. Broil about 4 minutes on each side, until the fish flakes easily when tested with a fork. Serve with lime or lemon coronets.

PER SERVING
Calories **210**, Saturated Fat **1g**, Total Fat **2g**, Sodium **445mg**, Cholesterol **52mg**, Protein **30g**, Carbohydrate **13g**, Fiber **1g**.

LIME CORONETS

1 *Push tip of a small knife through to center of fruit at an angle. Make next cut at the opposite angle to make a V shape.*

2 *Continue around fruit in a zigzag pattern. Twist gently and pull halves apart. Trim ends so coronets sit flat.*

Oven-Fried Fish with Toasted Coconut

If you want to reduce the amount of saturated fat, you could replace half the flaked coconut with dried bread crumbs and still have a crispy, coconut-flavored coating.

- Serves **4**
- Preparation Time **10 minutes**
- Cooking Time **10–12 minutes**

$^1/_2$ **cup nonfat plain yogurt**

1 large egg white

1 tablespoon honey

1 cup crushed shredded wheat cereal

$^1/_4$ **cup flaked coconut, toasted (see box, below)**

$^1/_2$ **teaspoon ground ginger**

$^1/_4$ **teaspoon garlic powder**

$^1/_4$ **teaspoon white pepper**

4 halibut or mahi mahi fillets (4–6 ounces each)

For the salsa

1 can (8 ounces) crushed pineapple

1 teaspoon red pepper flakes

$^1/_8$ **teaspoon pepper**

1 Preheat oven to 400°F. Place a wire rack, large enough to hold the fish without overlapping them, on a baking sheet. Lightly oil the rack.

2 In a medium bowl, whisk together the yogurt with the egg white and honey. On a sheet of wax paper, combine the shredded wheat cereal with the toasted coconut, ginger, garlic powder, and white pepper.

3 Dip fillets in coconut mixture, then in yogurt mixture, and then again in coconut mixture, pressing the mixture onto the flesh with your fingers to form an even layer.

Steamed broccoli and pineapple salsa make the perfect partners for **Oven-Fried Fish with Toasted Coconut.**

4 Place the coated fillets on the rack without overlapping them and bake 10 to 12 minutes, until coating is golden brown and the fish flakes easily when tested with a fork. Make the salsa: mix the pineapple, red pepper flakes, and pepper and serve with the fish.

PER SERVING
Calories **239**, Saturated Fat **2g**, Total Fat **5g**, Sodium **99mg**, Cholesterol **37mg**, Protein **27g**, Carbohydrate **22g**, Fiber **2g**.

HOW TO TOAST COCONUT

1 *Preheat the oven to 350° F. Spread a thin even layer of shredded coconut on a baking sheet and bake about 3 minutes, until brown at the edges.*

2 *Stir the half-toasted coconut on the baking sheet and then return to the oven about 3 minutes longer, until it is golden.*

GETTING AHEAD

If you're short of time, make a batch of toasted coconut the day before. If you make a double batch, you can store the remainder in a sealed container in the refrigerator up to 4 weeks.

Sole Baked in Parchment

Cooking technique ▪ *Baking in parchment or foil steams the fish and brings out the natural flavors. Simply wrap and bake until tender.*

Reduce fat ▪ *Parchment paper makes a very pretty presentation, but it requires a little more oil to keep the food from sticking. If you use aluminum foil, you can reduce the oil.*

● Serves **4** ● Preparation Time **20 minutes** ● Cooking Time **10–12 minutes**

PER SERVING
Calories **196**, Saturated Fat **1g**, Total Fat **9g**, Sodium **105mg**, Cholesterol **55mg**, Protein **24g**, Carbohydrate **6g**, Fiber **2g**.

1 lemon

2 tablespoons olive oil (1 tablespoon if using foil)

1 tablespoon dry white wine (optional)

$^1/_2$ teaspoon lemon pepper

$^1/_8$ teaspoon salt (optional)

1 pound slender asparagus (or medium, halved), trimmed and cut into 2-inch pieces

4 sole or flounder fillets (4–6 ounces each), fresh or frozen and thawed

1 Preheat the oven to 450°F. Prepare four 12-inch square pieces of parchment paper or aluminum foil: fold in half and cut out a half-heart shape on the fold.

2 Using a vegetable peeler, cut ½-inch strips of zest from the lemon. Cut each strip into thin matchsticks and place in a bowl with 2 tablespoons of lemon juice.

3 Stir the oil, wine, if using, lemon pepper, and salt into the lemon zest and juice. Add the asparagus and gently toss until well coated.

*The paper seals in the flavor and keeps the fish moist – **Sole Baked in Parchment**.*

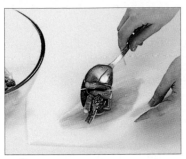

4 Place 1 fillet on a half of each parchment paper heart and top each with about a quarter of the asparagus and lemon mixture. Fold the paper over the asparagus.

5 Starting at one end, close the edges by making small pleats. Work around the length of the paper to seal the package. Fold the end piece under the package.

6 Bake on a baking sheet 10 to 12 minutes or until paper puffs and fish is cooked. Transfer to individual dishes, carefully open paper, and serve at once.

Bluefish Baked with Tomatoes

- Serves **4**
- Preparation Time **25 minutes**
- Cooking Time **35 minutes**

1–2 tablespoons olive oil

2 cloves garlic, finely chopped

1¼ pounds fennel or celery, trimmed and sliced

4-inch strip of orange zest, cut into matchsticks

Pepper

½ cup dry white wine or chicken stock

4 large plum tomatoes, peeled, seeded, and diced

4 bluefish or perch fillets (4–6 ounces each), fresh or frozen

1 Preheat oven to 450°F. Prepare 4 pieces parchment paper or foil as in master recipe.

2 In a nonstick skillet, heat oil. Sauté garlic, fennel, orange zest, and pepper 3 minutes. Add wine, cover, and simmer 5 minutes. Add tomatoes, cover, and simmer 5 minutes. Uncover and cook until most of liquid evaporates.

3 Place 1 fillet on each piece of paper, top with a quarter of mixture, and seal as in the master recipe.

4 Bake on a baking sheet 12 to 15 minutes or until paper puffs and fish is cooked. Serve as in master recipe.

PER SERVING
Calories **296**, Saturated Fat **2g**, Total Fat **9g**, Sodium **206mg**, Cholesterol **67mg**, Protein **26g**, Carbohydrate **20g**, Fiber **2g**.

Flounder Baked with Vegetables

- Serves **4**
- Preparation Time **25 minutes**
- Cooking Time **25 minutes**

1 tablespoon olive or canola oil

2 cloves garlic, finely chopped

2 slices ginger, cut into slivers

2 tablespoons reduced-sodium soy sauce

1 stalk celery, trimmed and cut into 3-inch matchsticks

1 carrot, peeled and cut into 3-inch matchsticks

2 scallions, cut into 3-inch matchsticks

4 flounder or sole fillets (4–6 ounces each), fresh or frozen

4 ounces tiny shrimp, peeled and deveined (optional)

1 Preheat oven to 450°F. Prepare 4 pieces of parchment paper or foil as in master recipe.

2 In a nonstick skillet, heat oil. Sauté garlic and ginger for 15 seconds. Stir in soy sauce; remove from the heat, add vegetables, and toss to coat.

3 Place 1 fillet on each paper; top with a quarter of vegetable mixture. Arrange shrimp on top and seal as in the master recipe.

4 Bake on a baking sheet 10 to 12 minutes or until paper puffs and fish is cooked. Serve as in master recipe.

PER SERVING
Calories **153**, Saturated Fat **1g**, Total Fat **5g**, Sodium **372mg**, Cholesterol **55mg**, Protein **23g**, Carbohydrate **4g**, Fiber **1g**.

Shellfish Baked with Artichokes

- Serves **4**
- Preparation Time **20 minutes**
- Cooking Time **20 minutes**

1–2 tablespoons olive oil

2 cloves garlic, finely chopped

¼ cup lemon juice

¼ teaspoon ground coriander or dried thyme

⅛ teaspoon each salt and pepper

12 ounces sea scallops or shrimp

16 medium shrimp, peeled and deveined (12 ounces)

1 package (10 ounces) frozen artichoke hearts or asparagus, thawed and well drained

2 tablespoons chopped parsley

1 Preheat oven to 400°F. Prepare 4 pieces of parchment paper or foil as in master recipe.

2 In a nonstick skillet, heat oil. Sauté garlic for 30 seconds. Remove the skillet from the heat and stir in lemon juice, coriander, salt, and pepper. Add shellfish and artichokes and toss to coat.

3 Place a quarter of the shell-fish mixture on the paper, sprinkle with parsley, and seal as in the master recipe.

4 Bake on ungreased baking sheet 12 to 14 minutes or until paper puffs and fish is cooked. Serve as in master recipe.

PER SERVING
Calories **213**, Saturated Fat **1g**, Total Fat **5g**, Sodium **422mg**, Cholesterol **159mg**, Protein **31g**, Carbohydrate **12g**, Fiber **0g**.

Poached Fish in Creole Sauce

Cooking technique ▪ *Poaching is an excellent way to cook fish without fat. Here the poaching liquid is a zesty Creole sauce, which not only tastes great – it keeps the fish moist and tender.*

Add nutrients ▪ *The spicy sauce gives you a triple serving of fiber-rich vegetables – celery, tomatoes, and sweet pepper. Use fresh parsley if you can. It's high in vitamin A and potassium, and it adds color.*

● Serves **4** ● Preparation Time **20 minutes** ● Cooking Time **45 minutes**

PER SERVING
Calories **364**, Saturated Fat **3g**, Total Fat **15g**, Sodium **525mg**, Cholesterol **99mg**, Protein **37g**, Carbohydrate **21g**, Fiber **4g**.

---

2 tablespoons olive or canola oil

6 scallions, white and green parts, sliced

2 cloves garlic, finely chopped

1 stalk celery, sliced

1 sweet green pepper, diced

1 onion, diced

2 tablespoons all-purpose flour

1 can (28 ounces) plum tomatoes, drained and chopped

1 tablespoon lemon juice

1 tablespoon Worcestershire sauce

¼ teaspoon dried thyme

¼ teaspoon cayenne pepper

1 teaspoon black pepper

2 cups fish or vegetable stock, page 18

½ cup chopped parsley or 2 tablespoons dried

4 firm white fish fillets, such as catfish, grouper, haddock, or cod (about 6 ounces each)

1 Make the sauce: In a large saucepan, heat the oil over moderate heat. Add the scallions, garlic, celery, green pepper, and onion. Cook, stirring frequently, about 5 minutes, until softened but not brown.

2 Add the flour to the vegetable mixture and stir to combine. Continue to cook, stirring, about 1 minute longer.

3 Add the tomatoes, lemon juice, Worcestershire sauce, thyme, cayenne, black pepper, and stock. Bring to a boil, stirring, then simmer, partially covered, 25 to 30 minutes.

4 Stir the parsley into the sauce, then remove about 1 cup of the sauce from the saucepan and reserve.

5 Add the fish fillets to the pan in a single layer. Pour the reserved sauce over the fillets.

6 Partially cover the pan and simmer the fish about 10 minutes, until the flesh flakes easily when tested with a fork. With a large slotted spatula, transfer fish to a serving dish and spoon the sauce over the fillets.

Poached Fish in Creole Sauce *is served here with Creamy Low-Fat Mashed Potatoes, page 185, and green beans, but it would also go well with rice.*

Poached Salmon Steaks with Horseradish and Chive Sauce

The horseradish and chive sauce in this simple dish is versatile – try it on beef steaks or roasts too.

- Serves **4**
- Preparation Time **10 minutes**
- Cooking Time **30 minutes**

---

2 cups 1% low-fat milk

1¹/₂ cups water

2 tablespoons lemon juice

1 small onion, thinly sliced

1 stalk celery with leaves, coarsely chopped

1 carrot, coarsely chopped

¹/₈ teaspoon salt (optional)

4 black peppercorns

4 salmon steaks (about 4 ounces each)

Horseradish and Chive Sauce (see box, right)

---

1 Pour the milk into a large nonstick skillet with the water, lemon juice, onion, celery, carrot, salt, and peppercorns. Bring to a boil over moderate heat, cover the skillet, and simmer the mixture about 10 minutes.

2 Add the salmon steaks to the skillet and return the liquid to a boil. Reduce the heat, cover the skillet, and poach the fish about 10 minutes or until the flesh flakes easily when tested with a fork.

3 Using a large slotted spatula, transfer the salmon steaks to a platter lined with paper towels. Allow to drain.

4 Transfer steaks to a serving platter and spoon the Horseradish and Chive sauce over them.

PER SERVING
Calories **262**, Saturated Fat **3g**, Total Fat **11g**, Sodium **200mg**, Cholesterol **75mg**, Protein **29g**, Carbohydrate **11g**, Fiber **1g**.

HORSERADISH AND CHIVE SAUCE

1 *Combine 1 tablespoon prepared horseradish, ¹/₂ cup each sour cream and low-fat mayonnaise, and 2 tablespoons chopped fresh or frozen chives.*

2 *Stir the ingredients together with a wooden spoon until evenly mixed. Season with black pepper to taste.*

Poached Fish in Orange-Pineapple Sauce

Grate the orange zest by using the finest side of the cheese grater. Shave off only the orange surface of the skin for the best flavor.

- Serves **4**
- Preparation Time **15 minutes**
- Cooking Time **20 minutes**

---

1 cup orange-pineapple or orange juice

1 teaspoon finely grated orange zest

2 teaspoons Dijon mustard

1 tablespoon chopped fresh tarragon or 1 teaspoon dried

4 ounces halibut or perch steaks (about 4 ounces each)

2 large carrots, cut into 2-inch lengths

2 tablespoons water

2 teaspoons cornstarch

¹/₈ teaspoon paprika

¹/₈ teaspoon salt (optional)

1 kiwi fruit, peeled and sliced or 4 small clusters of green grapes (optional)

---

1 Pour the orange-pineapple juice into a large nonstick skillet. Add the orange zest, mustard, and tarragon, and bring to a boil over moderate heat.

2 Add the fish steaks to the skillet, cover the skillet, and poach about 10 minutes or until the fish flakes easily when tested with a fork.

3 Transfer the fish steaks to a large platter, cover with aluminum foil, and keep them warm.

4 Strain the cooking liquid and return it to the skillet. Add the carrot strips and cook about 3 minutes or until crisp-tender.

5 In a small bowl, combine 2 tablespoons water with the cornstarch until smooth. Stir this mixture into the cooking liquid. Cook, stirring, about 2 minutes, until thickened. Stir in the paprika and salt, if using, and simmer about 1 minute longer.

6 Spoon the sauce over the fish and serve garnished with the kiwi slices or grapes, if using.

PER SERVING
Calories **202**, Saturated Fat **0g**, Total Fat **3g**, Sodium **175mg**, Cholesterol **36mg**, Protein **25g**, Carbohydrate **18g**, Fiber **3g**.

Slices of kiwi fruit and tangy orange zest add a tropical flavor.

Poached Fish Roll-Ups with Tomato, Basil, and Olive Sauce

If you purchase chopped frozen broccoli, chop it even more finely after it has thawed. You may wish to omit the sliced olives if you're watching your sodium intake.

- Serves **4**
- Preparation Time **20 minutes**
- Cooking Time **45 minutes**

---

4 sole or flounder fillets (about 5 ounces each)

1 tablespoon balsamic or red wine vinegar

2 tablespoons olive or canola oil

3 cloves garlic, finely chopped

2 tablespoons chopped fresh basil or 2 teaspoons dried

1 package (10 ounces) frozen broccoli, thawed, drained, and finely chopped

2 tablespoons dry bread crumbs

1 tablespoon grated Parmesan cheese

1 small onion, finely chopped

1 can (28 ounces) plum tomatoes in purée, chopped

1 cup fish stock, page 18

1/8 teaspoon pepper

1/4 cup sliced black olives

---

1 Place the fish on large platter or tray and sprinkle with the vinegar. Cover and refrigerate while you make the stuffing.

2 To make the stuffing: In a large nonstick skillet, heat half of the oil over moderate heat. Add half of the garlic and sauté, stirring, about 1 minute. Stir in the basil, broccoli, bread crumbs, and Parmesan cheese. Cook, stirring, until just heated through. Transfer to a bowl and allow to cool.

3 Wipe the skillet clean, then heat the remaining oil over moderate heat. Add the remaining garlic with the onion and sauté about 5 minutes, until soft but not browned. Stir in the tomatoes with the stock and pepper. Bring to a boil, then simmer, uncovered, about 10 minutes.

4 Meanwhile, roll up the fish fillets, filling each with a quarter of the stuffing (see box, below).

5 Stir olives into sauce, then add rolled fillets. Return the sauce to a boil, cover, and poach about 10 minutes or until the fish flakes easily when tested with a fork. Transfer the roll-ups to a platter, remove the toothpicks, and spoon the sauce around them.

PER SERVING
Calories **265**, Saturated Fat **1g**, Total Fat **5g**, Sodium **699mg**, Cholesterol **69mg**, Protein **33g**, Carbohydrate **21g**, Fiber **3g**.

A delicious duo – Squash Ribbons with Chili Peppers, page 188, and Poached Fish Roll-Ups with Tomato, Basil, and Olive Sauce.

HOW TO STUFF AND ROLL UP FISH FILLETS

1 *With a tablespoon, arrange the stuffing down the center of each fillet. Mound it slightly toward the wide end of the fillet.*

2 *Starting at the wide end, fold the fish over the filling, then continue rolling it up down the length of the fillet.*

3 *Secure the tapered end of the fish fillet firmly with a toothpick, threading it in and out of the fish to prevent it unrolling.*

Cod Stir-Fry with Mixed Vegetables

Cooking technique ■ *Cut the fish into uniform strips so that they cook evenly. Use very hot oil.*

● Serves **4** ● Preparation Time **10 minutes** plus marinating time ● Cooking Time **15 minutes**

PER SERVING
Calories **291**, Saturated Fat **1g**,
Total Fat **10g**, Sodium **541mg**,
Cholesterol **36mg**, Protein **28g**,
Carbohydrate **23g**, Fiber **3g**.

1 pound cod or halibut fillets

2 tablespoons reduced-sodium soy sauce

2 tablespoons cornstarch

2 tablespoons rice wine (optional)

1/4 cup chicken stock, page 18

1 teaspoon sugar

2 tablespoons canola oil

1 can (14 ounces) baby cocktail corn, drained

1 can (8 ounces) sliced water chestnuts, drained

2 cups broccoli florets

2 mild red chili peppers, finely chopped (optional)

1 Cut fish into 2-inch strips. In a bowl, blend 1 tablespoon each soy sauce and cornstarch with rice wine, if using. Stir in fish; cover and marinate about 30 minutes.

2 In a small bowl, combine the chicken stock with the remaining soy sauce and cornstarch and the sugar.

3 Heat a wok or large nonstick skillet over high heat until hot. Add 1 tablespoon oil and heat until the oil sizzles when a small piece of fish is added.

Cod Stir-Fry with Mixed Vegetables – a colorful Oriental-style dish with an interesting mix of tastes and textures.

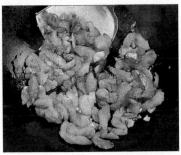

4 Add the fish to the oil. Using a metal spatula to turn the strips, stir-fry them about 3 minutes, until golden. Using a slotted spoon, transfer the fish to a plate.

5 Heat the remaining oil in the wok as in Step 3. Add corn, water chestnuts, broccoli, and chili peppers, if using, and stir-fry about 4 minutes.

6 Stir in the cornstarch mixture and cook, stirring constantly, about 1 minute. Return the fish to the wok and cook 1 minute longer. Serve at once.

Shrimp and Broccoli Stir-Fry with Peppers

- Serves **4**
- Preparation Time **15 minutes plus marinating time**
- Cooking Time **15 minutes**

2 tablespoons reduced-sodium soy sauce
1 tablespoon rice vinegar or sherry
1¹/₂ tablespoons cornstarch
³/₄ pound medium shrimp, peeled and deveined
³/₄ cup chicken stock, page 18
1 teaspoon sugar
2 tablespoons canola oil
3 cloves garlic, finely chopped
1 tablespoon finely chopped ginger
1 stalk celery, sliced diagonally
2 cups broccoli florets
1 sweet red or green pepper, cut into 2-inch strips
1¹/₂ cups sugar snap peas, trimmed

1 In a bowl, combine 1 tablespoon soy sauce, the rice vinegar, and ¹/₂ tablespoon cornstarch. Stir in shrimp; cover, and marinate about 15 minutes. In another bowl, combine ¹/₄ cup stock with remaining soy sauce and cornstarch and the sugar.

2 Heat 1 tablespoon oil in a wok or large nonstick skillet as in master recipe. Add shrimp and stir-fry about 3 minutes, until pink; transfer to a bowl.

3 Heat remaining oil in wok. Add garlic and ginger and stir-fry about 30 seconds. Add celery, broccoli, and pepper, and stir-fry about 2 minutes. Stir in remaining stock. Reduce heat, cover, and cook about 3 minutes. Add peas, cover, and cook about 2 minutes longer, until vegetables are tender.

4 Stir in the cornstarch mixture and cook, stirring constantly, about 1 minute. Stir in shrimp and cook about 1 minute longer or until just heated through.

PER SERVING
Calories **208**, Saturated Fat **1g**, Total Fat **8g**, Sodium **431mg**, Cholesterol **97mg**, Protein **17g**, Carbohydrate **16g**, Fiber **3g**.

Spicy Scallop Stir-Fry with Asparagus

- Serves **4**
- Preparation Time **15 minutes**
- Cooking Time **10 minutes**

¹/₃ cup chicken stock, page 18
2 tablespoons reduced-sodium soy sauce
1¹/₂ tablespoons rice wine (optional)
2 teaspoons Worcestershire sauce
1 teaspoon sugar
1 teaspoon grated lemon zest
1 small hot red chili pepper, finely chopped, or ¹/₄ teaspoon red pepper flakes
2 teaspoons cornstarch
2 tablespoons canola oil
3 cloves garlic, finely chopped
1 tablespoon finely chopped ginger
1 pound sea scallops, rinsed and halved
1 pound asparagus, cut diagonally into 1-inch pieces
1 small sweet yellow or red pepper, cut into ¹/₄-inch strips

1 In a small bowl, combine the chicken stock, soy sauce, rice wine, Worcestershire sauce, sugar, lemon zest, chili pepper, and cornstarch until blended.

2 Heat oil in a wok or large nonstick skillet as in Step 3 of the master recipe. Add the garlic and ginger and stir-fry about 15 seconds.

3 Add the scallops to the wok and stir-fry about 1 minute. Add the asparagus pieces and sweet pepper strips and stir-fry about 2 minutes longer.

4 Stir in the chicken stock and seasoning mixture. Reduce heat and cook, stirring constantly, about 3 minutes, until vegetables are tender and the sauce has thickened slightly.

PER SERVING
Calories **225**, Saturated Fat **1g**, Total Fat **8g**, Sodium **520mg**, Cholesterol **37mg**, Protein **24g**, Carbohydrate **14g**, Fiber **2g**.

Fish Baked on a Bed of Broccoli, Corn, and Red Pepper

Cooking technique ■ *Bake fish fillets on top of cut fresh vegetables to create an easy and nutritious one-dish dinner.*

● Serves **4** ● Preparation Time **15 minutes** ● Cooking Time **50 minutes**

PER SERVING
Calories **210**, Saturated Fat **1g**,
Total Fat **6g**, Sodium **340mg**,
Cholesterol **56mg**, Protein **25g**,
Carbohydrate **16g**, Fiber **3g**.

---

4 sole or any firm white fillets (4–6 ounces each), fresh or frozen and thawed

2 tablespoons fat-free Italian dressing or vinaigrette

1 tablespoon fine dry unseasoned bread crumbs

1 tablespoon grated Parmesan cheese

¹/₄ teaspoon paprika

1 tablespoon olive or canola oil

2 cups broccoli florets

1 cup fresh or frozen corn kernels, thawed

1 sweet red pepper, cut into thin strips

1 small red onion, thinly sliced

2 tablespoons chopped parsley or 2 teaspoons dried

1 tablespoon chopped fresh basil or 1 teaspoon dried

¹/₈ teaspoon each salt and pepper

1 Place the fish in a shallow baking dish and brush lightly with the Italian dressing. Cover and refrigerate.

2 In a small bowl, combine the bread crumbs with the Parmesan cheese and paprika until blended.

3 Preheat the oven to 425°F. Brush 4 individual or one 13" x 9" x 2" ovenproof dish with oil. In a large bowl, combine the broccoli, corn, red pepper, onion, parsley, basil, salt, and pepper.

4 Divide the vegetable mixture evenly among the dishes. Cover with aluminum foil and bake 35 to 40 minutes or until the vegetables are just tender.

5 Uncover the dishes and top vegetables with fish fillets. Cover again and bake 8 to 10 minutes or until fish is barely cooked and still moist in thickest part.

6 Uncover the dishes, sprinkle with the bread crumb mixture, and continue to bake, uncovered, 2 to 3 minutes longer or until the topping is golden.

Fish Baked on a Bed of Broccoli, Corn, and Red Pepper makes a quick-to-prepare
light meal that's as healthful as it is colorful.

Swordfish Baked on a Bed of Garlic Potatoes

Thick swordfish or salmon steaks will take longer to cook than more delicate fillets, but it's just as important not to overcook them. If you're a big garlic fan, double the amount listed here.

- Serves **4**
- Preparation Time **15 minutes**
- Cooking Time **35–50 minutes**

2 tablespoons coarse-grained mustard

2 tablespoons lemon juice

4 swordfish or salmon steaks (4 ounces each), ³/₄–1 inch thick, fresh or frozen and thawed

2 pounds red potatoes, peeled and very thinly sliced

2 cloves garlic, finely chopped

2 tablespoons olive or canola oil

¹/₈ teaspoon each salt and pepper

1 tomato, thinly sliced

1 In a small bowl, blend the mustard and lemon juice. Place the steaks in a shallow baking dish and brush with mustard mixture. Cover and refrigerate.

2 Preheat oven to 450°F. Place potatoes in a roasting pan with the garlic, oil, salt, and pepper and toss. Bake about 20 to 30 minutes or until potatoes begin to brown, turning once during cooking.

3 Top the potatoes with the fish steaks, mustard side up, and bake 10 to 15 minutes or until fish is barely cooked and still moist.

4 Arrange the tomato slices on top of the steaks and bake about 5 minutes longer or until the fish flakes easily when tested with a fork.

PER SERVING
Calories **414**, Saturated Fat **2g**, Total Fat **12g**, Sodium **369mg**, Cholesterol **44mg**, Protein **28g**, Carbohydrate **49g**, Fiber **4g**.

BONING A FISH STEAK

1 *Remove the skin by securing it with a fork. Then turn the fork outward and twist the skin around it.*

2 *With a fork or sharp knife, pierce the central bone. Then lift out the bone with its surrounding spines attached.*

Red Snapper Baked on a Bed of Spinach

Cut off the tough stems and wash the spinach thoroughly before cooking it. However, do not soak the leaves because that causes valuable water-soluble nutrients to be lost.

- Serves **4**
- Preparation Time **25 minutes**
- Cooking Time **25 minutes**

2 tablespoons olive or canola oil

1 onion, thinly sliced

2 cloves garlic, finely chopped

2 packages fresh spinach (10 ounces each), stemmed, washed, and drained

4 red snapper, rockfish, sea bass or tilefish fillets (4–6 ounces each), fresh or frozen and thawed

8 ounces mushrooms, sliced

¹/₂ cup chicken or vegetable stock, page 18

2 tablespoons low-fat sour cream

1 tablespoon chopped parsley or 1 teaspoon dried

¹/₈ teaspoon salt and pepper

Pinch of ground nutmeg

1 Preheat oven to 425°F. In a large skillet, heat 1 tablespoon of oil over moderate heat. Add onion and garlic and sauté until golden brown, about 7 minutes.

2 Stir in the spinach and cook about 2 minutes or until just wilted. Remove from heat and transfer the spinach to 13" x 9" x 2" baking dish or divide among 4 individual ovenproof dishes.

3 Top spinach with fish fillets, cover, and bake as in Step 5 of the master recipe.

4 Meanwhile, sauté the mushrooms in the remaining oil in the skillet about 5 minutes or until just tender. Add the stock and simmer for 1 minute. Remove from the heat and stir in the sour cream, parsley, salt, pepper, and nutmeg.

5 Uncover baking dish, pour mushroom sauce over each fillet, and bake, uncovered, 2 to 3 minutes longer.

PER SERVING
Calories **263**, Saturated Fat **1g**, Total Fat **11g**, Sodium **289mg**, Cholesterol **42mg**, Protein **30g**, Carbohydrate **14g**, Fiber **5g**.

A nutmeg grater provides a useful place to store your nutmeg. Always grate it freshly.

Fish Cooking Chart

This guide will help you determine the time needed for all methods of cooking whole fish, fillets, and stuffed fish. Cooking times are based on weight or thickness of fish.

	Fresh or thawed Fillets or Steaks	Frozen Fillets or Steaks	Dressed or Stuffed Whole Fish
Baking *Bake uncovered*	450°F 4–6 minutes per ¹/₂ inch thickness	450°F 9–11 minutes per ¹/₂ inch thickness	350°F 6–9 minutes per ¹/₂ pound
Broiling *Cook 4 inches from heat*	4–6 minutes per ¹/₂ inch thickness*	6–9 minutes per ¹/₂ inch thickness*	Not Recommended
Poaching *Simmer covered*	4–6 minutes per ¹/₂ inch thickness	6–9 minutes per ¹/₂ inch thickness	6–9 minutes per ¹/₂ pound
Pan-Frying *Cook in skillet*	3–4 minutes per side, up to ¹/₂ inch thickness; 5–6 minutes for 1 inch	Not Recommended	5–8 minutes on each side for 8–12 ounce fillet or steak

* *If more than ¹/₂ inch thick, turn once during cooking.*

TESTING FISH FOR DONENESS

For steaks: insert a fork into the fish, pulling the flesh apart gently. The fish should flake easily and be opaque throughout rather than translucent.

For fillets: with a fork, insert the tip into the fillet and lift up a little of the fish to see that it flakes easily and is opaque.

Cod Baked on a Bed of Cabbage and Tomatoes

Bacon renders a flavorful fat for cooking the vegetables. If you do not have a slice of it on hand, use a tablespoon of olive oil instead.

- Serves **4**
- Preparation Time **20 minutes**
- Cooking Time **45 minutes**

1 slice reduced-sodium bacon, coarsely chopped

2 carrots, thinly sliced

1 green cabbage (2 pounds), cored and coarsely shredded

1 onion, diced

¹/₂ cup chicken or vegetable stock, page 18

2 tablespoons cider vinegar or white wine vinegar

1 teaspoon sugar

1 tablespoon chopped fresh dill or 1 teaspoon dried

¹/₈ teaspoon each salt and pepper

8 ounces plum tomatoes, seeded and coarsely chopped

4 cod or halibut fillets (4–6 ounces each), fresh or frozen and thawed

Pinch of paprika

1 Preheat oven to 425°F. In a large saucepan, cook the bacon over moderate heat about 3 minutes or until the bacon is crisp and the fat is rendered. Using a slotted spoon, transfer the bacon to a plate. (See Cooking Tip.)

COOKING TIP

When you are crisping chopped bacon, use a slotted spoon to remove the bacon bits from the pan so that the fat drains off.

2 Add carrots, cabbage, onion, stock, vinegar, sugar, dill, salt, and pepper to the pan and cook, stirring, 7 to 10 minutes or until the cabbage is wilted and carrots are tender. Stir in the tomatoes and transfer to a 13" x 9" x 2" baking dish. Cover with foil and bake for 20 minutes.

3 Top the vegetables with the fish, cover, and bake as in Step 5 of the master recipe, 8 to 10 minutes. Uncover, sprinkle the paprika and crumble the bacon over the fish and bake, uncovered, 2 to 3 minutes or until golden as in Step 6 of the master recipe.

PER SERVING
Calories **203**, Saturated Fat **0g**, Total Fat **2g**, Sodium **221mg**, Cholesterol **50mg**, Protein **25g**, Carbohydrate **24g**, Fiber **7g**.

Potato and Zucchini Fish Loaf

Cooking technique ■ *Bake thin-sliced potatoes until crisp. Then layer them with fish, vegetables, and herbs to make a delicious one-dish meal that's high in protein, low in fat. These healthy potato chips can also be served on their own.*

- Serves **4** - Preparation Time **30 minutes**
  - Cooking Time **1½ hours**

PER SERVING
Calories **306**, Saturated Fat **2g**, Total Fat **11g**, Sodium **191mg**, Cholesterol **109mg**, Protein **28g**, Carbohydrate **26g**, Fiber **4g**.

---

4 cloves garlic, finely chopped

2 tablespoons chopped fresh parsley or basil

½ teaspoon pepper

8 firm white fish fillets, such as flounder, sole, or pike (2–3 ounces each)

1 tablespoon lemon juice

¼ teaspoon dried oregano

2 tablespoons olive or canola oil

2 large potatoes, peeled and very thinly sliced

2 large zucchini, thinly sliced

1 egg

1 tablespoon milk

8 ounces firm tomatoes, seeded and very thinly sliced

¼ cup sliced black olives

1 tablespoon grated Parmesan cheese

SLICING YELLOW SQUASH

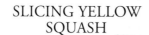

Use yellow squash as an alternative to zucchini. It will add an attractive yellow color to your fish loaf. Remove a thin slice from each end of the squash and discard, and then slice across as you would a zucchini, in fairly thin slices.

1 Preheat oven to 400°F. Mix garlic, parsley, and pepper. Place fish in a dish. Top with half of garlic mixture. Add lemon juice and oregano. Cover and chill.

2 Brush 2 baking sheets with 1 tablespoon oil; arrange the potato slices on them without overlapping and bake about 25 minutes, until crisp and brown.

3 In a nonstick skillet, heat the remaining oil over moderate heat. Sauté the remaining garlic mixture with the zucchini, about 4 minutes, until soft.

4 Using a metal spatula, remove the potatoes from the sheets and transfer them to a plate. Reduce oven temperature to 350°F.

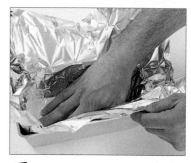

5 Line an 8½" x 4½" x 2½" loaf pan with oiled aluminum foil, allowing about 4 inches of foil to hang over sides of pan. In a bowl, whisk the egg and milk.

6 Arrange half of the potato slices in the base of the pan. Top with a third of the zucchini, half of the fish, and a third of the tomatoes and olives.

7 Brush with some egg mixture; top with half the cheese. Repeat layering zucchini, fish, tomatoes, olives, egg, and cheese. Finish with the potatoes.

8 Bake the loaf in the oven 55 to 60 minutes or until the fish is cooked. If potatoes on top start to become too dark, cover with overhanging foil.

9 To serve, carefully turn the loaf out of the pan onto a serving dish and remove the foil. Cut into slices.

Potato and Zucchini Fish Loaf *tastes as good as it looks. Serve it with a leafy tossed salad, as above, or sliced tomatoes.*

Potato, Onion, and Orange Fish Loaf

The fish loaf will be easier to invert onto a platter if you line the pan with foil. For extra insurance, spray the foil with vegetable oil cooking spray before filling the pan.

- Serves **4**
- Preparation Time **30 minutes**
- Cooking Time **1½ hours**

---

2 cloves garlic, finely chopped

2 tablespoons chopped cilantro or parsley

½ teaspoon pepper

4 catfish or red snapper fillets (4–6 ounces each)

1 tablespoon lime juice

2 tablespoons olive or canola oil

2 large sweet potatoes, peeled and very thinly sliced

2 large red onions, sliced

1 egg

1 tablespoon orange juice

1 large orange, peeled, thinly sliced, and seeded

¼ cup sliced black olives

---

1 Preheat oven to 400°F. Mix together the garlic, cilantro, and pepper. Place the fish in a dish and sprinkle with half of the garlic mixture. Add the lime juice, cover, and chill.

2 Bake the sweet potatoes as in Step 2 of the master recipe. Meanwhile, in a large nonstick skillet, heat the remaining oil over moderate heat. Add the remaining garlic mixture with the onion slices, and sauté about 5 minutes, until soft.

3 Line an 8½" x 4½" x 2½" loaf pan with oiled aluminum foil, allowing about 4 inches of foil to hang over the long sides of the pan. In a small bowl, whisk together the egg and orange juice.

4 Arrange half of the sweet-potato slices in a layer in the base of the pan. Top with a third of the onions, half of the fish, and a third of the orange slices and olives.

5 Brush with the egg mixture before topping with the next layer. Repeat to make a second layer of the onions, fish, orange slices, and olives. Then finish with the remaining onions, orange slices, olives, and potatoes.

6 Bake the fish loaf 55 to 60 minutes or until the fish is cooked. If the potatoes on top start to become too dark, cover with overhanging foil. To serve, carefully turn the loaf out of the pan onto a serving dish and remove the foil. Cut into slices.

PER SERVING
Calories **433**, Saturated Fat **3g**, Total Fat **16g**, Sodium **200mg**, Cholesterol **135mg**, Protein **31g**, Carbohydrate **42g**, Fiber **7g**.

Potato, Salmon, and Leek Fish Loaf

If you're cooking young carrots for the fish loaf, don't bother to peel them, but make sure you scrub them throroughly to remove any possible trace of pesticide.

- Serves **4**
- Preparation Time **30 minutes**
- Cooking Time **1½ hours**

---

2 cloves garlic, finely chopped

2 tablespoons chopped fresh dill or parsley

½ teaspoon pepper

4 salmon fillets (4–6 ounces each)

1 teaspoon finely grated lemon zest

1 tablespoon lemon juice

2 tablespoons olive or canola oil

2 large red potatoes, peeled and very thinly sliced

1 pound leeks, trimmed and thinly sliced

3 carrots, scrubbed

1 egg

1 tablespoon 1% low-fat milk

---

1 Preheat the oven to 400°F. Mix together the garlic, dill, and pepper. Place the fish in a dish and sprinkle with half of the garlic mixture. Add the lemon zest and juice. Cover and chill.

2 Bake the potatoes as in Step 2 of the master recipe. Meanwhile, in a large nonstick skillet, heat the remaining oil over moderate heat. Add the remaining garlic, dill, and pepper with the leeks and sauté about 5 minutes, until soft and just transparent.

3 Using a vegetable peeler, cut the carrots lengthwise into very long thin strips. Set aside. In a small bowl, whisk together the egg and milk.

4 Line an 8½" x 4½" x 2½" loaf pan with oiled aluminum foil, allowing about 4 inches of foil to hang over the long sides of the pan. Arrange half of the potatoes in the base of the pan. Top with a third of the leeks, half of the fish, and a third of the carrot strips.

5 Brush each layer with the egg mixture before topping with the next layer. Repeat to make a second layer of the leeks, fish, and carrot strips. Then finish with a layer of the remaining leeks, carrot strips, and potatoes.

6 Bake the fish loaf 55 to 60 minutes, until the fish is cooked. If the potatoes on top start to become too dark, cover with the overhanging foil. To serve, carefully turn the loaf out of the pan onto a serving dish and remove the foil. Cut into slices.

PER SERVING
Calories **493**, Saturated Fat **4g**, Total Fat **21g**, Sodium **130mg**, Cholesterol **141mg**, Protein **37g**, Carbohydrate **41g**, Fiber **6g**.

Potato, Cabbage, and Apple Fish Loaf

An easy way to cut potatoes thinly is to use the slicing side of a cheese grater. You can use a cheese grater to slice the apples too.

- Serves **4**
- Preparation Time **30 minutes**
- Cooking Time **1½ hours**

2 cloves garlic, finely chopped

2 tablespoons chopped fresh parsley

¹/₂ teaspoon pepper

4 cod or haddock fillets (4–6 ounces each)

1 tablespoon lemon juice

¹/₄ teaspoon caraway seeds

2 tablespoons olive oil

2 large potatoes, peeled and very thinly sliced

1 green cabbage (about 1¹/₂ pounds), shredded

1 egg

1 tablespoon 1% low-fat milk

2 apples, thinly sliced

1 Preheat oven to 400°F. Mix together garlic, parsley, and pepper. Place the fish in a dish and sprinkle with half of garlic mixture. Add lemon juice and caraway seeds. Cover and chill.

2 Bake the potatoes as in Step 2 of the master recipe. In a large nonstick skillet, heat remaining oil over moderate heat. Add remaining garlic mixture with cabbage, and sauté about 5 minutes, until just wilted.

3 Line an 8¹/₂ " x 4¹/₂ " x 2¹/₂ " loaf pan with oiled aluminum foil, allowing about 4 inches of foil to hang over the long sides of the pan. In a small bowl, whisk together the egg and milk.

4 Arrange half of the potatoes in base of the pan. Top with a third of the cabbage, half of the fish, and a third of the apple slices.

5 Brush with egg mixture before topping with the next layer. Repeat to make a second layer of the cabbage, fish, and apple slices. Then finish with a layer of the remaining cabbage, apple slices, and potatoes.

Potato, Cabbage, and Apple Fish Loaf is accompanied by Lemon Carrots with Watercress, page 172.

6 Bake the fish loaf 55 to 60 minutes, until the fish is cooked. If the potatoes on top start to become too dark, cover with the overhanging foil. To serve, carefully turn the loaf out of the pan onto a serving dish and remove the foil. Cut into slices.

PER SERVING
Calories **333**, Saturated Fat **2g**, Total Fat **9g**, Sodium **115mg**, Cholesterol **103mg**, Protein **26g**, Carbohydrate **38g**, Fiber **6g**.

HOW TO FILLET A FISH

1 *Holding the fish firmly with one hand and using a sharp knife, cut down the length of the fish along the backbone.*

2 *Cut through the fish, taking care to run the knife on top of the bone in order to remove the top fillet.*

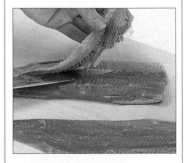

3 *Gently cut away the backbone and small bones from the bottom fillet. Remove the bones and use for fish stock. Remove the skin.*

Baked Deviled Crab

Reduce fat ▪ *Instead of frying crab and fish cakes, bake them in the oven. Use reduced-fat mayonnaise in place of some of the egg.*

● Serves **4** ● Preparation Time **20 minutes** ● Cooking Time **30 minutes**

PER SERVING
Calories **262**, Saturated Fat **3g**, Total Fat **16g**, Sodium **585mg**, Cholesterol **140mg**, Protein **23g**, Carbohydrate **5g**, Fiber **0g**.

1 egg	2 scallions, trimmed and sliced
1 pound lump crabmeat, picked over, or imitation crabmeat	$^1/_8$ teaspoon each pepper and hot red pepper sauce
2 tablespoons lemon juice	1 tablespoon dry sherry (optional)
$^1/_3$ cup reduced-fat mayonnaise	6 teaspoons olive or canola oil
1$^1/_2$ teaspoons Worcestershire sauce	2 tablespoons fine dry unseasoned bread crumbs
2 teaspoons coarse-grained mustard	Paprika

1 Bring a small pan of water to a boil and hard-cook the egg. Remove from the pan, cool, and peel.

2 In a large bowl, gently toss the crabmeat with the lemon juice until combined. Preheat the oven to 350°F.

3 In another bowl, mash the egg with the mayonnaise, Worcestershire sauce, mustard, scallions, pepper, hot red pepper sauce, and sherry, if using.

Perfect dinner partners – Baked Deviled Crab and a salad of avocado, orange, and endive.

4 Using a large metal spoon, lightly fold the egg mixture into the crabmeat until just combined.

5 Using 2 teaspoons of the oil, lightly coat 4 large crab or scallop shells, ramekins, or an 8" x 8" x 2" baking dish. Fill shells or dish with crab mixture.

6 Sprinkle bread crumbs and drizzle 1 teaspoon of oil over each. Lightly sprinkle with paprika and bake 25 to 30 minutes or until hot and lightly browned.

Quick Fish Cakes

- Serves **4**
- Preparation Time **10 minutes, plus chilling**
- Cooking Time **15 minutes**

1 egg white, well beaten

2 tablespoons reduced-fat mayonnaise

1 tablespoon Dijon mustard

1 scallion, finely chopped

$^1/_2$ teaspoon dry mustard

$^1/_4$ teaspoon celery seeds

$^1/_8$ teaspoon each salt and pepper

2 cans (6–7 ounces each) solid white tuna or salmon packed in water, drained and flaked, or 12 ounces cooked white fish, flaked

8 teaspoons wheat germ or bread crumbs

1 Preheat oven to 400°F. In a large bowl, combine egg white, mayonnaise, Dijon mustard, scallion, dry mustard, celery seeds, salt, and pepper. Gently fold in fish until just combined.

2 Shape into 8 even-sized patties and place on a nonstick baking sheet or a baking sheet covered with parchment paper. Sprinkle each cake with 1 teaspoon wheat germ. Cover and chill for 30 minutes.

3 Remove cover and bake 15 to 20 minutes or until hot and lightly browned.

PER SERVING
Calories **172**, Saturated Fat **1g**, Total Fat **5g**, Sodium **482mg**, Cholesterol **36mg**, Protein **25g**, Carbohydrate **4g**, Fiber **1g**.

Cod and Potato Cakes

- Serves **4**
- Preparation Time **20 minutes**
- Cooking Time **45 minutes**

1 pound cod fillets, fresh or frozen and thawed

1 onion, finely chopped

12 ounces all-purpose potatoes, peeled and cubed

$^1/_2$ cup 1% low-fat milk

$^1/_4$ cup water

$^1/_8$ teaspoon salt

$^1/_4$ teaspoon pepper

1 cup corn bread or regular bread stuffing

$^1/_4$ teaspoon each dried thyme and marjoram

3 egg whites

2 teaspoons white wine vinegar

1 package (10 ounces) frozen peas and carrots, thawed

1 tablespoon olive or canola oil

1 Remove any bones from fish and drain well. In a saucepan, combine onion, potatoes, milk, water, salt, and pepper and bring just to a boil over moderate heat. Reduce heat to low, cover, and simmer 20 minutes or until potatoes are tender.

2 Drain, reserving liquid. Return $^1/_4$ cup reserved liquid to potatoes in saucepan and mash to smooth consistency, adding more liquid if necessary.

3 In a food processor or blender, combine stuffing, thyme, and marjoram and process until fine. Transfer to a bowl. Flake fish into the cornbread crumbs and stir in mashed potatoes, egg whites, vinegar, and peas and carrots. Shape into eight 4-inch patties 2$^1/_2$ inches thick.

4 In a large nonstick skillet, heat 1$^1/_2$ teaspoons oil over moderate heat. Cook 4 patties, covered, 8 to 10 minutes, turning halfway through cooking time. Transfer to a warm serving platter and repeat with remaining oil and patties.

PER SERVING
Calories **300**, Saturated Fat **1g**, Total Fat **5g**, Sodium **338mg**, Cholesterol **51mg**, Protein **29g**, Carbohydrate **35g**, Fiber **5g**.

Shrimp Jambalaya

Reduce fat ▪ *For Creole flavor with less fat, substitute turkey sausage for the traditional pork sausage and use just ³/4 pound shrimp.*

● Serves **4** ● Preparation Time **15–20 minutes** ● Cooking Time **1 hour**

PER SERVING
Calories **376**, Saturated Fat **3g**,
Total Fat **8g**, Sodium **316mg**,
Cholesterol **113mg**, Protein **22g**,
Carbohydrate **54g**, Fiber **4g**.

2 slices reduced-sodium bacon
1 ounce turkey sausage, sliced
1 large onion, diced
2 cloves garlic, finely chopped
1 sweet green pepper, diced
2 stalks celery, diced
1³/4 cups chicken stock, page 18
1 can (14 ounces) reduced-sodium tomatoes

¹/4 cup chopped parsley
1 box (7 ounces) wild pecan rice or 1 cup long-grain rice
¹/2 teaspoon hot red pepper sauce
¹/2 teaspoon dried thyme
1 bay leaf
¹/4 teaspoon pepper
12 ounces medium shrimp, peeled and deveined

1 In a 4-quart saucepan, cook the bacon over moderate heat until crisp. Using a slotted spoon, transfer bacon to a plate.

2 Add the sausage slices to the pan and cook, stirring frequently, about 5 minutes or until browned. Transfer to the plate with the bacon.

3 Add onion, garlic, green pepper, and celery and sauté, stirring, about 5 minutes. If necessary, add a little stock to keep vegetables from browning.

*A healthy new version of an old Southern favorite – **Shrimp Jambalaya**.*

4 Stir the tomatoes, remaining stock, parsley, rice, hot red pepper sauce, thyme, bay leaf, and pepper into the vegetables.

5 Bring the mixture to a boil. Cover pan and simmer 20 to 30 minutes, until rice is just tender and most of the liquid has been absorbed.

6 Stir in shrimp, sausage, and bacon. Cover and continue to simmer about 5 minutes longer, until shrimp are pink and firm. Discard bay leaf.

Spicy Shrimp Jambalaya

- Serves **4**
- Preparation Time **20 minutes**
- Cooking Time **35 minutes**

2 tablespoons olive or canola oil

1 large onion, diced

2 cloves garlic, finely chopped

2 jalapeño peppers, chopped, or 2 canned green chili peppers

1 can (14 ounces) reduced-sodium tomatoes

2 tablespoons chopped cilantro or parsley

1¹/₂ cups chicken stock, page 18

1 cup long-grain rice

1 teaspoon sugar

1 pound medium shrimp, peeled and deveined

2 tablespoons lime juice

1 In a 4-quart saucepan, heat oil over moderate heat. Sauté onion and garlic as in master recipe.

2 Stir in peppers, tomatoes, cilantro, stock, rice, and sugar. Cover and simmer 20 to 30 minutes, until rice is tender and most of liquid has been absorbed.

3 Stir in shrimp and continue to cook about 5 minutes longer, until shrimp are pink and firm.

4 Add lime juice and stir gently to combine. Cook mixture about 1 minute longer.

PER SERVING
Calories **386**, Saturated Fat **1g**, Total Fat **9g**, Sodium **230mg**, Cholesterol **129mg**, Protein **23g**, Carbohydrate **52g**, Fiber **3g**.

Crab Jambalaya with Scallions

- Serves **4**
- Preparation Time **15 minutes**
- Cooking Time **30–35 minutes**

2 tablespoons olive or canola oil

¹/₂ cup sliced scallions

2 tablespoons chopped parsley

1 can (14 ounces) reduced-sodium tomatoes

1 cup chicken stock, page 18

¹/₂ cup dry white wine or chicken stock

1 cup long-grain rice or kasha

³/₄ teaspoon dried oregano, crumbled

¹/₄ teaspoon pepper

8 ounces cooked crabmeat, picked over

2 ounces feta cheese, cubed

1 In a 4-quart saucepan, heat the oil over moderate heat. Sauté scallions as in master recipe.

2 Stir in 1 tablespoon of parsley with tomatoes, stock, wine, rice, oregano, and pepper, and bring to a boil, stirring. Cover and simmer 20 to 30 minutes, until rice is softened and liquid is absorbed. (If using kasha, about 15 minutes.)

3 Stir in crab and simmer about 1 minute longer. Remove pan from the heat, stir in cheese, and sprinkle with remaining parsley.

PER SERVING
Calories **374**, Saturated Fat **3g**, Total Fat **12g**, Sodium **352mg**, Cholesterol **50mg**, Protein **18g**, Carbohydrate **44g**, Fiber **2g**.

Tuna Jambalaya with Barley

- Serves **4**
- Preparation Time **20 minutes**
- Cooking Time **40–45 minutes**

2 tablespoons olive or canola oil

2 onions, halved and sliced

3 cloves garlic, finely chopped

1 pound eggplant, cubed

4 ounces mushrooms, sliced

2 tablespoons chopped fresh dill or 2 teaspoons dried dill weed

¹/₂ teaspoon dried basil

1 can (14 ounces) diced tomatoes

2 cups fish or vegetable stock, page 18

1 cup quick-cooking barley or long-grain rice

1 pound tuna or swordfish steaks, cut into 1-inch cubes

1 In a 4-quart saucepan, heat oil over moderate heat. Sauté onions and garlic as in master recipe, about 4 minutes. Add eggplant, mushrooms, dill, and basil and cook about 4 minutes longer.

2 Stir in tomatoes, stock, and barley and bring to a boil. Cover and simmer 25 to 30 minutes, until eggplant and barley are soft.

3 Place the tuna on top of vegetable mixture in the saucepan, cover, and continue to simmer about 5 minutes longer, until the fish is cooked.

PER SERVING
Calories **511**, Saturated Fat **3g**, Total Fat **14g**, Sodium **260mg**, Cholesterol **43mg**, Protein **38g**, Carbohydrate **61g**, Fiber **15g**.

MEAT

The succulent flavor of roasted meat is one of life's pleasures. Fortunately, meat can still be part of a healthy diet if you eat it in smaller amounts with larger servings of vegetables. This reduces saturated fat and increases your intake of fiber and vitamins. The way you cook meat is important too, as it affects both nutrition and taste. This chapter shows simple, efficient techniques that retain the moisture, tenderness, and flavor of meat while reducing fat. But the proof is in the eating, and you'll find a wonderful variety of healthy recipes. For quick family suppers, there are nutritious stir-fries; for Sunday dinner, traditional roasts surrounded by vegetables; and for barbecues, grilled cutlets topped with a spicy fruit relish.

Teriyaki Grilled Steak with Asian Vegetables, page 140

Meat is one of our best sources of complete protein, B vitamins, and iron. Depending on the cut, however, it also contains moderate to high amounts of saturated fat and cholesterol. Although producers have responded by developing leaner meats with up to 25 percent less fat, health experts still recommend cutting back. A number of health-conscious Americans have responded by cutting out red meat altogether, but that can create other dietary problems.

Meat is especially rich in iron, which is particularly important for women, who tend to become anemic. Although iron is found in spinach and other vegetables, most of it is bound, which means the body is not able to use it all. Meat is also rich in vitamin B6, which strengthens the immune system, and like all animal foods, it is a good source of vitamin B12, which is needed to maintain a good blood supply. So the wisest course appears to be moderation – follow the USDA food pyramid and eat red meat just two or three times a week.

Buying and serving

Nutritionists also advise reducing portions to 3½ to 4 ounces per person. However, in real life that may not be as easy as it sounds. A pork chop thick enough for stuffing weighs about 8 ounces, and it's hard to find a 2-pound roast. And harder yet to serve just one slice per person.

The solution is easy: serve the larger portion of meat but count it as two servings for the week. An even wiser strategy is to think ahead and plan meals differently. If you're serving small pieces of meat, accompany it with more side dishes, like a hot crusty loaf of bread, green vegetables, oven-fried potatoes, and a salad. No one will go away from the table hungry, and you will have increased the nutritional value of the meal with extra fiber, vitamins, and minerals.

Is natural better?

Recently scientists have raised concerns that some of the hormones, growth enhancers, and antibiotics injected into cattle and hogs might taint the meat, causing illness in the humans who consume it. The FDA maintains that the amount of residues in meat is minuscule and therefore not harmful to your health. If you are still concerned, look for meats labeled natural or organic, which means that they have been raised without hormones, growth enhancers, and antibiotics. In any case, you should limit your consumption of organ meats. If there are residues, they tend to concentrate in the liver, kidneys, and other organs.

SELECTING LOW-FAT MEATS

Some cuts have less saturated fat and cholesterol than others. Choose wisely.

3½ ounces cooked	Calories	Fat g	Saturated Fat g	Cholesterol mg
Beef				
Blade roast	265	15	6	106
Flank steak	237	13	6	71
Prime rib	280	19	8	81
Short ribs	295	18	8	93
Tenderloin	232	12	5	84
Top round	207	6	2	90
Pork				
Center loin	199	9	3	79
Loin chop	182	7	2	91
Loin roast	187	7	3	77
Sirloin	216	10	4	86
Tenderloin	164	5	2	79
Lamb				
Leg	191	8	3	89
Shoulder	204	11	4	87

SAFETY FIRST

Despite government regulations for meat processing, many meats are contaminated with harmful bacteria. If the meat isn't kept cold enough or isn't cooked properly, the bacteria can multiply and pose a serious health threat, especially to infants and the elderly. Ground meats are particularly prone to contamination. However, there's no need for alarm. If you store and cook meats as directed below, you can enjoy the delicious taste of meat with no problems.

◆ Make sure your refrigerator maintains a temperature of 40°F.

◆ Store meat in the coldest part of the refrigerator, away from the door.

◆ Make sure meat is wrapped securely, so juices do not fall on other foods.

◆ Rewrap any meats that you plan to freeze.

◆ Store frozen meats at 0°F.

◆ Defrost meats in the microwave or the refrigerator – never at room temperature.

◆ Cook ground meat within 1 or 2 days of purchase, chops and roasts within 3 to 5 days.

◆ Do not eat meat raw.

◆ Be especially careful with ground meat – cook it until no longer pink.

◆ Do not partially cook meat ahead of time and finish cooking it later. Bacteria can multiply in half-cooked meat while it is in the refrigerator.

◆ After handling raw meat, wash counter and utensils with hot soapy water.

Cooking with less fat

Cut off any visible fat before you begin, and use the following techniques to reduce fat and retain nutrients.

Stir-frying relies on very high heat to seal and quickly cook thin strips of meat, so that they remain succulent. It requires very little fat and is an excellent way to preserve nutrients in fresh vegetables as well.

Braising in liquid is excellent for the leaner cuts of meat because it breaks down the fiber and makes them tender. Be sure to serve the pan juices, which contain all the nutrients from the meat, stock, and vegetables, but skim off any fat first.

Grilling and broiling require no added cooking oil. Better yet, the fat from the meat drips off. However, you may want to use a marinade containing just a little oil for flavor. For hints and tips on safe grilling, see box, right.

Roasting allows the fat to drip away from the meat. Instead of making gravy, flavor the roast with herbs and garlic, as shown below. Or serve the meat with salsa, chutney, or a low-fat sauce. Use a thermometer, and cook meat to the temperature called for in the recipe or in the chart on page 129. Do not serve meat rare.

Stuffing roasts and meat loaves allows you to serve a smaller portion of meat while still satisfying hearty appetites. And it gives you an opportunity to add flavor and nutrients with fruit, vegetables, grains, and nuts.

These cooking methods are all demonstrated in the chapter that follows. You will find mouthwatering recipes from many cuisines, from the American Southwest to the Mediterranean and even the Orient. All are lower in fat and calories than standard recipes, but still hearty and satisfying.

HEALTHY GRILLING TIPS

Grilled food has a wonderful flavor and can be enjoyed indoors or outdoors. However, there is a slight health risk. If the meat is fatty, the fat drips onto the heat source and forms cancer-causing substances that are picked up in the smoke and then deposited on the food. Charring meat also causes the same effect. If you follow these guidelines, you should not have a problem.

- ◆ Trim visible fat. Precook large pieces of meat, such as roasts, to reduce time on the grill.

- ◆ Line the grill with foil and punch holes in it to allow the fat and juices to drip through.

- ◆ Don't let the fire flare up, as harmful smoke may be produced.

- ◆ Don't use mesquite briquettes; they produce a hotter flame and are more likely to char the meat. Hickory gives a sweetish flavor that is good with beef, pork, lamb, and poultry.

- ◆ Baste with sauce or lemon juice rather than oil or fat.

- ◆ If the food is charred, remove any blackened area before eating.

- ◆ Limit your cook-outs to once a week.

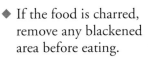

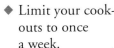

FLAVORING MEAT WITH GARLIC AND ROSEMARY

1 *Cut a few small sprigs of fresh rosemary, then peel and slice several garlic cloves. Using a small, sharp kitchen knife, make a series of deep cuts in the meat.*

2 *Insert of small sprig of rosemary and a slice of garlic into each cut in the meat prior to roasting. The pungent "pine" aroma of the rosemary, together with the garlic, will infuse the meat with great flavor.*

Herb-Roasted Beef

Cooking technique ▪ *A change in proportions is the secret here. Roast a generous serving of vegetables alongside a smaller piece of meat to create a nutritionally balanced meal.*

Reduce fat ▪ *Instead of gravy, add herbs for extra flavor. If fresh are not available, you can still get great taste by combining dried herbs with flat-leaf parsley.*

● Serves 6 ● Preparation Time **15 minutes** ● Cooking Time **1 hour 40 minutes**

PER SERVING
Calories **317**, Saturated Fat **3g**,
Total Fat **10g**, Sodium **278mg**,
Cholesterol **82mg**, Protein **39g**,
Carbohydrate **20g**, Fiber **7g**.

2 pounds lean boneless beef
rib roast

¹⁄₈ teaspoon each salt and pepper

1 cup fresh herbs, such as
parsley, basil, sage, rosemary,
thyme, and chives, or
1¹⁄₂ tablespoons dried

2 tablespoons Dijon mustard

1 tablespoon olive or canola oil

3 large onions, cut into eighths

6 small zucchini, cut into thirds

1 cauliflower, cut into florets

COOKING TIP
*To slice, hold the meat
steady with a two-pronged
fork. Using a well-sharpened
carving knife, cut across the
grain into thin or thick
slices, as preferred.*

1 Preheat the oven to 350°F. With a sharp knife, trim all the fat and cartilage from the beef roast. Season the meat with salt and pepper.

2 Place the herbs in a food processor with the Dijon mustard and process to chop very finely and combine, scraping down the sides of the bowl occasionally. Transfer to a small bowl.

3 Spoon the herb mixture onto the roast and, using a palette knife, spread it evenly to cover all sides of the meat. In a large roasting pan, place the oil and the herb-covered meat. Roast the meat for about 30 minutes.

4 Arrange the onions, zucchini, and cauliflower around the meat in the roasting pan and toss the vegetables to coat them thoroughly.

5 Roast the meat and vegetables about 1 hour or until a thermometer inserted in the center of the meat reads 160°F (for medium). Turn the vegetables occasionally so that they cook evenly.

6 Remove pan from oven. With a slotted spoon, transfer the vegetables to a serving dish and keep them warm. Transfer the roast to a carving platter, cover, and let stand for 5 minutes. Slice beef and serve with vegetables.

What could be better for Sunday dinner than **Herb-Roasted Beef** *served with its own pan vegetables and Roasted New Potatoes, page 185.*

Garlic-Roasted Lamb

Use fresh rosemary if possible (many supermarkets carry it). The flavor it imparts to the lamb will be far superior to that of dried. If you like, white potatoes may be substituted for the sweet potatoes, and turnips for the parsnips.

- Serves **6**
- Preparation Time **20 minutes**
- Cooking Time **1 hour 50 minutes**

Fresh rosemary looks like a sprig of pine needles.

---

1 shank half leg of lamb (about 3 pounds)

$^1/_8$ teaspoon each salt and pepper

---

8 cloves garlic, sliced in half lengthwise

---

2 large sprigs fresh rosemary or 2 teaspoons dried

---

2 teaspoons olive or canola oil

---

4 large sweet potatoes, peeled and cut into 1-inch cubes

---

6 parsnips, cut into 1-inch pieces

---

1 Preheat the oven to 325°F. With a sharp knife, trim all the fat and any cartilage from the lamb. Season the meat with salt and pepper.

2 With a small knife, make slits about 1 inch deep all over the leg of lamb. Using most of the garlic and all the rosemary, push a garlic half or a few rosemary leaves into each of the slits.

3 In a large roasting pan, combine oil with sweet potatoes, parsnips, and remaining garlic to coat well. Move the vegetables to the side of the pan and place the lamb in the center.

4 Roast the lamb and vegetables 1$^1/_2$ to 2 hours or until a thermometer inserted into the center of the meat reads 160°F (for medium). Turn the vegetables occasionally so that they cook evenly.

5 Remove pan from the oven. With a slotted spoon, transfer the vegetables to a serving dish and keep them warm. Transfer the lamb to a carving platter, cover with foil, and let stand for 5 minutes. Slice the roast lamb and serve with the vegetables.

> **COOKING TIP**
> *You can also flavor lamb by covering it with lemon slices before roasting.*

PER SERVING
Calories **482**, Saturated Fat **3g**, Total Fat **10g**, Sodium **188mg**, Cholesterol **122mg**, Protein **43g**, Carbohydrate **55g**, Fiber **11g**.

Roasted Ham and Apples with Butternut Squash

Since ham is high in sodium, make sure you watch your sodium intake from other meals on the day that you serve this dish.

- Serves **6**
- Preparation Time **25 minutes**
- Cooking Time **1 hour 25 minutes**

---

2 tablespoons margarine or butter

---

1 tablespoon Dijon mustard

---

2 tablespoons brown sugar

$^1/_2$ cup apple juice

---

1 smoked ham center slice, fully cooked (about 2 pounds)

---

2 pounds butternut squash, peeled and sliced $^1/_2$ inch thick

---

1 pound small white onions

---

3 small tart apples, sliced $^1/_2$ inch thick

---

1 Preheat the oven to 350°F. In a small saucepan, melt margarine, stir in mustard, brown sugar, and apple juice and simmer until sugar dissolves. Brush ham with most of apple juice mixture, cover, and refrigerate.

2 Meanwhile, in a large roasting pan, place squash, onions, apples, and remaining apple juice mixture. Cover with foil and roast for 50 minutes.

3 Uncover roasting pan and place ham on top of squash and onions.

4 Roast 30 minutes longer or until ham is heated through, basting halfway. Remove pan from the oven. With a slotted spoon, transfer the vegetables and apples to a serving dish and keep them warm. Transfer the roast ham to a carving platter, cover with foil, and let stand for 5 minutes. Slice the ham and serve with the vegetables and apples.

> **COOKING TIP**
>
> *To peel small onions quickly, plunge them into very hot water. Remove at once, then transfer to cold water and let cool before peeling.*

PER SERVING
Calories **413**, Saturated Fat **3g**, Total Fat **13g**, Sodium **1,937mg**, Cholesterol **80mg**, Protein **34g**, Carbohydrate **42g**, Fiber **5g**.

Butternut squash is an excellent source of beta carotene; apples provide fiber.

Herb-Roasted Pork with Turnips, Apples, and Onions

The fruit and vegetables add sweetness to this elegant roast, as well as a sizable amount of vitamin A and fiber. When cooking pork, it is important that the meat reaches an internal temperature of 170° F. Pork should always be served well done – never rare.

- Serves **8**
- Preparation Time **35 minutes**
- Cooking Time **2 hours 20 minutes**

---

3 pounds pork rib roast

$1/8$ teaspoon each salt and pepper

1 tablespoon olive or canola oil

1 tablespoon each chopped fresh sage and oregano or 1 teaspoon each dried

$1/4$ teaspoon ground cinnamon

$1/8$ teaspoon cayenne pepper

4 tart apples, cored and cut into cubes

2 large red onions, coarsely chopped

6 small turnips, quartered

---

1 Preheat the oven to 325°F. With a sharp knife, trim all the fat from the pork roast. Season the meat with salt and pepper.

2 Heat the oil in a small saucepan over moderate heat. Add the sage, oregano, cinnamon, and cayenne pepper and stir to combine. Remove from the heat.

3 Place the pork on a rack in a roasting pan. Lightly brush some of the oil and herb mixture over the meat and roast about 1 hour.

4 Scatter the apple, onion, and turnip pieces around the pork. Brush the meat, apples, and vegetables with more of the oil and herb mixture. Continue roasting about 1 hour 15 minutes longer or until a thermometer inserted into the meat reads 170°F and the apples, onions, and turnips are tender.

5 Remove pan from the oven. With a slotted spoon, transfer the apples and vegetables to a serving dish and keep them warm. Transfer the pork to a carving platter, cover with foil, and let stand for 5 minutes. Slice the roast pork and serve with the apples and vegetables.

COOKING TIP
If you don't have a meat thermometer, make a small slit in the center of the meat; it will be a light gray color if well done.

PER SERVING
Calories **366**, Saturated Fat **5g**, Total Fat **14g**, Sodium **206mg**, Cholesterol **107mg**, Protein **39g**, Carbohydrate **21g**, Fiber **5g**.

Cooking Times for Beef, Lamb, and Pork

Before roasting, season the meat and place on a rack over a roasting pan; this allows the fat to drain off. If using a marinade, brush on before roasting and once during roasting. To test for doneness, insert a meat thermometer into the thickest part of the meat, avoiding any bone. To ensure that the meat is cooked to your liking – rare, medium, or well done – check below for the desired internal temperature. Remove the meat from the oven just before the ideal temperature is reached because it will continue cooking for a few minutes. After the meat is done to your liking, cover it and let stand for about 15 minutes; this allows the meat to set and makes carving much easier.

BEEF	Pounds	Oven temp.°F	Med. Rare	Medium	Well Done
Standing Rib Roast	6–8	350	18/145	22/160	25/170
Rolled Rib	4–6	325	15/145	20/160	22/170
Shell Roast	6	325	15/145	18/160	20/170
Top Sirloin	4	325	20/145	25/160	30/170
Eye of Round	5	350	15/145	–	20/170

Note: *Ground beef should be cooked to 160°F. Never serve rare.*

LAMB			Medium	Well Done
Leg	5–8	350	25/160	30/170
Loin	3–4	350	35/160	45/170
Saddle	6–8	325	25/160	30/170
Rack*	3	350	35/160	40/170
Crown**	4–5	350	25/160	30/170
Shoulder†	4–6	325	25/160	30/170

* before trimming   ** unstuffed   † before boning

PORK			Minutes per pound	Internal °F
Center Loin	3–4	325	30–35	170
Blade or Sirloin	3–4	325	35–40	170
Rolled Loin	3–5	325	35–40	170
Whole Leg	12–16	325	30–35	170
Half Leg	5–8	325	35–40	170
Shoulder	4–6	325	20–25	170
Rump	6–10	325	25–30	170

Pork Loin Stuffed with Winter Fruits

Cooking technique ▪ *A sweet or spicy stuffing adds flavor to roasts, so you don't need gravy. And it makes a very satisfying meal with less meat. Ask your supermarket to bone the roast for you.*

Add fiber ▪ *Instead of sausage or nuts, make the stuffing with nutritious fruits and vegetables. In bread stuffings, replace the butter with chicken stock.*

● Serves **6** ● Preparation Time **20 minutes** ● Cooking Time **1½ hours**

PER SERVING
Calories **375**, Saturated Fat **4g**,
Total Fat **11g**, Sodium **170mg**,
Cholesterol **95mg**, Protein **35g**,
Carbohydrate **34g**, Fiber **4g**.

---

³/₄ cup chicken stock, page 18

1 cup pitted prunes, coarsely chopped

1 cup dried apricots, coarsely chopped

2 pounds boned pork loin

¹/₈ teaspoon each salt and pepper

1 clove garlic, finely chopped

1 teaspoon dried thyme

2 tablespoons Madeira or port wine (optional)

2 tablespoons dark molasses

1 In a small saucepan, bring the stock to a boil over moderate heat. Remove from the heat and stir in the prunes and apricots. Allow to soak at least 15 minutes or until very soft.

2 Meanwhile, preheat the oven to 325°F. With a sharp knife, trim all the fat from the pork loin. Open out the loin, and pat dry with paper towels. Season the inside with salt and pepper.

3 Drain the soaked fruit, reserving the liquid in a saucepan. Place the fruit along one of the long sides of the pork loin. Scatter the chopped garlic and thyme over the fruit.

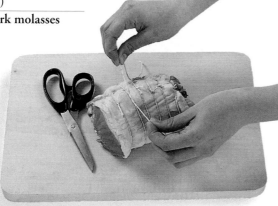

4 Fold the long edge of meat over the fruit and roll up the loin. With kitchen string, tie up the loin at regular intervals to seal in the stuffing. Trim excess string.

5 Place loin on a rack in a roasting pan, seam side down, and roast about 30 minutes. Meanwhile, add the Madeira or port wine, if using, and molasses to the reserved soaking liquid and bring to a boil to make the glaze.

6 Brush the glaze evenly over the pork loin. Roast the pork about 1 hour longer or until tender and the internal temperature of the meat reads 170°F, brushing with the glaze every 10 minutes.

*Mashed Turnips with Carrots, page 189, and green beans go beautifully with **Pork Loin Stuffed with Winter Fruits.**
The fruit complements the richness of the pork.*

Veal Breast Stuffed with Mushrooms

The subtle taste of veal pairs well with mushrooms.

- Serves **6**
- Preparation Time **20 minutes**
- Cooking Time **2 hours**

---

1 cup chicken stock, page 18, or water

1 ounce dried mushrooms (optional)

2¹/₂ pounds boned veal breast

Salt and pepper

2 teaspoons olive or canola oil

1 onion, finely chopped

2 stalks celery, finely chopped

8 ounces white mushrooms, trimmed and sliced

2 tablespoons chopped parsley

2 tablespoons fine dried bread crumbs

¹/₈ teaspoon each salt and pepper

2 tablespoons honey

1 Pour the chicken stock into a small saucepan and add the dried mushrooms, if using. Bring to a boil over moderate heat, remove from the heat, and allow to soak at least 15 minutes.

COOKING TIP
If you can't find any dried mushrooms, add 2 to 3 table-spoons low-sodium soy sauce to the stock for flavor. Make the glaze as directed in Step 6 with the soy-stock mixture.

2 Preheat the oven to 325°F. Using a sharp knife, trim all the fat from the veal breast, open out the breast, and pat dry with paper towels. Season the inside with a pinch each of salt and pepper.

3 In a nonstick skillet, heat the oil over moderate heat. Add the onion and celery and sauté about 5 minutes or until softened and lightly browned. Add the white mushrooms and cook, stirring often, about 10 minutes or until very soft and most of the liquid has cooked off.

4 Remove from the heat and stir in the parsley, bread crumbs, and ¹/₈ teaspoon each salt and pepper. Strain the dried mushrooms, if using, reserving the stock. Finely chop the dried mushrooms and stir into the cooked mushroom mixture.

5 Place the mushroom mixture along one of the short edges of the veal breast. Fold the long edge of meat over the stuffing and roll up the loin. With kitchen string, tie up the meat at regular intervals to seal in the stuffing.

6 Place veal on a rack in a roasting pan, seam side down, and roast about 30 minutes. Meanwhile, return reserved stock to a boil, add the honey and simmer about 5 minutes to make the glaze. Brush the glaze over the veal. Roast about 1 hour longer or until tender and the internal temperature of the meat reads 170°F, brushing with glaze every 10 minutes.

PER SERVING
Calories **288**, Saturated Fat **2g**, Total Fat **8g**, Sodium **304mg**, Cholesterol **151mg**, Protein **40g**, Carbohydrate **12g**, Fiber **1g**.

Leg of Lamb Stuffed with Spinach

Spinach and feta cheese add Mediterranean flair to this elegant main dish. Serve it with rice and a salad on the side. You can increase the amount of garlic if you like – it's very good for you.

- Serves **8**
- Preparation Time **20 minutes**
- Cooking Time **1¹/₂–2 hours**

3¹/₂ pounds shank half leg of lamb, butterflied

¹/₈ teaspoon each salt and pepper

2 packages (10 ounces each) frozen chopped spinach, thawed and drained

1 teaspoon olive or canola oil

1 shallot or small onion, finely chopped

2 cloves garlic, finely chopped

4 ounces feta or ricotta cheese

1 Preheat the oven to 375°F. Using a sharp knife, trim all the fat from the lamb, open out the butterflied leg, and pat dry with paper towels. Season the inside with salt and pepper.

2 In a sieve, press the spinach with a wooden spoon to squeeze out any remaining liquid (see page 74). Place spinach in a bowl.

3 In a small nonstick skillet, heat the oil over moderate heat. Add the shallot and garlic and sauté 3 to 4 minutes or until softened and lightly browned. Add to the bowl with the spinach.

4 Spread the spinach mixture on top of the surface of the butterflied lamb; crumble the cheese on top of the spinach. Roll up the butterflied lamb; with kitchen string, tie up the meat at regular intervals to seal in the stuffing.

5 Place the stuffed leg on a rack in a roasting pan seam side down and roast – 1¹/₂ to 2 hours or until internal temperature of the meat reads 160°F for medium, or 1³/₄ to 2¹/₄ hours or until the internal temperature reads 170°F for well done.

6 Remove from the oven and allow the lamb to rest about 10 minutes before slicing.

PER SERVING
Calories **321**, Saturated Fat **5g**, Total Fat **13g**, Sodium **388mg**, Cholesterol **139mg**, Protein **45g**, Carbohydrate **5g**, Fiber **2g**.

SELECTING CHEESES FOR HEALTHY EATING AND COOKING

In order to keep your fat intake down, look for cheeses with 4 grams of fat or less per ounce. For stuffings, sauces, and dressings use soft cheeses such as part-skim mozzarella, ricotta, string cheese and 1% low-fat cottage cheese.

For shredding and sprinkling on top of casseroles and salads, use hard cheeses such as low-fat Monterey Jack and Cheddar, and reduced-fat Muenster, Swiss, and Colby.

Pork Chops Stuffed with Apples and Pears

Applesauce is the classic partner for pork chops. In this imaginative new dish, the apples are combined with pears to make a high-fiber, fat-free stuffing. Apple juice is placed in the roasting pan to keep the meat moist while it cooks and to infuse the meat with apple flavor from both inside and out. Use a tart apple such as a Granny Smith in the stuffing for the best flavor.

- Serves **6**
- Preparation Time **20 minutes**
- Cooking Time **1½ hours**

---

2 teaspoons olive or canola oil

2 leeks or 1 small onion, trimmed and sliced

2 tart apples, peeled, cored, and diced

1 ripe pear, cored and diced

½ teaspoon dried sage

¾ cup unsweetened apple juice

¼ cup chicken stock, page 18

½ teaspoon finely grated orange zest

6 pork loin chops with bone, 1 inch thick (about 8 ounces each)

Vegetable oil cooking spray

---

1 Preheat the oven to 350°F. In a saucepan, heat the oil over moderate heat. Add the leeks and sauté 3 to 4 minutes or until softened and lightly browned. Add the apples, pear, and sage; sauté about 3 minutes longer. Stir in ½ cup apple juice and the stock, bring to a boil, reduce heat, and simmer, uncovered, about 2 minutes or until the fruit is slightly soft.

2 Drain the fruit mixture, reserving the liquid in the saucepan. Allow the fruit to cool slightly. Stir the orange zest into the fruit mixture.

3 Using a sharp knife, trim all the fat from the pork chops. Cut a pocket in the side of each chop and stuff with the fruit mixture (see box).

4 Coat a nonstick pan with vegetable oil cooking spray, add 3 chops, and cook on moderately high heat for 2 minutes on each side or until browned. Repeat with second batch. *Do not use spray near hot burner.*

5 Place the stuffed chops in a nonstick roasting pan, add the remaining apple juice, and roast about 1 hour or until tender and the internal temperature of the meat is 170°F. Transfer the chops to a platter, cover with aluminum foil, and keep them warm.

6 Spoon off most of the fat from the roasting pan. Stir in the reserved fruit poaching liquid and place over moderate heat. Bring to a boil, reduce heat, and simmer, stirring to loosen the brown bits on the pan, about 3 minutes or until a rich sauce forms.

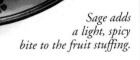
Sage adds a light, spicy bite to the fruit stuffing.

PER SERVING
Calories **384**, Saturated Fat **5g**, Total Fat **15g**, Sodium **133mg**, Cholesterol **113mg**, Protein **40g**, Carbohydrate **21g**, Fiber **3g**.

STUFFING PORK CHOPS

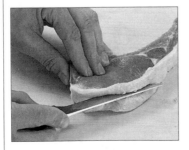

1 *Using a sharp knife, make a horizontal slit into the side of the chop until the knife blade reaches the bone.*

2 *Move the knife back and forth to make a pocket about 3 inches long, taking care not to go through to the outside of the meat at any point.*

3 *With a teaspoon, stuff the stuffing mixture into the pocket.*

Braised Beef Pot Roast

Cooking technique ▪ *Braising in liquid makes a roast very tender without drying it out. Add vegetables and you have a nutritious one-dish meal.*
Reduce fat ▪ *Serve the beef with the pan juices instead of gravy.*

● Serves 6 ● Preparation Time **20 minutes** ● Cooking Time **2 hours 45 minutes**

PER SERVING
Calories **414**, Saturated Fat **5g**,
Total Fat **13g**, Sodium **186mg**,
Cholesterol **138mg**, Protein **49g**,
Carbohydrate **17g**, Fiber **5g**.

2 pounds beef chuck roast

1 tablespoon olive or canola oil

2 large onions, cut into eighths

8 carrots, cut into 2-inch pieces

4 stalks celery, cut into
  2-inch pieces

1 cup red wine or ¼ cup red
  wine vinegar

1½ cups beef stock, page 18

1 bay leaf

½ teaspoon dried thyme

⅛ teaspoon each salt and pepper

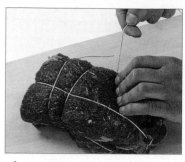

1 Trim the fat from the beef. Cut a piece of kitchen string about 4 times the length of the roast and tie it around the roast at regular intervals along its length.

2 In a large Dutch oven, heat oil over moderately high heat. Brown beef all over, turning it with a long-handled fork, about 10 minutes. Transfer to a plate.

3 Add vegetables to the pan and sauté, stirring frequently, about 7 minutes or until browned and slightly softened. Transfer the vegetables to a plate.

*A bountiful meal that's easy to make – **Braised Beef Pot Roast**.*

4 Return roast to pot with wine, stock, herbs, salt, and pepper. Stir to blend. Cover and simmer gently, turning beef every 30 minutes, about 2 hours.

5 Return the vegetables to the pot, cover, and continue to cook about 15 minutes or until the beef is very tender when pierced with a table fork.

6 Discard bay leaf. Transfer the beef to a chopping board and remove the strings. Slice the meat and serve with the vegetables and pot juices.

Braised Beef with Cabbage

- Serves 6
- Preparation Time 20 minutes
- Cooking Time 2 hours 50 minutes

2 pounds beef chuck roast

1 tablespoon olive or canola oil

2 large onions, coarsely chopped

2 cloves garlic, finely chopped

1 each small green and red cabbage, cored and cut into 8 wedges

1¹/₂ cups beef stock, page 18

¹/₂ cup red wine or beef stock

¹/₂ teaspoon caraway seeds

¹/₄ teaspoon ground ginger

¹/₈ teaspoon each salt and pepper

1 Prepare the beef as in Step 1 of the master recipe. Brown the beef as in Step 2 of the master recipe.

2 Add the onions and garlic and sauté as in Step 3 of the master recipe. Transfer to a plate. Cook cabbage wedges a few minutes on all sides until slightly softened. Add to the plate with the onions.

3 Return the beef to the pot with the stock, wine, caraway seeds, ginger, salt, and pepper. Stir to blend. Cover and simmer gently, turning beef every 30 minutes, about 2 hours. Return the vegetables to the pot and cook as in Step 5 of the master recipe. Serve as in Step 6 of the master recipe.

Braised Pork in Cider with Apples

- Serves 8
- Preparation Time 12 minutes
- Cooking Time 2¹/₂ hours

3 pounds smoked pork shoulder roll

2 teaspoons olive or canola oil

2 large onions, coarsely chopped

4 tart apples, cored and cut into rings

1 cup chicken stock, page 18

1 cup unsweetened apple cider or juice

¹/₈ teaspoon each salt and pepper

1 Prepare the pork as in Step 1 of the master recipe. Brown the pork as in Step 2 of the master recipe.

2 Add onions and sauté as in Step 3 of the master recipe. Add apple rings to pan and cook, stirring gently, about 4 minutes longer or until browned. Transfer onions and apples to a plate.

3 Return the pork to the pot with stock, apple cider, salt, and pepper. Stir to blend. Cover and simmer gently, turning pork every 30 minutes, about 1¹/₂ hours.

4 Add onions and apples to pot, cover, and cook 30 to 40 minutes or until pork is tender. Serve as in Step 6 of master recipe.

Braised Lamb Shanks with Tomatoes

- Serves 6
- Preparation Time 25 minutes
- Cooking Time 2–2¹/₂ hours

6 lamb shanks (10 ounces each)

1 tablespoon olive or canola oil

3 large onions, coarsely chopped

3 stalks celery, sliced

2 cloves garlic, finely chopped

1 pound fresh tomatoes, diced

1 can (28 ounces) crushed tomatoes

1 tablespoon each chopped fresh rosemary and oregano or 1 teaspoon each dried

1 cup beef stock, page 18

¹/₂ cup sliced black olives

¹/₄ teaspoon pepper

1 Trim fat from lamb. Brown the lamb shanks, 2 at a time, as in Step 2 of the master recipe. Transfer to a plate.

2 Add onions, celery, and garlic to the pot and sauté as in Step 3 of the master recipe. Stir in all the tomatoes, herbs, stock, olives, and pepper.

3 Add lamb to tomato mixture. Bring to a boil, cover, and simmer, stirring occasionally, 1¹/₂ to 2 hours or until meat is tender when pierced with a fork. Serve as in Step 6 of master recipe.

Braised Pork Chops with Oranges

Cooking technique ■ *Simmer chops until tender in a flavorful blend of stock and fruit juice.*
Add nutrients ■ *Cook vegetables with the chops to make a healthful one-dish meal.*

● Serves **4** ● Preparation Time **15 minutes** ● Cooking Time **1 hour**

PER SERVING
Calories **358**, Saturated Fat **4g**,
Total Fat **13g**, Sodium **220mg**,
Cholesterol **85mg**, Protein **33g**,
Carbohydrate **26g**, Fiber **6g**.

4 lean center-cut pork chops, ³/₄ inch thick (6 ounces each)	¹/₂ teaspoon dried sage, crumbled
2¹/₂ tablespoons all-purpose flour	¹/₈ teaspoon each salt and pepper
1 tablespoon olive or canola oil	1 pound carrots, cut into 2-inch pieces
³/₄ cup chicken stock, page 18	2 oranges, peeled and cut across into slices
¹/₂ cup orange juice	

1 With a sharp knife, trim any fat from the pork chops. Very lightly dredge the chops in flour by placing them, one at a time, in a bag with the flour and shaking.

2 In a large nonstick skillet, heat the oil over moderately high heat. Add the chops and sauté 2 to 3 minutes or until thoroughly browned on each side, turning them once.

COOKING TIP

To test if the oil is hot enough for frying, add a cube of bread — it should turn golden.

---

*The piquant citrus flavor enhances **Braised Pork Chops with Oranges**. Serve with roasted sweet potatoes.*

3 With a large spatula, transfer the chops to a platter, cover with foil, and keep them warm. Pour or wipe the fat from the skillet with a paper towel, and return the skillet to the heat. Stir the chicken stock, orange juice, sage, salt, and pepper into the pan juices and bring to a boil, stirring occasionally.

4 Return the chops to the skillet, top with carrots, cover, and simmer about 35 minutes or until the chops are almost cooked through. Push carrots to the edges of the skillet, place the orange slices on top of the chops, and cook about 10 minutes longer or until the orange slices become slightly soft.

Braised Pork Chops with Sweet Potatoes

- Serves **4**
- Preparation Time **15 minutes**
- Cooking Time **1 hour**

4 lean center-cut pork chops, $^3/_4$ inch thick (6 ounces each)

2$^1/_2$ tablespoons all-purpose flour

1 tablespoon olive or canola oil

1 cup chicken stock, page 18

1 cup unsweetened apple juice

2 tablespoons apple brandy (optional)

$^1/_2$ teaspoon dried thyme

$^1/_8$ teaspoon each salt and pepper

1$^1/_2$ pounds sweet potatoes, cut across into $^1/_4$-inch slices

1 Trim pork and dredge in flour as in Step 1 of the master recipe.

2 Sauté the pork chops as in Step 2 of the master recipe.

3 Keep chops warm, return skillet to the heat, and add the chicken stock, apple juice, apple brandy, if using, thyme, salt, and pepper as in Step 3 of the master recipe.

4 Return chops to the skillet with potatoes, cover, and simmer about 45 minutes or until the chops are cooked through and the juices run clear.

PER SERVING
Calories **471**, Saturated Fat **4g**, Total Fat **13g**, Sodium **209mg**, Cholesterol **85mg**, Protein **34g**, Carbohydrate **52g**, Fiber **5g**.

Braised Lamb Chops with Baby Vegetables

- Serves **4**
- Preparation Time **15 minutes**
- Cooking Time **1 hour**

4 lamb shoulder blade chops, $^3/_4$ inch thick (6 ounces each)

2$^1/_2$ tablespoons all-purpose flour

1 tablespoon olive or canola oil

$^1/_4$ teaspoon dried rosemary

2 cups beef stock, page 18

$^1/_8$ teaspoon each salt and pepper

8 small new potatoes, halved

8 ounces baby carrots or regular carrots, sliced

8 ounces sugar snap peas

1 tablespoon chopped fresh mint, dill, or parsley (optional)

1 Trim the lamb and dredge in flour as in Step 1 of the master recipe. Sauté lamb with the rosemary as in Step 2 of the master recipe.

2 Keep chops warm; return skillet to the heat and add stock, salt, and pepper as in Step 3 of the master recipe.

3 Return chops to skillet with new potatoes and carrots, cover, and simmer about 45 minutes or until chops are almost cooked.

4 Add sugar snap peas and fresh herbs, if using, and simmer about 5 minutes longer.

PER SERVING
Calories **428**, Saturated Fat **5g**, Total Fat **16g**, Sodium **190mg**, Cholesterol **89mg**, Protein **33g**, Carbohydrate **36g**, Fiber **4g**.

Braised Veal Steaks with Mushrooms

- Serves **4**
- Preparation Time **15 minutes**
- Cooking Time **1 hour**

4 veal shoulder blade steaks, $^3/_4$ inch thick (6 ounces each)

2$^1/_2$ tablespoons all-purpose flour

1 tablespoon olive or canola oil

1$^1/_2$ cups beef stock, page 18

$^1/_2$ cup red wine or chicken stock

$^1/_8$ teaspoon each salt and pepper

8 ounces turnips, cubed

4 stalks celery, diced

8 ounces mushrooms, halved

2 tablespoons chopped parsley

1 Trim the veal and dredge in flour as in Step 1 of the master recipe. Sauté as in Step 2 of the master recipe.

2 Keep steaks warm. Return skillet to the heat and add stock, wine, salt, and pepper as in Step 3 of the master recipe.

3 Return steaks to skillet with turnips and celery, cover, and simmer about 25 minutes or until steaks are half cooked.

4 Add the mushrooms and simmer about 20 minutes longer or until the steaks are cooked through and the juices run clear. Stir in chopped parsley.

PER SERVING
Calories **294**, Saturated Fat **2g**, Total Fat **10g**, Sodium **291mg**, Cholesterol **146mg**, Protein **37g**, Carbohydrate **11g**, Fiber **3g**.

Grilled Steak and Vegetables

Cooking technique ▪ *Grilling is an ideal way to cook steak because the fat drips away. Begin with a low-fat cut such as flank steak or London broil and buy 4 to 6 ounces per person. Then put your favorite vegetables on the grill for more vitamins and fiber. See page 125 for tips on healthy grilling.*

Add flavor ▪ *The marinade infuses the meat with the taste of the herbs and spices.*

● Serves 4 ● Preparation Time **20 minutes plus marinating time** ● Cooking Time **20 minutes**

PER SERVING
Calories **327**, Saturated Fat **6g**,
Total Fat **18g**, Sodium **271mg**,
Cholesterol **57mg**, Protein **27g**,
Carbohydrate **16g**, Fiber **5g**.

---

4 lean London broil or flank steaks (4 ounces each)

3 tablespoons olive or canola oil

3 tablespoons red wine vinegar

2 tablespoons Dijon mustard

2 cloves garlic, finely chopped

1 teaspoon each dried basil and oregano

1/8 teaspoon hot red pepper flakes

1/8 teaspoon each salt and pepper

2 sweet red or green peppers, cut lengthwise into 1-inch strips

3 zucchini, each cut lengthwise into 4 strips

2 red or yellow onions, cut across into 1/2-inch slices

1 Using a sharp knife, trim all the fat from the steaks.

2 Make the marinade: In a small bowl, combine the oil with the vinegar, mustard, garlic, basil, oregano, hot pepper flakes, salt, and pepper until blended.

3 Place the steaks in a dish just large enough to hold them and pour the marinade over. Turn the meat in the marinade to coat it thoroughly. Cover the dish and marinate in the refrigerator at least 2 hours.

4 Remove the meat from the refrigerator and allow to come to room temperature. Pour off the marinade into a small bowl. Preheat a charcoal grill or broiler, setting the rack 4 to 5 inches from the heat.

5 Add the steaks to the grill or broiler and cook according to taste, about 6 minutes on each side for medium. Meanwhile, using a small brush, coat the vegetable pieces with the marinade mixture.

6 Transfer the steaks to a platter, cover with foil, and keep warm. Add the vegetables to the grill or broiler and cook until browned and softened, turning once and brushing twice with the remaining marinade.

Grilled Steak and Vegetables *can be cooked equally well on a grill pan or broiler as well as an outdoor barbecue.*
Serve with a fresh green salad.

Teriyaki Grilled Steak with Asian Vegetables

Once the vegetables have been brushed with the marinade mixture and grilled, discard any remaining marinade. Uncooked marinade is no longer safe after exposure to meat.

- Serves **6**
- Preparation Time **20 minutes** plus marinating time
- Cooking Time **20 minutes**

---

6 lean London broil or flank steaks (4 ounces each)

3–4 tablespoons olive or canola oil

2 tablespoons reduced-sodium soy sauce

1 tablespoon rice vinegar or dry sherry (optional)

1 tablespoon finely chopped fresh ginger

1 clove garlic, finely chopped

1/4 teaspoon pepper

2 Japanese (slender) or 1 small regular eggplant, cut across into 1/4-inch slices

1 can (15 ounces) baby corn, drained and rinsed

2 bunches scallions, trimmed and halved crosswise

1 Using a sharp knife, trim all the fat from the steaks.

2 Make the marinade: In a small bowl, combine 3 tablespoons of the oil with the soy sauce, rice vinegar, ginger, garlic, and pepper until blended.

3 Place the steaks in a dish just large enough to hold them and pour the marinade over. Turn the meat in the marinade to coat it thoroughly. Cover the dish and marinate in the refrigerator at least 2 hours.

4 Remove the meat from the refrigerator and allow to come to room temperature. Pour off the marinade into a small bowl. Preheat a charcoal grill or broiler, setting the rack 4 to 5 inches from the heat.

5 Add the steaks to the grill or broiler and cook according to taste, about 6 minutes on each side for medium. Meanwhile, using a small brush, coat the eggplant, corn, and scallions with the marinade mixture.

6 Transfer the steaks to a platter, cover with foil, and keep warm. Add the vegetables to the grill or broiler and cook until browned and softened, turning once and brushing with any remaining marinade or olive oil.

> **COOKING TIP**
> *Place the vegetables on a piece of aluminum foil to prevent them from falling through the grill.*

PER SERVING
Calories **356**, Saturated Fat **5g**, Total Fat **16g**, Sodium **227mg**, Cholesterol **57mg**, Protein **28g**, Carbohydrate **29g**, Fiber **7g**.

Jamaican Grilled Pork Steak

Sliced sweet potatoes and bananas make a rich-tasting, low-fat accompaniment to grilled pork.

- Serves **6**
- Preparation Time **20 minutes** plus marinating time
- Cooking Time **20 minutes**

---

6 pork shoulder blade steaks (4 ounces each)

2 cloves garlic, coarsely chopped

2 scallions, cut into pieces

1 tablespoon olive or canola oil, more as necessary

2 teaspoons lime or lemon juice

2 teaspoons dark brown sugar

1 teaspoon chopped fresh ginger or 1/4 teaspoon dried

1/2 teaspoon each ground allspice and cinnamon

1/8 teaspoon each salt, black pepper, and cayenne pepper

3 large sweet potatoes, cooked and cut across into 1/2-inch slices

3 bananas, cut lengthwise in half

1 Using a sharp knife, trim all the fat from the meat.

2 Make the marinade: In a food processor or blender, combine the garlic with the scallions, oil, lime juice, sugar, ginger, spices, salt, and peppers. Process until smooth.

3 Spread the marinade all over the meat so that it is well covered. Place the meat in a dish, cover, and marinate in the refrigerator at least 2 hours.

4 Preheat a charcoal grill or broiler, setting the rack 4 to 5 inches from the heat. Remove the meat from the refrigerator and let come to room temperature.

5 Remove the excess marinade and add the pork to the grill or broiler. Cook the pork, making sure that the meat in the thickest part is no longer pink.

6 Transfer the pork to a platter, cover with foil, and keep warm. Brush the sweet potato slices and banana with the remaining marinade and add to the grill or broiler. Cook 4 to 6 minutes or until browned and softened, brushing occasionally with any remaining marinade or olive oil.

PER SERVING
Calories **329**, Saturated Fat **4g**, Total Fat **12g**, Sodium **140mg**, Cholesterol **76mg**, Protein **24g**, Carbohydrate **33g**, Fiber **3g**.

Ginger and lime give an authentic Caribbean flavor.

Grilled Pork Fajitas

This Tex-Mex classic works equally well when made with flank steak. If you have time, serve the filling in tortilla bowls (see box) – kids love them. Garnish with tomato salsa and a dollop of low-fat sour cream.

- Serves **6**
- Preparation Time **35 minutes** plus marinating time
- Cooking Time **30 minutes**

---

6 pork shoulder blade steaks (4 ounces each)

¹/₈ teaspoon each salt, pepper, and ground cumin

2 tablespoons lime or lemon juice

2 tablespoons olive or canola oil, more as necessary

2 tablespoons chopped fresh cilantro or parsley

1 tablespoon red wine vinegar

2 cloves garlic, finely chopped

2 large red or yellow onions, sliced into rings

2 sweet red or green peppers, cut into ¹/₄-inch strips

3 zucchini, thinly sliced diagonally

12 flour tortillas (10" diameter)

1 Using a sharp knife, trim all the fat from the pork. Season the meat with the salt, pepper, and cumin.

2 Make the marinade: In a small bowl, combine the lime juice, oil, cilantro, vinegar, and garlic until blended. Place the meat in a small dish and pour the marinade over it. Turn the meat so it is thoroughly coated. Cover and marinate in the refrigerator at least 2 hours.

3 Preheat a charcoal grill or broiler, setting the rack 4 to 5 inches from the heat. Remove the meat from the refrigerator and allow to come to room temperature. Spoon the marinade into a small bowl.

4 Add the pork to the grill or broiler and cook about 7 minutes on each side or until cooked through. Meanwhile, using a small brush, coat the onions, peppers, and zucchini with the marinade.

5 Transfer the pork to a platter, cover with foil, and keep warm. Place the vegetables on a piece of foil, lay on the grill or broiler, and grill 5 to 6 minutes on each side or until browned and softened, brushing occasionally with any remaining marinade or olive oil.

Grilled Pork Fajitas are lightly spiced with lime, cumin, and garlic.

6 Thinly slice the pork across the grain. Wrap tortillas in aluminum foil and place on a plate over a pan of simmering water for about 5 minutes. Mound some of the sliced meat and vegetables along the center of each tortilla and fold the edges over the filling mixture.

PER SERVING
Calories **458**, Saturated Fat **4g**, Total Fat **17g**, Sodium **30mg**, Cholesterol **76mg**, Protein **138g**, Carbohydrate **47g**, Fiber **5g**.

MAKING TORTILLA BOWLS

1 *Place a tortilla over an upturned heatproof bowl and invert a second bowl on top.*

2 *Bake in the oven at 350°F for 5 to 7 minutes until golden and crisp. Remove the bowls.*

3 *Holding the tortilla bowl very carefully, add the desired filling, then serve.*

Grilled Beef with Peach Relish

Reduce fat ▪ *If you like steak slathered with sauce, you'll love this healthy version. Begin with a lean cut of meat, then tenderize it in a vinegar marinade. Grill – with no added fat – on a barbecue or stovetop grill or in a broiler.*

Add nutrients ▪ *Top with a luscious fruit relish or vegetable sauce for extra vitamins.*

• Serves 4 • Preparation Time **20 minutes plus marinating time** • Cooking Time **7 minutes**

PER SERVING
Calories **235**, Saturated Fat **2g**, Total Fat **7g**, Sodium **127mg**, Cholesterol **61mg**, Protein **26g**, Carbohydrate **17g**, Fiber **2g**.

4 thin slices lean beef top round (about 4 ounces each)	1 pound fresh peaches or mango
⅛ teaspoon each salt and pepper	1 tablespoon honey
2 teaspoons olive or canola oil	1 teaspoon lemon juice
1 teaspoon red wine vinegar	1 teaspoon finely chopped fresh ginger or ¼ teaspoon ground
2 scallions, finely chopped	⅛ teaspoon hot red pepper flakes

1 With a sharp knife, trim fat from steaks. Place 2 steaks between 2 sheets of wax paper and lightly pound with a rolling pin. Season with salt and pepper.

2 Make the marinade mixture: In a small bowl, combine the oil with the vinegar and scallions. Place the meat on a shallow plate and spoon the marinade over it.

3 Turn the meat in the mixture to coat thoroughly. Allow the meat to marinate in the refrigerator at least 1 hour.

*The fruit provides just the right sweet but piquant flavor – **Grilled Beef with Peach Relish**.*

4 Meanwhile, make the peach relish: Peel the peaches and coarsely chop them either in a food processor or by hand.

5 Place the chopped peaches in a bowl and combine with the honey, lemon juice, ginger, and hot pepper flakes. Cover and allow to stand at least 30 minutes.

6 Heat a cast-iron grill pan until very hot and a drop of water evaporates immediately. Grill steaks about 2 minutes on each side. Serve with the peach relish.

Grilled Beef with Mushroom Gravy

- Serves **4**
- Preparation Time **15 minutes**
- Cooking Time **25 minutes**

4 thin slices lean beef top round (about 4 ounces each)
¹/₈ teaspoon each salt and pepper
2 teaspoons olive or canola oil
1 clove garlic, finely chopped
8 ounces fresh mushrooms, sliced
¹/₂ cup beef stock, page 18
¹/₃ cup low-fat sour cream
2 tablespoons chopped parsley

1 Prepare the steaks as in Step 1 of the master recipe.

2 In a nonstick skillet, heat oil over moderate heat. Sauté garlic about 2 minutes. Add mushrooms and sauté about 5 minutes.

3 Stir in stock, bring to a boil, cover, and gently simmer about 5 minutes or until mushrooms are very soft. Stir in sour cream, cover, and remove from the heat.

4 Prepare grill pan as in Step 6 of the master recipe. Add steaks and cook about 2 minutes on each side or until cooked through. (Divide into batches if necessary.)

5 Stir the parsley into mushroom gravy and serve with the steaks.

PER SERVING
Calories **246**, Saturated Fat **2g**, Total Fat **13g**, Sodium **160mg**, Cholesterol **61mg**, Protein **26g**, Carbohydrate **3g**, Fiber **1g**.

Grilled Pork Cutlets in Barbecue Sauce

- Serves **4**
- Preparation Time **10 minutes**
- Cooking Time **20 minutes**

1 pound lean pork tenderloin, cut across into 8 thin slices
¹/₈ teaspoon each salt and pepper
1 can (14 ounces) crushed plum tomatoes
¹/₃ cup unsweetened apple juice
2 tablespoons dark brown sugar
1 tablespoon cider vinegar
¹/₄ teaspoon hot red pepper sauce

1 Prepare the meat as in Step 1 of the master recipe.

2 Make the barbecue sauce: In a saucepan, combine the tomatoes with the apple juice, sugar, vinegar, and hot red pepper sauce. Bring to a boil over moderate heat and gently simmer about 10 minutes or until a rich sauce forms.

3 Prepare grill pan as in Step 6 of the master recipe. Add the pork slices and cook about 2 minutes on each side or until cooked through.

4 Transfer to a platter and pour the barbecue sauce over pork.

PER SERVING
Calories **182**, Saturated Fat **1g**, Total Fat **3g**, Sodium **288mg**, Cholesterol **74mg**, Protein **25g**, Carbohydrate **14g**, Fiber **1g**.

Grilled Pork Cutlets with Cranberries

- Serves **4**
- Preparation Time **15 minutes**
- Cooking Time **25 minutes**

1 pound lean pork tenderloin, cut across into 8 thin slices
¹/₄ teaspoon ground ginger
¹/₈ teaspoon each salt and pepper
1 package (12 ounces) frozen cranberries, thawed
¹/₂ cup orange juice
¹/₂ cup chicken stock, page 18
1 teaspoon grated orange zest
2 sweet apples, cored and cut across into rings

1 Prepare the meat as in Step 1 of the master recipe, seasoning meat with ginger, salt, and pepper.

2 Make the cranberry sauce: In a saucepan, combine cranberries, orange juice, stock, and orange zest. Gently simmer about 10 minutes, until a rich sauce forms.

3 Prepare grill pan as in Step 6 of the master recipe. Cook pork about 2 minutes on each side, until cooked through. Transfer to a platter, cover, and keep warm. Grill apples 2 to 3 minutes on each side.

4 Transfer apples to the platter. Serve the pork with the cranberry sauce and grilled apples.

PER SERVING
Calories **226**, Saturated Fat **1g**, Total Fat **3g**, Sodium **140mg**, Cholesterol **74mg**, Protein **25g**, Carbohydrate **25g**, Fiber **2g**.

Pork Stir-Fry with Scallions

Cooking technique ■ *Stir-frying over high heat sears the meat, making it juicy and tender. The vegetables stay colorful, crisp, and nutritious.*
Reduce fat ■ *Make sure the oil is very hot so that it is not absorbed by the food.*

● Serves **4** ● Preparation Time **15 minutes** plus marinating time ● Cooking Time **10 minutes**

PER SERVING
Calories **237**, Saturated Fat **3g**,
Total Fat **10g**, Sodium **343mg**,
Cholesterol **71mg**, Protein **28g**,
Carbohydrate **7g**, Fiber **2g**.

1 pound boneless pork loin
¹/₂ cup beef stock, page 18
2 tablespoons reduced-sodium soy sauce
1 tablespoon rice vinegar or dry sherry (optional)
2¹/₂ teaspoons cornstarch

¹/₈ teaspoon hot red pepper flakes
¹/₄ teaspoon pepper
2 teaspoons canola oil
2 tablespoons thinly sliced fresh ginger
12 ounces scallions, trimmed and diagonally cut into 1-inch pieces

1 Using a sharp knife, trim all the fat from the pork. Holding the knife at a 45° angle, cut the pork across the grain into paper-thin slices.

2 In a medium bowl, make the marinade: Combine the beef stock with the soy sauce, vinegar, cornstarch, pepper flakes, and pepper; stir until blended.

3 Add the pork to the marinade and toss together to coat thoroughly. Cover the bowl and marinate in the refrigerator, stirring occasionally, at least 1 hour.

Pork Stir-Fry with Scallions *can be served with noodles or rice. For an easy garnish, sprinkle with sesame seeds.*

4 Heat a nonstick wok or large skillet over high heat. Heat oil until it sizzles when a piece of ginger is added. Stir-fry remaining pieces of ginger for 15 seconds.

5 Add the scallions and stir-fry about 2 minutes or until they are slightly browned and softened. Transfer to a plate and reserve.

6 Reserve marinade; stir-fry pork 2 to 3 minutes. Return ginger and scallions to wok, add marinade, and cook 3 to 4 minutes or until sauce thickens.

Pork Stir-Fry with Snow Peas

- Serves **4**
- Preparation Time **20 minutes**
- Cooking Time **10 minutes**

1 pound boneless pork loin or beef flank steak

8 ounces sliced fresh mushrooms or ¹/₂ ounce dried

¹/₂ cup chicken stock, page 18

3 teaspoons canola oil

Dash of hot chili oil (optional)

1 large onion, thinly sliced

1 sweet red or green pepper, thinly sliced

2 teaspoons cornstarch

8 ounces snow peas

¹/₈ teaspoon each salt and pepper

1 Trim and slice pork as in Step 1 of the master recipe.

2 If using dried mushrooms, soak in stock according to package directions. Drain, reserving stock, and slice. Set aside.

3 Heat 2 teaspoons of oil and chili oil, if using, as in Step 4 of master recipe, testing oil with onion. Add onion, sweet pepper, and mushrooms. Stir-fry as in Step 5 of master recipe.

4 Blend cornstarch into stock. Heat remaining oil; stir-fry pork 2 to 3 minutes. Add vegetables, stock, snow peas, salt, and pepper and stir-fry 3 to 4 minutes.

PER SERVING
Calories **280**, Saturated Fat **3g**, Total Fat **12g**, Sodium **165mg**, Cholesterol **71mg**, Protein **29g**, Carbohydrate **14g**, Fiber **2g**.

Beef Stir-Fry with Broccoli Rabe

- Serves **4**
- Preparation Time **15 minutes** plus marinating time
- Cooking Time **10 minutes**

1 pound lean London broil or flank steak

¹/₂ cup beef stock, page 18

2 tablespoons reduced-sodium soy sauce

1 tablespoon sherry (optional)

2¹/₂ teaspoons cornstarch

¹/₄ teaspoon pepper

2 teaspoons canola oil

4 cloves garlic, finely sliced

1 pound broccoli rabe or broccoli, cut into 2-inch pieces

1 sweet red pepper, sliced

1 Trim and slice beef as in Step 1 of the master recipe.

2 Make the marinade: Combine stock, soy sauce, sherry, if using, cornstarch, and pepper. Marinate beef as in Step 3 of master recipe.

3 Heat oil and stir-fry garlic 15 seconds; add broccoli rabe and sweet pepper and stir-fry 2 minutes as in Step 5 of master recipe.

4 Reserve marinade and stir-fry meat 2 to 3 minutes. Add vegetables and marinade and cook 1 to 2 minutes or until sauce thickens.

PER SERVING
Calories **265**, Saturated Fat **5g**, Total Fat **13g**, Sodium **379mg**, Cholesterol **57mg**, Protein **28g**, Carbohydrate **10g**, Fiber **4g**.

Lamb and Napa Cabbage Stir-Fry

- Serves **6**
- Preparation Time **15 minutes** plus marinating time
- Cooking Time **10 minutes**

1 pound lean lamb shoulder

¹/₂ cup beef stock, page 18

2 tablespoons lime juice

¹/₄ teaspoon hot red pepper flakes

2 teaspoons minced fresh ginger

2¹/₂ teaspoons cornstarch

2 teaspoons canola oil

2 cloves garlic, finely chopped

1 small head Napa (Chinese) cabbage, cored and shredded

¹/₈ teaspoon each salt and pepper

¹/₄ cup toasted cashews or unsalted peanuts (optional)

1 Trim and slice lamb as in Step 1 of the master recipe.

2 In a bowl, make the marinade: Combine stock, lime juice, hot red pepper flakes, ginger, and cornstarch. Marinate lamb as in Step 3 of the master recipe.

3 Stir-fry garlic as in Step 4, and cabbage as in Step 5 of the master recipe.

4 Reserve marinade and stir-fry meat 2 to 3 minutes; add cabbage, marinade, salt, pepper, and nuts, if using, and cook 1 to 2 minutes or until sauce thickens.

PER SERVING
Calories **143**, Saturated Fat **2g**, Total Fat **7g**, Sodium **105mg**, Cholesterol **50mg**, Protein **16g**, Carbohydrate **4g**, Fiber **2g**.

Mexican Pork Stew

Reduce fat ▪ *To make a lean and healthful stew, use just 4 ounces of meat per person. Add beans or legumes for more protein.*

Add nutrients ▪ *The dried beans boost the fiber, while the sweet peppers and tomatoes contribute vitamin C, and the onions add folacin.*

• Serves **6** • Preparation Time **25 minutes** • Cooking Time **2½ hours**

PER SERVING
Calories **309**, Saturated Fat **3g**, Total Fat **11g**, Sodium **376mg**, Cholesterol **57mg**, Protein **25g**, Carbohydrate **33g**, Fiber **9g**.

- 1½ pounds boneless pork shoulder
- 1 dried hot or mild chili pepper, such as ancho or pasilla
- 1½ tablespoons olive or canola oil
- 2 sweet green peppers, diced
- 2 large onions, coarsely chopped
- 2 cloves garlic, finely chopped
- ½ teaspoon ground cumin
- 1 tablespoon all-purpose flour
- 1 can (28 ounces) crushed tomatoes
- 2 cups chicken or beef stock, page 18
- 1 tablespoon unsweetened cocoa
- 1 can (16 ounces) red kidney beans, drained and rinsed
- ⅛ teaspoon each salt and pepper

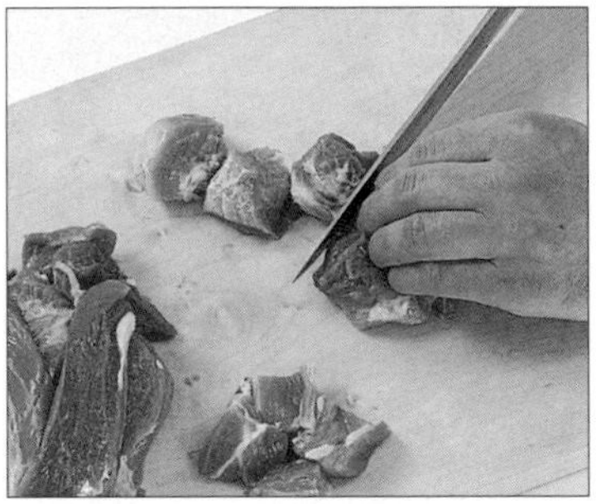

1 Using a sharp knife, trim all the fat and cartilage from the pork. Cut the meat into 1-inch strips, then cut the strips across into 1-inch cubes.

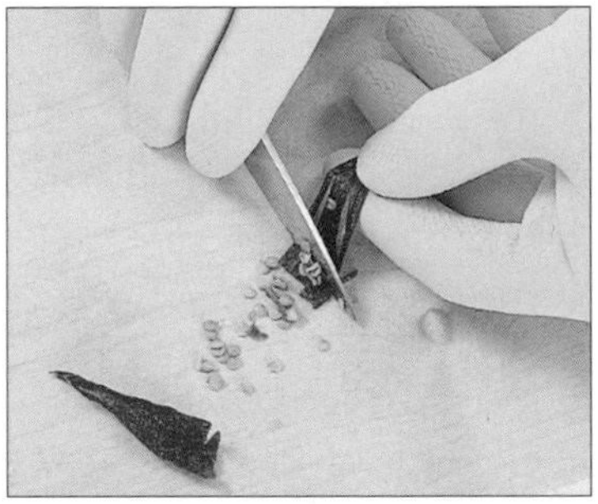

2 Place the chili pepper in a small bowl and cover with boiling water. Allow to soak at least 20 minutes or until very soft. Drain the chili pepper and, wearing rubber gloves, remove the core and seeds and finely chop.

3 In a Dutch oven, heat 1 tablespoon oil over moderately high heat. Sauté green peppers, onions, and garlic, stirring, about 10 minutes or until golden. Stir in cumin and cook 1 to 2 minutes longer or until fragrant.

4 Using a slotted spoon, transfer the vegetables to a plate. Heat remaining oil over moderately high heat. Sauté the pork, stirring, 5 to 7 minutes or until well browned on all sides. Sprinkle with the flour and cook, stirring, about 1 to 2 minutes longer.

5 Return the vegetables to the Dutch oven with the chili pepper, canned tomatoes, and stock. Bring to a boil, then cover with the lid and simmer very gently about 2 hours or until the pork is very tender when pierced with a table fork.

6 Place cocoa in a small bowl. Add about ½ cup of the cooking liquid and stir to blend well. Stir mixture back into Dutch oven with the beans and season with salt and pepper. Simmer about 5 minutes longer to heat through and blend the flavors.

*The secret ingredient in **Mexican Pork Stew** is a touch of chocolate, which blends with the spices to create dark, rich flavor.*
Serve it with Home-Style Corn Bread, page 310.

Old-Fashioned Beef Stew

For a new twist on a traditional beef stew – and more fiber –
try adding the black beans. If you prefer, you can use
red or white kidney beans.

- Serves 6
- Preparation Time **20 minutes**
- Cooking Time **2¹/₂ hours**

1¹/₂ **pounds boneless lean**
beef chuck steak

1¹/₂ **tablespoons olive or**
canola oil

6 **carrots, thickly sliced**
diagonally

2 **sweet green or red peppers,**
cubed

8 **ounces frozen pearl onions,**
thawed

1 **tablespoon all-purpose flour**

1–2 **cups beef stock, page 18**

1 **cup dark beer or beef stock**

1 **can (28 ounces) crushed**
tomatoes

1 **bay leaf**

1 **can (16 ounces) black beans,**
drained and rinsed (optional)

¹/₈ **teaspoon each salt and pepper**

1 Using a sharp knife, trim all the
fat and cartilage from the beef.
Cut the meat into 1-inch cubes.

2 In a Dutch oven, heat
1 tablespoon oil over high heat.
Sauté the carrots, sweet peppers,
and onions about 10 minutes
or until browned. Remove from
heat and, with a slotted spoon,
transfer the vegetables to a
plate and reserve.

3 Heat remaining oil in the Dutch
oven. Add the beef cubes and
sauté, stirring, about 3 minutes or
until well browned on all sides.
Sprinkle the flour over the meat
and cook 1 to 2 minutes longer.

4 Return the vegetables to
the Dutch oven with 1 cup of
stock and the beer, tomatoes,
and bay leaf. Bring to a boil,
cover, and gently simmer about
2 to 2¹/₂ hours or until the beef
is very tender when pierced with
a table fork. Add up to 1 cup
additional stock if stew becomes
too thick. Remove bay leaf, stir
in black beans, and cook about
5 minutes or until heated through.
Season with salt and pepper.

PER SERVING
Calories **350**, Saturated Fat **4g**,
Total Fat **12g**, Sodium **349mg**,
Cholesterol **103mg**, Protein **38g**,
Carbohydrate **20g**, Fiber **4g**.

TRIMMING MEAT

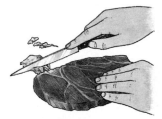

1 *With a sharp knife, trim off*
all the cartilage and fat.

2 *Cut the meat into even*
strips and then into cubes.

Spiced Beef Stew with Dried Fruit

This British-inspired stew combines beef, fruit, and
spices with delicious results. The barley
increases the fiber.

- Serves 6
- Preparation Time **10 minutes**
- Cooking Time **2¹/₂ hours**

1¹/₂ **pounds lean chuck steak**

1¹/₂ **tablespoons olive or**
canola oil

2 **large onions, thinly sliced**

1 **tablespoon all-purpose flour**

¹/₂ **teaspoon each ground cumin**
and coriander

1¹/₂–2¹/₂ **cups beef stock,**
page 18

1 **can (28 ounces) crushed**
tomatoes

¹/₂ **cup pearl barley**

¹/₂ **cup pitted dried apricots,**
halved

¹/₂ **cup pitted prunes, halved**

¹/₈ **teaspoon each salt and pepper**

1 Using a sharp knife, trim all the
fat and cartilage from the beef.
Cut the meat into 1-inch cubes.

2 In a Dutch oven, heat
1 tablespoon oil over moderate
heat. Sauté the onions about
10 minutes or until well browned.
With a slotted spoon, transfer
the onions to a plate.

3 Heat the remaining oil in
the Dutch oven. Add the beef
cubes and sauté, stirring, about
3 minutes or until well browned
on all sides. Sprinkle the flour
and ground spices over the
meat and cook 1 to 2 minutes
longer or until the flour and
spices are absorbed.

4 Return the onions to the
Dutch oven with 1¹/₂ cups of
stock and the tomatoes. Bring to
a boil, cover, and gently simmer
about 1 hour or until the beef is
half cooked. Stir in the barley,
apricots, and prunes and season
with salt and pepper. Cover the
stew and cook about 1 to 1¹/₂
hours longer or until the meat
is very tender when pierced
with a table fork. Add up to
1 cup additional stock if stew
becomes too thick.

PER SERVING
Calories **424**, Saturated Fat **4g**,
Total Fat **12g**, Sodium **325mg**,
Cholesterol **103mg**, Protein **40g**,
Carbohydrate **40g**, Fiber **7g**.

Dried prunes and apricots are
good sources of fiber and iron.

Mediterranean Lamb Stew

Rosemary, basil, and garlic provide the seasoning in this aromatic stew, so you can use less salt.

- Serves **6**
- Preparation Time **20 minutes**
- Cooking Time **2 hours 40 minutes**

1¹/₂ pounds boned lean lamb shoulder

1¹/₂ tablespoons olive or canola oil

2 large onions, sliced

2 cloves garlic, finely chopped

1 tablespoon all-purpose flour

2 teaspoons chopped fresh rosemary or 1 teaspoon dried

1–2 cups beef stock, page 18

1¹/₂ cups reduced-sodium tomato juice

1 can (16 ounces) canned chick-peas, drained and rinsed

2 zucchini, cubed

1 pint cherry tomatoes, halved

¹/₈ teaspoon each salt and pepper

2 teaspoons chopped fresh basil or 1 teaspoon dried

1 Using a sharp knife, trim all the fat and cartilage from the lamb. Cut the meat into 1-inch cubes.

2 In a Dutch oven, heat 1 table-spoon oil over moderate heat. Add the onions and garlic and sauté about 10 minutes or until well browned. With a slotted spoon transfer to a plate.

3 In the Dutch oven, heat the remaining oil over moderately high heat. Sauté the lamb, stirring, about 3 minutes or until well browned on all sides. Sprinkle the flour and rosemary over the meat and cook about 1¹/₂ minutes longer or until flour is absorbed.

4 Return the onions to the Dutch oven with 1 cup of stock and the tomato juice. Bring to a boil, cover, and gently simmer about 1 hour or until the lamb is half cooked. Stir in chick-peas and continue cooking 1 to 1¹/₄ hours longer or until the meat is almost tender. Stir in zucchini, cherry tomatoes, salt, pepper, and basil. Add up to 1 cup additional stock if stew becomes too thick. Cook about 15 minutes longer or until meat is very tender when pierced with a table fork.

PER SERVING
Calories **332**, Saturated Fat **3g**, Total Fat **13g**, Sodium **439mg**, Cholesterol **75mg**, Protein **29g**, Carbohydrate **26g**, Fiber **7g**.

*Tomatoes, zucchini, and chick-peas add color and flavor to **Mediterranean Lamb Stew** – serve it with crusty bread rolls.*

LOW-FAT WAYS TO THICKEN STEWS

1 *Sprinkle stew with 1 table-spoon of all-purpose flour. Stir into the juices and simmer until thickened.*

2 *Blend 1 tablespoon of corn-starch with 2 tablespoons of water. Stir into the stew and simmer until thickened.*

GETTING AHEAD

Stews are ideal make-aheads because the flavor of the meat intensifies, and the herbs and spices become more fragrant. Prepare the stew as directed and refrigerate overnight in a covered casserole. If your recipe requires adding fresh vegetables at the last minute, prepare them in advance and refrigerate in sealed plastic bags. When ready to serve, reheat the stew until very hot, adding any last-minute vegetables as directed.

Spinach-Stuffed Meat Loaf

Reduce fat ■ *Extend lean ground beef with ground turkey and a spinach stuffing.*
Add nutrients ■ *Roast fresh vegetables around the meat loaf to make a nutritious sauce.*

● Serves **6** ● Preparation Time **30 minutes** ● Cooking Time **1½ hours**

PER SERVING
Calories **294**, Saturated Fat **2g**,
Total Fat **6g**, Sodium **405mg**,
Cholesterol **71mg**, Protein **32g**,
Carbohydrate **28g**, Fiber **2g**.

1 pound lean ground beef
8 ounces lean ground turkey
1 small onion, finely chopped
½ cup fresh bread crumbs
⅛ teaspoon garlic salt
1 tablespoon tomato paste
1 egg white
½ cup part-skim ricotta cheese

1 package (10 ounces) frozen
  chopped spinach, thawed
  and drained
⅛ teaspoon each salt and pepper
2 large onions, thinly sliced
2 carrots, coarsely chopped
1 can (28 ounces) crushed
  tomatoes

1 In a bowl, mix beef, turkey,
chopped onion, bread crumbs,
garlic salt, and tomato paste. In
another bowl, mix egg white,
ricotta, spinach, salt, and pepper.

2 Preheat oven to 350°F.
Turn out the beef mixture
onto a large sheet of wax paper,
and form into a 9- by 10-inch
rectangle with your hands.

3 Spoon the spinach stuffing
lengthwise down the center
of the meat, leaving about 1 inch
uncovered at each short end.

Spinach-Stuffed Meat Loaf *is served with a pan tomato sauce and Creamy Low-Fat Mashed Potatoes, page 185.*

4 With the help of the wax paper, lift the long edges of the meat. Fold the meat over the stuffing to enclose it.

5 Using your fingers, pinch the edges of the meat together. Place loaf seam side down in a nonstick roasting pan. Add onions, carrots, and tomatoes to pan.

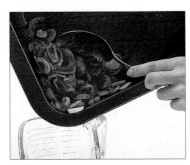

6 Bake about 1½ hours or until meat and vegetables are cooked. Transfer meat to platter. Purée vegetables in a blender and serve sauce with the meat loaf.

Meat Loaf with Vegetable Stuffing

- Serves **6**
- Preparation Time **20 minutes**
- Cooking Time **1½ hours**

1 pound lean ground beef

8 ounces lean ground pork

1 small onion, finely chopped

½ cup fresh bread crumbs

1 tablespoon tomato paste

⅛ teaspoon garlic salt

1 package (10 ounces) frozen peas and carrots, thawed

1 egg white

½ cup part-skim ricotta cheese

⅛ teaspoon each salt and pepper

1½ cups reduced-sodium tomato sauce (optional)

1 Preheat the oven to 350°F. In a bowl, mix beef, pork, onion, bread crumbs, tomato paste, and garlic salt.

2 In another bowl, combine vegetables with egg white, ricotta cheese, salt, and pepper.

3 Form meat into a rectangle, spoon on stuffing, and seal meat around as in the master recipe. Bake about 1½ hours or until meat is cooked. Heat the tomato sauce, if using, and serve with the meat loaf.

PER SERVING
Calories **253**, Saturated Fat **1g**, Total Fat **5g**, Sodium **416mg**, Cholesterol **69mg**, Protein **30g**, Carbohydrate **21g**, Fiber **4g**.

Lamb Meat Loaf on a Bed of Cabbage

- Serves **6**
- Preparation Time **15 minutes**
- Cooking Time **1½ hours**

1 teaspoon olive or canola oil

1 large onion, finely chopped

1 stalk celery, finely chopped

1 clove garlic, finely chopped

1 pound lean ground lamb

8 ounces lean ground beef

1 cup cooked long-grain rice

2 teaspoons Worcestershire sauce

⅛ teaspoon each salt and pepper

1 head green cabbage, cored and shredded

⅔ cup beef stock, page 18

1 Preheat oven to 350°F. Heat oil in skillet over moderate heat. Sauté onion, celery, and garlic about 4 minutes. Cool slightly.

2 In a bowl, mix lamb with beef, rice, Worcestershire sauce, salt, pepper, and onion mixture. Form into a loaf about 8 by 3 inches.

3 Place cabbage in nonstick roasting pan. Place meat loaf on top and pour stock over. Bake about 1½ hours or until meat is cooked. Transfer meat loaf and cabbage to serving platter.

PER SERVING
Calories **255**, Saturated Fat **5g**, Total Fat **12g**, Sodium **170mg**, Cholesterol **75mg**, Protein **31g**, Carbohydrate **25g**, Fiber **5g**.

Mini Pork Loaves with Apricots

- Serves **6**
- Preparation Time **25 minutes**
- Cooking Time **30 minutes**

½ cup dried pitted apricots

1 pound lean ground pork

8 ounces lean ground turkey

1 cup cooked long-grain rice or couscous

2 stalks celery, finely chopped

1 egg white

½ teaspoon dried sage, crumbled

¼ teaspoon dried oregano

⅛ teaspoon each salt and pepper

6 ripe plum tomatoes

1 Preheat oven to 350°F. Soak apricots in a bowl of boiling water about 10 minutes. Drain, dry with paper towels, and coarsely chop.

2 In a bowl, combine pork with turkey, rice, celery, egg white, sage, oregano, salt, and pepper. Stir in chopped apricots.

3 Divide meat into 6 portions. Form into small loaves and transfer to a nonstick roasting pan.

4 Thinly slice tomatoes. Arrange slices on top of each mini loaf. Bake about 30 minutes or until meat is cooked.

PER SERVING
Calories **250**, Saturated Fat **4g**, Total Fat **11g**, Sodium **130mg**, Cholesterol **80mg**, Protein **28g**, Carbohydrate **23g**, Fiber **3g**.

Italian Meatballs in Tomato Sauce

Cooking technique ▪ *Use 4 ounces of meat per person and extend it with bread crumbs. Then smother the meatballs in a vitamin-rich sauce and serve over pasta or noodles.*

Reduce fat ▪ *Replace some of the meat with low-fat ground turkey. Instead of frying the meatballs, brown them in the oven – the fat will drip off. For binding, use an egg white.*

● Serves 4 ● Preparation Time **25 minutes** ● Cooking Time **50 minutes**

PER SERVING
Calories **281**, Saturated Fat **3g**,
Total Fat **10g**, Sodium **523mg**,
Cholesterol **70mg**, Protein **29g**,
Carbohydrate **21g**, Fiber **4g**.

1½ teaspoons olive or canola oil

2 cloves garlic, finely chopped

2 stalks celery, finely chopped

8 ounces lean ground beef

8 ounces lean ground pork or turkey

½ cup fresh bread crumbs

1 egg white

¼ teaspoon each dried oregano and basil

Vegetable oil cooking spray

1 can (28 ounces) crushed tomatoes

2 onions, finely chopped

2 tablespoons tomato paste

½ cup sliced black olives (optional)

2 tablespoons chopped parsley or 1 tablespoon dried

⅛ teaspoon pepper

1 Preheat oven to 350°F. In a small skillet, heat the oil over moderate heat. Add the garlic and celery and sauté about 5 minutes or until softened and lightly browned. Remove from the heat and allow to cool slightly.

2 In a bowl, combine the ground beef, ground pork, bread crumbs, egg white, oregano, and basil. Stir in the celery mixture until just combined.

3 Using your hands, shape the mixture into 16 meatballs about 1½ inches across (it is easier to shape the meatballs if you wet your hands first).

4 Spray a rack with vegetable oil cooking spray. Place the meatballs on the rack over a baking tray, and bake 10 to 15 minutes or until well browned on all sides, turning occasionally. Transfer to a plate and reserve.

5 Meanwhile, in a large non-stick skillet over moderate heat, combine the tomatoes, onions, and tomato paste and bring to a boil. Cover and simmer the mixture about 12 minutes or until slightly thickened.

6 Return the meatballs to the skillet with the black olives, if using. Cover and cook about 20 minutes longer or until cooked through. Stir the parsley into the tomato sauce and season with pepper.

Italian Meatballs in Tomato Sauce *is teamed with a bowl of hot pasta. Penne is shown here,
but spaghetti, fusilli, or wagon wheels would also be good.*

German Meatballs in Cream Sauce

Chop the onion very fine to help the meatballs hold together. Cover the baking tray with pierced foil so the fat drips off.

- Serves **4**
- Preparation Time **20 minutes**
- Cooking Time **45 minutes**

Caraway seeds

Capers

---

1 pound lean ground pork

$^1/_2$ cup fresh whole-wheat bread crumbs

1 onion, finely chopped

1 egg white

$^1/_4$ teaspoon paprika

$^1/_4$ teaspoon crushed caraway or fennel seeds

Vegetable oil cooking spray

1 can (14 ounces) crushed tomatoes

1 cup beef stock, page 18

1 tablespoon finely chopped capers (optional)

$^1/_4$ cup low-fat sour cream

$^1/_8$ teaspoon each salt and pepper

---

1 In a bowl, combine the ground pork, bread crumbs, onion, egg white, paprika, and caraway or fennel seeds until just mixed.

2 Using your hands, shape the mixture into 24 meatballs about 1 inch across (it is easier to shape the meatballs if you wet your hands first).

3 Spray a rack with vegetable-oil cooking spray. Place the meatballs on the rack over a baking tray, and bake about 10 minutes or until well browned on all sides, turning occasionally. Transfer to a plate and reserve.

4 In a large nonstick skillet over moderate heat, combine the tomatoes, beef stock, and capers, if using, and bring to a boil. Simmer the mixture about 5 minutes or until slightly thickened.

5 Add the meatballs to the skillet, cover, and cook about 25 minutes longer or until cooked through. Stir in the sour cream and season with salt and pepper.

COOKING TIP

Crush caraway seeds with the end of a rolling pin and use immediately – do not store.

PER SERVING
Calories **265**, Saturated Fat **3g**, Total Fat **13g**, Sodium **373mg**, Cholesterol **76mg**, Protein **25g**, Carbohydrate **11g**, Fiber **2g**.

Hawaiian Meatballs in Sweet and Sour Sauce

The oats extend the meat, and they add fiber.

- Serves **4**
- Preparation Time **15 minutes**
- Cooking Time **45 minutes**

---

1 pound lean ground pork

$^1/_3$ cup quick-cooking oats

$^1/_4$ teaspoon ground ginger

2 tablespoons chopped scallions

1 egg white

2 teaspoons reduced-sodium soy sauce

Vegetable oil cooking spray

$1^1/_2$ teaspoons olive or canola oil

1 large sweet red or green pepper, diced

1 cup beef stock, page 18

$^1/_2$ cup crushed unsweetened pineapple

2 teaspoons red wine vinegar

$^1/_8$ teaspoon each salt and pepper

---

1 In a bowl, combine the ground pork with the oats, ginger, scallions, egg white, and soy sauce until just mixed.

2 Using your hands, shape the mixture into 24 meatballs about 1 inch across (it is easier to shape the meatballs if you wet your hands first).

3 Spray a rack with vegetable oil cooking spray. Place the meatballs on the rack over a baking tray, and bake about 10 minutes or until well browned on all sides, turning occasionally. Transfer to a plate and reserve.

4 In a large nonstick skillet, heat the oil over moderate heat. Add the sweet pepper to the skillet and sauté 5 to 7 minutes or until softened and browned. Stir in the stock, pineapple, and vinegar and bring to a boil. Simmer the mixture about 7 minutes or until slightly thickened.

5 Add the meatballs to the skillet, cover, and simmer about 15 minutes or until cooked through. Season with salt and pepper.

PER SERVING
Calories **268**, Saturated Fat **4g**, Total Fat **12g**, Sodium **256mg**, Cholesterol **76mg**, Protein **26g**, Carbohydrate **13g**, Fiber **2g**.

Use fresh, unblemished scallions and sweet peppers for maximum vitamins and flavor.

Grilled Meatball Kabobs

Place a sheet of aluminum foil over the grill and prick holes through it. Place the kabobs on the foil and they will get all of the smoky barbecue flavor without falling through. Serve them with potatoes or rice and salad.

- Serves **4**
- Preparation Time **35 minutes**
- Cooking Time **15 minutes**

---

1 pound finely ground lamb or beef

¹/₂ cup fresh bread crumbs

1 small onion, minced

4 ounces mushrooms, very finely chopped

2 egg whites

¹/₂ teaspoon Worcestershire sauce

¹/₈ teaspoon each ground cumin and cayenne pepper

1 pint cherry tomatoes

1 large sweet green pepper, cut into 1-inch pieces

8 ounces frozen pearl onions, thawed

1¹/₂ tablespoons olive or canola oil

---

1 Preheat the grill or broiler. In a bowl, combine ground lamb, bread crumbs, onion, mushrooms, egg whites, Worcestershire sauce, cumin, and cayenne pepper.

2 Wet hands, and shape the meat mixture into 24 meatballs about 1 inch across. Onto 12 thin skewers, thread the cherry tomatoes, green pepper, pearl onions, and meatballs.

3 Place a sheet of foil on the grill or broiler pan and prick with a fork. Place the meatball and vegetable kabobs on top and brush with oil.

COOKING TIP
When threading meatballs or vegetables onto the skewers, leave a small space between each one. This helps them to cook evenly and quickly.

4 Cook the meatball and vegetable kabobs about 15 minutes, turning once and brushing with oil, or until well browned on all sides and the meat juices run clear.

PER SERVING
Calories **438**, Saturated Fat **12g**, Total Fat **32g**, Sodium **139mg**, Cholesterol **84mg**, Protein **23g**, Carbohydrate **14g**, Fiber **3g**.

Watercress and a baked potato make a meal of **Grilled Meatball Kabobs.**

TIPS FOR MAKING KABOBS

For vegetable kabobs, cut the vegetables to roughly the same size so that they all cook at the same time. Serve on the side with grilled meatballs.

The meatball mixture breaks up easily, so use thin skewers to avoid this. For flavor and color, alternate the meatballs with a selection of vegetables.

GETTING AHEAD

If you are using frozen ground lamb or beef, thaw it overnight in the refrigerator. If you are making the meatballs from fresh ground meat, they will improve in flavor if you make the mixture the day before and refrigerate it for about 8 hours. Chilling also makes the ground meat mixture firmer and easier to handle, so that when you form it into meatballs it will be easier to mold and less likely to break apart. To chill the ground meat mixture on the same day as cooking, place it in the freezer for about an hour.

Beef and Turkey Chili

Reduce fat ▪ *For a chili with real beef flavor and less fat, use a combination of two parts beef to one part turkey. Then sauté the meat in its own juices – you don't need added oil. While the vegetables are cooking, drain the meat to remove still more fat.*

Add nutrients ▪ *Corn, kidney beans, and other vegetables add fiber as well as vitamins.*

● Serves **6** ● Preparation Time **20 minutes** ● Cooking Time **50–60 minutes**

PER SERVING
Calories **340**, Saturated Fat **2g**,
Total Fat **7g**, Sodium **546mg**,
Cholesterol **68mg**, Protein **34g**,
Carbohydrate **37g**, Fiber **8g**.

1 pound lean ground beef

8 ounces lean ground turkey

1 tablespoon olive or canola oil

2 large onions, coarsely chopped

3 cloves garlic, finely chopped

3 sweet red or green peppers, coarsely chopped

1 tablespoon chili powder or more to taste

1 teaspoon each ground cumin and coriander

1 can (28 ounces) crushed tomatoes

Dash of hot red pepper sauce (optional)

¹/₈ teaspoon pepper

1 package (10 ounces) frozen corn kernels, thawed

1 can (16 ounces) red kidney beans, drained and rinsed

1 Heat a Dutch oven over moderately high heat until hot. Add the beef and turkey and sauté, stirring frequently, about 7 minutes or until the meat has lost its pink color and has released its juices.

2 Remove from the heat and spoon the meat into a sieve set over a bowl. Allow all the fat to drain from the meat; it will take at least 10 minutes.

3 Meanwhile, in the Dutch oven, heat the oil over moderate heat. Add the onions and garlic and sauté 5 to 7 minutes or until softened and golden brown.

4 Stir in the sweet peppers, chili powder, and spices and cook about 5 minutes longer or until the peppers are slightly soft. Return the meat to the pan.

5 Stir in the crushed tomatoes, hot red pepper sauce, if using, and pepper and bring to a boil. Partially cover and simmer, stirring occasionally, 20 to 30 minutes or until the sauce thickens.

6 Stir in the corn kernels and kidney beans. Cover and cook about 5 minutes longer to heat through.

*Chili powder and ground cumin give **Beef and Turkey Chili** real Mexican flavor.
If you like your chili fiery hot, add 1 or 2 teaspoons more chili powder.*

Spicy Beef and Turkey Tacos

This spicy Mexican-style meat filling makes delicious burritos too. Just spoon over warmed flour tortillas.

- Serves 8
- Preparation Time 25 minutes
- Cooking Time 45 minutes

---

1 pound lean ground beef

8 ounces lean ground turkey

1 tablespoon olive or canola oil

1 onion, coarsely chopped

3 cloves garlic, finely chopped

1 sweet red or green pepper, coarsely chopped

1 tablespoon chili powder or more to taste

1 can (16 ounces) crushed tomatoes, drained

$^1/_8$ teaspoon each salt and pepper

16 taco shells

3 cups shredded iceberg lettuce

$^1/_2$ cup shredded jalapeño cheese or low-fat Cheddar cheese

---

1 Heat a Dutch oven over moderately high heat until hot. Add the beef and turkey and sauté, stirring frequently, about 7 minutes or until the meat has lost its pink color and has released it juices. Remove from the heat and spoon the meat into a sieve set over a bowl (see box). Drain the meat at least 10 minutes.

2 Meanwhile, in the Dutch oven, heat the oil over moderate heat. Add the onion and garlic and sauté 5 to 7 minutes or until softened and golden brown.

3 Stir in the sweet pepper and chili powder and cook about 5 minutes longer or until the pepper is slightly soft. Return the meat to the pan.

4 Preheat the oven according to taco shell package directions. Stir the tomatoes, salt, and pepper into the pan and bring to a boil. Cover and simmer, stirring occasionally, about 15 minutes or until a rich stew has formed.

5 Place the taco shells on a baking sheet and warm according to package directions.

6 Divide meat mixture among the taco shells, then sprinkle some of the lettuce and cheese on top.

PER SERVING
Calories **293**, Saturated Fat **3g**,
Total Fat **12g**, Sodium **257mg**,
Cholesterol **61mg**, Protein **26g**,
Carbohydrate **21g**, Fiber **3g**.

Warm the taco shells thoroughly without baking them.

Down-Home Beef Hash

Our low-fat version tastes just as good as the one Grandma used to make, but it's much better for you; serve for brunch or supper.

- Serves 6
- Preparation Time 30 minutes
- Cooking Time 45–50 minutes

---

1 pound lean ground beef

8 ounces lean ground turkey

1 tablespoon olive or canola oil

2 large onions, coarsely chopped

2 cloves garlic, finely chopped

2 large carrots, coarsely chopped

2 stalks celery, diced

1 cup beef stock, page 18

1 teaspoon Worcestershire sauce

$^1/_8$ teaspoon each salt and pepper

$1^1/_2$ pounds all-purpose potatoes, peeled and cubed

1 tablespoon chopped parsley

---

1 Heat a large broiler-safe skillet over moderately high heat until hot. Add the beef and turkey and sauté, stirring frequently, about 7 minutes or until the meat has lost its pink color and has released its juices. Remove from the heat and spoon the meat into a sieve set over a bowl. Allow all the fat to drain from the meat at least 10 minutes.

2 Meanwhile, in the skillet, heat the oil over moderately high heat. Add the onions, garlic, carrots, and celery and sauté about 10 minutes or until softened and golden brown. Return the meat to the skillet.

3 Stir in the beef stock, Worcestershire sauce, salt, and pepper and bring to a boil. Simmer, stirring occasionally, about 15 minutes or until most of the liquid has cooked off and all the vegetables are tender.

4 Preheat the broiler. Meanwhile, bring the potatoes to a boil in a pan of water and cook until tender. Remove from the heat and drain well.

5 Add the potatoes and parsley to the skillet and gently toss together with the meat mixture. Place the skillet under the broiler and cook until browned on top.

PER SERVING
Calories **310**, Saturated Fat **2g**,
Total Fat **7g**, Sodium **148mg**,
Cholesterol **68mg**, Protein **30g**,
Carbohydrate **33g**, Fiber **4g**.

COOKING TIP
Pat the vegetables dry before you put them in the skillet, or they will spatter.

DRAINING GROUND MEAT

Spoon the cooked ground meat into a sieve set over a bowl and allow all the fat to drain off.

Hearty Beef, Turkey, and Mashed Potato Pie

Sweet potatoes are a rich source of vitamin A.

- Serves **6**
- Preparation Time **30 minutes**
- Cooking Time **1 hour**

---

1 pound lean ground beef

8 ounces lean ground turkey

1 tablespoon olive or canola oil

2 large onions, coarsely chopped

2 cloves garlic, finely chopped

2 large carrots, coarsely chopped

1 can (28 ounces) crushed tomatoes

¹/₂ teaspoon dried thyme

¹/₈ teaspoon each salt and pepper

2 pounds sweet or all-purpose potatoes or rutabaga, peeled and sliced ¹/₂ inch thick

¹/₄ cup 1% low-fat milk

2 tablespoons chopped parsley

1 Heat a Dutch oven over moderately high heat until hot. Add the beef and turkey and sauté, stirring frequently, about 7 minutes or until the meat is no longer pink and has released its juices. Remove from the heat and spoon the meat into a sieve set over a bowl. Allow all the fat to drain from the meat at least 10 minutes.

2 Meanwhile, in the Dutch oven, heat the oil over moderately high heat. Add the onions, garlic, and carrots and sauté about 10 minutes or until softened and golden brown. Return the meat to the pan.

3 Stir in the crushed tomatoes, thyme, salt, and pepper and bring to a boil. Cover and simmer, stirring occasionally, about 25 minutes or until a rich stew has formed.

4 Preheat the oven to 400°F. Meanwhile, simmer sweet potatoes in a pan of boiling water about 10 minutes or until tender. Drain, return to the saucepan, and mash them with the milk until smooth. Stir in the chopped parsley.

5 Transfer the meat mixture to a 13" x 9" x 2" baking dish and smooth out to an even layer.

6 Spread the mashed sweet potatoes over the meat and smooth the surface with a spatula. Bake 12 to 15 minutes or until heated through and bubbling around the edges.

PER SERVING
Calories **393**, Saturated Fat **2g**, Total Fat **7g**, Sodium **360mg**, Cholesterol **68mg**, Protein **31g**, Carbohydrate **52g**, Fiber **8g**.

Hearty Beef, Turkey, and Mashed Potato Pie: You can make the topping with white or sweet potatoes, or with rutabaga, as shown here.

MAKING DESIGNS WITH MASHED POTATO TOPPINGS

For rosettes, use a piping bag fitted with a star tube.

For scallops, make tile-like indentations with the tip of a spoon.

For a crisscross pattern, draw a fork tip across the surface.

VEGETABLES

Vegetables add color, texture, and variety to our meals and offer huge health benefits. They are high in fiber, low in fat, and a good source of vitamins and minerals. The A–Z Vegetable Primer in this chapter shows you how to select the best produce and store it for maximum freshness. It will also help you identify vegetables that may be unfamiliar, like kale and Chinese cabbage. You'll find serving suggestions, as well as tips for preparing each vegetable, and you'll learn which cooking techniques to use. Best of all, you'll discover new recipes – from tempting side dishes to hearty Zucchini Cheese Lasagne, which is a meal in itself. Enjoy!

Salmon and Shrimp Spinach Roll-Ups, page 197,
Baked Asparagus with Lemon Sauce, page 165, and
Steamed Leeks with Tomatoes, page 177

In addition to eating at least three to five servings each day, medical experts recommend that you eat vegetables from each of the four basic groups. This will ensure that you get all the vitamins and minerals you need.

Vegetable know-how

The easiest way to identify vegetables is by the parts that we eat, which are the root, stalk, leaves, and flower. Each has its own nutritional advantages and makes a unique contribution to a healthy diet.

Root vegetables, such as potatoes, beets, carrots, and turnips, are literally the root of the plant. They grow underground, where they absorb large amounts of nutrients. Sweet potatoes and carrots are exceptionally high in beta carotene, while white potatoes are high in vitamin C.

Leafy green vegetables, such as spinach, collard greens, kale, and salad greens, are literally the leaves of the plant. They are usually low in calories and high in vitamins. Most leafy greens, but especially collards and kale, are a superb source of calcium. They are also high in vitamin C.

The pod vegetables – lima beans, green peas, and snow peas, contain the seeds of the plant. Like all seeds, they are high in protein and carbohydrate, so they're a good source of energy. They are also rich in B vitamins, zinc, potassium, and iron. Snow peas supply less protein but more calcium and iron than shelled green peas.

The stalk and flower vegetables, such as cauliflower, broccoli, and Brussels sprouts, are good sources of potassium and vitamin C. They are also members of the cruciferous family of vegetables, which in several recent studies has been linked to reducing the risk of stomach and colon cancer.

Cooking vegetables

Gone are the days of overcooked and soggy vegetables. The recipes in this chapter use a variety of cooking techniques designed to retain nutrients and bring out the most flavor.

Baking is ideal for moist vegetables like potatoes, tomatoes, sweet peppers, and squashes because it requires no added cooking oil.

Boiling is the best way to cook root vegetables like beets, parsnips, and turnips, which need long, slow cooking. However, vitamins are lost in the cooking water. If you are going to boil green vegetables, plunge them into boiling water and cook quickly so that they retain their color and texture.

Braising means to cook in a small amount of liquid. It is particularly healthful because the vitamins leach into the liquid, which should be served with the vegetables as a sauce. Braising is ideal for fennel, cabbage, onions, and celery.

Broiling is a quick way to cook moist vegetables like eggplant, tomatoes, and onions. If you wish, you can add herbs or a little oil for flavor.

PEELS AND PESTICIDES

Medical experts have raised concern that over a long period of time, the pesticides used to spray vegetables might be dangerous to the human beings who ingest them. The FDA claims that they monitor residue levels and remove any produce that is unsafe. Furthermore, many nutritionists argue that any risks are far outweighed by the health gains of including plenty of fruit and vegetables in our diet. If you are concerned about pesticides, you will be able to find certified organic produce in most supermarkets – although it is often more expensive. Otherwise, take these simple steps to reduce possible contamination:

- ◆ Buy from local producers so that the vegetables have not been shipped long distances. The longer the storage, the greater the loss in flavor and nutrients. Domestically grown produce will be picked when ripe and fresh.

- ◆ Wash fruits and vegetables thoroughly and scrub them, if possible, with a brush kept specially for the purpose.

- ◆ Discard the outer leaves of leafy vegetables, and wash the remaining leaves thoroughly.

- ◆ Avoid buying potatoes that have green patches, which indicate they have been exposed to light during storage and have developed a naturally occurring toxin known as solanine under the skin. Small patches of green that develop after purchase can be cut away, but if there is extensive greening, the potato should be discarded.

- ◆ Peel any fruits or vegetables that appear to be waxed – most commonly cucumbers, peppers, turnips, and apples. The wax contains a fungicide.

Grilling over wood or charcoal adds smoky flavor and is an especially good way to cook peppers, zucchini, summer squash, and other moist vegetables. Use some oil to keep the vegetables from drying out. Corn cobs can be soaked in water and grilled. Remove the silk but retain the husk to prevent charring.

Oven roasting caramelizes root vegetables such as potatoes, beets, and parsnips, giving them a sweet, nutlike flavor. It is

more healthful than cooking vegetables around a roast, where they absorb the fat. Use just enough olive oil to coat the vegetables and cook at fairly high heat (400°–425°F).

Steaming is particularly healthful because most of the nutrients are retained. Place the vegetables in a basket and cook over – not in – boiling water until crisp-tender. It works best for quick- cooking vegetables like zucchini, new potatoes, and baby carrots.

Stir-frying preserves nutrients because the vegetables are cooked quickly at high heat, sealing in the juices. It requires very little oil and is particularly good with crisp vegetables like carrots and cauliflower because it keeps them moist and crunchy. Always cut vegetables into small uniform pieces and keep stirring and turning them with a spatula so that they cook quickly and evenly.

Freezing fresh vegetables

If you grow your own vegetables, you'll find it's simple to freeze them. Make sure to pick them at the peak of flavor. Then blanch them – either by boiling or steaming – until crisp-tender (see chart below for times). Place in freezer bags or plastic freezer containers, seal tightly, and label. Freeze at 0°F for up to 6 months.

BLANCHING TIMES FOR FREEZING VEGETABLES

Vegetable	Minutes To Boil	Minutes To Steam
Asparagus	–	4
Beans, green	$2^{1}/_{2}$	3
Beans, lima	$1^{1}/_{2}$	2
Broccoli florets	$3–4^{1}/_{2}$	3–5
Brussels sprouts	$3–4^{1}/_{2}$	3–5
Carrots	3	$3^{1}/_{2}$
Corn on the cob	6–10	7–11
Peas, green	$1^{1}/_{2}–2^{1}/_{2}$	2–3
Spinach	$2^{1}/_{2}$	–

THE HEALTH BENEFITS OF VEGETABLES

Fresh vegetables are exceptionally high in five important vitamins and minerals.

Vitamin/Mineral	Benefits	Best Sources
Beta carotene	Converts to vitamin A in the body. Vitamin A keeps hair and skin healthy, helps night vision, promotes proper bone and teeth growth. Beta carotene also reduces the risk of heart disease and cancers of the stomach, mouth, and lung.	Carrots, sweet potatoes, pumpkin, spinach, broccoli, most dark green leafy vegetables.
Vitamin B group	Help you absorb and metabolize carbohydrates, protein, and fats. Help in the formation of red blood cells. Maintain functioning of the skin, nerves, and digestive system. Vitamin B6 enhances immune responses in the elderly.	Kidney beans, sweet potatoes, baked potatoes with skin.
Vitamin C	Helps in healing and aids absorption of iron and calcium. A powerful antioxidant that can neutralize free radicals thought to be responsible for cancers and heart disease.	Broccoli, sweet red pepper, kale, asparagus.
Calcium	An essential mineral for healthy bones and teeth, muscle contractions, regulation of blood pressure, and prevention of osteoporosis.	Watercress, cabbage, broccoli.
Potassium	Helps regulate and maintain blood pressure and water balance in the body. It is essential for muscle contractions, nerve impulses, and healthy functioning of the heart.	Potatoes, cauliflower, tomatoes, and frozen peas.

Artichokes

A good source of calcium, potassium, and beta carotene and also high in protein and fiber.

AT THEIR BEST   March, April, and May.

STORING   Place in a plastic bag with a few drops of water and refrigerate up to 3 days.

COOKING   Bring about 1 inch of water to a boil in a large nonreactive saucepan over high heat. Meanwhile, rub all the cut surfaces of the prepared artichokes with the juice of 1 lemon. Add the artichokes, standing them upright on their stem ends. Cover the saucepan with the lid, reduce the heat to moderate, and gently steam the artichokes about 30 minutes, until they are tender and you can easily pull out a leaf. Remove the artichokes from the saucepan with a slotted spoon and allow to stand until cool enough to handle.

Lemon juice prevents discoloration.

SERVING   Steamed artichokes can be served as a first course or a side dish. Prepare and steam the artichokes as directed in the instructions (see box), then serve them hot or cold with a sauce (see right). To eat, place each artichoke on an individual plate and pull off the leaves one at a time, starting with the bottom outside leaves. Dip the fleshy base of the leaf into the sauce and pull through the teeth to scrape off the pulp. Discard the remaining part of the leaves. Once all the leaves have been removed and the furry center (choke) is reached, cut off the tiny hairs with a knife and discard. Then cut the remaining artichoke heart into pieces with a knife and eat with the vinaigrette or sauce.

NUTRITIONAL VALUES   One artichoke: Calories **60**, Sodium **114mg**, Protein **4g**, Carbohydrate **13g**, Fiber **10g**.

◆ **LOOK FOR**
Tightly closed thick green leaves.

Plump heads that are heavy in relation to their size.

PREPARING ARTICHOKES

1 *Snap the stem from the artichoke so the fibers are pulled out with the stem. Then trim the base of artichoke with a sharp knife so that it will sit flat on the work surface.*

2 *Pull off outer leaves and trim the thorny tips. With a sharp knife, cut off about ³/₄ inch from the pointed top in the center of the artichoke.*

Tarragon Vinaigrette

• Juice of 1 lemon • 1 tablespoon finely chopped fresh tarragon • 1 tablespoon Dijon mustard or 1 teaspoon dry • Pinch of pepper • ¹/₂ cup olive oil

In a bowl, combine lemon juice, tarragon, mustard, and pepper. Gradually whisk in olive oil until thoroughly blended. Makes ³/₄ cup.
*Per tablespoon: Calories **82**, Fiber **0g**, Saturated Fat **1g**, Total Fat **9g**, Sodium **10mg**, Cholesterol **0mg**, Carbohydrate **1g**, Protein **0g**.*

Creamy Garlic Sauce

• 1 cup nonfat plain yogurt • 1 tablespoon snipped fresh chives • 1 clove garlic • ¹/₂ teaspoon finely grated lemon zest • ¹/₈ teaspoon cayenne pepper

In a bowl, combine all the ingredients. Cover and refrigerate at least 2 hours. Discard the garlic. Makes 1 cup.
*Per tablespoon: Calories **9**, Fiber **0g**, Saturated Fat **0g**, Total Fat **0g**, Sodium **11mg**, Cholesterol **0mg**, Carbohydrate **1g**, Protein **1g**.*

Asparagus

High in vitamin C and also a good source of beta carotene and potassium.

AT THEIR BEST   March, April, May, and June.

STORING   Wrap the stalks in damp paper towels and then in a plastic bag. Store in the crisper drawer of the refrigerator up to 4 days.

PREPARING   Snap off the ends of the stalks and discard. Peel the spears to remove the scales, if you like, so that the stalks cook at the same rate as the tips. Soak the spears in a bowl of cold water to refresh them.

COOKING   Cook the spears either tied in a bundle or loose. When tied in a bundle, they can be steamed upright in a tall saucepan and the tips will not overcook. It is also easier to remove them from the pan. To cook in a bundle, tie a serving-sized number of spears together with string or a twist-tie.

Bring 3 to 4 inches of water to a boil in a large nonreactive pan of water over high heat, and stand the asparagus in the boiling water. To cook them loose, bring about 2 inches of water to a boil in a wide, shallow nonreactive saucepan and add the asparagus. Cooking times for both methods will be approximately 3 to 5 minutes for small asparagus, 5 to 8 minutes for medium, and 10 to 12 minutes for large. The stalks should be tender but still quite firm to the touch. Remove from the pan and drain well.

SERVING   Serve asparagus at room temperature or cold; run them under cold water immediately after draining so that they stop cooking. Serve them as a side vegetable or first course with vinaigrette dressing, sauce, or seasoning mixture.

NUTRITIONAL VALUES   ¹/₂ cup cooked: Calories **23**, Sodium **4mg**, Protein **2g**, Carbohydrate **4g**, Fiber **2g**.

Asparagus with Parmesan Cheese

• 1 pound asparagus, prepared as directed • 1 tablespoon olive or canola oil • ¹/₃ cup dry bread crumbs (or whole-wheat) • 1 tablespoon grated Parmesan cheese • ¹/₈ teaspoon each salt and pepper • Pinch of paprika

Cut the asparagus spears on the diagonal into 1-inch pieces. Steam as directed 4 to 5 minutes, until crisp-tender. Keep them warm. Meanwhile, in a large nonstick skillet, heat the oil over moderate heat until hot and the oil sizzles when a few bread crumbs are added. Add the bread crumbs and cook 2 to 3 minutes, stirring constantly, until they start to turn golden. Remove the skillet from the heat and stir in the Parmesan, salt, pepper, and paprika. Add the asparagus pieces and toss to coat well. Serves 4.
*Per serving: Calories **90**, Fiber **2g**, Saturated Fat **1g**, Total Fat **4g**, Sodium **159mg**, Cholesterol **2mg**, Carbohydrate **10g**, Protein **5g**.*

Baked Asparagus with Lemon Sauce

• 1 lemon • ¹/₂ cup vegetable or chicken stock, page 18 • 1 tablespoon olive or canola oil • ¹/₈ teaspoon each salt and pepper • 1 pound asparagus, prepared as directed

Preheat the oven to 350°F. Into a small bowl, finely grate the zest and squeeze the juice of the lemon. Add the stock, oil, salt, and pepper and whisk to combine thoroughly. In a shallow baking dish, arrange the asparagus with all the spears facing the same way. Pour the lemon mixture over the spears so that they are all coated. Tightly cover the dish with aluminum foil or a lid and bake 20 to 25 minutes, until the asparagus are tender. Serves 4.
*Per serving: Calories **55**, Fiber **1g**, Saturated Fat **1g**, Total Fat **4g**, Sodium **76mg**, Cholesterol **0mg**, Carbohydrate **5g**, Protein **3g**.*

◆ **LOOK FOR**
Firm plump spears that are green almost to the end of the stalk.

The tips should be tightly closed.

Beans: Green and Lima

Green: a good source of vitamin C. Lima: contain iron and fiber.

AT THEIR BEST July, August, and September.

STORING Keep, unwashed, in a plastic bag in the refrigerator up to 3 days.

PREPARING Rinse green beans under cold water, then snap off and discard the stem ends as well as the tail ends, if you like. Small green beans can be cooked whole, and large ones can be cut into halves or small pieces. Shell lima beans by cutting off the end of the pod and opening to remove the beans. Rinse the beans after shelling.

Snap off the stem ends of green beans before cooking.

◆ **LOOK FOR**

Small, plump, firm pods with velvety, shiny skins and small seeds.

Lima beans should be plump, green, and free of blemishes.

COOKING Green beans can be steamed or boiled. To steam, place in a steamer basket and set in a saucepan over 2 inches of boiling water. Cover and steam about 8 minutes, until tender but still firm. To boil, half-fill a saucepan with water and bring to a boil. Add beans and return to a boil. Boil about 5 minutes, until tender but still firm. Boil lima beans for about 20 minutes.

SERVING Beans can be served hot as a side vegetable. They can be tossed with seasonings, a light sauce, or a little olive oil. Green beans can be served in a salad; run them under cold water after draining to stop cooking.

NUTRITIONAL VALUES Green beans, ½ cup cooked: Calories **23**, Sodium **2mg**, Protein **1g**, Carbohydrate **5g**, Fiber **2g**. Lima beans, ½ cup cooked: Calories **108**, Sodium **2mg**, Protein **7g**, Carbohydrate **20g**, Fiber **9g**.

Green Beans with Tomatoes and Herbs

- 1 tablespoon olive or canola oil • 1 clove garlic, finely chopped • 1 small onion, finely chopped • 1 can (14 ounces) crushed tomatoes • ¼ teaspoon dried basil • ⅛ teaspoon pepper • 1 pound green beans, prepared as directed

In a large nonstick skillet, heat the oil over moderate heat. Add the garlic and onion and cook, stirring, about 5 minutes, until softened and golden. Stir in the tomatoes with basil and pepper and cook, stirring frequently, about 2 minutes longer. Stir in the green beans so that they are all coated with the tomato mixture. Cover the skillet and cook about 6 minutes, until the beans are crisp-tender. Serves 4.
*Per serving: Calories **105**, Fiber **5g**, Saturated Fat **0g**, Total Fat **4g**, Sodium **112mg**, Cholesterol **0mg**, Carbohydrate **18g**, Protein **4g**.*

Creamy Lima Beans with Mustard

- 1½ pounds fresh lima beans, shelled, or 1 package (10 ounces) frozen baby lima beans, thawed • ¼ cup low-fat sour cream • 2 teaspoons Dijon mustard • 2 tablespoons chopped parsley • ⅛ teaspoon each salt and pepper

Bring a medium saucepan of water to a boil over high heat. Add the lima beans, cover the pan, and cook about 10 minutes, until tender. Remove from the heat and drain the beans. In a large bowl, combine the sour cream with the mustard, parsley, salt, and pepper until blended. Add the hot beans and toss to coat well with the sour cream mixture. Serves 4.
*Per serving: Calories **96**, Fiber **6g**, Saturated Fat **1g**, Total Fat **1g**, Sodium **125mg**, Cholesterol **3mg**, Carbohydrate **16g**, Protein **6g**.*

Beets

A good source of vitamin C as well as potassium.

AT THEIR BEST July to October.

STORING Cut off greens 1 inch from beet; store and cook as for spinach. Place unwashed beets in a plastic bag and store in the refrigerator up to 1 week.

PREPARING Gently scrub the beets but do not trim or peel so that they retain color and flavor while cooking.

COOKING Boil or bake: To boil 1 pound of whole beets, place in a pan and cover with cold water. Cover, bring to a boil, and simmer 40 to 50 minutes or until tender. For baby beets, boil for 20 minutes or until tender. To bake, preheat the oven to 350°F, wrap in aluminum foil, and cook about 1 hour.

SERVING Drain and cool under cold water. Wearing rubber gloves, peel by rubbing off the skins with your fingers. Slice or cut into pieces, then toss with seasonings or a light sauce. Serve hot or cold.

NUTRITIONAL VALUES ¹/₂ cup cooked: Calories **26**, Sodium **42mg**, Protein **1g**, Carbohydrate **6g**, Fiber **2g**.

◆ **LOOK FOR**
Firm beets with deep-colored, unblemished skins. The leaves should be dark green and not wilted.

Baked Beets with Orange Sauce

• 1¹/₄ pounds beets, prepared as directed • 1 orange • 1 tablespoon olive oil • 1 teaspoon prepared horseradish, drained • ¹/₂ teaspoon dried dill weed • ¹/₈ teaspoon each salt and pepper

Preheat oven to 325°F. Wrap beets in foil and bake as directed. Finely grate zest and squeeze juice from orange into a bowl. Stir in oil, horseradish, dill, salt, and pepper. Cool and peel beets as directed. Cut them into ¹/₄ inch matchsticks. Add beets to orange mixture and toss to coat. Serves 4.
*Per serving: Calories **74**, Fiber **2g**, Saturated Fat **0g**, Total Fat **4g**, Sodium **117mg**, Cholesterol **0mg**, Carbohydrate **10g**, Protein **1g**.*

Belgian Endive

Good source of beta carotene and fiber.

AT THEIR BEST September to May.

STORING Do not trim or wash. Place in an open plastic bag and store in the refrigerator up to 3 days.

PREPARING Trim the stem and remove any wilted leaves. Either peel the leaves from core or cut lengthwise in half.

COOKING To steam, cut across into chunks and place in a steamer. Cook about 8 minutes or until tender. To braise, heat a little olive oil in a covered skillet. Cut the endive in half lengthwise and cook, cut side down, about 3 minutes or until golden. Add stock just to cover. Cover and gently cook 20 to 30 minutes or until very tender.

SERVING Belgian endive can be served raw in salads and appetizers or served hot as a side vegetable.

NUTRITIONAL VALUES ¹/₂ cup raw: Calories **4**, Sodium **6mg**, Protein **0g**, Carbohydrate **1g**, Fiber **0g**.

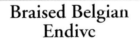

Braised Belgian Endive

◆ **LOOK FOR**
Medium heads that feel crisp and heavy.

• 4 Belgian endive • 1 orange • 1 tablespoon olive or canola oil • ¹/₂ cup vegetable stock, page 18 • ¹/₈ teaspoon each salt and pepper

Preheat the oven to 350°F. Trim endive and cut lengthwise in half. Arrange endive, cut side down, in a 13" x 9" x 2" dish. Grate zest and squeeze juice of orange into a small bowl. Add the oil, stock, salt, and pepper and whisk to combine. Pour over endive and cover dish. Bake about 50 to 60 minutes or until very soft. Serves 4.
*Per serving: Calories **55**, Fiber **1g**, Saturated Fat **0g**, Total Fat **4g**, Sodium **85mg**, Cholesterol **0mg**, Carbohydrate **6g**, Protein **1g**.*

Leaves should be white and pale green around the edges.

Broccoli

Very high in B vitamins and also a good source of beta carotene, vitamin C, fiber, and folacin.

AT THEIR BEST All year.

STORING Do not wash. Place in an open plastic bag or wrap in damp paper towels and store in the refrigerator up to 5 days.

COOKING Broccoli florets and stalks can be steamed or boiled. To steam them, place the stalks in a steamer basket, then cover with the florets and set over about 1 inch of boiling water in a saucepan. Cover the saucepan and steam the broccoli about 8 minutes, until tender but still bright green. To boil the broccoli, bring a saucepan of water to a boil, add the broccoli stalks and return to a boil, then add the florets and boil about 3 minutes longer, until they are all tender.

SERVING To serve as a side vegetable: Drain the broccoli and either toss with seasonings and herbs (such as cilantro, dill, mustard, nutmeg, or oregano), a light sauce, or simply a pinch of salt and pepper. Serve hot. Broccoli can also be added to casseroles or used in soups.

NUTRITIONAL VALUES ½ cup cooked: Calories **22**, Sodium **20mg**, Protein **2g**, Carbohydrate **4g**, Fiber **2g**.

◆ **LOOK FOR**
Compact heads with clusters of tightly closed dark green florets.

Heads should feel heavy in relation to their size and the stalk should feel firm. Avoid yellowing florets and woody stalks.

Stir-Fried Broccoli with Sesame Seeds

• 1 tablespoon sesame seeds •
1 tablespoon canola oil •
1 tablespoon reduced-sodium soy sauce • ⅛ teaspoon hot red pepper flakes • 1 bunch broccoli (about 1½ pounds), florets and stalks prepared as directed • ¼ cup vegetable stock, page 18, or water • ⅛ teaspoon each salt and pepper

Heat a large nonstick skillet. Add sesame seeds and toast them, shaking the pan constantly, 1 to 2 minutes or until seeds turn golden. Remove skillet from the heat and transfer seeds to a plate. Return skillet to the heat, add oil and soy sauce, if using, and hot red pepper flakes, and stir to combine. Add broccoli florets and stir-fry about 2 minutes.

Add stock and cover the skillet. Cook broccoli 1 to 2 minutes longer or until crisp-tender. Stir in sesame seeds and season with salt and pepper. Serves 4.
Per serving: Calories **106**, *Fiber* **3g**, *Saturated Fat* **1g**, *Total Fat* **8g**, *Sodium* **101mg**, *Cholesterol* **0mg**, *Carbohydrate* **7g**, *Protein* **4g**.

PREPARING BROCCOLI

1 *Trim the ends of the stalks. If serving raw, leave to crisp in a bowl of cold water no longer than 10 minutes.*

2 *Cut the florets from the stalks. Peel the stalks with a sharp knife or vegetable peeler, then cut into pieces for cooking.*

Brussels Sprouts

High in vitamin C, beta carotene, and fiber.

AT THEIR BEST   Winter months, after the first frost.

STORING   Pull off any discolored leaves, place the unwashed Brussels sprouts in an open plastic bag, and store in the refrigerator up to 3 days. If you store longer, they will develop a strong flavor.

COOKING   Brussels sprouts can be steamed or boiled. To steam them, place in a steamer basket and set over about 1 inch of boiling water in a saucepan. Cover the saucepan and steam the sprouts about 10 minutes or until they are tender when pierced with the tip of a fork. To boil the sprouts, bring 1 inch of water to a boil in a saucepan, add the sprouts, return to a boil, and cook about 8 minutes longer.

SERVING   Drain the sprouts, then toss with seasonings, herbs and spices (such as caraway, dill, mustard, or ground nutmeg), a little olive oil, or simply a pinch of salt and pepper. Serve hot as a side vegetable, or use combined with cooked carrots, squash, or chestnuts.

NUTRITIONAL VALUES   ¹/₂ cup cooked: Calories 30, Sodium 16mg, Protein 2g, Carbohydrate 7g, Fiber 3g.

◆ **LOOK FOR**
Small, tightly closed heads that have a bright green color.

They should have no yellowing or wilted leaves nor any strong smell.

PREPARING BRUSSELS SPROUTS

1 *Trim the stem ends and pull off any wilted leaves.*

2 *With a small knife, cut an X in the base of the stem so that the core will cook at the same speed as the leaves.*

Puréed Brussels Sprouts

• 2 cups vegetable stock, page 18 • 2 packages (10 ounces each) Brussels sprouts, prepared as directed • 1 onion, sliced • ¹/₂ cup low-fat sour cream • ¹/₂ cup plain nonfat yogurt • ¹/₈ teaspoon each ground nutmeg, salt, and pepper

In a large saucepan, bring stock to a boil. Add Brussels sprouts and onion. Return to a boil, cover, and cook about 10 minutes or until very tender. Using a slotted spoon, transfer sprouts and onions to a food processor or blender. Process until very finely chopped. Add enough stock to form a smooth purée. Add sour cream, yogurt, nutmeg, salt, and pepper and process to combine. Return to saucepan, set over low heat, and gently warm through. Serves 4.
Per serving: Calories 159, Fiber 5g, Saturated Fat 0g, Total Fat 7g, Sodium 179mg, Cholesterol 1mg, Carbohydrate 19g, Protein 7g.

Brussels Sprouts with Chestnuts

• 2 packages (10 ounces each) Brussels sprouts, prepared as directed • 2 teaspoons olive or canola oil • 2 cups cooked and peeled chestnuts or 1 can (10 ounces) • ¹/₃ cup vegetable stock, page 18 • 1 scallion, finely chopped • ¹/₈ teaspoon each salt and pepper • Pinch of ground nutmeg

In a large saucepan, bring 1 inch of water to a boil. Add the Brussels sprouts, return to a boil, reduce the heat, cover, and cook 6 to 8 minutes or until just tender. Drain.

Meanwhile, in a large skillet, heat the oil over moderate heat. Add the chestnuts and toss to coat well. Add the sprouts to the skillet with the stock and stir to combine. Cover the skillet and cook 2 to 3 minutes longer or until the sprouts are tender. Stir in the chopped scallion and season with salt, pepper, and nutmeg. Serves 4.
Per serving: Calories 272, Fiber 10g, Saturated Fat 1g, Total Fat 4g, Sodium 107mg, Cholesterol 0mg, Carbohydrate 54g, Protein 9g.

Cabbage: Green, Red, Savoy, and Napa

High in vitamin C and fiber.

AT THEIR BEST All year.

VARIETIES The most common variety is the green cabbage which is usually trimmed of the outer leaves, leaving a pale green solid head. It is the variety normally used for making sauerkraut. Red cabbage is similar in texture but tastes sweeter. It must be cooked longer than green cabbage; combine it with an acid ingredient such as apple or orange if you want it to keep its color. Savoy cabbage has curly outer leaves and a more delicate flavor than green cabbage. Hollowed out, it can make a container for party dips. Napa cabbage is a Chinese variety and is popular in stir-fries and salads.

STORING Place the unwashed cabbage in a plastic bag and store in the refrigerator up to 1 week. To store part of a cabbage, wrap it in plastic wrap and store in the refrigerator up to 2 days.

COOKING Cabbage can be steamed, boiled, or braised. To steam cabbage, place the shredded leaves in a steamer basket over 1 inch of boiling water in a saucepan. Cover the pan and steam the cabbage about 12 minutes, until tender. To boil cabbage, bring a large saucepan with 1 inch of water to a boil, add the cabbage, shredded or in wedges, and return to a boil. Cover and cook the cabbage about 5 minutes longer, until tender. To braise shredded cabbage, sauté in a covered casserole in a little olive or canola oil. Then add stock almost to cover and cook, covered, about 1 hour, until tender.

SERVING Cabbage can be eaten raw in salads or cooked and served hot as a side vegetable with herbs, seasonings, or simply a pinch of salt and pepper. It can also be used in stir-fries, stews, soups, and other recipes.

NUTRITIONAL VALUES Green cabbage, ½ cup raw: Calories 8, Sodium 6mg, Protein 0g, Carbohydrate 2g, Fiber 1g.
½ cup cooked: Calories 15, Sodium 14mg, Protein 1g, Carbohydrate 4g, Fiber 2g.

PREPARING CABBAGE

1 *Peel off and discard the outer leaves. With a large sharp knife, cut the cabbage lengthwise in half.*

2 *Cut out the core from each half. Cut the halves across into quarters.*

3 *Using a sharp knife, carefully shred the cabbage quarters as finely as required.*

Green Cabbage with Caraway Seeds

- 1 tablespoon olive or canola oil • 2 leeks or small onions, trimmed and finely chopped • 1 teaspoon caraway, celery, or fennel seeds • 1 cabbage (about 1½ pounds), prepared as directed • ½ cup vegetable or chicken stock, page 18 • ⅛ teaspoon each salt and pepper

In a large nonstick skillet, heat the oil over moderate heat. Add the leeks and sauté 2 to 3 minutes or until softened, (if using onions, sauté 4 to 5 minutes). Stir in the caraway seeds and cook about 2 minutes longer. Add the shredded cabbage and the stock to the skillet. Cover the skillet and steam the cabbage, stirring occasionally, about 10 minutes or until tender. Season with salt and pepper, and toss before serving. Serves 4.
Per serving: Calories 93, Fiber 5g, Saturated Fat 1g, Total Fat 4g, Sodium 108mg, Cholesterol 0mg, Carbohydrate 14g, Protein 3g.

Sweet and Sour Braised Red Cabbage

• 1 orange • 1 tablespoon olive or canola oil • 2 red onions, coarsely chopped • 1 tart apple, peeled, cored, and diced • 2 tablespoons brown sugar • 2 tablespoons red wine vinegar • ¼ cup vegetable or chicken stock, page 18 • 1 red cabbage (about 1 pound), prepared as directed • ⅛ teaspoon each salt and pepper

In a small bowl, finely grate the zest and squeeze the juice of the orange. In a Dutch oven, heat the oil over moderate heat. Add the onions and sauté about 4 minutes or until softened. Add the apple, brown sugar, vinegar, orange zest and juice, and the stock to the pan; stir to combine. Once the mixture has come to a boil, add the cabbage and toss to coat. Cover the pan and cook the cabbage, stirring occasionally, about 10 minutes or until tender. Season with salt and pepper. Serves 4.
Per serving: Calories **143**, *Fiber* **6g**, *Saturated Fat* **0g**, *Total Fat* **4g**, *Sodium* **101mg**, *Cholesterol* **0mg**, *Carbohydrate* **27g**, *Protein* **4g**.

Baked Cabbage Wedges with Ginger

• ½ cup vegetable or chicken stock, page 18 • ⅓ cup dry white wine or vegetable or chicken stock • ¼ teaspoon ground ginger • ⅛ teaspoon each salt and pepper • 1 cabbage, cored and cut into 6 wedges • 1 tablespoon chopped fresh chives or parsley

Preheat the oven to 350°F. In a small saucepan, combine the stock with wine, ginger, salt, and pepper, and bring to a boil over moderate heat. Arrange the cabbage wedges in a wide, shallow casserole, spoon some of the liquid over the cabbage to coat well, and pour the remaining liquid into the casserole. Cover the casserole and bake 20 to 25 minutes or until the cabbage is soft. Sprinkle the chives over the cabbage and serve. Serves 4.
Per serving: Calories **49**, *Fiber* **3g**, *Saturated Fat* **0g**, *Total Fat* **0g**, *Sodium* **100mg**, *Cholesterol* **0mg**, *Carbohydrate* **8g**, *Protein* **2g**.

◆ **LOOK FOR**
Firm heads that feel heavy in relation to their size.

Green cabbage

Red cabbage

Napa cabbage

Stir-Fried Chinese Cabbage

• 2 teaspoons canola oil • 1 teaspoon Oriental sesame oil (optional) • 2 tablespoons finely chopped garlic • 1 head (about 1½ pounds) Napa cabbage, shredded • 1 tablespoon reduced-sodium soy sauce • 1 tablespoon toasted sesame seeds • ⅛ teaspoon pepper

Heat a wok or large heavy skillet over high heat. Add the oils and heat until the oil sizzles when a small piece of garlic is added.

Add the remaining garlic and stir-fry about 2 minutes or until fragrant. Add the shredded cabbage and stir-fry about 5 minutes or until slightly wilted. Add the soy sauce. Stir-fry 3 to 5 minutes longer or until the cabbage is crisp-tender. Stir in the sesame seeds and season with pepper. Serves 6.
Per serving: Calories **56**, *Fiber* **2g**, *Saturated Fat* **0g**, *Total Fat* **3g**, *Sodium* **118mg**, *Cholesterol* **0mg**, *Carbohydrate* **6g**, *Protein* **2g**.

Savoy cabbage

The outer leaves should have a bright color, feel firm, and not be wilted or torn.

Carrots

An excellent source of vitamin C and beta carotene.

AT THEIR BEST All year.

STORING Cut off the tops, place carrots, unwashed, in a plastic bag, and store in the refrigerator 1 to 2 weeks.

PREPARING Trim the tops and roots. Scrub young carrots; peel large carrots, then cut into slices, dice, or sticks.

COOKING Carrots can be steamed, boiled, or roasted. Steam over 1 inch of boiling water about 10 minutes or until tender. To boil, add the carrots to boiling water, return to a boil, and cook about 8 minutes or until tender. To roast, preheat the oven to 350°F, coat the carrots lightly in oil, and roast about 35 minutes or until tender.

SERVING Carrots can be eaten raw or cooked as a side vegetable with herbs or seasonings. They can also be used in stir-fries, stews, or soups.

NUTRITIONAL VALUES ½ cup cooked: Calories **35**, Sodium **52mg**, Protein **1g**, Carbohydrate **8g**, Fiber **3g**.

◆ **LOOK FOR**
Firm, smooth carrots; small ones are sweeter. Buy carrots with green tops still on – they are fresher.

Lemon Carrots with Watercress

• 1 lemon • 1 teaspoon sugar
• ⅛ teaspoon each salt and pepper • 1 pound carrots, thinly sliced • 1½ tablespoons olive oil
• 1 bunch watercress leaves

Finely grate zest and squeeze juice of lemon into a bowl. Stir in sugar, salt, and pepper. Steam carrots as directed, 6 minutes. In a large skillet, heat oil over moderate heat. Add carrots and toss to coat. Stir in lemon mixture and watercress and sauté 2 to 3 minutes or until carrots are tender. Serves 4.
*Per serving: Calories **104**, Fiber **4g**, Saturated Fat **1g**, Total Fat **5g**, Sodium **113mg**, Cholesterol **0mg**, Carbohydrate **14g**, Protein **2g**.*

Cauliflower

High in vitamin C, carbohydrate, and potassium.

◆ **LOOK FOR**
Firm, creamy-colored heads that feel heavy in relation to their size, with fresh, green leaves.

AT THEIR BEST October to April.

STORING Do not wash. Place in an open plastic bag and store in the refrigerator up to 5 days.

PREPARING Cut off leaves and trim stem. Break florets from core and cut florets into smaller pieces if you like.

COOKING Cauliflower can be steamed or boiled. Steam small florets, covered, about 8 minutes or until tender. To boil, add florets to boiling water and return to a boil; cook 5 to 10 minutes or until tender.

SERVING Cauliflower can be eaten raw in salads or served hot as a side vegetable. Add it to stews and soups.

NUTRITIONAL VALUES ½ cup cooked: Calories **15**, Sodium **4mg**, Protein **1g**, Carbohydrate **3g**, Fiber **1g**.

Cauliflower Provençal

• 1 cauliflower • 1 sweet red pepper, diced • 2 tomatoes, coarsely chopped • ⅓ cup vegetable stock, page 18
• ¼ cup sliced black olives •
⅛ teaspoon each salt and pepper

Prepare and steam cauliflower as directed 9 to 10 minutes or until just tender. In a saucepan, combine red pepper, tomatoes, and stock. Bring to a boil over moderate heat. Cover pan and cook, stirring, about 3 minutes or until peppers are almost tender. Add cauliflower and olives and toss to coat. Cover pan and continue to cook, stirring, 2 to 3 minutes or until cauliflower is tender. Season with salt and pepper. Serves 4.
*Per serving: Calories **74**, Fiber **1g**, Saturated Fat **0g**, Total Fat **1g**, Sodium **127mg**, Cholesterol **0mg**, Carbohydrate **14g**, Protein **5g**.*

Celery

Good source of folacin and very low in calories although quite high in sodium.

AT THEIR BEST All year.

STORING Rinse under cold water and drain. Place in an open plastic bag and store in the refrigerator up to 1 week.

PREPARING Separate the stalks and wash thoroughly under cold water. Drain well, then peel and chop (see box). Alternatively, cut into 2-inch lengths, then cut lengthwise into strips. Reserve the leaves, then chop them and add to soups or stews toward the end of cooking.

COOKING Celery can be steamed, boiled, braised, or stir-fried. To steam, cut across into slices or lengthwise into thin strips, then place in a steamer basket over 1 inch of boiling water. Cover the pan and steam the celery about 10 minutes or until tender. To boil celery, bring a large saucepan of water to a boil, add the celery slices or strips, and return to a boil. Cook the celery 8 to 10 minutes or until tender. To braise, sauté 2- to 3-inch pieces in a little olive or canola oil in a covered casserole. Add stock to almost cover and cook gently, covered, about 15 minutes or until tender.

SERVING Celery can be eaten raw as a snack or in salads. It can also be cooked and served hot as a side vegetable with herbs, seasonings, or simply a pinch of salt and pepper. It can be used in stews, soups, and stir-fries.

NUTRITIONAL VALUES 1/2 cup raw: Calories **10**, Sodium **52mg**, Protein **0g**, Carbohydrate **2g**, Fiber **1g**.

◆ **LOOK FOR**
Firm, crisp stalks that are medium-size and pale green in color.

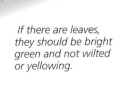

If there are leaves, they should be bright green and not wilted or yellowing.

PREPARING CELERY

1 *Peel the outer stalks with a vegetable peeler to remove the tough strings if you like.*

2 *Cut the celery stalks across into thin or thick slices.*

Celery Baked with Parmesan Cheese

• 1 large bunch celery, stalks washed and trimmed • 1 clove garlic, finely chopped • 1 small sweet red pepper, finely chopped • 1/2 cup chicken stock, page 18 • 2 tablespoons grated Parmesan cheese

Preheat oven to 350°F. Cut celery stalks across into 4-inch pieces and arrange in a single layer in a 14 1/2" x 10 1/2" x 2" broiler-safe pan. Sprinkle with garlic and red pepper, then pour stock over. Cover dish and bake 40 to 50 minutes, until celery is very soft. Preheat broiler. Uncover dish and sprinkle cheese over celery and broil about 5 minutes, until golden brown. Serves 4.
Per serving: Calories **40**, *Fiber* **2g**, *Saturated Fat* **0g**, *Total Fat* **1g**, *Sodium* **180mg**, *Cholesterol* **2mg**, *Carbohydrate* **6g**, *Protein* **3g**.

Celery Medley

• 1 bunch celery, trimmed and sliced • 8 ounces broccoli, cut into florets • 1 teaspoon olive oil • 4 scallions, sliced • 1 sweet red pepper, thinly sliced • 2 tablespoons reduced-sodium soy sauce

Boil celery as directed until almost tender. Add broccoli and cook for 5 minutes or until just tender. Drain well. In a saucepan, heat oil and add celery, broccoli, scallions, and sweet red pepper. Stir-fry for 3 minutes, add soy sauce, warm through, and serve at once. Serves 4.
Per serving: Calories **54**, *Fiber* **4g**, *Saturated Fat* **0g**, *Total Fat* **2g**, *Sodium* **385mg**, *Cholesterol* **0mg**, *Carbohydrate* **9g**, *Protein* **4g**.

Corn

Good source of protein, carbohydrate, potassium, and fiber.

AT THEIR BEST May to September.

STORING Do not remove the husks. Place in a plastic bag and store in the refrigerator up to 2 days. Fresh corn is best cooked and eaten the same day because the sugar will start turning to starch after picking.

COOKING Corn can be boiled, steamed, or grilled. To steam, place the shucked ears in a steamer over 1 inch boiling water. Cover and steam about 6 minutes or until the kernels are tender. To boil, add the corn to boiling water and return to a boil. Cook about 4 minutes or until the kernels are tender. To grill, soak the ears in cold water at least 10 minutes. Shuck the corn and wrap in aluminum foil or leave them in their husks, but remove the silks. Place over hot coals and cook about 20 minutes, turning occasionally.

SERVING Serve whole corn topped with a pat of butter or polyunsaturated margarine. Sprinkle with a pinch of salt and pepper. Serve corn kernels hot as a side dish or in other recipes. They can also be used in salads or relishes.

NUTRITIONAL VALUES ½ cup cooked: Calories **87**, Sodium **14mg**, Protein **3g**, Carbohydrate **21g**, Fiber **4g**.

◆ **LOOK FOR**
Fresh ears with green husks. Kernels should be plump and firm; the color ranges from yellow to creamy white, which is sweeter than yellow.

REMOVING HUSKS AND KERNELS FROM CORN

1 *Pull off the husks and silks from the cob and trim the stem. Any remaining silks can be brushed off with your fingers.*

2 *Stand the cob on the stem and hold firmly; working downward, slice off the kernels with a large sharp knife.*

Corn Succotash

- 1 tablespoon olive or canola oil
- 1 small onion, finely chopped •
1 cup frozen baby lima beans •
¹/₃ cup chicken stock, page 18 •
2 cups corn kernels • ¹/₄ cup buttermilk or 1% low-fat milk
- 1 tablespoon chopped fresh basil or parsley • ¹/₈ teaspoon each salt and pepper

In a saucepan, heat oil over moderate heat. Add onion and sauté, stirring, until softened but not brown. Stir in lima beans and chicken stock and bring to a boil. Cover pan and simmer 5 to 6 minutes or until beans are almost tender. Add corn and return to a boil. Cover and simmer 3 minutes or until vegetables are tender. Stir in buttermilk and cook about 1 minute longer, until heated through. Remove from the heat and add basil, salt, and pepper. Serves 4.
*Per serving: Calories **155**, Fiber **4g**, Saturated Fat **1g**, Total Fat **4g**, Sodium **121mg**, Cholesterol **1mg**, Carbohydrate **28g**, Protein **6g**.*

Corn Pudding

- ¹/₂ teaspoon olive or canola oil • 1 slice reduced-sodium bacon, coarsely chopped •
2 leeks, trimmed and chopped •
1 small sweet red pepper, finely chopped • 2 cups corn kernels •
2 cups cubed bread • ³/₄ cup 1% low-fat milk • 1 egg •
1 egg white • ¹/₄ teaspoon dry mustard • ¹/₈ teaspoon each salt and pepper

Lightly grease a 1¹/₂-quart baking dish or casserole with oil. Preheat oven to 350°F. In a nonstick skillet, cook bacon over moderate heat until crisp and fat is rendered. Add leeks and sweet pepper and sauté 3 to 4 minutes or until softened. Remove from the heat and pour into baking dish. Stir in corn and bread. In a bowl, whisk milk, egg, egg white, mustard, salt, and pepper. Pour mixture into baking dish and stir to combine. Bake pudding 30 to 40 minutes or until puffed and cooked through. Serves 4.
*Per serving: Calories **195**, Fiber **4g**, Saturated Fat **1g**, Total Fat **4g**, Sodium **217mg**, Cholesterol **56mg**, Carbohydrate **35g**, Protein **9g**.*

Cucumber

Very low in calories and, with the peel, a good source of fiber.

AT THEIR BEST   All year.

STORING   Store in the refrigerator up to 1 week. Wrap cut cucumbers in plastic and refrigerate up to 5 days.

PREPARING   Regular cucumbers have a tough skin that is often coated with wax – peel off the skin and discard it. Kirby, or pickling, and English cucumbers are not waxed and completely edible. Slice or dice cucumbers or cut in strips.

COOKING   Cut cucumbers across into thick slices and steam or sauté. To steam, place in a steamer basket, cover, and cook about 3 minutes or until tender. To sauté, heat a little olive oil in a skillet, add the cucumber with a pinch of salt and pepper, and cook, stirring, about 5 minutes or until tender.

SERVING   Marinate thinly sliced cucumbers as a salad. Slices are good in sandwiches and as a garnish. Toss steamed or sautéed cucumbers with seasonings.

NUTRITIONAL VALUES   With skin, ¹/₂ cup raw: Calories **7**, Sodium **1mg**, Protein **0g**, Carbohydrate **2g**, Fiber **0.5g**.

Sautéed Cucumber with Dill

• ¹/₂ lemon • 1 tablespoon olive oil • 2 cucumbers, sliced • 1 tablespoon chopped fresh dill • ¹/₈ teaspoon each salt and pepper

In a bowl, finely grate zest and squeeze lemon juice. In a skillet, heat oil over moderate heat. Sauté cucumbers, stirring, 6 to 8 minutes or until soft. Stir in lemon juice, zest, dill, salt, and pepper. Reduce heat and cook about 2 minutes longer. Serves 4.
Per serving: Calories 52, Fiber 2g, Saturated Fat 1g, Total Fat 5g, Sodium 2mg, Cholesterol 0mg, Carbohydrate 5g, Protein 1g.

◆ **LOOK FOR**
Firm cucumbers with dark green skin.

Kirby cucumbers are smaller, with bumpy skin; English are long and thin.

Eggplant

High in complex carbohydrates and folacin.

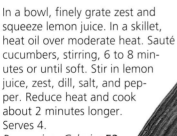

◆ **LOOK FOR**
Firm eggplants with shiny skin that feel heavy. Soft, wrinkled eggplant may taste bitter.

AT THEIR BEST   July to October.

STORING   Store, unwashed, in an open plastic bag in the refrigerator up to 5 days.

PREPARING   Cut off the stem and, if you like, peel. Cut across or lengthwise into slices and then cubes. For baking, cut eggplant lengthwise in half. The flesh will discolor quickly, so prepare just before cooking. Today's varieties are not normally bitter, and there is no need to salt, unless large.

COOKING   Bake eggplant halves, cut sides brushed with oil, in a 400°F oven about 30 minutes or until tender. Sauté 1-inch cubes in a little olive oil over moderate heat, stirring, about 10 minutes or until tender. Broil eggplant halves or slices, brushed with oil, under a preheated broiler, 5 inches from the heat, 5 minutes on each side or until golden brown.

SERVING   Eggplant is always cooked, either as a side vegetable or in a stew or baked dish. Puréed, it makes a dip for crudités.

NUTRITIONAL VALUES   ¹/₂ cup cooked: Calories **22**, Sodium **2mg**, Protein **1g**, Carbohydrate **5g**, Fiber **3g**.

Broiled Eggplant with Lemon Pepper

• 1 eggplant, thickly sliced and cut into ¹/₂-inch strips • 2 tablespoons olive oil • 1 teaspoon lemon pepper • ¹/₈ teaspoon salt • ¹/₄ cup plain nonfat yogurt

Preheat broiler, setting rack about 4 inches from the heat. In a bowl, combine eggplant with oil, lemon pepper, and salt, and coat well.

Transfer to a roasting pan and broil, stirring occasionally, about 10 minutes or until browned and very soft. Transfer to a serving bowl and stir in yogurt. Serves 4.
Per serving: Calories 113, Fiber 6g, Saturated Fat 1g, Total Fat 7g, Sodium 84mg, Cholesterol 0mg, Carbohydrate 13g, Protein 3g.

Fennel

High in vitamin C and beta carotene and a source of potassium, fiber, and iron.

◆ **LOOK FOR**
Heavy, firm white bulbs, free of bruises, with a crisp outer layer and feathery green leaves.

AT THEIR BEST October to April.

STORING Place the unwashed fennel in an open plastic bag and store in the refrigerator up to 1 week.

PREPARING Trim stalk and root end, reserving fronds if you like. Cut the bulb lengthwise in half and cut out the core. Leave whole or cut into quarters or slices.

COOKING Steam fennel, cut into 1-inch slices, over boiling water about 15 minutes, until tender. Braise cored fennel quarters in a covered skillet or casserole with a little stock, turning them occasionally, about 20 minutes or until the fennel is very tender.

SERVING Finely shredded, serve raw in salads. Cut stalks into strips and serve as a crudité. Serve cooked fennel as a side dish or in soups or stews. The fronds make a licorice-flavored seasoning for salads.

NUTRITIONAL VALUES Per serving: Calories **28**, Sodium **47mg**, Protein **1g**, Carbohydrate **4g**, Fiber **2g**.

Herb-Roasted Fennel

• **2 heads fennel** • **2 tablespoons olive or canola oil** • **¹/₄ teaspoon dried mixed herbs** • **¹/₈ teaspoon each salt and pepper** • **¹/₂ cup dry white wine or chicken stock**

Preheat oven to 375°F. Quarter fennel as directed. In a bowl, combine oil with herbs, salt, and pepper; add fennel and toss to coat. Roast in a nonstick roasting pan 30 minutes. Add wine and roast 30 to 35 minutes longer or until tender. Serves 4.
*Per serving: Calories **193**, Fiber **3g**, Saturated Fat **1g**, Total Fat **7g**, Sodium **263mg**, Cholesterol **0mg**, Carbohydrate **18g**, Protein **4g**.*

Greens

Good sources of beta carotene, vitamin C, and potassium.

AT THEIR BEST Winter months.

VARIETIES Kale is related to cabbage but has frilly leaves. Collard greens are a type of kale, and the taste is similar to spinach; mustard greens are peppery, so use sparingly. Escarole is a variety of endive and has a slightly bitter flavor. Swiss chard is a member of the beet family and has a spinach flavor.

STORING Greens can be refrigerated in an open plastic bag in the refrigerator up to 2 days.

COOKING To steam greens, place about ¹/₄ inch of water in a heavy wide saucepan. Add the prepared greens and cover. Bring the water to a boil over moderate heat and cook, covered, until the leaves are wilted and slightly soft. Stir, cover again, and cook a few minutes longer or until very soft. You can add the raw torn leaves to a variety of recipes.

SERVING The tender greens, such as Swiss chard, escarole, and mustard greens, can be served raw in salads. You can serve cooked greens as a vegetable side dish, flavored with garlic if you like, or you can add them to soups, stew, and stir-fries.

NUTRITIONAL VALUES **Collard greens**, ¹/₂ cup cooked: Calories **17**, Sodium **10mg**, Protein **1g**, Carbohydrate **4g**, Fiber **2g**.

SHREDDING GREENS

1 *Wash the leaves and drain well. Stack the leaves in a pile and roll them up in a bundle.*

2 *Cut the roll across into slices to shred the leaves.*

◆ **LOOK FOR**
Firm, crisp green leaves with no yellow or brown patches.

Collard greens

Mustard greens

Escarole

Swiss chard

Kale

Small leaves will be younger and more tender.

Leeks

A good source of fiber, folacin, vitamin C, and iron.

AT THEIR BEST October to March.

STORING Do not wash or trim the leeks. Place in a plastic bag and store in the refrigerator up to 1 week.

PREPARING Wash under cold water, opening out the layers so that the water can wash out any grit and dirt between them. Drain well and slice or finely chop.

COOKING Leeks can be braised, grilled, baked, stir-fried, steamed, or boiled. Using leeks as a base for soups and stews adds a slightly sweet-savory flavor.

SERVING Serve leeks hot or at room temperature, add to stews, or serve in a low-fat cheese sauce.

NUTRITIONAL VALUES ¹/₂ cup cooked: Calories **16**, Sodium **5mg**, Protein **0g**, Carbohydrate **4g**, Fiber **2g**.

Spicy Greens with Bacon

• 2 slices reduced-sodium bacon, coarsely chopped • 1 small onion, finely chopped • 1 clove garlic, finely chopped • ¹/₈ teaspoon hot red pepper flakes • 1¹/₂ pounds greens, prepared as directed • ¹/₄ cup chicken, beef, or vegetable stock, page 18 • ¹/₈ teaspoon each salt and pepper

Heat a large heavy skillet over moderate heat. Add the bacon and cook, stirring, about 5 minutes or until browned and all the fat is rendered. Using a slotted spoon, transfer the bacon to a plate. Add the onion and garlic to the skillet and sauté, stirring, about 4 minutes or until softened. Stir in the hot red pepper flakes, then add the greens, pour the stock over, and quickly cover the skillet with a lid. Cook, stirring occasionally, about 10 minutes or until the leaves are wilted and quite soft. Stir in the bacon and season with salt and pepper. Serves 4.
Per serving: Calories **67**, *Fiber* **3g**, *Saturated Fat* **0g**, *Total Fat* **1g**, *Sodium* **137mg**, *Cholesterol* **2mg**, *Carbohydrate* **12g**, *Protein* **4g**.

Steamed Leeks with Tomatoes

• 8 tomatoes, coarsely chopped •
2 cloves garlic, finely chopped •
1 tablespoon olive or canola oil
• ¹/₄ teaspoon grated lemon zest
¹/₈ teaspoon each salt and pepper
• 8 leeks, halved and rinsed

In a skillet, combine tomatoes with garlic, oil, lemon zest, salt, and pepper. Cover and cook over moderate heat about 5 minutes. Arrange leeks on top, cover, and cook about 10 minutes or until soft. Serves 4.
Per serving: Calories **230**, *Fiber* **9g**, *Saturated Fat* **1g**, *Total Fat* **5g**, *Sodium* **138mg**, *Cholesterol* **0mg**, *Carbohydrate* **46g**, *Protein* **6g**.

PREPARING LEEKS

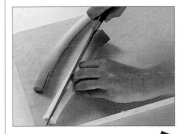

Trim ends. Halve lengthwise and discard the outer layer.

◆ **LOOK FOR**
Medium to small leeks with a white base.

The leaves should be green and should have crisp clean ends.

Mushrooms

A good source of riboflavin and niacin, and low in sodium.

AT THEIR BEST All year. Wild mushrooms in spring and fall.

STORING Eat them as fresh as possible. If necessary, store in the refrigerator in a paper bag for up to 2 days.

PREPARING Gently clean with a damp paper towel or wash under cold water and pat dry. Trim or remove stems. Leave whole, quarter, slice, or chop.

COOKING Sauté in hot oil, stirring, about 2 minutes so that they stay firm. Braise with a little stock or wine, covered, for about 5 minutes. Bake in a moderate oven, drizzled with a little oil and sprinkled with a little stock, for about 20 minutes, until tender.

SERVING Serve as a hot side dish or appetizer or in sauces seasoned with pepper, garlic, lemon, or onion. Slice raw button mushrooms into salads. Wild chanterelles (trumpet-shaped) are good with chicken – use porcini (parasol-shaped) or morels (conical-shaped) in pasta sauces and risottos.

NUTRITIONAL VALUES ¹/₂ cup raw: Calories 9, Sodium 1mg, Protein 1g, Carbohydrate 2g, Fiber 0g.

◆ **LOOK FOR**
Firm dry-skinned mushrooms. Colors vary from white to brown.

Marinated Mushrooms

• 1 pound large brown mushrooms • 2 tablespoons olive or canola oil • 1 tablespoon chopped fresh herbs • 1 teaspoon lemon juice • ¹/₄ teaspoon hot red pepper flakes • ¹/₈ teaspoon each salt and pepper

Preheat broiler. Trim mushroom stems. Arrange mushrooms, stem side down, on rack over a broiler pan. Brush generously with oil and broil until slightly soft. Transfer to a bowl and stir in remaining ingredients; marinate at least 2 hours. Serves 4.
Per serving: Calories 89, Fiber 2g, Saturated Fat 1g, Total Fat 7g, Sodium 72mg, Cholesterol 0mg, Carbohydrate 6g, Protein 2g.

Okra

High in calcium, all the B vitamins, as well as fiber.

◆ **LOOK FOR**
Tender, young, plump pods up to 6 inches long.

AT THEIR BEST From May to October, but available all year.

STORING Refrigerate and use within 2 days.

PREPARING Rinse under cold water and cut off the stems without opening the pod to expose the seeds. Leave the pods whole or thickly slice.

COOKING Simmer okra 5 to 10 minutes, until soft but not mushy and still bright green. Once sliced, okra's familiar slippery texture will be released as it cooks. Sliced okra can be sautéed with onions and tomatoes.

SERVING Serve as a cooked side dish, either hot or cold. When added to Creole dishes such as gumbo, it helps thicken the stew.

NUTRITIONAL VALUES 1 pod cooked: Calories 3, Sodium 0mg, Protein 0g, Carbohydrate 1g, Fiber 0g.

Stewed Okra with Chili Peppers

• 1 pound small okra, prepared as directed • 1 tablespoon olive or canola oil • 1 large onion, sliced • 1 teaspoon finely chopped fresh or canned jalapeño pepper, • 2 large ripe tomatoes, coarsely chopped • ¹/₄ cup water • ¹/₈ teaspoon salt and pepper

Steam the okra over boiling water about 3 minutes, until just tender. Heat the oil in a large nonstick skillet over moderate heat. Add the onion and sauté, stirring, 7 to 9 minutes, until softened and golden brown. Stir in the jalapeño pepper, tomatoes, and water, and cook 3 to 5 minutes, stirring occasionally, until the tomatoes are very soft. Add okra to the skillet with the salt and pepper and cook 3 to 5 minutes longer, until the okra are very soft. Serves 4.
Per serving: Calories 102, Fiber 3g, Saturated Fat 1g, Total Fat 4g, Sodium 92mg, Cholesterol 0mg, Carbohydrate 16g, Protein 3g.

Onions

A fair source of vitamin C and folacin, providing about 20% of your Daily Value per cup.

AT THEIR BEST All year.

VARIETIES The yellow onion is strongly flavored; the Bermuda, Spanish, Vidalia, and red onions are much sweeter. Scallions, also known as green onions, are high in vitamins C and A. They have small white bulbs with long green tops and have a strong chive-garlic flavor. Shallots have a mild, subtle flavor and tender texture.

STORING Store in a cool, dry place for up to 4 weeks.

PREPARING To peel pearl onions easily, boil for 1 minute in water, cool under cold running water, and slip off the skins.

COOKING Onions can be sautéed, broiled, steamed, braised, or baked. Sautéed, they will first become translucent, then turn golden brown. Don't allow them to burn or turn dark brown or the taste will be spoiled. Scallions and shallots can be finely chopped and sautéed in a little oil to add a wonderful flavor to sauces, vinaigrettes, stir-fries, and soups. Small pearl onions can be cooked in an herb sauce and make a flavorful addition to stews.

SERVING Baked and sautéed onions can be served with meat, poultry, and fish dishes and as an integral part of a wide variety of recipes. Use the sweeter varieties of onion raw in salads or on hamburgers. Scallions can be sliced and used raw in salads; both white and green parts can be used. The dark green ends can be sliced and used as a flavorful garnish for poultry, fish, meats, soups, and stews. Shallots can be peeled and cooked whole as a side dish. Serve pearl onions in herb and cream sauces to accompany turkey and chicken or add them to stews.

NUTRITIONAL VALUES Onions, 1/2 cup raw: Calories 30, Sodium 2mg, Protein 1g, Carbohydrate 7g, Fiber 1g.
1/2 cup cooked: Calories 46, Sodium 3mg, Protein 1g, Carbohydrate 11g, Fiber 2g.
Scallions, 1/2 cup raw: Calories 16, Sodium 8mg, Protein 1g, Carbohydrate 4g, Fiber 1g.
Shallots, 1/2 cup raw: Calories 58, Sodium 10mg, Protein 2g, Carbohydrate 13g, Fiber 1g.

CHOPPING AN ONION

1 *Trim the top and root ends leaving a little of the root attached to hold the onion together, then peel and halve it lengthwise.*

2 *Make horizontal and then vertical slices toward but not through the root end. Slice across to make dice, discarding the root end. You can then finely chop the onion if you like.*

Baked Spanish Onions

• 3 large Spanish onions, trimmed and cut across into 1/2-inch slices • 1 1/2 tablespoons olive or canola oil • 2 tablespoons toasted pine nuts (optional) • 1 teaspoon finely grated orange zest • 1 tablespoon chopped fresh chives or scallion tops • 1/8 teaspoon each salt and pepper

Preheat the oven to 350°F. Brush both sides of the onion slices with the oil and arrange them, overlapping slightly, in a nonstick jelly-roll pan. Sprinkle the pine nuts, orange zest, chives, salt, and pepper over the onion slices. Cover the pan with aluminum foil and bake the onions about 1 hour, until very soft and some juices have been released. Serves 4.
Per serving: Calories **136**, *Fiber* **4g**, *Saturated Fat* **1g**, *Total Fat* **5g**, *Sodium* **74mg**, *Cholesterol* **0mg**, *Carbohydrate* **21g**, *Protein* **3g**.

Shallots

Pearl onions

Red onions

◆ **LOOK FOR**
Firm onions with a smooth, papery skin; avoid onions that feel soft or are starting to sprout.

Yellow onion

Parsnips

High in fiber, folacin, and carbohydrate.

AT THEIR BEST   During fall and winter, but available year round.

STORING   Refrigerate, unwashed, in an open plastic bag and use within 1 to 2 weeks as long as they still feel firm.

PREPARING   With larger parsnips, cut across in half and then cut the wider part lengthwise in half. For soups and stews, cut into thick slices or chunks.

COOKING   You can cook large pieces of parsnip around roast meats or poultry for the last hour of cooking. Parsnips, cut into chunks, can be added to soups and stews for about 30 minutes. You can also boil or steam parsnips over a little boiling water about 20 minutes, until soft, then purée them and season simply with a little salt and pepper. Matchstick strips of parsnip can be baked in the oven, then tossed with a little olive oil and brown sugar, as you would do for glazed carrots.

Stirring roast parsnip matchsticks

SERVING   Serve puréed parsnips as an alternative to mashed potatoes with meat, turkey, or chicken. Roast or baked parsnips are best served alongside a traditional roast poultry or meat dish. Add to other seasonal vegetables, then simmer in stock and purée to make a silky-smooth soup.

NUTRITIONAL VALUES   ¹/₂ cup cooked: Calories **63**, Sodium **8mg**, Protein **1g**, Carbohydrate **15g**, Fiber **3g**.

PEELING AND CHOPPING PARSNIPS

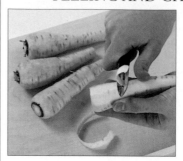

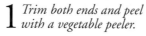

1 *Trim both ends and peel with a vegetable peeler.*

2 *Cut the parsnips lengthwise in half and then across into chunks.*

Puréed Parsnips with Ginger

• 1¹/₂ pounds parsnips, cut into 2-inch pieces • 1 cup vegetable or chicken stock, page 18 • 1 teaspoon finely chopped fresh ginger or ¹/₄ teaspoon ground • 2 tablespoons low-fat sour cream • ¹/₈ teaspoon each salt and pepper

In a medium saucepan, combine the parsnips with the stock and ginger. Cover the pan and bring to a boil over moderate heat. Simmer the parsnips in the stock about 15 minutes, until very soft. Transfer the parsnips with about half of the stock to a blender or food processor and purée until smooth. Gradually add the remaining stock until you have the desired consistency. Add the sour cream, salt, and pepper and process to combine. Serves 4.
Per serving: Calories **132**, *Fiber* **7g**, *Saturated Fat* **0g**, *Total Fat* **1g**, *Sodium* **106mg**, *Cholesterol* **0mg**, *Carbohydrate* **30g**, *Protein* **3g**.

◆ **LOOK FOR**
Medium-size parsnips that are firm and crisp, free of blemishes, and smooth skinned.

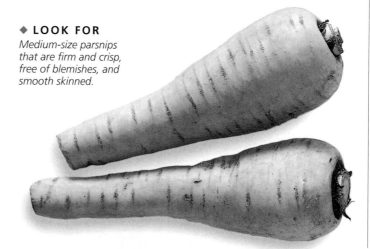

Peas

High in vitamin C and iron, and a fairly good source of beta carotene.

Green peas

Snow peas

To open the pod, press it gently between your thumb and forefinger, then gently push the peas out with your thumb.

◆ LOOK FOR
Green peas should have firm, bright green pods, well filled with plump peas. Avoid wilted or wrinkled pods.

AT THEIR BEST
January to August, but available all year.

VARIETIES
Snow peas are flat and a little limp, with edible pods. Sugar snap peas (a cross between the green pea and the snow pea) are rounder but also entirely edible. They should be very crisp.

STORING
Eat peas as fresh as possible; the sugar turns to starch in storage. You can refrigerate the pods in a plastic bag up to 4 days. Shelled green peas will freeze, but eat snow and sugar snap peas fresh.

PREPARING
Rinse shelled green peas under cold running water and drain. Rinse snow peas under cold water, break off the stem end, and pull off the string down the pod. Prepare sugar snap peas in a similar way but pull off the string from both sides.

COOKING
Green peas only need very brief cooking in about 1 inch of boiling water for about 5 minutes. Older green peas can be boiled until tender and then puréed with a little vegetable or chicken stock and sautéed onion. Either steam or boil snow and sugar snap peas for only 2 to 3 minutes. You can stir-fry snow peas for 2 to 3 minutes; if you want to sauté sugar snap peas, blanch them for a minute in boiling water, then refresh under cold water and dry thoroughly before sautéing.

SERVING
Green peas tossed with butter and mint make the classic accompaniment to a myriad of meat and fish dishes. Snow and sugar snap peas are used in Asian recipes, or served as a side dish with Chinese-style entrées.

NUTRITIONAL VALUES
Green peas, 1/2 cup cooked: Calories **67**, Sodium **2mg**, Protein **4g**, Carbohydrate **13g**, Fiber **4g**.

French-Style Peas

• 1 slice reduced-sodium bacon, finely chopped, or 1 tablespoon olive oil • 2 scallions, sliced • 2 cups fresh or frozen green peas • 1/2 cup vegetable or chicken stock, page 18 • 2 cups shredded romaine lettuce leaves • 1/8 teaspoon each salt and pepper

In a medium saucepan, cook the bacon over moderate heat about 2 1/2 minutes, stirring, until crisp and the fat is rendered. Remove bacon and reserve. Add the sliced scallions and sauté about 1 1/2 minutes, until softened. Stir in the peas, add the stock, and bring to a boil. Cover the pan and simmer about 5 minutes. Stir in the lettuce leaves with the salt and pepper and cook, stirring, until the lettuce is very wilted and heated through. Sprinkle the bacon on top and serve. Serves 4.
Per serving: Calories 43, Fiber 2g, Saturated Fat 0g, Total Fat 1g, Sodium 95mg, Cholesterol 1mg, Carbohydrate 7g, Protein 3g.

Stir-Fried Snow Peas with Bean Sprouts

• 1 tablespoon canola oil • 2 leeks, trimmed and sliced • 1 clove garlic, finely chopped • 12 ounces snow peas, trimmed as directed • 1 1/2 cups bean sprouts • 2 teaspoons reduced sodium soy sauce • 1/8 teaspoon pepper

In a large nonstick skillet or wok, heat the oil over high heat. Add the leeks and garlic and stir-fry, stirring constantly, about 2 minutes, until leeks are slightly soft. Add snow peas and stir-fry about 2 minutes, until they are crisp-tender and bright green. Add the bean sprouts and stir-fry about 2 minutes longer. Add the soy sauce and pepper; continue cooking 2 to 3 minutes longer, until the bean sprouts are slightly soft and have released some liquid. Serves 4.
Per serving: Calories 118, Fiber 2g, Saturated Fat 0g, Total Fat 4g, Sodium 106mg, Cholesterol 0mg, Carbohydrate 18g, Protein 5g.

Peppers

High in vitamin C (ounce for ounce they contain over twice as much as citrus fruit) and beta carotene.

AT THEIR BEST All year; home grown from March to October, and imported from September to March.

VARIETIES Sweet, or bell, peppers are found in a range of colors – yellow, orange, purple, and red – the riper versions of green peppers. Hot chili peppers have tastes varying from very hot to mild. The hottest is the Scotch bonnet or habanero, which is small, red, round, and very fiery. The medium-hot jalapeño peppers are slender and tapered, with a dark green color. Anaheim chili peppers, eaten in both green and red stages, range in flavor from mild to medium-hot. They are often stuffed and used for chiles rellenos.

STORING Store sweet green peppers unwashed in the crisper draw of the refrigerator up to 1 week; riper colored sweet peppers will keep slightly less well. Chili peppers will keep in a paper bag or wrapped in paper towels in the refrigerator up to 2 weeks.

PREPARING When preparing hot chili peppers, be sure to wear rubber gloves and handle them carefully. Capsaicin (the substance that makes them taste hot) can irritate your skin and will cause a burning sensation if it gets into your eyes, so avoid touching your eyes and face and wipe the cutting board well after use. To reduce the heat of a chili pepper, remove the seeds and membranes. To peel peppers, blacken the skins under the broiler, then cool in a paper bag and peel with a small knife.

COOKING Sauté sweet peppers in a little olive or canola oil; they combine well with onions and tomatoes. Stuffed sweet peppers should be parboiled first for about 10 minutes, then stuffed and baked for about 15 minutes. Roast cored and seeded sweet peppers in a moderate oven, brushed with a little oil, until very soft. Sweet peppers can also be broiled or grilled. Add a subtle flavor or a fiery kick to stews, hot or cold sauces, salads, and cooked vegetables by adding finely chopped mild to hot chili peppers.

SERVING Sweet peppers are excellent for stuffing with vegetable, rice, or meat fillings. They are an integral part of Mediterranean dishes such as ratatouille, Mexican dishes such as chili, and Creole dishes such as gumbo. They are used in many other casseroles and sauces, and they can also be served cooked by themselves. Raw sweet peppers, thinly sliced or chopped, add color, flavor, and a refreshing crunch to salads and cold salsas. Or slice thickly and serve with dips.

NUTRITIONAL VALUES Green peppers, ½ cup raw: Calories **14**, Sodium **1mg**, Protein **0g**, Carbohydrate **3g**, Fiber **1g**. ½ cup cooked: Calories **19**, Sodium **1mg**, Protein **1g**, Carbohydrate **5g**, Fiber **1g**.

Broil the skin of peppers before peeling.

To stuff sweet peppers, cut a thin slice from the bottom of the pepper so that it stands upright, and cut off the top. With a small spoon, scoop out the seeds and white ribs.

SEEDING AND DICING SWEET PEPPERS

1 *If sweet peppers are to be sliced or diced, first cut them in half lengthwise. Then cut out the core, removing the white ribs and seeds at the same time.*

2 *Slice the pepper halves lengthwise into strips, then gather the strips together and cut across into dice.*

Roasted Sweet Peppers

- 1 pound sweet peppers: red, green, yellow, or a combination • 2 tablespoons olive or canola oil • 1 clove garlic, finely chopped • 2 tablespoons chopped fresh basil, thyme, oregano, or sage or 1 teaspoon dried • 1/8 teaspoon each salt and pepper • 1 tablespoon balsamic or red wine vinegar

Preheat the oven to 400°F. Remove core and seeds from the peppers and cut the flesh into 1-inch strips. In a large bowl, combine the peppers with the oil, garlic, herbs, salt, and pepper. Transfer to a non-stick baking dish and roast, stirring occasionally, about 30 minutes or until very soft. Remove from the oven and stir in the vinegar while the peppers are still hot. Serves 4.
Per serving: Calories **89**, *Fiber* **2g**, *Saturated Fat* **1g**, *Total Fat* **7g**, *Sodium* **69mg**, *Cholesterol* **0mg**,

Sweet Pepper and Corn Salsa

- 1 each sweet green and red pepper • 1 cup frozen corn kernels, thawed • 2 tablespoons olive oil • Finely grated zest and juice of 1 lime • 1/8 teaspoon each salt and pepper • Dash of hot red pepper sauce • 2 tablespoons chopped parsley

Cut sweet peppers in half lengthwise. Remove core and seeds and place, skin side up, on a baking sheet. Broil 4 inches from the heat for 10 minutes, until the skins are blackened. Let cool and peel. Chop into small dice and transfer to a bowl. Add corn and mix well. In a small bowl, combine olive oil, lime zest and juice, salt, pepper, hot red pepper sauce, and parsley. Mix together, then pour over the peppers and corn. Toss together to mix; serve with broiled chicken breasts or as a dip. Serves 4.
Per serving: Calories **115**, *Fiber* **2g**, *Saturated Fat* **1g**, *Total Fat* **7g**, *Sodium* **75mg**, *Cholesterol* **0mg**, *Carbohydrate* **13g**, *Protein* **2g**.

◆ **LOOK FOR**
Sweet, or bell, peppers should be firm, shiny, and plump, with a smooth skin and no soft spots.

Stuffed Chili Peppers

- 4 large chili peppers or Italian frying peppers, halved lengthwise and seeded • 2 tablespoons olive or canola oil • 1 sweet red pepper, diced • 1 clove garlic, finely chopped • 1 small red onion, diced • 2 stalks celery, diced • 1/4 cup chopped fresh cilantro or parsley • 1/8 teaspoon each salt and pepper

Preheat oven to 350°F. Place the pepper halves, cut side down, in a roasting pan. Brush with half of the oil. Roast the peppers about 10 minutes or until slightly softened. Meanwhile, heat the remaining oil in a skillet over moderate heat. Add the sweet pepper, garlic, red onion, and celery. Sauté the vegetables about 5 minutes or until softened. Stir in the chopped cilantro, salt, and pepper. Spoon the mixture into the chili peppers, mounding the filling. Return to the oven and bake about 10 minutes longer or until the chili peppers are tender. Serves 4.
Per serving: Calories **118**, *Fiber* **3g**, *Saturated Fat* **1g**, *Total Fat* **7g**, *Sodium* **75mg**, *Cholesterol* **0mg**, *Carbohydrate* **14g**, *Protein* **3g**.

Hot chili peppers are smaller and are available in a variety of colors, shapes, and sizes.

Red jalapeños

Green jalapeños

Potatoes and Sweet Potatoes

High in vitamin C, beta carotene, and potassium.

AT THEIR BEST
All year. New potatoes in the spring and summer.

VARIETIES
Use russet potatoes for baking and oven frying; all-purpose potatoes for boiling, roasting, and salads.

STORING
Take them out of plastic bags if you purchase them this way. Store in a well-ventilated, cool, dark place up to 2 weeks; do not refrigerate.

PREPARING
Scrub baking potatoes. If you choose to peel all-purpose potatoes for boiling or roasting, use a potato peeler and remove just a thin layer of flesh with the peelings. Any green parts should be cut away; if green is widespread, discard the potato. Peeled potatoes should be immersed in cold water immediately to prevent discoloring.

COOKING
You can boil white or sweet potatoes for 15 to 30 minutes, depending on their size. Boil or steam new potatoes in their skins about 20 minutes. Bake large white or sweet potatoes in a moderate oven (350°F) in their skins about 1 hour or until they feel soft when squeezed. (If you are in a hurry, microwave the potato until it is nearly done, then finish it off in a hot oven for about 10 minutes to give it a crispy skin.) Roast all-purpose or new potatoes around meat or poultry roasts, basting them with the pan juices. If you prefer, you can parboil the potatoes for 10 minutes, then add to the roasting pan for the last hour.

SERVING
Cold potatoes can be used in salads with herb or vinaigrette dressing. Oven fries and baked potatoes make the ideal accompaniment to burgers and grilled poultry or meat. Baked potatoes can make the basis for the entire main course, topped with corn, beans, cheese, or low-fat sour cream. Boiled potatoes can be mashed or served sprinkled with herbs. Add cubed potatoes to casseroles and soups to thicken the liquid.

NUTRITIONAL VALUES
All-purpose potato, baked with skin: Calories **200**, Sodium **16mg**, Protein **5g**, Carbohydrate **15g**, Fiber **5g**. Peeled, cooked: Calories **116**, Sodium **7mg**, Protein **2g**, Carbohydrate **27g**, Fiber **2g**. Sweet potato, peeled, cooked: Calories **158**, Sodium **20mg**, Protein **2g**, Carbohydrate **38g**, Fiber **5g**.

PREPARING NEW POTATOES

1 Because most nutrients are directly beneath the skin, don't peel new potatoes; just scrub and cook.

2 Cut large potatoes in quarters if necessary. Steam new potatoes in their skins to retain flavor, texture, and vitamin C.

Fiesta Potato Bake

• 4 baking potatoes • 1 tablespoon olive or canola oil • 1 onion, coarsely chopped • 1 sweet red or green pepper, coarsely chopped • 2 stalks celery, sliced • 1/2 cup buttermilk or 1% low-fat milk • 2 tablespoons grated Parmesan cheese (optional) • 12 ounces lean ground beef or turkey • 1/2 teaspoon chili powder • 1/8 teaspoon each salt and pepper

Bake potatoes as directed. About 5 minutes before they are done, heat oil in a large nonstick skillet over moderate heat. Add onion and sauté for 3 minutes, until slightly softened. Add sweet pepper and celery and sauté 2 to 3 minutes longer or until crisp-tender. Meanwhile, slit open top of potatoes, leaving bottoms intact. Scoop out flesh and place in a bowl. Add milk and cheese, if using, and mash with a fork until fairly smooth. Fill potato shells with mixture and keep them warm. Add ground beef, chili powder, salt, and pepper to skillet. Stir with a spatula to break up beef and cook, stirring occasionally, about 3 minutes or until beef is cooked through. Spoon mixture over the potatoes and serve. Serves 4.
Per serving: Calories **326**, *Fiber* **5g**, *Saturated Fat* **2g**, *Total Fat* **7g**, *Sodium* **173mg**, *Cholesterol* **50mg**, *Carbohydrate* **14g**, *Protein* **24g**.

Roasted New Potatoes

- 1¹/₂ pounds small new potatoes, scrubbed • 3 cloves garlic, thinly sliced • 2 tablespoons olive or canola oil • ¹/₂ teaspoon crumbled rosemary (optional)

Preheat the oven to 400°F. In a large bowl, combine the potatoes with the garlic, oil, and rosemary, if using. Transfer to a roasting pan and roast about 45 minutes or until golden and cooked through. Serves 8.

Per serving: Calories **219**, *Fiber* **6g**, *Saturated Fat* **1g**, *Total Fat* **8g**, *Sodium* **16mg**, *Cholesterol* **0mg**, *Carbohydrate* **35g**, *Protein* **3g**.

◆ LOOK FOR

Firm, smooth-skinned, solid potatoes. Avoid potatoes that are blemished or sprouting and those with a green color, which will be bitter.

Red potatoes

Long white (all-purpose)

Round red

Russet potatoes

New potatoes

Sweet potatoes are often tapered in shape

Creamy Low-Fat Mashed Potatoes

- 1¹/₂ pounds russet potatoes, peeled and cut into 2-inch pieces • 1 tablespoon olive or canola oil • 3 tablespoons low-fat sour cream or plain nonfat yogurt • ¹/₈ teaspoon each salt and pepper

Place the potatoes in a large saucepan and cover with water. Bring to a boil over moderate heat and simmer 20 to 30 minutes or until the potatoes are very tender. Drain the potatoes, reserving about 1 cup of the cooking liquid. Either pass the potatoes through a ricer or mash them in the saucepan. Stir in the oil, sour cream, salt, and pepper until well blended. Gradually stir in some of the reserved cooking liquid until the potatoes become creamy and smooth. Serves 4.
Per serving: Calories **126**, *Fiber* **2g**, *Saturated Fat* **1g**, *Total Fat* **4g**, *Sodium* **83mg**, *Cholesterol* **2mg**, *Carbohydrate* **20g**, *Protein* **3g**.

Oven Fries

- 2 pounds large baking potatoes or sweet potatoes, scrubbed but unpeeled • 2 teaspoons olive or canola oil • ¹/₈ teaspoon each salt and pepper

Place 2 baking sheets in the oven and preheat the oven to 450°F. Cut the potatoes lengthwise into ¹/₂-inch slices, then cut the slices lengthwise into ¹/₂-inch strips. In a large bowl, combine the oil with the salt and pepper. Add the potatoes and toss well so that they are evenly coated. Arrange the potatoes in a single layer on the hot baking sheets and bake, turning once, 30 to 35 minutes or until browned, crisp, and cooked through. Serves 4.
Per serving:
Calories **150**, *Fiber* **3g**, *Saturated Fat* **0g**, *Total Fat* **2g**, *Sodium* **72mg**, *Cholesterol* **0mg**, *Carbohydrate* **29g**, *Protein* **4g**.

Radishes

A good source of vitamin C. Use for texture and flavor.

AT THEIR BEST In spring and summer. Red radishes are at their hottest in the summer.

STORING Wrap loosely and refrigerate up to 1 week. To crisp them up, soak in iced water 1 to 2 hours.

PREPARING Trim off the roots and green tops. Either slice, chop, grate, or leave radishes whole as required.

COOKING Steam whole radishes for about 10 minutes or until crisp-tender, adding a pinch of black pepper and a little olive oil if you like. Add sliced or halved raw radishes to stir-fries and summer vegetable stews. Long white radishes can be grated or cut into julienne strips for hot or cold Oriental recipes.

SERVING Serve radishes raw in salads and sandwiches or as a snack. They can also be steamed and served as a side vegetable or in recipes.

NUTRITIONAL VALUES ¹/₂ cup raw: Calories **10**, Sodium **14mg**, Protein **0g**, Carbohydrate **2g**, Fiber **1g**.

◆ **LOOK FOR**
Firm red or white radishes, with smooth skins and uniform shape. Leaves should be deep green color.

White radish or daikon

Steamed Radishes with Dill

• 2 bunches radishes, trimmed
• 1 scallion, thinly sliced •
1¹/₂ tablespoons olive or canola oil • 1 tablespoon chopped fresh dill • ¹/₈ teaspoon each salt and pepper

Steam radishes as directed for about 6 minutes. Scatter scallion over radishes, cover, and continue steaming for another 3 minutes. Combine oil with dill, salt, and pepper in a bowl. Add radishes and toss well to coat. Serves 4.
Per serving: Calories 55, Fiber 1g, Saturated Fat 1g, Total Fat 5g, Sodium 78mg, Cholesterol 0mg, Carbohydrate 2g, Protein 0g.

Spinach

High in beta carotene; a source of vitamin C and iron.

AT THEIR BEST Late spring and early summer.

STORING Wrap in plastic bags and refrigerate up to 3 days.

PREPARING Tear off the tough stems and discard. Wash in several changes of cold water and drain well. Dry spinach to be used raw in salads.

COOKING Bring a little water to a boil in a saucepan. Pack in the spinach, cover, and steam 1 to 2 minutes or until wilted. Drain and toss with seasonings and a little olive oil if you like. Sauté spinach in a little olive oil with chopped onion and garlic about 4 minutes or until wilted.

SERVING The leaves can be eaten raw in salads or used as a garnish. Serve steamed spinach as a side dish, in Florentine recipes with eggs or fish, or as a filling for crêpes. It also makes a delicious soup.

NUTRITIONAL VALUES ¹/₂ cup raw: Calories **6**, Sodium **22mg**, Protein **1g**, Carbohydrate **1g**, Fiber **1g**.

◆ **LOOK FOR**
Crisp, dark green, tender young leaves with no yellow or wilting patches.

Spinach Sauté with Mushrooms

• 2 tablespoons olive oil •
1 clove garlic, finely chopped
• 10 ounces mushrooms, thinly sliced • 1 bag (10 ounces) spinach, prepared as directed
• 1 tablespoon lemon juice
• ¹/₈ teaspoon hot red pepper flakes • ¹/₈ teaspoon each salt and pepper

Heat oil in a skillet; cook garlic and mushrooms, stirring, 3 minutes. Add spinach, cover, and steam 3 minutes. Stir in lemon juice, pepper flakes, salt, and pepper and cook 2 minutes longer. Serves 4.
Per serving: Calories 92, Fiber 3g, Saturated Fat 1g, Total Fat 7g, Sodium 114mg, Cholesterol 0mg, Carbohydrate 6g, Protein 3g.

Squash, Winter

High in beta carotene as well as vitamin C.

AT THEIR BEST Fall, but available all year.

VARIETIES Acorn squash has sweet, slightly dry flesh and deeply ridged skin. Butternut has rich, sweet flesh that is a deep orange color. Pumpkins have a deep orange, hard skin. Choose the smaller sugar pumpkins with sweeter, coarse-grained flesh.

STORING Uncut, they keep in a cool, dry place for up to 1 month. Once cut into pieces, they can be tightly wrapped and refrigerated up to 2 weeks.

PREPARING See box (right). The skin is more easily removed after cooking.

COOKING Bake squash slices or chunks in a roasting pan at 350°F for about 45 minutes, or steam for about 40 minutes. Smaller acorn or golden nugget squash can be cut in half and baked upside down for about 1 hour.

SERVING Serve as a cooked side-dish vegetable. The flavor of the flesh is mild, so you can combine squash with other ingredients such as ginger, garlic, spices, herbs, and honey. After baking, purée the flesh and flavor it as you like. Puréed squash makes a velvety soup with stock and flavoring vegetables.

NUTRITIONAL VALUES Acorn and butternut squash, ½ cup cooked: Calories **42**, Sodium **4mg**, Protein **1g**, Carbohydrate **11g**, Fiber **3g**.
Pumpkin, ½ cup cooked: Calories **25**, Sodium **1mg**, Protein **1g**, Carbohydrate **6g**, Fiber **2g**.

◆ **LOOK FOR**
Acorn squash that are hard-skinned green or orange with a streaked, furrowed skin. Avoid ones with soft spots.

PREPARING WINTER SQUASH

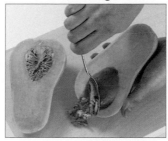

1 *With a knife, cut off stem and halve lengthwise. With a spoon, scoop out all the seeds.*

2 *Cut the halves lengthwise into quarters and then cut the flesh into chunks.*

Baked Acorn Squash Rings

• 2 large acorn squash • 1 tablespoon olive or canola oil • ⅛ teaspoon each salt and pepper • 2 tablespoons honey • 3 tablespoons coarsely chopped pecans

Preheat the oven to 350°F. Halve the squash crosswise and scrape out the seeds. Cut into ¾-inch rings. Brush the slices on all sides with the oil and arrange in a single layer on a nonstick baking sheet. Season with the salt and pepper. Bake about 15 minutes or until slightly soft. Turn the rings over, drizzle with the honey, and sprinkle with the pecans. Continue baking about 20 to 35 minutes longer or until very soft. Serves 4.
*Per serving: Calories **182**, Fiber **4g**, Saturated Fat **1g**, Total Fat **7g**, Sodium **73mg**, Cholesterol **0mg**, Carbohydrate **32g**, Protein **2g**.*

Butternut has a smooth, hard, beige-colored skin and feels heavy in relation to its size.

Squash, Summer

Good sources of vitamin C.

Pattypan
squash

◆ **LOOK FOR**
*Firm yellow squash and green
zucchini that feel heavy.*

*Avoid squash that are bruised
or pitted. Smaller squash
will be sweeter.*

AT THEIR BEST   Spring and summer, although available all year.

VARIETIES   Soft-skinned summer squash include zucchini, yellow squash, and small pattypan squash.

STORING   Unwashed in the refrigerator for 3 to 4 days.

PREPARING   Trim both ends, cut lengthwise into halves or quarters, and then into slices or strips. For stuffing, cut lengthwise in half and scoop out the seeds.

COOKING   Steam about 5 minutes or until tender. Sauté in oil with onions or carrots. Steam halved squash, then stuff with rice, vegetable, or meat mixtures and bake about 30 minutes. Combine with tomatoes, onions, and sweet peppers in ratatouille. Use as a filling in savory pies and tarts. Simmer in stock to make a summer soup served hot or chilled.

NUTRITIONAL VALUES   Zucchini, ½ cup cooked: Calories **14**, Sodium **3mg**, Protein **1g**, Carbohydrate **4g**, Fiber **1g**.

Squash Ribbons with Chili Peppers

• 1½ **pounds summer squash** •
1 **red onion, thinly sliced** • 1
**teaspoon finely chopped red or
green chili pepper** • 2 **teaspoons
lime or lemon juice** • ⅛ **teaspoon each salt and pepper**

Trim squash. With vegetable
peeler, shave squash into long
strips. Pile ribbons over onion

in a steamer basket and steam
about 3 minutes or until tender.
Transfer to a bowl, add chili pep-
per, lime juice, salt, and pepper,
and toss to coat. Cover and let
stand for a few minutes. Serves 4.
*Per serving: Calories 38, Fiber 2g,
Saturated Fat 0g, Total Fat 0g,
Sodium 73mg, Cholesterol 0mg,
Carbohydrate 8g, Protein 2g.*

Tomatoes

High in beta carotene and vitamin C.

AT THEIR BEST   Local vine-ripened tomatoes in the summer; cherry and imported tomatoes available all year.

VARIETIES   The most common tomato is usually red and rounded and is juicy yet firm. Yellow tomatoes have less flavor than red; green tomatoes are unripe red tomatoes, are less sweet, and are usual-ly cooked. Cherry tomatoes are perfect in salads. Use plum tomatoes for cooking or canning.

STORING   At room temperature, out of direct sunlight. Use ripe tomatoes within 1 or 2 days. To ripen, place in a closed paper bag with an apple and leave at room temperature.

PREPARING   To seed, cut crosswise in half and, with a teaspoon, scoop out the seeds. Slice or dice tomatoes with a serrated knife.

COOKING   Broil halved beefsteak or plum tomatoes or stuff with a vegetable or seafood mixture, then bake. Sauté with onions, garlic, or other vegetables. Tomatoes make the basis for soups and casseroles as well as sauces for pasta and fish. Raw, they are a staple for salads and sandwiches.

NUTRITIONAL VALUES   ½ cup raw: Calories **13**, Sodium **6mg**, Protein **1g**, Carbohydrate **3g**, Fiber **1g**.

PEELING TOMATOES

1 *With a sharp knife, cut
a small cross in the skin.
Blanch the tomatoes in boiling
water for about 30 seconds.*

2 *Plunge them into cold
water. With a sharp knife,
peel the skins from the point
where the cross-shaped cut
was made.*

Roasted Tomatoes with Herbs

• 4 ripe tomatoes • 1 tablespoon olive or canola oil • 1 tablespoon chopped parsley • 1 tablespoon chopped fresh basil or 1 teaspoon dried • 2 cloves garlic, finely chopped • 1/8 teaspoon pepper

Preheat the oven to 375°F. Remove the stem end from the tomatoes and halve each tomato crosswise. Brush them all over with the oil and arrange, cut side up, in a nonstick roasting pan. Roast about 8 minutes or until slightly soft. Sprinkle evenly with the herbs, garlic, and pepper and roast 5 to 10 minutes longer or until very soft. Serves 4.
Per serving: Calories 63, Fiber 2g, Saturated Fat 1g, Total Fat 4g, Sodium 14mg, Cholesterol 0mg, Carbohydrate 7g, Protein 1g.

Chinese Stir-Fried Cherry Tomatoes

• 1 tablespoon canola oil • 1 teaspoon Oriental sesame oil (optional) • 1 teaspoon finely chopped fresh ginger or 1 scallion, sliced diagonally • 2 pints cherry tomatoes • 1 cup shredded white radish (daikon) • 1 tablespoon reduced-sodium soy sauce • 1/8 teaspoon pepper

Heat oil in a wok or skillet. Add sesame oil, if using, with ginger and stir-fry about 2 minutes, until fragrant. Add tomatoes and stir-fry 2 to 3 minutes, until they begin to split and soften. Add radish, soy sauce, and pepper and toss to coat. Continue stir-frying about 3 minutes longer. Serves 4.
Per serving: Calories 87, Fiber 3g, Saturated Fat 1g, Total Fat 5g, Sodium 171mg, Cholesterol 0mg, Carbohydrate 10g, Protein 2g.

Cherry tomatoes

Common tomato

Plum tomatoes

◆ **LOOK FOR**
Smooth, firm, deep-colored tomatoes that are plump and well shaped.

Turnips

A source of vitamin C and carbohydrate.

◆ **LOOK FOR**
Firm, smooth vegetables that feel heavy. Choose young turnips about 2 inches across. Turnip tops should be a deep green color.

AT THEIR BEST Fall and winter.

VARIETIES Turnips have a white and purple skin. The vegetable called yellow turnip is not a turnip but rutabaga; it has a sweeter, stronger flavor. Prepare and cook in the same way.

STORING Refrigerate greens separately in a plastic bag; use as soon as possible. Use turnips within 1 week.

PREPARING Slice off both ends. Scrub baby turnips but peel older turnips, then quarter, slice, or dice them.

COOKING Boil or steam about 15 minutes, until tender; toss in olive oil and seasoning. Roast turnips with meat or poultry for about 30 minutes. Sauté sliced turnips in oil, then bake for about 30 minutes with seasoning and sliced onion. Cook young turnip greens like collard greens (see page 176).

SERVING Serve delicately flavored turnips with pork, duck, game, or roast meat and poultry. Glaze boiled sliced turnips with oil and sugar. Purée turnips with carrots or apples to serve with meats.

NUTRITIONAL VALUES 1/2 cup cooked: *Calories 14, Sodium 39mg, Protein 1g, Carbohydrate 4g, Fiber 2g.*

Mashed Turnips with Carrots

• 1 pound turnips, diced • 2 large carrots, sliced • 1 tablespoon olive or canola oil • 2 tablespoons low-fat sour cream • 1/8 teaspoon each salt and pepper • Pinch of ground nutmeg

Bring a large saucepan of water to a boil. Add turnips and carrots and boil for 20 minutes. Drain and either pass through a ricer or mash. Return pan to very low heat and add oil with sour cream, salt, pepper, and nutmeg. Stir together 3 to 5 minutes, until heated through. Serves 4.
Per serving: Calories 98, Fiber 4g, Saturated Fat 1g, Total Fat 4g, Sodium 167mg, Cholesterol 1mg, Carbohydrate 14g, Protein 2g.

Vegetable and Cheese Lasagne

Reduce fat ▪ *Replace the traditional ground meat with a layer of vegetables. Use low-fat cheeses.*
Reduce sodium ▪ *No salt is added because there is salt in the tomato paste.*
Save time ▪ *Use 4 cups of your favorite prepared spaghetti sauce and omit Step 1.*
Bring the water for the lasagne noodles to a boil while you complete Step 2.

● Serves **6** ● Preparation Time **35 minutes** ● Cooking Time **1 hour 40 minutes**

PER SERVING
Calories **428**, Saturated Fat **7g**,
Total Fat **15g**, Sodium **514mg**,
Cholesterol **34mg**, Protein **23g**,
Carbohydrate **53g**, Fiber **6g**.

2 tablespoons olive or canola oil

2 large onions, coarsely chopped

2 cloves garlic, finely chopped

1 can (28 ounces) crushed tomatoes

2 tablespoons tomato paste

¹/₂ teaspoon each dried oregano and basil

3 zucchini, diced

2 large carrots, diced

2 stalks celery, diced

9 thick or 12 narrow lasagne noodles (8–10 ounces)

1 container (15 ounces) part-skim ricotta cheese

1 egg white

2 tablespoons finely chopped parsley

3 ounces part-skim mozzarella cheese, sliced

2 tablespoons grated Parmesan cheese

1 In a saucepan, heat 1 tablespoon oil over moderate heat. Sauté onions and garlic, stirring, about 5 minutes or until softened. Add tomatoes, tomato paste, and herbs. Simmer, stirring occasionally, about 15 minutes or until cooked to a thick sauce.

2 Meanwhile, in a nonstick skillet, heat the remaining oil over moderate heat and sauté the zucchini, carrots, and celery, stirring frequently, about 7 minutes or until slightly softened.

3 Bring a large pot of water to a boil. Add the lasagne and cook until barely tender, according to package directions. Drain, rinse, and drain well again. In a small bowl, combine the ricotta cheese, egg white, and parsley.

4 Preheat the oven to 350°F. Spread about a quarter of the tomato sauce into the base of a 13" x 9" x 2" baking dish. Arrange a third of the lasagne over the sauce in an even layer.

5 Spread half the ricotta-cheese mixture over pasta; scatter half the vegetables on top. Repeat layers of tomato sauce, lasagne, ricotta-cheese mixture, and vegetables. End with a layer of tomato sauce and lasagne.

6 Spread the remaining sauce over the final layer of pasta and scatter the mozzarella and Parmesan cheese over it. Bake about 45 minutes or until browned around the edges.

An ideal party dish or family supper –
Vegetable and Cheese Lasagne.

Roasted Vegetable Lasagne

Roasted vegetables add fiber and vitamins to this hearty lasagne. Serve them on their own for an excellent side dish.

- Serves **6**
- Preparation Time **25 minutes**
- Cooking Time **2¼ hours**

---

1 large eggplant, cubed

2 zucchini, cubed

1 large sweet red or green pepper, cubed

2 large carrots, diced

2 tablespoons olive or canola oil

2 large onions, coarsely chopped

2 cloves garlic, finely chopped

1 can (28 ounces) crushed tomatoes

2 tablespoons tomato paste

1 can (8 ounces) reduced-sodium tomato sauce

½ teaspoon each dried rosemary and thyme

9 thick or 12 narrow lasagne noodles (8–10 ounces)

1 container (15 ounces) part-skim ricotta cheese

1 egg white

2 tablespoons chopped parsley

3 ounces part-skim mozzarella cheese, sliced

2 tablespoons grated Parmesan cheese

1 Preheat the oven to 450°F. In a large nonstick roasting pan, combine eggplant, zucchini, sweet pepper, and carrots. Add 1 tablespoon oil and toss to coat. Roast the vegetables, stirring occasionally, about 45 minutes or until browned and very soft. Reduce oven temperature to 350°F.

2 Meanwhile, in a skillet heat remaining oil over moderate heat and sauté onions and garlic about 5 minutes or until soft. Add tomatoes, tomato paste, tomato sauce, and herbs. Simmer, stirring occasionally, about 15 minutes or until cooked to a thick sauce.

3 Bring a large pot of water to a boil. Add the lasagne and cook until barely tender, according to package directions. Drain, rinse, and drain well again. In a small bowl, combine ricotta cheese, egg white, and parsley.

4 Spread about a quarter of the tomato sauce into the base of a 13" x 9" x 2" baking dish. Arrange about a third of the lasagne over the sauce in an even layer.

5 Spread half of the ricotta mixture over the pasta, scatter the roasted vegetables over the top, then spoon a third of the remaining sauce over it. Top with half of the remaining pasta and repeat to make another layer.

6 Spread the remaining sauce over the final layer of pasta and scatter the mozzarella and Parmesan cheese over them. Bake about 45 minutes or until browned around the edges.

PER SERVING
Calories **469**, Saturated Fat **7g**, Total Fat **15g**, Sodium **743mg**, Cholesterol **34mg**, Protein **24g**, Carbohydrate **62g**, Fiber **8g**.

Broccoli Mushroom Lasagne

If you choose to use the ham in this dish, remember that the sodium level will be pushed up.

- Serves **6**
- Preparation Time **30 minutes**
- Cooking Time **1 hour 20 minutes**

---

1 tablespoon olive or canola oil

2 large onions, coarsely chopped

1 large sweet red or green pepper, thinly sliced

2 cloves garlic, finely chopped

10–12 ounces mushrooms, sliced

1 can (28 ounces) crushed tomatoes

2 tablespoons tomato paste

1 can (8 ounces) reduced-sodium tomato sauce

½ teaspoon dried basil

1 container (15 ounces) part-skim ricotta cheese

1 egg white

2 tablespoons chopped parsley

9 thick or 12 narrow lasagne noodles (8–10 ounces)

1 package (10 ounces) frozen chopped broccoli, thawed and well drained

3 ounces reduced-fat, reduced-sodium ham, thinly sliced (optional)

3 ounces part-skim mozzarella cheese, sliced

2 tablespoons grated Parmesan cheese

1 In a saucepan, heat oil over moderate heat. Sauté onions, sweet pepper, and garlic about 7 minutes. Add mushrooms and cook 5 minutes longer. Stir in tomatoes, tomato paste, tomato sauce, and basil. Simmer, stirring occasionally, about 15 minutes or until cooked to a thick sauce.

2 Preheat the oven to 350°F. In a small bowl, combine ricotta cheese, egg white, and parsley. Spread about a quarter of the vegetable-tomato sauce into the base of a 13" x 9" x 2" baking dish.

3 Bring a large pot of water to a boil. Cook lasagne according to package directions until barely tender. Drain, rinse, and drain again. Arrange a third of the lasagne noodles over the sauce in an even layer. Spread half the ricotta cheese mixture over the pasta and top with half of the broccoli and half of the ham slices, if using.

> **COOKING TIP**
> *Make sure you use the drained lasagne immediately or the pasta will stick together and be difficult to separate.*

4 Spoon a third of the remaining vegetable-tomato sauce over the layers in the baking dish. Top with half of the remaining lasagne noodles, the remaining cheese, broccoli, and ham, if using, and finish with the remaining lasagne and sauce.

5 Scatter the mozzarella and Parmesan cheese over the top. Bake until browned around the edges, about 45 minutes.

PER SERVING
Calories **420**, Saturated Fat **6g**, Total Fat **13g**, Sodium **512mg**, Cholesterol **34mg**, Protein **24g**, Carbohydrate **54g**, Fiber **6g**.

Eggplant Cannelloni with Ham and Mozzarella

Eggplant is very low in calories and contains hardly any fat, making it an ideal partner for cheese and ham.

- Serves **6**
- Preparation Time **30 minutes**
- Cooking Time **1½ hours**

---

3 large eggplants (1 pound each)

2 tablespoons olive or canola oil

2 large onions, coarsely chopped

1 large sweet red or green pepper, thinly sliced

2 cloves garlic, finely chopped

10 ounces mushrooms, chopped

1 can (28 ounces) crushed tomatoes

2 tablespoons tomato paste

1 can (8 ounces) reduced-sodium tomato sauce

½ teaspoon dried basil

1 cup part-skim ricotta cheese

6 thin slices reduced-sodium, reduced-fat ham

12 large basil leaves (optional)

6 ounces part-skim mozzarella cheese, cut into 12 (2" x ½" x ½") sticks

2 tablespoons grated Parmesan cheese

---

1 Preheat oven to 450°F. Cut each eggplant into 6 lengthwise slices; discard outer slices. With 1 tablespoon oil, brush slices and bake on nonstick baking sheets 15 to 20 minutes on each side.

2 Meanwhile, in a saucepan, heat remaining oil over moderate heat. Sauté onions, sweet peppers, and garlic about 7 minutes or until soft. Add mushrooms and cook about 5 minutes longer.

3 Stir in tomatoes, tomato paste, tomato sauce, and basil. Simmer, stirring occasionally, about 15 minutes or until cooked to a thick sauce.

4 Prepare the eggplant rolls (see box, right), spreading each with a little ricotta cheese and laying ½ slice of ham on top, then 1 basil leaf, if using. Place 1 mozzarella stick at the stem end of each slice and roll up.

5 Spoon about half of the tomato sauce into the base of a 13" x 9" x 2" baking dish and set the eggplant rolls on top, making sure the seams are underneath.

6 Pour the remaining tomato sauce over the eggplant rolls in the baking dish and sprinkle with the grated Parmesan cheese. Bake about 45 minutes or until the cheese is browned and the sauce is bubbling around the edges.

COOKING TIP
To avoid bitterness, sprinkle eggplant slices with salt and leave for 30 minutes. Rinse, drain, and pat them dry.

PER SERVING
Calories **371**, Saturated Fat **7g**, Total Fat **16g**, Sodium **712mg**, Cholesterol **45mg**, Protein **24g**, Carbohydrate **37g**, Fiber **10g**.

MAKING EGGPLANT CANNELLONI

1 *Spread each eggplant slice with a little ricotta cheese and top with the ham and basil leaf, if using.*

2 *Place 1 stick of mozzarella at the stem end, then carefully roll up each eggplant slice.*

Thin slices of eggplant are rolled around cheese and ham, then baked in a tomato and mushroom sauce.

193

Vegetable Ratatouille

Cooking technique ■ *Sauté the vegetables in batches so that they brown nicely and don't get mushy. For a meatless main dish, serve over rice or couscous.*

● Serves **4** ● Preparation Time **20 minutes** ● Cooking time **55–60 minutes**

PER SERVING
Calories **342**, Saturated Fat **2g**,
Total Fat **13g**, Sodium **651mg**,
Cholesterol **0mg**, Protein **12g**,
Carbohydrate **50g**, Fiber **16g**.

3 tablespoons olive or canola oil

2 large onions, coarsely chopped

2 cloves garlic, finely chopped

2 sweet red, green, or yellow peppers, diced

4 zucchini or yellow squash, sliced

1 large eggplant, diced

1 can (16 ounces) crushed or diced tomatoes

1 can (16 ounces) chick-peas, drained and rinsed

1 teaspoon each dried oregano, basil, and thyme

$1/8$ teaspoon each salt and pepper

2 tablespoons chopped parsley

1 In a Dutch oven, heat 2 tablespoons of oil over moderate heat. Add onions and garlic; sauté, stirring, about 7 minutes or until softened and golden.

2 Add sweet peppers and sauté, stirring, about 7 minutes or until browned. Remove from the heat; using a slotted spoon, transfer mixture to a bowl.

3 Return Dutch oven to the heat. Sauté zucchini, stirring frequently, about 7 minutes or until softened. Transfer to the bowl with the onions and peppers.

Vegetable Ratatouille is sure to please, either as a side dish or the main event.

4 Heat the remaining oil in the Dutch oven. Add the eggplant and sauté, stirring constantly, for about 6 minutes or until the eggplant is slightly softened.

5 Return all the sautéed vegetables to the Dutch oven with the tomatoes, chickpeas, dried herbs, salt, and pepper and stir to combine.

6 Cover and simmer gently for 25 to 30 minutes or until the vegetables are soft. Stir in parsley. Serve hot or allow to cool and serve at room temperature.

Spicy Vegetables

- Serves **4**
- Preparation Time **15 minutes**
- Cooking Time **50 minutes**

3 tablespoons olive or canola oil

2 large onions, sliced

2 cloves garlic, finely chopped

2 large carrots, diced

¹/₄ teaspoon ground cumin

Pinch each nutmeg, ground ginger, and hot red pepper flakes

2 small parsnips, diced

2 cups reduced-sodium tomato juice

1 each zucchini and yellow squash, sliced

1 can (16 ounces) chick-peas, drained and rinsed

¹/₂ cup dark raisins

¹/₈ teaspoon pepper

1 Heat the oil and sauté onions and garlic in as in Step 1 of the master recipe.

2 Sauté carrots about 5 minutes or until softened. Stir in the spices and cook about 3 minutes longer.

3 Stir in parsnips and tomato juice. Cover and simmer gently 10 to 12 minutes or until vegetables are almost cooked.

4 Stir in zucchini, yellow squash, and chick-peas. Cover and simmer about 20 minutes or until the vegetables are very soft. Stir in raisins and pepper.

PER SERVING
Calories **417**, Saturated Fat **2g**, Total Fat **13g**, Sodium **563mg**, Cholesterol **0mg**, Protein **11g**, Carbohydrate **71g**, Fiber **17g**.

Vegetable Curry

- Serves **4**
- Preparation Time **20 minutes**
- Cooking Time **45–50 minutes**

2 tablespoons olive or canola oil

2 large onions, coarsely chopped

2 cloves garlic, finely chopped

1 tablespoon curry powder

2 large carrots, diced

1 eggplant, diced

3 cups cauliflower florets

2 cups vegetable stock, page 18

1 can (6 ounces) tomato paste

1 package (10 ounces) frozen baby lima beans

2 teaspoons lemon juice

2 tablespoons chopped fresh cilantro or parsley

¹/₂ cup plain nonfat yogurt

1 Heat the oil and sauté onions and garlic as in Step 1 of master recipe. Stir in curry powder and cook about 3 minutes longer, until fragrant.

2 Sauté carrots and eggplant 6 to 7 minutes or until softened. Stir in cauliflower with stock and tomato paste. Cover and simmer gently 15 to 20 minutes or until vegetables are almost cooked.

3 Stir in lima beans, cover, and simmer about 10 minutes or until vegetables are soft.

4 Stir in the lemon juice and cilantro. Top each serving with 2 tablespoons of yogurt.

PER SERVING
Calories **305**, Saturated Fat **1g**, Total Fat **8g**, Sodium **457mg**, Cholesterol **1mg**, Protein **12g**, Carbohydrate **52g**, Fiber **14g**.

Vegetable Chili

- Serves **4**
- Preparation Time **20 minutes**
- Cooking Time **45–55 minutes**

2 tablespoons olive or canola oil

2 large onions, coarsely chopped

2 cloves garlic, finely chopped

1 tablespoon chili powder

2 stalks celery, diced

2 large carrots, diced

1 sweet red or green pepper, diced

1 can (16 ounces) crushed or diced tomatoes

1 cup vegetable stock, page 18

2 yellow squash, sliced

1 can (16 ounces) red kidney beans, drained and rinsed

1 cup frozen corn kernels

2 tablespoons chopped parsley

¹/₂ cup low-fat sour cream

1 Heat oil and sauté onions and garlic as in Step 1 of master recipe. Stir in chili powder and cook 2 to 3 minutes longer.

2 Sauté celery, carrots, and sweet pepper, stirring frequently, 6 to 7 minutes or until softened.

3 Add tomatoes and stock; bring to a boil. Add squash, kidney beans, and corn. Cover and simmer, stirring occasionally, 25 to 30 minutes or until tender.

4 Stir in the parsley and top each serving with sour cream.

PER SERVING
Calories **374**, Saturated Fat **1g**, Total Fat **14g**, Sodium **661mg**, Cholesterol **0mg**, Protein **13g**, Carbohydrate **54g**, Fiber **14g**.

Spinach Ricotta Roll-Ups

Cooking technique ■ *For this savory version of a jelly roll, make a thin "cake" with spinach and egg whites. Spread the filling on top, then roll and slice.*

● Serves 3 ● Preparation Time **25 minutes** ● Cooking Time **15 minutes**

PER SERVING
Calories **215**, Saturated Fat **5g**, Total Fat **12g**, Sodium **33mg**, Cholesterol **3mg**, Protein **17g**, Carbohydrate **11g**, Fiber **1g**.

For the roll-up mixture

1 package (10 ounces) frozen chopped spinach, thawed and drained

1 tablespoon olive or canola oil

1 tablespoon all-purpose flour

1/3 cup 1% low-fat milk

1/8 teaspoon ground nutmeg

Salt and pepper

3 egg whites

For the filling

1 cup part-skim ricotta cheese

2 tablespoons chopped herbs, such as parsley, basil, or thyme

1 tablespoon grated Parmesan cheese

1 Heat oven to 375°F. Line a 15½" x 10½" x ¾" baking pan with parchment paper. In a food processor or with a knife, chop spinach. Transfer to a bowl.

2 In a small saucepan, combine the oil and flour over moderately low heat and cook about 2 minutes, stirring constantly. Remove from the heat.

3 Stir in milk, nutmeg, and pinch of salt and pepper. Return to the heat and bring to a boil. Cook about 1 minute, stirring, until thickened and smooth.

Spinach Ricotta Roll-Ups makes an impressive lunch or brunch dish.

4 Scrape flour mixture into a bowl, stir in spinach, and allow to cool. Meanwhile, in another bowl, whisk the egg whites until soft peaks form.

7 Meanwhile, in a small bowl, combine the ricotta cheese with the herbs, Parmesan cheese, and a pinch of salt and pepper until smooth.

5 Spoon a quarter of the egg whites into spinach mixture and gently fold to combine. Stir mixture back into remaining egg whites and carefully combine.

8 When the baked spinach mixture is cool, spoon on the herb filling and spread it all the way to the edges.

6 Spread mixture in pan. Bake about 10 minutes, until risen and firm to the touch. Turn out onto a clean dish towel and allow to cool. Remove paper.

9 Starting with one of the short sides, roll up the baked spinach mixture so the seam finishes underneath. Cut across into 9 equal slices.

Provençal Spinach Roll-Ups

- Serves **3**
- Preparation Time **35 minutes**
- Cooking Time **20 minutes**

Spinach roll-up mixture, as in master recipe
1 tablespoon olive or canola oil
1 small onion, finely chopped
1 clove garlic, finely chopped
$^1/_2$ cup sliced sweet red or green pepper
8 ounces mushrooms, chopped
1 cup canned crushed tomatoes
2 tablespoons chopped parsley
$^1/_8$ teaspoon salt and pepper

1 Prepare roll-up as in Steps 1 to 6 of the master recipe. In a skillet, heat the oil over moderate heat. Add onion and garlic and sauté about 4 minutes or until softened.

2 Stir in sweet pepper and sauté about 2 minutes or until softened. Add mushrooms and cook about 2 minutes longer or until soft.

3 Stir in tomatoes and cook, uncovered, stirring, about 12 minutes or until soft and sauce has thickened. Stir in parsley and season with salt and pepper.

4 Remove from the heat and allow to cool slightly. Spread over the cooked spinach mixture, roll up, and slice as in master recipe.

PER SERVING
Calories **197**, Saturated Fat **1g**, Total Fat **10g**, Sodium **283mg**, Cholesterol **1mg**, Protein **10g**, Carbohydrate **21g**, Fiber **5g**.

Salmon and Shrimp Spinach Roll-Ups

- Serves **3**
- Preparation Time **25 minutes**
- Cooking Time **15 minutes**

Spinach roll-up mixture, as in master recipe
$^1/_2$ cup part-skim ricotta cheese
4 ounces cooked tiny shrimp, coarsely chopped
1 teaspoon tomato paste
$^1/_2$ teaspoon lemon juice
$^1/_8$ teaspoon pepper
Pinch of paprika
1 can (8 ounces) boneless, skinless salmon, packed in water

1 Prepare roll-up as in Steps 1 to 6 of the master recipe. In a bowl, combine ricotta cheese with shrimp, tomato paste, lemon juice, pepper, and paprika.

2 Drain the salmon, reserving the liquid. Flake the salmon into pieces and gently stir into the ricotta mixture. If the mixture is very stiff, you can soften it with 1 to 2 tablespoons of the salmon liquid.

3 Spread the filling over the cooked spinach mixture, roll up, and slice as in Step 9 of the master recipe.

PER SERVING
Calories **300**, Saturated Fat **4g**, Total Fat **14g**, Sodium **615mg**, Cholesterol **108mg**, Protein **33g**, Carbohydrate **9g**, Fiber **1g**.

Vegetable and Nut Loaf

Cooking technique ■ *Mix chopped nuts with vegetables and bake like a meat loaf. Use any combination of unsalted nuts — they are all good sources of vitamins.*

● Serves **6** ● Preparation Time **15 minutes** ● Cooking Time **55 minutes**

PER SERVING
Calories **325**, Saturated Fat **3g**,
Total Fat **21g**, Sodium **174mg**,
Cholesterol **36mg**, Protein **11g**,
Carbohydrate **28g**, Fiber **8g**.

2 large onions, quartered
3 sticks celery, cut into pieces
1 pound carrots, cut into pieces
1/4 teaspoon dried rosemary
2 teaspoons olive or canola oil
1 1/2 cups unsalted mixed nuts, such as peanuts or cashews
2 tablespoons chopped parsley

2 teaspoons ketchup
1 egg plus 1 egg white
1/8 teaspoon each salt and pepper
1 cup fine fresh whole-wheat bread crumbs
2 tablespoons fresh white bread crumbs

1 Preheat the oven to 350°F. In a food processor, combine onions, celery, carrots, and rosemary, and finely chop, scraping sides of the bowl occasionally.

2 In a large nonstick skillet, heat oil over moderate heat. Add the chopped vegetables and sauté, stirring occasionally, about 5 minutes or until slightly soft.

3 Finely chop the nuts in the food processor and add to the vegetables with the parsley. Remove the pan from the heat and allow to cool slightly.

Vegetable and Nut Loaf makes a high-protein lunch or dinner. It's speedy to prepare too.

4 In a small bowl combine the ketchup with the egg, egg white, salt, and pepper until blended.

5 Stir the whole-wheat bread crumbs into the vegetable and nut mixture to combine. Pour in the egg and ketchup and mix well.

6 Pack mixture into a nonstick or foil-lined 8¹/₂" x 3¹/₂" x 2¹/₂" loaf pan. Sprinkle white bread crumbs on top. Bake about 50 minutes or until firm to touch.

Cheesy Nut Patties

- Serves **4**
- Preparation Time **10 minutes**
- Cooking Time **10 minutes**

1 large onion, quartered
2 stalks celery, cut into pieces
2 teaspoons olive or canola oil
1 cup unsalted mixed nuts
2 tablespoons chopped parsley or 1¹/₂ teaspoons dried
1 egg plus 1 egg white
¹/₈ teaspoon each salt and pepper
³/₄ cup fine fresh bread crumbs
¹/₂ cup finely shredded low-fat Swiss cheese

1 Chop the onion and celery in a food processor as in Step 1 of the master recipe.

2 Sauté the chopped vegetables as in Step 2 of the master recipe.

3 Chop the nuts and add to the vegetables with the parsley as in Step 3 of the master recipe.

4 In a bowl, combine egg, egg white, salt, and pepper until blended. Stir bread crumbs and cheese into vegetable mixture to combine. Stir in the egg mixture.

5 Preheat broiler. With wet hands, form 4 compact patties. Broil about 4 inches from the heat for 2 to 3 minutes on each side or until browned and firm.

PER SERVING
Calories **347**, Saturated Fat **6g**, Total Fat **26g**, Sodium **200mg**, Cholesterol **66mg**, Protein **14g**, Carbohydrate **19g**, Fiber **5g**.

Lentil and Walnut Loaf

- Serves **4**
- Preparation Time **15 minutes**
- Cooking Time **1¹/₄ hours**

1 cup red lentils
2–3 cups water or stock
1 onion, quartered
2 stalks celery, cut into pieces
1 large sweet red or green pepper, cut into eighths
2 teaspoons olive or canola oil
¹/₄ teaspoon ground cumin
³/₄ cup walnut pieces
2 tablespoons parsley
1 cup fine fresh bread crumbs
1 egg white
¹/₈ teaspoon each salt and pepper

1 In a saucepan, combine lentils and water and bring to a boil. Partially cover and simmer about 15 minutes or until lentils are soft.

2 In a food processor, chop onion, celery, and sweet pepper as in Step 1 of the master recipe.

3 Preheat oven to 350°F. Sauté the vegetables with the cumin as in Step 2 of the master recipe. Finely chop walnuts and add to the vegetables with the parsley. Transfer to a large bowl.

4 Drain lentils; stir into vegetables with the bread crumbs, egg white, salt, and pepper. Bake as in Step 6 of the master recipe.

PER SERVING
Calories **388**, Saturated Fat **2g**, Total Fat **17g**, Sodium **169mg**, Cholesterol **0mg**, Protein **19g**, Carbohydrate **43g**, Fiber **9g**.

Turkey and Carrot Nut Loaf

- Serves **6**
- Preparation Time **20 minutes**
- Cooking Time **1 hour**

2 teaspoons olive or canola oil
1 pound carrots, coarsely shredded
2 cloves garlic, finely chopped
8 ounces mushrooms, finely chopped
1¹/₂ cups unsalted mixed nuts
8 ounces lean ground turkey
1 cup cooked long-grain rice
1 egg white
2 scallions, chopped
¹/₈ teaspoon each salt and pepper

1 In a large skillet, heat the oil over moderate heat. Add the carrots and garlic and sauté about 5 minutes or until slightly softened. Stir in the mushrooms and cook about 3 minutes longer or until softened.

2 In a food processor, finely chop the nuts. Remove the vegetables from the heat and stir in the nuts with the turkey, rice, egg white, scallions, salt, and pepper until blended.

3 Pack the mixture into a nonstick or foil-lined 8¹/₂" x 3¹/₂" x 2¹/₂" loaf pan. Bake about 50 minutes or until firm to the touch in the center.

PER SERVING
Calories **361**, Saturated Fat **4g**, Total Fat **22g**, Sodium **98mg**, Cholesterol **27mg**, Protein **17g**, Carbohydrate **28g**, Fiber **6g**.

GRAINS & BEANS

*From Italian risotto to spicy chili, grains
and beans are comfort food at its best – hot, hearty,
and satisfying. But the best news is that they are two
of the healthiest foods you can eat. Grains are an
excellent source of complex carbohydrates, while beans
are high in soluble fiber, which is thought to reduce
the risk of heart disease. And this chapter tells you all you
need to know about storing and cooking grains and
beans, from old standbys like rice and kidney beans
to new arrivals like couscous. Above all, you'll enjoy
delicious dishes. So dip into this chapter and
discover a whole new way of eating healthy!*

Couscous-Stuffed Yellow Squash, page 216

For people who would like to reduce their intake of saturated fat, grains combined with beans make a healthy alternative to meat. Grains are a nutritional powerhouse, high in complex carbohydrates, fiber, vitamins, and iron. Legumes (dried beans, peas, and lentils) are a rich source of protein, carbohydrates, iron, calcium, potassium, and B vitamins.

Rich in fiber

Because they are high in complex carbohydrates, beans take a long time to digest, and the blood sugar level rises slowly. Studies have shown that diabetics who eat large quantities of beans often can reduce their intake of insulin. Both grains and beans are high in fiber, which is important to good health. Soluble fiber helps lower blood cholesterol levels, while insoluble fiber helps prevent constipation and protects against colon cancer, diverticulitis, and hemorrhoids.

Oatmeal, which contains a soluble fiber called beta glucan, has been shown especially effective in reducing serum cholesterol.

Buying and storing

Both grains and beans can be stored for long periods but not indefinitely. Whole grains contain oils that turn rancid, while beans that are too old will be tough. So always buy grains and legumes from a store with a brisk turnover to ensure freshness, and check the freshness date. Store legumes in the original packaging or in airtight containers for up to 1 year in a cool place or indefinitely in the freezer. Grains should also be stored in the original packaging or airtight containers. Keep whole grains for 1 month in a cool, dry place, up to 5 months in the refrigerator, and indefinitely in the freezer. Store refined grains as for white rice (see box, right).

Preparing

Both grains and beans should be rinsed before cooking to remove any grit. Check beans and remove any shriveled or broken pods. Most refined grains can be cooked immediately in water, but a few of the whole grains, such as wheat berries, must be soaked first. The recipe or package will give directions. You must soak dried beans for at least 8 hours to hydrate them, or you can use the quick-soak method on page 227. Lentils and split peas do not have to be soaked.

MAKING PERFECT RICE

- ◆ Sprinkle rice with lemon juice rather than salt to help keep the rice white.

- ◆ Measure liquid carefully. Too much liquid, and rice will be sticky; too little, and the rice will burn.

- ◆ Test for doneness by squeezing rice grains between the fingers. The rice should be tender, with no hard center.

- ◆ Never stir rice while it is cooking – it breaks up the holes that allow the steam to escape.

- ◆ Keep white rice almost indefinitely in an airtight container in a cool, dry place. Store brown rice for up to 6 months.

- ◆ Do not let rice or any leftover foods sit out after cooking. Refrigerate quickly in an airtight container.

WHY YOU SHOULD EAT GRAINS AND BEANS

Grains and beans are the perfect health food – high in fiber and complex carbohydrate, low in fat, and a good source of protein when served together. (See box, page 11, on how to combine protein.)

GRAINS

½ cup cooked	Fiber g	Protein g	Calories
White rice	1.0	2.8	132
Brown rice	1.7	2.5	108
Arborio rice	1.3	2.4	134
Wild rice	1.3	3.3	83
Barley	4.4	1.8	97
Bulgur	3.4	2.8	76
Polenta	1.0	10.2	60
Couscous	4.1	3.4	100
Steel-cut oats	1.0	3.0	73
Rolled oats	1.0	3.0	73

LEGUMES

½ cup cooked	Fiber g	Protein g	Calories
Black beans	3.6	7.6	114
Black-eyed peas	5.5	2.6	80
Chick-peas	2.9	7.3	135
Red kidney beans	4.5	7.7	113
White kidney beans	3.1	7.7	113
Lentils, whole	4.9	8.9	116
Pinto beans	4.0	7.0	118
Navy beans	3.3	7.9	130
Great Northern beans	4.9	7.0	105
Split peas	5.7	8.2	116

Cooking times and yields

Grains: For 1 cup of grain, use 2 cups of liquid. For 1 cup barley, use 3 cups liquid. For polenta, use 1 cup of cornmeal to 3–3¹/₂ cups liquid. Cook breakfast cereal grains in water or 1% low-fat milk.

Rice: For 1 cup of brown rice, use 2¹/₂ cups of liquid. For 1 cup of long-grain white rice, use 2 cups liquid.

Beans: For 1 cup of any dried beans or peas, use 3 cups of liquid. Soaking is required for all except lentils. Red and black beans may have a toxin on their skins, made harmless by 10 minutes of vigorous boiling. Always season beans after cooking; if added during cooking, salt toughens the skins and prolongs cooking time.

Black-eyed Peas
Cooking Time: 35–45 minutes
Yield: 3 cups

Wild Rice
Cooking Time: 35–40 minutes
Yield: 4 cups

Black Beans
Cooking Time: 1¹/₂ hours
Yield: 2¹/₂ cups

Arborio Rice (Risotto)
Cooking Time: 20–30 minutes
Yield: 3 cups

Chick-peas
Cooking Time: 1¹/₂–2 hours
Yield: 2¹/₂ cups

Red Kidney Beans
Cooking Time: ³/₄–1¹/₄ hours
Yield: 2¹/₂ cups

Barley
Cooking Time: 35–45 minutes
Yield: 3 cups

Cracked Wheat
Cooking Time: 20 minutes
Yield: 2¹/₂ cups

Long-Grain Brown Rice
Cooking Time: 35 minutes
Yield: 3 cups

Lentils
Cooking Time: 20–25 minutes
Yield: 3 cups

Bulgur
Cooking Time: 20–25 minutes
Yield: 3 cups

Polenta
Cooking Time: 35–45 minutes
Yield: 3 cups

Long-Grain White Rice
Cooking Time: 20 minutes
Yield: 3 cups

Navy Beans
Cooking Time: 1–1¹/₂ hours
Yield: 3 cups

Couscous
Cooking Time: 5–10 minutes
Yield: 1¹/₂–2 cups

Steel-Cut Oats
Cooking Time: 20–25 minutes
Yield: 2¹/₂ cups

Rolled Oats
Cooking Time: 10 minutes
Yield: 1³/₄ cups

Pinto Beans
Cooking Time: 1–1¹/₂ hours
Yield: 2¹/₂ cups

White Kidney Beans
Cooking Time: ³/₄–1¹/₄ hours
Yield: 2¹/₂ cups

Basic Cheese Risotto

Cooking technique ▪ *To get the soft, chewy texture of perfect risotto, add the stock gradually, stirring frequently after each addition until all the liquid is absorbed.*

About Arborio rice ▪ *The classic Italian risotto is made with Arborio, a short-grain polished rice. However, long-grain or basmati rice would also work well.*

● Serves **4** ● Preparation Time **5–7 minutes** ● Cooking Time **35 minutes**

PER SERVING
Calories **326**, Saturated Fat **2g**,
Total Fat **11g**, Sodium **263mg**,
Cholesterol **9mg**, Protein **12g**,
Carbohydrate **44g**, Fiber **1g**.

2 tablespoons olive or canola oil
2 small onions, finely chopped
1 shallot, finely chopped
1 cup Arborio, long-grain, or basmati rice
3–4 cups chicken stock, page 18

1/4 cup shredded reduced-fat Cheddar cheese
2 tablespoons grated Parmesan cheese
1/8 teaspoon each salt and pepper

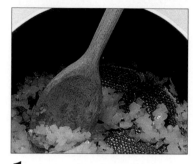

1 In a large saucepan, heat the oil over moderate heat. Sauté chopped onions and shallot, stirring, about 5 minutes or until soft but not browned.

2 Add rice to pan and stir well to coat thoroughly with the oil mixture. Cook, stirring, 2 to 3 minutes longer or until the rice becomes almost translucent.

3 With a ladle, pour about 1/2 cup of the chicken stock into the rice mixture and stir well to combine.

*A meal that's sure to win compliments – **Basic Cheese Risotto** served with bread, tomatoes, and mozzarella cheese.*

4 Bring the stock to a boil, then gently simmer, uncovered and stirring occasionally, until most of the liquid is absorbed.

5 Repeat the process, adding about ½ cup stock at a time, until rice is almost tender but still firm to the bite, or *al dente*, using as much stock as necessary.

6 Remove from the heat, cover the pan, and allow to stand about 5 minutes. Stir in both cheeses, season with salt and pepper, and serve at once.

Risotto Primavera

- Serves **4**
- Preparation Time **15 minutes**
- Cooking Time **35–40 minutes**

2 tablespoons olive or canola oil
2 small onions, finely chopped
2 yellow squash, sliced
2 carrots, sliced
4 ounces snow peas, halved
1 cup Arborio, long-grain, or basmati rice
3–4 cups chicken stock, page 18
2 tablespoons grated Parmesan cheese
1 teaspoon lemon juice
¹/₈ teaspoon each salt and pepper

1 Sauté the onions as in Step 1 of the master recipe. Add the squash, carrots, and snow peas to the pan and sauté, stirring, about 5 minutes longer or until the vegetables are crisp-tender. With a slotted spoon, transfer vegetables to a plate.

2 Add the rice to the saucepan and cook as in Step 2 of the master recipe. Add stock and simmer, stirring, as in Steps 3 and 4 of the master recipe.

3 Add more stock as in Step 5 of the master recipe. Stir in reserved vegetables, cheese, lemon juice, salt, and pepper. Remove from the heat, cover pan, and allow to stand about 5 minutes.

PER SERVING
Calories **344**, Saturated Fat **2g**, Total Fat **10g**, Sodium **244mg**, Cholesterol **2mg**, Protein **10g**, Carbohydrate **56g**, Fiber **5g**.

Shrimp and Scallion Risotto

- Serves **4**
- Preparation Time **15 minutes**
- Cooking Time **35–40 minutes**

2 tablespoons olive or canola oil
8 ounces small shrimp, peeled and deveined
3–4 cups fish stock, page 18
2 small onions, finely chopped
1 cup Arborio, long-grain, or basmati rice
6 scallions, thinly sliced
1 teaspoon lemon juice
¹/₈ teaspoon each salt and pepper

1 Heat oil in a large nonstick saucepan over moderate heat. Add the shrimp with about 2 tablespoons of the stock and sauté, stirring, 2 to 3 minutes or until shrimp turn pink.

2 With a slotted spoon, transfer shrimp to a plate and reserve. Add onions to pan and sauté about 5 minutes or until soft.

3 Add the rice to the saucepan and cook as in Step 2 of the master recipe. Add stock and simmer, stirring, as in Steps 3 and 4 of the master recipe.

4 Add more stock as in Step 5 of the master recipe. Stir in reserved shrimp, scallions, lemon juice, salt, and pepper. Remove from the heat, cover, and allow to stand about 5 minutes.

PER SERVING
Calories **330**, Saturated Fat **1g**, Total Fat **9g**, Sodium **256mg**, Cholesterol **87mg**, Protein **18g**, Carbohydrate **44g**, Fiber **2g**.

Chicken Risotto with Asparagus

- Serves **4**
- Preparation Time **20 minutes**
- Cooking Time **35–40 minutes**

3–4 cups chicken stock, page 18
3 boneless, skinless chicken breast halves (about ³/₄ pound)
2 tablespoons olive or canola oil
2 small onions, finely chopped
2 stalks celery, diced
1 cup Arborio, long-grain, or basmati rice
12 ounces asparagus, cut into 2-inch pieces
2 tablespoons grated Parmesan cheese
1 teaspoon lemon juice
¹/₈ teaspoon each salt and pepper

1 Bring the stock to a boil in a saucepan and poach the chicken; shred chicken and reserve stock.

2 Sauté the onions and celery as in Step 1 of the master recipe.

3 Add rice to saucepan and cook as in Step 2 of master recipe. Add stock and simmer, stirring, as in Steps 3 and 4 of master recipe.

4 Add more stock as in Step 5 of the master recipe. Add asparagus with last ½ cup of stock. Stir in chicken, cheese, lemon juice, salt, and pepper. Remove from the heat, cover, and allow to stand about 5 minutes.

PER SERVING
Calories **399**, Saturated Fat **2g**, Total Fat **10g**, Sodium **311mg**, Cholesterol **52mg**, Protein **30g**, Carbohydrate **48g**, Fiber **3g**.

Nutted Lemon Barley

Cooking technique ▪ *For a savory side dish, simmer barley until tender in an aromatic spiced broth.*
About barley ▪ *This slightly chewy grain is rich in soluble fiber, which can help lower cholesterol. The most common type is pearl barley, whole kernels that have been milled to remove the husk and polished. You can add barley to soups or serve like rice.*

● Serves 8 ● Preparation Time **10 minutes** ● Cooking Time **55–60 minutes**

PER SERVING
Calories **169**, Saturated Fat **1g**,
Total Fat **5g**, Sodium **71mg**,
Cholesterol **0mg**, Protein **4g**,
Carbohydrate **28g**, Fiber **5g**.

2 tablespoons olive or canola oil

2 onions, finely chopped

3 stalks celery, finely chopped

1 cup pearl barley, rinsed

2¹/₂ cups chicken stock, page 18

1 teaspoon finely grated lemon zest

¹/₂ teaspoon dried oregano

¹/₈ teaspoon each salt and pepper

2 tablespoons sunflower seeds or pine nuts

1 tablespoon fresh lemon juice

¹/₄ cup golden raisins

2 tablespoons chopped parsley

COOKING TIP
When done, the barley should be tender, with a slightly resilient center. If you prefer a softer texture, cook a little longer.

1 In a wide heavy saucepan, heat the oil over moderate heat. Add the onions and celery and sauté, stirring, about 7 minutes or until softened and lightly browned.

2 Stir in the barley until well coated with the oil. Pour in the stock and add the lemon zest, oregano, salt, and pepper.

3 Bring the stock to a boil, then reduce the heat; cover the pan and simmer, stirring occasionally, about 40 minutes or until the barley is nearly cooked through and almost all the liquid is absorbed.

4 Meanwhile, toast the sunflower seeds in a dry nonstick skillet over moderate heat, stirring frequently or shaking the pan until they are golden brown. Remove from the heat and transfer to a plate.

5 Stir the lemon juice and raisins into the barley mixture and cover the saucepan. Remove the saucepan from the heat and allow the mixture to stand about 5 minutes longer.

6 Gently stir the toasted sunflower seeds with the chopped parsley into the barley until just mixed.

Nutted Lemon Barley *makes a tasty change from potatoes.*
Serve it with grilled pork, lamb chops, or poultry.

Barley with Scallions

This simple dish goes well with chops or roasts. It's adaptable too, because barley blends with many flavors. For variety, stir in a chopped tomato, a cup of cooked vegetables, or leftover meat.

- Serves 6
- Preparation Time 5 minutes
- Cooking Time 55 minutes

2 tablespoons olive or canola oil

4 stalks celery, finely chopped

1 cup pearl barley, rinsed

1 1/2 cups chicken stock, page 18

1 1/2 cups water

1 bunch scallions, sliced

1/8 teaspoon each salt and pepper

1 In a wide heavy saucepan, heat the oil over moderate heat. Add the celery and sauté, stirring, about 7 minutes or until softened and lightly browned.

2 Add the barley and cook, stirring, until well coated with the oil. Stir in half of the stock. Bring to a boil over moderate heat and simmer, stirring occasionally, until the liquid is absorbed.

3 Add the remaining stock and water in 3 more batches, stirring constantly, until almost all the liquid is absorbed and the barley is nearly tender.

4 Stir in the scallions, salt, and pepper. Cover the pan, remove from the heat, and let stand about 5 minutes longer.

PER SERVING
Calories 170, Saturated Fat 1g, Total Fat 5g, Sodium 90mg, Cholesterol 0mg, Protein 4g, Carbohydrate 28g, Fiber 6g.

Scallions have a mild, onionlike flavor. Use both the green and white parts after trimming the tops.

COOKING TIP
The barley is sautéed in oil before it is cooked to add more flavor to the pilaf.

Baked Barley, Peas, and Mushrooms

Like most grains, barley must be cooked slowly so that the grains absorb the liquid before it evaporates. In this recipe slow cooking is done by baking rather than simmering.

- Serves 6
- Preparation Time 15 minutes
- Cooking Time 1 hour 5 minutes

PER SERVING
Calories 223, Saturated Fat 1g, Total Fat 6g, Sodium 115mg, Cholesterol 0mg, Protein 7g, Carbohydrate 38g, Fiber 5g.

2 tablespoons olive or canola oil

2 large carrots, sliced

1 onion, finely chopped

8 ounces fresh mushrooms, sliced

1 cup pearl barley, rinsed

2 cups chicken stock, page 18

1/4 teaspoon dried thyme

1/8 teaspoon each salt and pepper

1 cup frozen peas, thawed

2 tablespoons chopped parsley

1 Preheat the oven to 325°F. In a flameproof casserole, heat the oil over moderate heat. Add the carrots and onion and sauté, stirring, 4 to 5 minutes or until slightly soft.

2 Stir in the sliced mushrooms. Cook, stirring, about 4 minutes longer or until the mushrooms are slightly soft.

3 Stir in the barley with the stock, thyme, salt, and pepper and bring to a boil. Cover the casserole and bake, stirring occasionally, about 30 minutes. Add the peas and cook for another 10 minutes or until the barley is tender and all the liquid is absorbed.

4 Stir in the chopped parsley before serving.

QUICK WAYS TO CHOP PARSLEY

Use a very sharp kitchen knife and hold the center of the blade against the board. Then chop while moving the knife across the parsley.

Use a curved bladed knife, or mezzaluna, and rock it back and forth over the parsley on the chopping board until it is finely chopped.

Tex-Mex Turkey, Corn, and Barley Casserole

If you do not have cooked turkey on hand, sauté a couple of turkey cutlets, then chop fine before adding them to the barley mixture. Cooked ham or chicken can also be used in place of the turkey.

- Serves **4**
- Preparation Time **10–12** minutes
- Cooking Time **1 hour 15 minutes**

---

2 tablespoons olive or canola oil

---

2 onions, coarsely chopped

---

1 large sweet red or green pepper, coarsely chopped

---

1 teaspoon finely chopped hot chili pepper

---

1 cup pearl barley, sorted and rinsed

1³/₄ cups chicken stock, page 18

---

1 can (14 ounces) crushed tomatoes

---

¹/₈ teaspoon each salt and pepper

---

2 cups shredded cooked turkey

---

1 cup frozen corn kernels, thawed

---

1 Preheat the oven to 325°F. In a flameproof casserole, heat the oil over moderate heat. Sauté the onions, sweet pepper, and chili pepper, stirring, about 7 minutes or until softened and lightly browned.

2 Add the barley and cook, stirring, until well coated with the oil. Pour in the chicken stock and the crushed tomatoes, and season with salt and pepper.

3 Bring to a boil, then stir in the turkey. Cover the casserole and cook in the oven, stirring occasionally, about 55 minutes or until almost all the liquid has been absorbed and the barley is nearly tender.

4 Stir in the corn kernels, cover the casserole, and cook 5 to 10 minutes longer, until heated through.

PER SERVING
Calories **475**, Saturated Fat **2g**, Total Fat **9g**, Sodium **262mg**, Cholesterol **53mg**, Protein **31g**, Carbohydrate **65g**, Fiber **14g**.

SHREDDING TURKEY

1 *Remove the skin from cooked turkey to reduce the fat content. Trim away any visible fat.*

2 *Gently pull the meat away from the bone; if tender, it should come off easily. Using your fingers, shred the meat by pulling the fibers apart.*

Tex-Mex Turkey, Corn, and Barley Casserole is an excellent way to use up leftover turkey.

GETTING AHEAD

The night before, you can shred the turkey and chop the onions, sweet pepper, and chili pepper. Store in the refrigerator in sealed bags until needed. You can also make this dish a day ahead – the flavors will blend and intensify. Follow the recipe, then cover, refrigerate, and reheat.

Cracked Wheat Pilaf

Cooking technique ▪ *This nutty-tasting grain is a delicious switch from rice. For a side dish, cook it with stock and vegetables; for an entrée, add meat.*

About cracked wheat ▪ *Made from wheat berries, cracked wheat is high in fiber and protein. Look for it in supermarkets and health food stores.*

● Serves **8** ● Preparation Time **15 minutes** ● Cooking Time **40–45 minutes**

PER SERVING
Calories **125**, Saturated Fat **1g**,
Total Fat **4g**, Sodium **83mg**,
Cholesterol **0mg**, Protein **3g**,
Carbohydrate **21g**, Fiber **5g**.

1 cup cracked wheat	1¹/₂ cups reduced-sodium tomato juice
2 tablespoons olive or canola oil	1 tomato, coarsely chopped
3 onions, thinly sliced	2 tablespoons chopped fresh basil or 1 tablespoon dried
1 clove garlic, finely chopped	¹/₈ teaspoon each salt and pepper
1¹/₂ cups vegetable stock, page 18	

1 Place the cracked wheat in a fine sieve and rinse under cold running water. Stir so that all the grains are well rinsed, then drain.

2 In a large nonstick skillet, heat oil. Sauté onions and garlic, stirring frequently, until softened and very brown. Stir in the stock and tomato juice.

3 Bring to a boil; add wheat. Cover and simmer, stirring occasionally, about 15 minutes. Stir in tomato, basil, salt, and pepper. Simmer a few minutes longer, until liquid is absorbed.

Cracked Wheat Pilaf is richly flavored with tomatoes and basil. Serve it with grilled meats or poultry.

Creamy Vegetable Wheat Pilaf

- Serves **8**
- Preparation Time **20 minutes**
- Cooking Time **35–40 minutes**

1 cup cracked wheat
2 tablespoons olive or canola oil
3 onions, thinly sliced
3 carrots, sliced
3 stalks celery, sliced
2 small parsnips, diced
1 clove garlic, finely chopped
2¹/₂ cups vegetable stock, page 18
¹/₂ cup low-fat sour cream
2 tablespoons chopped parsley
¹/₈ teaspoon each salt and pepper

1 Rinse the cracked wheat as in Step 1 of the master recipe.

2 In a large nonstick skillet, heat oil over moderate heat. Sauté onions, carrots, celery, parsnips, and garlic, stirring frequently, until browned. Stir in stock.

3 Bring to a boil; add wheat and stir well to combine. Return to a boil, cover, and gently simmer, stirring frequently, about 20 minutes or until the wheat is tender and the liquid is absorbed.

4 Stir in the sour cream and parsley and season with salt and pepper.

PER SERVING
Calories **164**, Saturated Fat **1g**, Total Fat **5g**, Sodium **99mg**, Cholesterol **3mg**, Protein **5g**, Carbohydrate **28g**, Fiber **7g**.

Wheat and Mushroom Gratin

- Serves **8**
- Preparation Time **20 minutes**
- Cooking Time **35–40 minutes**

1 cup cracked wheat
2 tablespoons olive or canola oil
2 leeks, trimmed and chopped
1 clove garlic, finely chopped
1 pound mushrooms, sliced
2¹/₂ cups vegetable stock, page 18
2 tablespoons chopped parsley
¹/₈ teaspoon each salt and pepper
¹/₄ cup shredded reduced-fat Cheddar cheese

1 Rinse the cracked wheat as in Step 1 of the master recipe.

2 In a large nonstick skillet, heat oil over moderate heat. Sauté leeks and garlic, stirring frequently, 5 to 6 minutes or until browned. Add mushrooms and cook 4 to 5 minutes. Stir in stock.

3 Bring to a boil; add wheat and stir well to combine. Return to a boil, cover, and gently simmer, stirring frequently, about 20 minutes or until the wheat is tender and the liquid is absorbed.

4 Preheat broiler. Stir in parsley, salt, and pepper. Transfer to an 8" x 8" x 2" baking dish, sprinkle with cheese, and broil about 3 minutes or until well browned.

PER SERVING
Calories **126**, Saturated Fat **1g**, Total Fat **5g**, Sodium **88mg**, Cholesterol **3mg**, Protein **5g**, Carbohydrate **19g**, Fiber **5g**.

Chicken, Walnut, and Cracked Wheat Casserole

- Serves **4**
- Preparation Time **15 minutes**
- Cooking Time **35–40 minutes**

1 cup cracked wheat
2 tablespoons olive or canola oil
4 boneless, skinless chicken breast halves (about 1 pound), diced
2 onions, coarsely chopped
¹/₂ teaspoon chili powder
2¹/₂ cups vegetable stock, page 18
2 tablespoons chopped walnuts
2 tablespoons chopped fresh mint or 2 teaspoons dried
¹/₈ teaspoon each salt and pepper

1 Rinse the cracked wheat as in Step 1 of the master recipe.

2 Meanwhile, in a large nonstick skillet, heat 1 tablespoon oil over moderately high heat. Add chicken and brown well, turning once, 5 to 6 minutes. Transfer to a plate.

3 Reduce heat to moderate. In remaining oil, sauté onions with chili powder about 5 minutes or until softened.

4 Return chicken to skillet with wheat. Pour in stock and bring to a boil, then cover and gently simmer, stirring occasionally, about 20 minutes or until wheat and chicken are tender and liquid is absorbed.

5 Stir in the walnuts, mint, salt, and pepper.

PER SERVING
Calories **393**, Saturated Fat **2g**, Total Fat **12g**, Sodium **181mg**, Cholesterol **66mg**, Protein **32g**, Carbohydrate **42g**, Fiber **3g**.

Chicken, Walnut, and Cracked Wheat Casserole is of Turkish origin.

Rice Pilaf with Artichokes

Cooking technique ▪ *Simmer the rice slowly so that it absorbs all of the flavor from the stock and vegetables. Add nuts, cheese, beans, or meat for protein.*

Add nutrients ▪ *If you prefer to make this dish with high-fiber brown rice, cook it about 20 minutes longer or according to package directions.*

● Serves **6** ● Preparation Time **15 minutes** ● Cooking Time **40 minutes**

PER SERVING
Calories **214**, Saturated Fat **1g**,
Total Fat **6g**, Sodium **132mg**,
Cholesterol **2mg**, Protein **6g**,
Carbohydrate **36g**, Fiber **5g**.

1 cup long-grain white rice	1 cup water
2 tablespoons olive or canola oil	1 package (9 ounces) frozen artichoke hearts, thawed
2 large onions, finely chopped	
3 stalks celery, finely chopped	2 tablespoons finely grated Parmesan cheese
1 cup vegetable or chicken stock, page 18	1/8 teaspoon each salt and pepper

1 Place the rice in a sieve and rinse well under cold running water, gently stirring to rinse all the grains. Set the sieve over a bowl and allow to drain well.

2 In a heavy nonstick skillet, heat oil over moderate heat. Add onions and celery and sauté, stirring, about 5 minutes or until soft but not browned.

3 Add the drained rice to the softened vegetables and sauté, stirring gently, about 2 minutes or until well coated.

*Perfect for lunch or supper – **Rice Pilaf with Artichokes** served with tomatoes and mozzarella cheese.*

4 Stir in stock and water until combined. Cover the skillet and simmer gently about 20 minutes or until rice is almost tender and most of liquid is absorbed.

5 Cut each artichoke heart lengthwise in half. Stir them into the rice. Cover skillet and simmer 5 to 7 minutes or until rice and artichokes are tender.

6 Remove from the heat, add the cheese, and season with the salt and pepper. Gently stir the rice pilaf just to mix.

Spicy Rice Pilaf

- Serves **6**
- Preparation Time **10 minutes**
- Cooking Time **35–40 minutes**

1 cup long-grain white rice

2 tablespoons olive or canola oil

2 onions, thinly sliced

1 sweet red or green pepper, cut into matchsticks

1–2 tablespoons curry powder

1 cup vegetable or chicken stock, page 18

1 cup water

1 package (10 ounces) frozen peas

¹/₂ cup golden raisins

¹/₄ cup slivered almonds

¹/₈ teaspoon each salt and pepper

1 Rinse and drain rice as in Step 1 of the master recipe.

2 In a heavy nonstick skillet, heat oil over moderate heat. Sauté onions and sweet pepper, stirring, 8 to 10 minutes or until soft.

3 Stir in curry powder and cook a few minutes longer or until fragrant. Add rice and sauté, stirring, about 1 minute or until well coated. Add stock and water and cook as in Step 4 of master recipe.

4 Stir in peas and raisins. Cover skillet and simmer about 5 minutes or until rice is tender.

5 Remove from heat and stir in almonds, salt, and pepper.

PER SERVING
Calories **295**, Saturated Fat **1g**, Total Fat **8g**, Sodium **115mg**, Cholesterol **0mg**, Protein **7g**, Carbohydrate **50g**, Fiber **6g**.

Two-Rice Pilaf

- Serves **8**
- Preparation Time **20 minutes**
- Cooking Time **60–65 minutes**

1 cup long-grain brown rice

¹/₂ cup wild rice

2 slices reduced-sodium bacon, finely chopped

8 ounces mushrooms, sliced

3 carrots, diced

1 onion, coarsely chopped

4 stalks celery, sliced

1¹/₂ cups vegetable or chicken stock, page 18

1¹/₂ cups water

2 tablespoons freeze-dried chives

¹/₈ teaspoon each salt and pepper

1 Place both types of rice in a sieve and rinse and drain as in Step 1 of the master recipe.

2 Cook bacon in a heavy nonstick skillet over moderate heat, stirring, 2 to 3 minutes. With a slotted spoon, transfer bacon to a plate and reserve.

3 Add mushrooms, carrots, onion, and celery to the pan and sauté about 10 minutes.

4 Add rice and sauté about 1 minute. Add stock and water and cook 45 to 50 minutes as in Step 4 of the master recipe.

5 Remove from heat and stir in chives, bacon, salt, and pepper.

PER SERVING
Calories **170**, Saturated Fat **1g**, Total Fat **3g**, Sodium **117mg**, Cholesterol **5mg**, Protein **5g**, Carbohydrate **31g**, Fiber **3g**.

Tex-Mex Rice

- Serves **8**
- Preparation Time **20 minutes**
- Cooking Time **40–45 minutes**

1¹/₂ cups long-grain white rice

8 ounces lean ground turkey

2 large red onions, sliced

2 sweet green peppers, diced

2 stalks celery, diced

1–2 tablespoons chili powder

1¹/₂ cups chicken stock, page 18

1¹/₂ cups spicy tomato juice

1¹/₂ cups frozen corn kernels

1 can (15 ounces) red kidney beans, drained and rinsed

¹/₈ teaspoon each salt and pepper

2 tablespoons chopped cilantro

1 Rinse and drain rice as in Step 1 of the master recipe.

2 Heat a nonstick skillet over moderate heat. Add turkey and cook, stirring, about 5 minutes. Remove from heat. With a slotted spoon, transfer meat to a bowl and reserve.

3 Sauté onions, sweet peppers, and celery, stirring, about 8 minutes. Stir in chili powder and cook about 2 minutes longer. Add rice and sauté about 1 minute.

4 Return meat to skillet. Stir in stock and tomato juice and cook as in Step 4 of the master recipe. Stir in corn, beans, salt, and pepper. Cook until rice is tender. Add cilantro and serve.

PER SERVING
Calories **274**, Saturated Fat **0g**, Total Fat **2g**, Sodium **441mg**, Cholesterol **18mg**, Protein **15g**, Carbohydrate **51g**, Fiber **6g**.

Couscous with Summer Vegetables

Cooking technique ▪ *For an easy casserole, sauté onions, vegetables, and spices, then add couscous and stock. Let sit 5 minutes, fluff with a fork, and serve.*

About couscous ▪ *This pale yellow grain is made from hulled durum wheat. In North Africa, where it originated, couscous is steamed for 30 minutes. However, the instant couscous sold in supermarkets cooks in just 5 minutes. Serve with stews, meats, and stir-fries as a tasty alternative to rice.*

● Serves **8** ● Preparation Time **12 minutes** ● Cooking Time **20–25 minutes**

PER SERVING
Calories **170**, Saturated Fat **0g**,
Total Fat **4g**, Sodium **80mg**,
Cholesterol **0mg**, Protein **4g**,
Carbohydrate **30g**, Fiber **2g**.

2 tablespoons olive or canola oil

3 stalks celery, diced

3 carrots, diced

1 zucchini, sliced

1 yellow squash, sliced

¹⁄₄ cup shredded fresh basil or
   1 tablespoon dried

¹⁄₈ teaspoon each salt and pepper

Hot red pepper sauce

1¹⁄₂ cups couscous

2 cups vegetable or chicken
   stock, page 18

1 In a large saucepan, heat the oil. Add the celery and carrots and sauté, stirring, about 7 minutes or until softened but not browned.

2 Add the zucchini and squash and cook, stirring, 2 to 4 minutes longer or until slightly softened.

3 Add the basil with the salt, pepper, and a few dashes of hot red pepper sauce and toss to mix.

4 Add the couscous to the saucepan and, with a wooden spoon, gently mix with the vegetables to coat the couscous grains well.

5 Pour the stock into the saucepan and gently mix. Bring the stock to a boil, then cover the saucepan and remove from the heat.

6 Allow the couscous to stand about 5 minutes or until the couscous grains are tender and all the liquid is absorbed. With a fork, lightly fluff up the couscous to separate the grains.

Couscous with Summer Vegetables – *only the name is exotic. Couscous tastes a little like pasta, and it is delicious with simple American foods like chops and beans.*

Toasted Couscous with Almonds and Raisins

Sweet, crunchy, and slightly spicy, this delectable dish goes well with meat or curried dishes.

- Serves **8**
- Preparation Time **5 minutes**
- Cooking Time **20–25 minutes**

1^1/$_2$ cups couscous
^{1}/$_4$ cup slivered almonds
2 cups vegetable or chicken stock, page 18
2 stalks celery, diced
^{1}/$_8$ teaspoon each salt and pepper
Pinch each of ground cumin and cayenne pepper
^{1}/$_2$ cup seedless raisins

Toasted slivered almonds and seedless raisins add contrasting textures.

1 Heat a large nonstick skillet over moderate heat. Add the couscous and toast the grains, stirring or shaking the pan frequently, until the grains become brown and fragrant. Transfer to a plate.

COOKING TIP

Toasting the couscous gives it a rich, nutty flavor. Stir frequently to make sure it browns evenly.

2 Add the almonds to the hot skillet and toast them in the same way, stirring frequently. Transfer them to another plate.

3 Bring the stock to a boil with the celery, salt, pepper, cumin, and cayenne. Simmer about 3 minutes or until the celery is slightly softened.

4 Add the couscous and raisins to the saucepan and stir gently just to mix. Cover the pan, remove from the heat, and allow to stand about 5 minutes or until the couscous is tender.

5 Add the almonds to the couscous and, with a fork, stir the mixture lightly to fluff up the grains.

PER SERVING
Calories **196**, Saturated Fat **0g**, Total Fat **4g**, Sodium **67mg**, Cholesterol **0mg**, Protein **5g**, Carbohydrate **34g**, Fiber **2g**.

Couscous-Stuffed Yellow Squash

Spoon Spicy Pepper Sauce (see box) over each serving, then sprinkle with shredded low-fat mozzarella cheese.

- Serves **6**
- Preparation Time **25 minutes**
- Cooking Time **35–50 minutes**

1 tablespoon olive or canola oil
2 small onions, finely chopped
1 sweet green pepper, chopped
2 cloves garlic, finely chopped
4 ounces reduced-sodium, reduced-fat baked ham, diced
^{3}/$_4$ cup vegetable or chicken stock, page 18
1^1/$_4$ cups reduced-sodium tomato juice
^{1}/$_8$ teaspoon each salt and pepper
1 cup couscous
1 can (15 ounces) red kidney beans, drained and rinsed
6 yellow squash, halved lengthwise and seeded

1 Preheat oven to 350°F. In a large nonstick skillet, heat oil and sauté onions, sweet pepper, and garlic about 7 minutes.

2 Stir in diced ham and cook, stirring frequently, 3 to 4 minutes.

3 Add stock, ^{3}/$_4$ cup tomato juice, salt, and pepper. Bring to a boil. Stir in couscous just to combine.

4 Cover, remove from the heat, and let stand 5 minutes or until couscous is tender and the liquid is absorbed. Stir in remaining tomato juice and the beans and, with a fork, lightly fluff up the grains.

5 Mound the stuffing into the squash. Place in a roasting pan and bake about 25 to 40 minutes or until tender.

PER SERVING
Calories **329**, Saturated Fat **1g**, Total Fat **5g**, Sodium **436mg**, Cholesterol **10mg**, Protein **16g**, Carbohydrate **58g**, Fiber **15g**.

SPICY PEPPER SAUCE

1 *In 1 tablespoon olive oil, sauté 1 sweet red pepper and 1 onion, finely chopped, for 5 to 7 minutes. Add 1 can (8 ounces) reduced-sodium tomato sauce, 2 teaspoons soft brown sugar, ^{1}/$_8$ teaspoon each salt and pepper, 2 tablespoons red wine vinegar, and ^{1}/$_2$ teaspoon hot red pepper sauce.*

2 *Cook for 10 minutes or until the sauce is thickened. Cool slightly, then blend in a food processor until the sauce is smooth. Add 1 tablespoon of chopped parsley, stir, and transfer to a serving bowl.*

Couscous with Moroccan Chicken Stew

Moroccans traditionally cook this spicy dish in a pot called a couscoussier, which allows the moisture from the stew to steam the couscous. If you have time, try grinding your own spices – the taste and aroma are well worth it.

- Serves **6**
- Preparation Time **15 minutes**
- Cooking Time **45 minutes**

---

2 cups reduced-sodium tomato juice

$^1/_4$ cup water

$^1/_4$ teaspoon each cumin seeds and coriander seeds or $^1/_8$ teaspoon each ground

$^1/_8$ teaspoon each hot red pepper flakes, salt, and pepper

$1^1/_2$ cups couscous

1 can (14 ounces) chick-peas, drained and rinsed

1 tablespoon olive or canola oil

2 large onions, coarsely chopped

4 boneless, skinless chicken breast halves (about 1 pound), thickly sliced

4 zucchini, diced

1 can (14 ounces) crushed tomatoes

COOKING TIP
If you prefer a thicker stew, replace the tomato juice with 2 cups of canned crushed tomatoes.

1 In a large nonstick saucepan, combine the tomato juice with the watér. Bring to a boil over moderately high heat.

2 Meanwhile, crush the cumin and coriander seeds with the hot red pepper flakes, salt, and pepper (see box right). Add the spices to the tomato mixture, cover, and slowly simmer about 10 minutes.

3 Preheat the oven to 375°F. Pour the couscous into the tomato mixture and stir gently just to combine. Cover the pan, remove from the heat, and allow to stand about 5 minutes or until the couscous is tender and the liquid is absorbed. Add the chick-peas and, with a fork, lightly stir the mixture to fluff up the grains. Spoon the mixture into a 13" x 9" x 2" baking dish in an even layer.

4 Meanwhile, in a nonstick skillet, heat the oil; add the onions and sauté about 5 minutes or until browned. Add the chicken and sauté 5 minutes. Add zucchini and crushed tomatoes and bring to a boil.

5 Spoon the chicken and vegetables over the couscous, and bake about 20 minutes or until the chicken and zucchini are tender.

PER SERVING
Calories **430**, Saturated Fat **1g**, Total Fat **4g**, Sodium **347mg**, Cholesterol **66mg**, Protein **38g**, Carbohydrate **60g**, Fiber **1g**.

Grilled eggplant slices are the perfect accompaniment to **Couscous with Morrocan Chicken Stew.**

THREE WAYS TO CRUSH SPICES

Place the spices in an electric coffee grinder and grind on high for 2–3 minutes.

Place the spices in a mortar and grind them firmly with the pestle into a coarse powder.

Place the spices in a plastic bag and, holding one end closed, crush them with a rolling pin.

Bulgur Vegetable Medley

Cooking technique ▪ *You can either simmer bulgur like rice or soak it in hot stock until tender. Serve it with vegetables for a side dish, meat for an entrée.*

About bulgur ▪ *An exceptionally good source of fiber, bulgur is made from cracked wheat that has been cooked, dried, and granulated.*

● Serves **6** ● Preparation Time **10 minutes plus standing time** ● Cooking Time **20 minutes**

PER SERVING
Calories **172**, Saturated Fat **1g**, Total Fat **5g**, Sodium **91mg**, Cholesterol **0mg**, Protein **5g**, Carbohydrate **29g**, Fiber **8g**.

1 1/2 **cups vegetable or chicken stock, page 18**

1 **cup bulgur wheat**

2 **tablespoons olive or canola oil**

2 **onions, thinly sliced**

4 **stalks celery, thinly sliced**

1/4 **teaspoon dried oregano**

1 **sweet red pepper, diced**

4 **ounces green beans, sliced**

2 **yellow squash, sliced**

1/4 **cup water**

1/8 **teaspoon each salt and pepper**

1 Bring stock to a boil in a saucepan. Stir in bulgur, cover, remove from heat, and let stand 15 to 20 minutes or until bulgur is soft and liquid is absorbed.

2 In a skillet, heat the oil over moderate heat. Add onions, celery, and oregano and sauté, stirring, for 7 minutes. Add sweet pepper and sauté 3 minutes.

3 Add beans, squash, and water. Cook vegetables 5 to 7 minutes. Fluff up bulgur with a fork. Gently stir into vegetables. Season with salt and pepper.

*A symphony of flavors and colors – **Bulgur Vegetable Medley** accompanied by grilled fish.*

Bulgur-Stuffed Acorn Squash

This dish is a healthful meal in itself. Acorn squash is a good source of beta carotene. The lean ground beef combined with the bulgur gives you 26 grams of protein.

- Serves **4**
- Preparation Time **20 minutes**
- Cooking Time **1 hour 12 minutes**

8 ounces lean ground beef

2 leeks or small onions, trimmed and sliced

2 cloves garlic, finely chopped

1 can (14 ounces) crushed tomatoes

¼ teaspoon each dried basil and thyme

1 cup bulgur wheat

⅛ teaspoon each salt and pepper

4 acorn squash, halved and seeded

1 Preheat oven to 350°F. Heat a large nonstick skillet over moderate heat. Add beef and cook, stirring, about 4 minutes or until browned. With a slotted spoon, transfer beef to a plate.

2 Spoon off all but 1 teaspoon of fat from skillet. Add leeks and garlic and sauté about 5 minutes or until browned.

> **COOKING TIP**
> *Removing most of the beef fat from the skillet reduces the saturated fat.*

3 Add the tomatoes and dried herbs to the skillet and bring to a boil. Stir in the bulgur. Cover and gently simmer about 15 minutes.

4 Stir in the beef and season with the salt and pepper. Stuff the mixture into squash (see box) and place in a roasting pan. Bake about 45 minutes or until tender.

PER SERVING
Calories **491**, Saturated Fat **3g**, Total Fat **7g**, Sodium **233mg**, Cholesterol **43mg**, Protein **26g**, Carbohydrate **94g**, Fiber **13g**.

STUFFING ACORN SQUASH

Slice the squash lengthwise and scoop out the seeds. Cut a thin slice from base of each half so it will sit flat. Spoon the filling into each half.

Bulgur, Carrot, and Broccoli Medley

- Serves **6**
- Preparation Time **15 minutes**
- Cooking Time **30–35 minutes**

2 tablespoons olive or canola oil

3 carrots, diced

2 onions, coarsely chopped

1 cup bulgur wheat

2 cups vegetable or chicken stock, page 18

1 teaspoon finely grated lemon zest

1 large head broccoli, cut into small florets

⅛ teaspoon each salt and pepper

1 In a large nonstick skillet, heat the oil over moderate heat. Add the carrots and onions and sauté, stirring, 7 to 9 minutes or until softened and lightly browned.

*To make a nourishing meal, serve **Bulgur, Carrot, and Broccoli Medley** with beans or legumes to complete the protein.*

2 Add the bulgur, stock, and lemon zest to the skillet. Bring to a boil, cover, and simmer 10 to 12 minutes or until all the liquid is absorbed and the bulgur is almost tender.

3 Lightly fluff up the bulgur with a fork. Add the broccoli florets to the skillet. Cover and cook about 10 minutes longer or until the broccoli and bulgur are tender. Season with salt and pepper.

PER SERVING
Calories **178**, Saturated Fat **1g**, Total Fat **5g**, Sodium **103mg**, Cholesterol **0mg**, Protein **6g**, Carbohydrate **30g**, Fiber **9g**.

Herbed Polenta

Cooking technique ▪ *There are two ways to make this Italian peasant dish. You can cook the cornmeal until thick, add vegetables, and serve like a stew. Or you can chill the cornmeal, cut into rounds, and broil.*

Save time ▪ *Quick to make, polenta rounds offer a nice change from biscuits.*

● Serves **6** ● Preparation Time **5 minutes plus chilling time** ● Cooking Time **25 minutes**

PER SERVING
Calories **128**, Saturated Fat **1g**, Total Fat **2g**, Sodium **128mg**, Cholesterol **5mg**, Protein **6g**, Carbohydrate **22g**, Fiber **2g**.

1 cup yellow cornmeal

2 cups water

2 cups 1% low-fat milk

¹/₈ teaspoon each salt and pepper

2 tablespoons chopped parsley, chives, or basil

2 tablespoons finely grated Parmesan cheese

1 Combine cornmeal with 1 cup water in a small bowl. Bring milk and remaining water to a boil in a nonstick saucepan. Season with the salt and pepper.

2 Reduce heat slightly and slowly stir cornmeal into milk mixture. Cook, stirring constantly, about 5 minutes or until mixture boils and thickens slightly.

3 Reduce the heat to very low and simmer the polenta gently, stirring frequently, about 10 minutes or until the mixture is smooth and thickened.

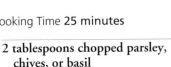

*Comfort food Italian style – **Herbed Polenta** served with a robust pork stew.*

4 Remove the saucepan from the heat. Add the chopped herbs and cheese and stir well to mix thoroughly.

5 Turn the polenta out onto a nonstick baking pan and spread to a depth of ¼ inch with a palette knife. Chill for 2 hours to set. Preheat the broiler.

6 With a cookie cutter, cut rounds from polenta. Use trimmings to make more. Or cut into 6 wedges. Broil on a rack about 5 minutes, until golden.

Grilled Polenta with Mushroom Sauce

- Serves **6**
- Preparation Time **20 minutes plus chilling time**
- Cooking Time **40 minutes**

---

1 cup yellow cornmeal

1 cup water

3 cups vegetable or chicken stock, page 18

¹/₈ teaspoon each salt and pepper

2 tablespoons olive or canola oil

2 leeks, trimmed and coarsely chopped

1 clove garlic, finely chopped

12 ounces mushrooms, sliced

¹/₂ cup red wine or vegetable stock

¹/₂ teaspoon dried thyme

2 tablespoons finely grated Parmesan cheese

1 In a small bowl, combine cornmeal with water. Place stock in a nonstick saucepan and season with the salt and pepper. Bring to a boil over high heat.

2 Slowly pour in cornmeal, stirring constantly. Simmer polenta gently, stirring constantly, about 10 minutes or until mixture is smooth and thickened.

3 Remove from the heat and allow to stand about 5 minutes. Grease a 9-inch pie plate with 1 teaspoon of oil. Pour in polenta and spread out. Cover with plastic wrap and chill for 2 hours to set.

4 Heat remaining oil in a nonstick skillet over moderate heat. Sauté leeks and garlic until softened. Add mushrooms and sauté about 5 minutes longer or until softened. Add wine and thyme and simmer about 10 minutes or until a rich sauce has formed.

5 Preheat the broiler. Sprinkle the polenta with cheese and cut into 6 wedges. Set triangles on a broiler rack and broil about 5 minutes, until golden brown. Transfer polenta triangles to a serving platter and spoon the mushroom sauce over.

PER SERVING
Calories **179**, Saturated Fat **1g**, Total Fat **6g**, Sodium **123mg**, Cholesterol **2mg**, Protein **5g**, Carbohydrate **25g**, Fiber **2g**.

Mediterranean Polenta

For stick-to-the-ribs goodness, make polenta the traditional way – thick and creamy. Serve it with meat, poultry, or bread and a salad.

- Serves **6**
- Preparation Time **10 minutes**
- Cooking Time **25 minutes**

---

1 cup yellow cornmeal

1 cup water

3 cups vegetable or chicken stock, page 18

2 teaspoons dried basil, oregano, or thyme

¹/₈ teaspoon each salt and pepper

3 tomatoes, diced

2 zucchini, diced

1 sweet red or green pepper, diced

2 tablespoons olive oil

1 In a small bowl, combine the cornmeal and water. Combine the stock, dried herbs, salt, and pepper in a nonstick saucepan. Bring to a boil over moderate heat.

2 Reduce the heat slightly and slowly stir the cornmeal into the stock mixture in a steady stream. Cook, stirring constantly, about 5 minutes or until the mixture comes to a boil and thickens slightly. Reduce the heat to very low and simmer, stirring frequently, about 10 minutes or until the mixture is smooth and thickened.

3 Stir the diced vegetables and the oil into the polenta and continue cooking about 4 minutes longer or until the vegetables are cooked and the polenta is thickened. Remove from the heat, cover, and let stand about 5 minutes.

PER SERVING
Calories **160**, Saturated Fat **1g**, Total Fat **5g**, Sodium **85mg**, Cholesterol **0mg**, Protein **4g**, Carbohydrate **26g**, Fiber **4g**.

Granola with Fruit and Nuts

Cooking technique ■ *Toast oats to make granola or cook with milk for a nutritious hot cereal.*
Add nutrients ■ *Stir in fruit for vitamin C, nuts for vitamin E.*
About oats ■ *Rolled oats are sold as "old-fashioned" oatmeal and cook in 5 minutes. The longer-cooking steel-cut oats are sold as Irish oatmeal.*

● Serves **10** ● Preparation Time **30 minutes** ● Cooking Time **50–55 minutes**

PER SERVING
Calories **331**, Saturated Fat **1g**, Total Fat **10g**, Sodium **4mg**, Cholesterol **0mg**, Protein **12g**, Carbohydrate **54g**, Fiber **8g**.

¹/₄ cup honey	¹/₂ cup sliced almonds
¹/₄ cup apple juice	2 sweet apples or 1 cup chopped dried apples
4 cups rolled oats	
1 cup flaked wheat or rolled oats	¹/₂ cup seedless raisins
1 cup wheat germ	¹/₂ cup sunflower seeds

1 Preheat oven to 325°F. In a saucepan, combine honey with apple juice. Heat, stirring, until almost boiling. Remove from the heat and allow to cool.

2 In a roasting pan, combine oats, flaked wheat, wheat germ, and almonds. Pour honey mixture over and toss until well mixed and the grains are coated.

3 Roast grain mixture, stirring occasionally, for 30 minutes or until the grains are toasted. Remove from oven and allow to cool, stirring occasionally.

Granola with Fruit and Nuts is packed with fiber – a delicious and healthy way to start the day.

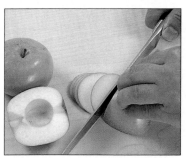

4 Reduce oven temperature to 250°F. Halve and core apples and cut halves into very thin slices. Arrange the slices on 2 baking sheets in a single layer.

5 Cook the apple slices in the oven, turning them once, about 15 to 20 minutes or until partly dried out. Allow slices to cool slightly, then chop coarsely.

6 In a bowl, combine grain mixture with apples, raisins, and sunflower seeds. When cooled, store, refrigerated, in an airtight container for up to 1 month.

Granola with Cranberries

- Serves **10**
- Preparation Time **30 minutes**
- Cooking Time **50–55 minutes**

¹/₄ cup honey

¹/₄ cup apple juice

5 cups rolled oats

1 cup toasted wheat germ

¹/₂ cup chopped almonds

2 Bosc pears or ¹/₂ cup chopped dried pears

1 tablespoon lemon juice

¹/₂ cup dried cranberries

¹/₂ cup toasted pumpkin seeds

1 Preheat oven to 325°F. Combine honey and apple juice as in Step 1 of the master recipe.

2 In a roasting pan, combine oats, wheat germ, and almonds. Pour honey mixture over and toss as in Step 2 of the master recipe.

3 Roast the grain mixture as in Step 3 of the master recipe.

4 If using fresh pears, slice, arrange on baking sheets, then sprinkle with lemon juice and cook as in Steps 4 and 5 of the master recipe.

5 In a bowl, combine grain mixture with pears, cranberries, and pumpkin seeds. When completely cooled, store, refrigerated, in an airtight jar for up to 1 month.

PER SERVING
Calories **319**, Saturated Fat **1g**,
Total Fat **8g**, Sodium **5mg**,
Cholesterol **0mg**, Protein **12g**,
Carbohydrate **53g**, Fiber **7g**.

Fruited Oatmeal

- Serves **4**
- Preparation Time **10–15 minutes**
- Cooking Time **45–50 minutes**

1¹/₂ cups water

1 cup 1% low-fat milk

1 cup steel-cut (Irish) oats

2 tablespoons honey

1 cup fresh blueberries

¹/₂ cup fresh raspberries

¹/₄ cup toasted chopped hazelnuts or almonds

1 In a large heavy nonstick saucepan, combine the water and milk. Bring to a boil over moderate heat. Stir in the oats and reduce the heat slightly.

2 Simmer the mixture, stirring, about 3 minutes or until starting to thicken. Then cover the pan and simmer the oats very gently 20 to 25 minutes longer or until fully cooked.

3 Remove from the heat, stir in the honey, and allow to stand, covered, about 5 minutes. Serve with the fruits and nuts sprinkled on top.

PER SERVING
Calories **222**, Saturated Fat **1g**,
Total Fat **7g**, Sodium **37mg**,
Cholesterol **2mg**, Protein **7g**,
Carbohydrate **37g**, Fiber **5g**.

Oatmeal Indian Pudding

- Serves **6**
- Preparation Time **8 minutes**
- Cooking Time **30–35 minutes**

1 quart 1% low-fat milk

¹/₂ cup rolled oats

¹/₂ cup yellow cornmeal

¹/₂ teaspoon ground cinnamon

¹/₈ teaspoon ground nutmeg

¹/₃ cup molasses

2 egg whites

¹/₂ cup golden raisins (optional)

1 In a large nonstick saucepan, heat the milk over moderate heat until almost boiling.

2 Stir in the oats, cornmeal, cinnamon, and nutmeg. Bring the mixture to a boil, then reduce the heat, cover the pan, and simmer, stirring occasionally, about 15 minutes or until cooked through. Remove from the heat and allow to stand about 5 minutes.

3 Meanwhile, combine the molasses with the egg whites until blended. Stir into the oat mixture. Return to moderately low heat, stirring constantly, until the mixture starts to bubble. Stir in raisins, if using. Remove from the heat and serve at once with low-fat milk or vanilla yogurt.

PER SERVING
Calories **222**, Saturated Fat **1g**,
Total Fat **2g**, Sodium **120mg**,
Cholesterol **7mg**, Protein **9g**,
Carbohydrate **42g**, Fiber **3g**.

Slow-Baked White Beans with Sage

Cooking technique ■ *Slow baking makes the beans tender yet firm. Serve them as a side dish or in stuffed peppers. For a quick meatless meal, boil the beans and toss with pasta.*

About white beans ■ *Great Northerns are best in the master recipe, as they are especially firm. However, you can use any white bean — white kidneys, navys, or great Northerns, in the variations.*

● Serves **4** ● Preparation Time **5 minutes plus soaking time** ● Cooking Time **1 hour 40 minutes**

PER SERVING
Calories **217**, Saturated Fat **1g**, Total Fat **4g**, Sodium **107mg**, Cholesterol **0mg**, Protein **12g**, Carbohydrate **35g**, Fiber **2g**.

1 cup dried great Northern beans

¹/₂ bunch fresh sage leaves or 2 tablespoons dried

2 cups vegetable or chicken stock, page 18

2 cups cold water

1 tablespoon olive or canola oil

¹/₈ teaspoon each salt and pepper

1 Place the beans in a large bowl and cover generously with cold water. Cover the bowl with a plate and allow to stand at least 8 hours or overnight or use the quick-soak method, page 227. Drain beans.

2 Pile the sage leaves together on a chopping board and, using a sharp knife, cut them across into thin shreds.

3 Preheat the oven to 375°F. In a large saucepan or skillet, bring the stock and 2 cups cold water to a boil. Add the beans and the sage, return to a boil, and boil 10 minutes.

COOKING TIP
Cook beans and legumes at a fast boil for the first 10 minutes. This removes any toxins that may be present.

4 Transfer the seasoned beans and liquid to a casserole, cover, and bake 45 minutes to 1 hour or until the beans are tender when tested with a fork and most of the liquid has been absorbed.

5 If the mixture is still very liquid, remove the lid and cook about 10 minutes longer, stirring occasionally.

6 Remove the casserole from the oven. Drizzle with the oil, season with salt and pepper, and stir well to combine.

Slow-Baked White Beans with Sage *goes well with ham, poultry, or pork. You'll need just
a small serving of meat because the beans provide more protein.*

White Beans with Pasta, Carrots, and Parsley Pesto

Even pesto — that irresistible Italian nut and herb sauce — can be part of a low-fat diet when you make it with just 2 tablespoons oil, as in this recipe. Traditionalists can substitute basil and pine nuts for the parsley and walnuts if they prefer.

- Serves **4**
- Preparation Time **20 minutes** plus soaking time
- Cooking Time **1 hour 10 minutes**

1 cup dried white beans
2 cups vegetable or chicken stock, page 18
2 cups cold water
2 large carrots, diced
1 bay leaf
8 ounces penne or ziti
1 cup parsley, stems removed
¼ cup walnuts
2 tablespoons grated Parmesan cheese
2 tablespoons olive or canola oil
⅛ teaspoon each salt and pepper

1 Place the white beans in a large bowl and cover generously with cold water. Cover the bowl with a plate and allow to stand at least 8 hours or overnight or use the quick-soak method, page 227. Drain the white beans.

2 In a large saucepan, bring the stock and 2 cups cold water to a boil. Add the carrots, reduce the heat, and simmer until just tender. Using a slotted spoon, transfer the carrots to a small bowl and reserve.

White Beans with Pasta, Carrots, and Parsley Pesto makes an easy light lunch or supper.

3 Return the stock and water to a boil. Add the white beans and bay leaf. Return to a boil and reduce the heat to moderately low.

4 Partially cover and simmer the beans 45 minutes to 1 hour, stirring occasionally, or until the beans are fork-tender and most of the liquid has been absorbed. If too liquid, remove cover during the last 10 minutes of cooking. Discard the bay leaf.

5 Bring a stockpot of water to a boil. Add the pasta and cook according to package directions or until tender. Drain and refresh the pasta under cold water.

COOKING TIP
To prevent the pasta from becoming soggy, always cook it without a lid on the pan.

6 Meanwhile, make the pesto with parsley, walnuts, Parmesan cheese, and oil (see box, right).

7 In a large serving bowl, toss the cooked beans and carrots with the pasta. Toss with the parsley pesto to coat thoroughly, and season with salt and pepper.

PER SERVING
Calories **551**, Saturated Fat **2g**, Total Fat **14g**, Sodium **194mg**, Cholesterol **2mg**, Protein **22g**, Carbohydrate **86g**, Fiber **7g**.

MAKING PARSLEY PESTO

1 *Place the parsley, walnuts, Parmesan cheese, and oil in the food processor and blend for a few seconds on high speed.*

2 *Process until smooth, scraping down the sides of the bowl of the food processor to ensure that all the ingredients are thoroughly processed.*

GETTING AHEAD

To save time later, make the parsley pesto the day before and refrigerate in a covered bowl until needed. Or make double the quantity and store the extra in a tightly sealed container in the refrigerator for up to 1 week. Pesto also adds piquancy to rice dishes.

White Bean, Tomato, and Mushroom Casserole

This robust casserole is delicious with broiled meat or fish. For a meatless main dish, serve it with rice, bread, or a little cheese to complete the protein.

- Serves **4**
- Preparation Time **15 minutes** plus soaking time
- Cooking Time **3–3¹/₂ hours**

1 cup dried white beans
2¹/₂ cups cold water
1 can (14 ounces) crushed tomatoes
2 tablespoons olive or canola oil
8 ounces mushrooms, halved
2 large onions, sliced
2 cloves garlic, finely chopped
¹/₄ cup chopped fresh basil or 1¹/₂ teaspoons dried
¹/₈ teaspoon each salt and pepper

1 Place the white beans in a large bowl and cover generously with cold water. Cover the bowl with a plate and allow to stand at least 8 hours or overnight or use the quick-soak method (see box, right). Drain beans.

2 Preheat the oven to 375°F. Place 2¹/₂ cups cold water, the crushed tomatoes, and the beans in a flameproof casserole. Bring to a boil and boil 10 minutes, stirring occasionally.

3 Transfer the casserole to the oven, cover, and bake 2¹/₂ to 3 hours, stirring occasionally, or until the beans are fork-tender but not mushy and most of the liquid has been absorbed.

4 In a large nonstick skillet, heat the oil over moderate heat. Add the mushrooms, onions, and garlic and sauté about 5 minutes or until soft.

5 Remove casserole from the oven and, using a slotted spoon, add the vegetables to the bean mixture and stir to combine. Stir in the chopped basil and season with salt and pepper.

PER SERVING
Calories **336**, Saturated Fat **1g**, Total Fat **8g**, Sodium **189mg**, Cholesterol **0mg**, Protein **16g**, Carbohydrate **54g**, Fiber **7g**.

QUICK-SOAK METHOD

If you forget to soak dried beans or are short of time, use this method. In a large pan of water, bring the beans to a boil. Remove the pan from the heat and let stand 1 to 2 hours. Drain the beans, rinse, then cook in fresh water until tender – see page 203 for cooking times and yields.

White Bean-Stuffed Peppers with Swiss Cheese

Stuffed red peppers make a tasty and attractive company dish. Arrange them on a pretty plate lined with lettuce or sprigs of parsley.

- Serves **4**
- Preparation Time **30 minutes** plus soaking time
- Cooking Time **2 hours**

1 cup dried white beans
2 tablespoons olive or canola oil
4 ounces mushrooms, sliced
2 red onions, sliced
2 cloves garlic, finely chopped
2 stalks celery, sliced
2 cups vegetable or chicken stock, page 18
2 cups cold water
2 tablespoons chopped parsley
¹/₈ teaspoon each salt and pepper
4 large sweet red or green peppers, halved lengthwise
¹/₂ cup shredded reduced-fat Monterey Jack cheese

1 Place the white beans in a large bowl and cover generously with cold water. Cover the bowl with a plate and allow to stand at least 8 hours or overnight or use the quick-soak method (see box, left). Drain the beans.

2 In a large nonstick skillet, heat half the oil over moderate heat. Sauté the mushrooms, onions, garlic, and celery about 7 minutes or until slightly softened. Using a slotted spoon, transfer to a plate.

3 Preheat the oven to 375°F. Add the stock and 2 cups cold water to the skillet and bring to a boil. Add the beans and boil 10 minutes.

4 Transfer the beans and sautéed vegetables to a casserole and stir in the parsley. Cover and bake about 1 hour, stirring occasionally, or until the beans are tender when tested with a fork and most of the liquid has been absorbed. If still very liquid, uncover and bake 10 minutes longer, stirring occasionally. Remove from oven and season with salt and pepper.

COOKING TIP
If you want to reduce the cooking time in the oven, blanch the peppers first in boiling water for 5 minutes. Drain and fill as directed.

---

5 Place the sweet peppers, cut side up, in a large roasting pan and drizzle with the remaining oil.

6 Fill each pepper with some of the cooked white bean mixture, top with the grated cheese, and return to the oven. Bake 35 to 45 minutes or until the peppers are tender and the cheese has melted.

PER SERVING
Calories **393**, Saturated Fat **3g**, Total Fat **11g**, Sodium **243mg**, Cholesterol **10mg**, Protein **20g**, Carbohydrate **59g**, Fiber **7g**.

Tex-Mex Red Beans

Cooking technique ▪ *Simmer the beans until tender. Add vegetables and serve with rice or corn bread for a meatless main dish; make a hearty casserole with sausage and rice; or use the beans as a filling for enchiladas.*

Add nutrients ▪ *Like all dried beans, red kidneys are a good source of iron.*

● Serves **6** ● Preparation Time **15 minutes plus soaking time** ● Cooking Time **1½ hours**

PER SERVING
Calories **201**, Saturated Fat **1g**, Total Fat **5g**, Sodium **131mg**, Cholesterol **9mg**, Protein **10g**, Carbohydrate **32g**, Fiber **10g**.

1 cup dried red kidney beans

2 tablespoons olive or canola oil

2 onions, coarsely chopped

2 cloves garlic, finely chopped

2 sweet red or green peppers, chopped

1 can (14 ounces) crushed tomatoes

1 bay leaf

¼ teaspoon dried thyme

⅛ teaspoon each ground cumin, salt, and pepper

1 cup vegetable stock, page 18

*It's down-home good – **Tex-Mex Red Beans** served with Home-style Corn Bread, page 310.*

1 Cover beans with cold water and let stand 8 hours or use quick-soak method, page 227. Drain. In a large pot, boil beans in 2 quarts water for 10 minutes, then simmer 45 minutes. Drain.

2 In a Dutch oven, heat oil. Sauté onions and garlic, stirring, 5 minutes. Add sweet peppers and sauté 5 minutes.

3 Add tomatoes, herbs, cumin, salt, and pepper, stir, and bring to a boil. Stir in beans and stock. Simmer, partially covered, for 20 minutes. Discard bay leaf.

Red Beans, Sausage, and Rice

A small amount of sausage is used for flavor, and it is blanched to remove the fat. You can add extra fiber by using brown rice, but check the cooking time on the package because it will take longer to cook than white rice.

- Serves **6**
- Preparation Time **10 minutes** plus soaking time
- Cooking Time **1 hour 40 minutes**

---

1 cup dried red kidney beans

2 tablespoons olive or canola oil

2 large onions, coarsely chopped

2 stalks celery, coarsely chopped

2 cups vegetable or chicken stock, page 18

1 bay leaf

8 ounces turkey sausage links

1 cup long-grain white rice

$^1/_8$ teaspoon each salt and pepper

Dash of hot red pepper sauce

---

1 Place the kidney beans in a large bowl and cover generously with cold water. Cover the bowl with a plate and allow to stand at least 8 hours or overnight, or use the quick soak method, page 227. Drain the beans.

2 Heat the oil in a large heavy saucepan over moderate heat. Add the onions and celery and sauté, stirring, about 5 minutes or until softened and slightly browned.

3 Add the beans with 1 quart water, stock, and bay leaf. Bring the mixture to a boil and boil 10 minutes. Partially cover the pan and simmer, stirring occasionally, 35 to 45 minutes or until tender. Remove and discard the bay leaf.

4 Meanwhile, place the sausages in a large saucepan, cover with water, and bring to a boil. Simmer about 15 minutes or until cooked. Drain and allow to cool. Carefully remove sausage casings and cut sausages into thin slices.

> ### COOKING TIP
> *To make it easier to remove the casings, using a sharp knife, make a shallow cut along the length of the sausage. Then peel off the casing with your fingers.*

5 Add the rice to the pan with the beans and season with the salt, pepper, and hot pepper sauce. Return to a boil and simmer 10 to 15 minutes longer or until the beans and rice are cooked. Add sausage slices and simmer about 5 minutes or until heated through.

PER SERVING
Calories **364**, Saturated Fat **2g**, Total Fat **10g**, Sodium **488mg**, Cholesterol **29mg**, Protein **17g**, Carbohydrate **51g**, Fiber **8g**.

Red Bean Enchiladas

- Serves **4**
- Preparation Time **35 minutes** plus soaking time
- Cooking Time **1 hour**

---

1 cup dried red kidney beans

2 tablespoons olive or canola oil

2 large onions, coarsely chopped

2 cloves garlic, finely chopped

8 ounces mushrooms, sliced

1 sweet red pepper, chopped

1 small fresh chili pepper, finely chopped

1 can (14 ounces) crushed tomatoes

$^1/_2$ teaspoon chili powder

$^1/_8$ teaspoon each salt and pepper

8 flour tortillas (8" diameter)

$^1/_4$ cup shredded reduced-fat Monterey Jack cheese

Sweet Pepper and Corn Salsa, page 183, or prepared salsa

---

1 Prepare kidney beans as in Step 1 of master recipe, cooking beans for about 1 hour or until tender.

2 Meanwhile, heat oil in a nonstick skillet. Sauté onions and garlic 5 minutes. Add mushrooms, sweet pepper, and chili pepper and sauté 5 minutes. Add tomatoes, chili powder, salt, and pepper and simmer about 20 minutes.

3 Preheat oven to 375°F. Place tortillas on a plate over a pan of simmering water. Cover and warm through for 5 minutes.

4 Add beans to vegetable mixture and stir. Divide mixture between the tortillas and roll them up.

5 Place enchiladas in a 13" x 9" x 2" baking pan and scatter cheese on top. Bake about 5 minutes or until cheese is melted. Serve with salsa on top.

PER SERVING
Calories **665**, Saturated Fat **4g**, Total Fat **22g**, Sodium **591mg**, Cholesterol **5mg**, Protein **25g**, Carbohydrate **104g**, Fiber **21g**.

Enjoy the Mexican flavor of **Red Bean Enchiladas.**

Black-eyed Pea Casserole

Cooking technique ■ *There are two ways to prepare black-eyed peas. You can slow cook them with vegetables, as in the Ham Casserole and master recipe. Or you can boil the peas until tender and add to pasta or rice dishes.*

● Serves 8 ● Preparation Time 15–20 minutes plus soaking time ● Cooking Time 1 hour 10 minutes

PER SERVING
Calories **340**, Saturated Fat **1g**, Total Fat **7g**, Sodium **154mg**, Cholesterol **0mg**, Protein **15g**, Carbohydrate **57g**, Fiber **18g**.

1 cup dried black-eyed peas

2 tablespoons olive or canola oil

2 each large onions and carrots, coarsely chopped

4 stalks celery, coarsely chopped

2 cloves garlic, finely chopped

3 cups vegetable stock, page 18

8 ounces each potatoes and turnips, peeled and cubed

1/2 teaspoon each dried thyme and rosemary

1/8 teaspoon each salt and pepper

1 Soak peas overnight or use quick-soak method, page 227. Drain. In a Dutch oven, heat oil and sauté onions, carrots, celery, and garlic for 5 to 8 minutes.

2 Add 1 quart water and the stock to the Dutch oven with the peas, potatoes, turnips, and herbs. Bring the mixture to a boil and boil 10 minutes.

3 Partially cover casserole and simmer 45 minutes or until peas are tender. Uncover, season with salt and pepper, and simmer about 10 minutes longer.

Black-eyed Pea Casserole, Roasted Sweet Peppers, page 183, and Couscous with Summer Vegetables, page 214.

Black-eyed Peas and Shrimp

- Serves **4**
- Preparation Time **20 minutes** plus soaking time
- Cooking Time **50 minutes**

1 cup dried black-eyed peas

3 cups vegetable stock, page 18

2 tablespoons olive or canola oil

2 stalks celery, coarsely chopped

2 sweet red or green peppers, sliced

1 large onion, thinly sliced

8 ounces slender asparagus spears, cut into 1-inch pieces

8 ounces medium shrimp, peeled and deveined

2 tablespoons chopped parsley

$^1/_8$ teaspoon each salt and pepper

1 Cover peas with cold water and let stand 8 hours or use quick-soak method, page 227. Drain.

2 In a saucepan, place peas, stock, and 1 quart water; boil 10 minutes. Cover and simmer 25 minutes or until tender; drain.

3 In a Dutch oven, heat oil over moderate heat. Add celery, sweet peppers, and onion and sauté, stirring, about 5 minutes.

4 Stir in asparagus and sauté about 5 minutes. Add shrimp and sauté about 5 minutes longer or until pink. Add peas and stir in parsley, salt, and pepper.

PER SERVING
Calories **318**, Saturated Fat **1g**, Total Fat **9g**, Sodium **224mg**, Cholesterol **86mg**, Protein **25g**, Carbohydrate **38g**, Fiber **14g**.

Black-eyed Peas and Pasta

- Serves **4**
- Preparation Time **15 minutes** plus soaking time
- Cooking Time **1 hour**

1 cup dried black-eyed peas

1 bay leaf

8 ounces fusilli or penne

2 tablespoons olive or canola oil

2 onions, coarsely chopped

2 cloves garlic, finely chopped

8 ounces mushrooms, chopped

1 can (14 ounces) crushed tomatoes

2 teaspoons dried basil

$^1/_2$ cup shredded part-skim mozzarella cheese

$^1/_8$ teaspoon each salt and pepper

1 Cover peas with cold water and let stand 8 hours or use quick-soak method, page 227. Drain.

2 In a pan, place peas, 1 quart water, bay leaf; boil 10 minutes. Cover; simmer 25 minutes or until tender. Drain; remove bay leaf.

3 Cook pasta according to package directions. Meanwhile, heat oil in a skillet. Sauté onions and garlic 5 minutes. Add mushrooms; sauté 5 minutes. Add tomatoes and basil and simmer 8 minutes.

4 Drain and rinse pasta. Stir cheese, salt, pepper, beans, and pasta into the sauce.

PER SERVING
Calories **526**, Saturated Fat **2g**, Total Fat **10g**, Sodium **252mg**, Cholesterol **8mg**, Protein **24g**, Carbohydrate **86g**, Fiber **18g**.

Black-eyed Pea and Ham Casserole

- Serves **4**
- Preparation Time **15 minutes** plus soaking time
- Cooking Time **1 hour**

1 cup dried black-eyed peas

2 tablespoons olive or canola oil

12 ounces reduced-sodium, reduced-fat baked ham, cubed

2 onions, coarsely chopped

2 sweet red or green peppers, coarsely chopped

1 can (14 ounces) crushed tomatoes

3 cups chicken stock, page 18

1 bay leaf

$^1/_8$ teaspoon pepper

2 tablespoons chopped parsley

1 Cover peas with cold water and let stand 8 hours or use quick-soak method, page 227. Drain.

2 Preheat the oven to 350°F. In a Dutch oven, heat the oil over moderate heat. Add the ham and sauté about 5 minutes or until browned. Add the onions and sweet peppers and sauté, stirring, about 5 minutes or until softened and slightly browned.

3 Add the peas, tomatoes, stock, 2 cups water, and bay leaf. Bring to a boil and boil for 10 minutes. Cover casserole and bake 50 minutes or until vegetables and beans are tender and most of the liquid is absorbed.

4 Remove and discard the bay leaf. Season the casserole with pepper and serve sprinkled with parsley.

PER SERVING
Calories **379**, Saturated Fat **3g**, Total Fat **13g**, Sodium **899mg**, Cholesterol **45mg**, Protein **26g**, Carbohydrate **41g**, Fiber **11g**.

Black-eyed Pea and Ham Casserole is a meal in itself.

Chick-peas with Potatoes

Cooking technique ■ *Simmer chick-peas until tender. Combine them with potatoes, yogurt, and spices to make a hearty side dish, or purée with garlic for a low-fat sandwich spread. You can also toss them into salads for extra protein.*

● Serves **6** ● Preparation Time **20 minutes plus soaking time** ● Cooking Time **2 hours 10 minutes**

PER SERVING
Calories **362**, Saturated Fat **1g**, Total Fat **7g**, Sodium **86mg**, Cholesterol **1mg**, Protein **10g**, Carbohydrate **42g**, Fiber **10g**.

1 cup dried chick-peas
1 pound potatoes, peeled and cut into $1/2$-inch cubes
2 tablespoons olive or canola oil
1 large onion, coarsely chopped
2 large carrots, coarsely chopped
2 tablespoons chopped parsley

1 tablespoon freeze-dried chives
1 teaspoon dried basil
$1/2$ cup plain nonfat yogurt
2 teaspoons lemon juice
$1/4$ teaspoon dry mustard
$1/8$ teaspoon each salt and pepper

1 Place chick-peas in a bowl and cover with cold water. Cover and let stand at least 8 hours or overnight or use the quick-soak method, page 227. Drain.

2 In a saucepan, bring 2 quarts water to a boil. Add chick-peas and return to a boil. Partially cover and simmer 2 hours or until tender. Drain; transfer to a bowl.

3 Meanwhile, bring another pan of water to a boil; add the potatoes and cook 8 to 10 minutes or until tender. Drain well and add to the chick-peas.

Chick-peas with Potatoes *is delicious with lamb chops or as a meatless main dish. Serve with yogurt on the side.*

4 In a nonstick skillet, heat the oil over moderate heat. Add the onion and carrots and sauté 8 to 10 minutes or until softened and slightly browned.

5 Add the herbs to the onion mixture and stir to combine. Remove from the heat and stir in the yogurt, lemon juice, mustard, salt, and pepper.

6 Pour the vegetable and yogurt mixture over the chick-peas and potatoes and stir to coat well.

Chick-pea and Roasted Garlic Spread on Pita

- Serves **4**
- Preparation Time **20 minutes plus soaking time**
- Cooking Time **2 hours**

---

1 cup dried chick-peas or 2 cups canned, drained and rinsed

1 large head garlic

2–3 tablespoons olive or canola oil

4 pita breads (7" diameter), split into 8 rounds

2 tablespoons lemon juice

$1/8$ teaspoon each salt and pepper

1 cup loosely packed parsley leaves

3 tomatoes, sliced

Parsley leaves for garnish

Black pepper

1 tablespoon toasted sesame seeds (optional)

---

1 Prepare the chick-peas as in Steps 1 and 2 of the master recipe.

2 Meanwhile, preheat the oven to 375°F. Cut off tip of garlic head and place on a sheet of aluminum foil. Drizzle with 2 teaspoons of oil. Pull up edges of foil and twist together to seal garlic into a package. Bake 30 to 40 minutes or until very soft. Allow to cool.

3 Place pita rounds on 2 baking sheets and bake for 7 minutes or until crisp but not browned.

4 Carefully squeeze the garlic cloves from their skins and place in a food processor with their oil. Add chick-peas, lemon juice, salt, pepper, and remaining oil. Process the mixture, scraping down sides of bowl occasionally, until a semi-smooth paste is formed. Add parsley and continue to process until finely chopped.

5 Spread mixture on each pita round. Top with tomato slices. Garnish with parsley leaves and sprinkle with black pepper and toasted sesame seeds.

PER SERVING
Calories **460**, Saturated Fat **2g**, Total Fat **12g**, Sodium **431mg**, Cholesterol **0mg**, Protein **18g**, Carbohydrate **73g**, Fiber **12g**.

Chick-pea and Marinated Tuna Salad

- Serves **4**
- Preparation Time **1 hour 10 minutes plus soaking time**
- Cooking Time **2 hours–2 hours 20 minutes**

---

1 cup dried chick-peas

$1/4$ cup olive or canola oil

2 tablespoons lemon juice

1 teaspoon each dried rosemary and thyme

$1/8$ teaspoon each salt and pepper

1 pound fresh tuna steaks or 2 cans (7 ounces each) chunk light tuna in water, drained

2 sweet red, yellow, or green peppers, halved

2 large red onions, thinly sliced into rings

1 large tomato, diced

---

1 Prepare the chick-peas as in Steps 1 and 2 of the master recipe.

2 In a small bowl, make the marinade: Combine oil with lemon juice, rosemary, thyme, salt, and pepper. In a shallow roasting pan or baking dish, place the tuna. Brush 2 tablespoons of the marinade over the fish. Cover and refrigerate about 1 hour.

3 Meanwhile, preheat the broiler then broil and peel the peppers (see page 182). Cut the peppers lengthwise into $1/4$-inch strips.

4 Broil the fresh tuna about 4 minutes on each side or until cooked through. Remove from the broiler and cut into 1-inch cubes. If using canned tuna, omit this step.

5 In a large bowl, combine the chick-peas with the tuna, pepper strips, onions, tomato, and remaining marinade. Refrigerate until chilled or serve at room temperature.

PER SERVING
Calories **542**, Saturated Fat **4g**, Total Fat **23g**, Sodium **133mg**, Cholesterol **43mg**, Protein **37g**, Carbohydrate **48g**, Fiber **13g**.

Black Bean Vegetable Chili

Cooking technique ▪ *Simmer black beans until tender. Use them for chili or refried beans. For variety, add Oriental spices and serve as a side dish.*

● Serves 6 ● Preparation Time 15 minutes plus soaking time ● Cooking Time 1³/₄ hours

PER SERVING
Calories **351**, Saturated Fat **1g**, Total Fat **6g**, Sodium **205mg**, Cholesterol **0mg**, Protein **18g**, Carbohydrate **60g**, Fiber **15g**.

2 cups dried black beans (turtle beans)
2 tablespoons olive or canola oil
1 onion, coarsely chopped
2 cloves garlic, finely chopped
1 large carrot, coarsely chopped
2 stalks celery, coarsely chopped
1 small turnip, coarsely chopped

1 tablespoon chili powder
¹/₈ teaspoon each salt and pepper
1 can (14 ounces) crushed tomatoes
1 cup vegetable stock, page 18
1 cup fresh or frozen corn kernels
¹/₄ cup chopped parsley

1 Cover beans with cold water and let stand 8 hours or use quick-soak method, page 227. Drain. In a saucepan, boil beans in 2 quarts water, cover, then simmer 1¹/₂ hours. Drain.

2 Heat oil in a nonstick skillet; sauté onion and garlic, stirring, about 4 minutes. Add carrot, celery, turnip, chili powder, salt, and pepper; sauté 8 minutes.

3 Stir in beans, tomatoes, stock, and corn. Cover and simmer 8 to 10 minutes. Add parsley and stir to combine.

Black Bean Vegetable Chili *is served south-of-the-border style in taco shells with salsa and shredded lettuce.*

Refried Black Beans

Serve as a side dish with chicken or as a meatless entrée accompanied by taco chips, salsa, and guacamole. You can substitute 1 teaspoon ground cumin and ¹/₄ cup chopped parsley for the cilantro.

- Serves **6**
- Preparation Time **10 minutes** plus soaking time
- Cooking Time **2 hours**

---

2 cups dried black beans (turtle beans)

1 slice reduced-sodium bacon, coarsely chopped

1 small onion, sliced

3 stalks celery, sliced

1 cup vegetable stock, page 18

1 bunch cilantro, stems separated and leaves chopped

¹/₈ teaspoon each salt and pepper

2 tablespoons olive or canola oil

2 teaspoons chili powder

¹/₂ cup plain nonfat yogurt

---

1 Prepare the beans as in Step 1 of the master recipe.

2 In a large nonstick skillet, cook the chopped bacon over high heat 2 to 3 minutes or until the fat is rendered. Using a slotted spoon, discard the bacon.

3 Add the sliced onion and celery to the pan and sauté 5 minutes or until the vegetables are soft. Add the beans, stock, and cilantro stems to the pan. Cook about 20 to 25 minutes or until the beans are very soft, adding a little water if needed.

4 Drain the beans and discard cilantro stems. When the beans are cool, purée them in a food processor or use a potato masher. Season with salt and pepper.

5 In a skillet, heat the oil with the chili powder over moderately high heat for 1 to 2 minutes. Fry the mashed beans in the oil (see box, below). Serve the refried black beans topped with yogurt and chopped cilantro leaves.

PER SERVING
Calories **297**, Saturated Fat **1g**, Total Fat **6g**, Sodium **126mg**, Cholesterol **1mg**, Protein **17g**, Carbohydrate **46g**, Fiber **7g**.

REFRYING BEANS

1 *Using a potato masher, mash the beans until they are fairly coarse in consistency.*

2 *Fry the mashed beans and, using a slotted spatula, turn them over like a pancake.*

Oriental Black Beans

Fresh ginger and sesame seeds flavor this Asian-inspired dish. Serve it with poultry or make a meatless meal with Oriental noodles.

- Serves **8**
- Preparation Time **15 minutes** plus soaking time
- Cooking Time **1³/₄ hours**

---

2 cups dried black beans (turtle beans)

2-inch piece fresh ginger, peeled and cut into slices

¹/₄ cup sesame seeds

2 tablespoons olive or canola oil

1 tablespoon dark sesame oil

1 large sweet red or green pepper, coarsely chopped

4 scallions, sliced

¹/₈ teaspoon each salt and pepper

---

1 Prepare the beans as in Step 1 of the master recipe, simmering the beans with the ginger. Remove and discard the ginger.

2 Preheat oven to 350°F. Spread out the sesame seeds on a baking sheet in an even layer. Toast them in the oven 4 to 5 minutes or until golden brown. Transfer to a plate.

3 In a heavy nonstick skillet, heat both oils over moderate heat. Sauté sweet pepper and scallions, stirring, about 5 minutes.

4 Add the cooked beans to the vegetable mixture, season with salt and pepper, and heat through, stirring gently. Serve sprinkled with the toasted sesame seeds.

PER SERVING
Calories **251**, Saturated Fat **1g**, Total Fat **8g**, Sodium **49mg**, Cholesterol **0mg**, Protein **12g**, Carbohydrate **32g**, Fiber **8g**.

Enjoy a taste of the Far East – ***Oriental Black Beans*** *accompanied by Celery Medley, page 173.*

235

Spicy Pinto Beans

Cooking technique ▪ *Simmer or slow bake pinto beans until tender, adding vegetables for flavor. You can serve Spicy Pinto Beans with rice or corn bread for a meatless meal; add cheese to make a high-protein meatless casserole; or use the beans in fajitas.*
Add fiber ▪ *Pinto beans are exceptionally high in fiber.*

• Serves 6 • Preparation Time **12 minutes plus soaking time** • Cooking Time **1½ – 2 hours**

PER SERVING
Calories **222**, Saturated Fat **1g**,
Total Fat **6g**, Sodium **115mg**,
Cholesterol **0mg**, Protein **10g**,
Carbohydrate **36g**, Fiber **11g**.

| 1 cup dried pinto beans |
| 2 tablespoons olive or canola oil |
| 3 large onions, coarsely chopped |
| 2 large carrots, coarsely chopped |
| 2 tablespoons chili powder |
| 2 cups vegetable or chicken stock, page 18 |
| 2 cups cold water |
| Dash of hot red pepper sauce |
| ⅛ teaspoon each salt and pepper |

COOKING TIP
It's best not to add salt to beans and lentils until the end of cooking time; otherwise they become tough.

1 Place the pinto beans in a large bowl and cover generously with cold water. Cover the bowl with a plate and allow to stand at least 8 hours or overnight or use the quick- soak method, page 227. Drain the pinto beans.

2 In a large Dutch oven, heat the oil over moderate heat. Add the onions, carrots, and chili powder and sauté, stirring, about 5 minutes or until the vegetables are slightly softened.

3 Stir in the stock and the 2 cups cold water and bring to a boil. Add the pinto beans, return to a boil, and boil 10 minutes.

4 Partially cover the Dutch oven and simmer, stirring occasionally, 1 to 1½ hours or until the pinto beans are tender when tested with a fork and most of the liquid has been absorbed.

5 If the mixture is still very liquid, remove the lid and raise the heat slightly; boil, stirring occasionally, until the beans have absorbed most of the liquid, about 5 to 10 minutes.

6 Remove from the heat and stir in the hot red pepper sauce. Season with the salt and pepper.

*If you like it hot, you'll love **Spicy Pinto Beans**, served here with grilled zucchini, rice, tortilla chips, and low-fat sour cream.*

Pinto Bean and Tomato Casserole

Molasses adds mellow sweetness to this meatless casserole. If desired, you can omit the rice and serve the beans as an accompaniment to hamburgers or barbecued chicken.

- Serves **4**
- Preparation Time **10 minutes** plus soaking time
- Cooking Time **1½ to 2 hours**

---

1 cup dried pinto beans

2 tablespoons olive or canola oil

2 large onions, coarsely chopped

2 cloves garlic, finely chopped

2 cups vegetable or chicken stock, page 18

1 can (14 ounces) crushed tomatoes

2 tablespoons molasses

1 cup brown or long-grain rice

¹/₈ teaspoon each salt and pepper

¹/₂ cup shredded reduced-fat Cheddar cheese

---

1 Soak and drain the pinto beans as in Step 1 of the master recipe.

2 Preheat the oven to 325°F. In a large casserole, heat the oil over moderate heat. Add the onions and garlic and sauté, stirring, about 5 minutes or until slightly softened. Stir in the stock and tomatoes and bring to a boil. Add the molasses and pinto beans, return to a boil, and boil 10 minutes.

3 Cover the casserole and bake, stirring occasionally, about 1 hour or until the pinto beans are tender. If still very liquid, remove the lid and bake, stirring occasionally, until the beans have absorbed most of the liquid.

4 Before the beans are done, cook rice according to package directions. Remove beans from oven and season with the salt and pepper. Serve beans over rice and sprinkle with the cheese.

PER SERVING
Calories **539**, Saturated Fat **3g**, Total Fat **11g**, Sodium **226mg**, Cholesterol **10mg**, Protein **23g**, Carbohydrate **91g**, Fiber **18g**.

COOKING TIP
Soaking, draining, and cooking beans in fresh water helps to eliminate the digestive problems associated with beans.

Pinto beans were named by the Spanish for their "painted" look.

Spicy Pinto Bean and Turkey Fajitas

- Serves **6**
- Preparation Time **20 minutes** plus soaking time
- Cooking Time **1½ to 2 hours**

---

1 cup dried pinto beans

2 cups vegetable or chicken stock, page 18

2 cups cold water

2 tablespoons chili powder

2 tablespoons olive or canola oil

8 ounces turkey breast, cut into strips

2 large onions, sliced

2 large sweet red, green, or yellow peppers, sliced

¹/₈ teaspoon each salt and pepper

12 flour tortillas (8" diameter), warmed

1 cup low-fat sour cream (optional)

---

1 Soak and drain the pinto beans as in Step 1 of the master recipe. In a large saucepan, bring the stock and 2 cups cold water to a boil. Add the chili powder and pinto beans, bring to a boil, and boil 10 minutes.

2 Partially cover pan and simmer 1 to 1½ hours or until beans are tender when tested with a fork and most of the liquid has been absorbed. If still very liquid, uncover and boil for 10 minutes.

3 Meanwhile, in a skillet, heat the oil over high heat. Add the turkey, onions, and sweet peppers and sauté, stirring, about 10 minutes or until the turkey and vegetables are browned and tender. Season with the salt and pepper.

4 Fill the warmed tortillas with equal amounts of the spicy bean mixture, then the turkey mixture, and loosely roll up (see box, below). Serve with the sour cream, if using.

PER SERVING
Calories **478**, Saturated Fat **3g**, Total Fat **13g**, Sodium **350mg**, Cholesterol **30mg**, Protein **25g**, Carbohydrate **70g**, Fiber **13g**.

FOLDING A TORTILLA

1 *Using a spoon, place some filling on the center of the tortilla. Fold one edge of the tortilla in toward the center.*

2 *With the folded edge toward you, fold the two sides in over the filling so that they overlap slightly.*

Layered Mexican Torta

You can also use this bean and meat mixture for burritos. Warm the flour tortillas, place the filling on top, and serve with salsa.

- Serves **4**
- Preparation Time **15 minutes** plus soaking time
- Cooking Time **2 to 2½ hours**

1 cup dried pinto beans

2 cups vegetable or chicken stock, page 18

2 cups cold water

2 tablespoons chili powder

8 ounces lean ground beef

2 large onions, sliced

2 large sweet red, green, or yellow peppers, sliced

1 can (14 ounces) crushed tomatoes

⅛ teaspoon each salt and pepper

4 flour tortillas (8" diameter)

½ cup sliced scallions

1 cup low-fat sour cream

1 Soak and drain the pinto beans as in Step 1 of the master recipe. In a large saucepan, bring the stock and 2 cups cold water to a boil. Add the chili powder and pinto beans, bring to a boil, and boil 10 minutes.

2 Partially cover the saucepan and simmer 1 to 1½ hours or until the pinto beans are tender when tested with a fork and most of the liquid has been absorbed. If still very liquid, uncover and boil 10 minutes longer.

3 Heat a large nonstick skillet over moderate heat. Add the beef and sauté until browned. Add the onions and sweet peppers and sauté about 10 minutes or until browned. Stir in the tomatoes and simmer, uncovered, stirring occasionally, about 6 minutes or until the mixture is quite thick. Season with the salt and pepper.

4 Preheat the oven to 350°F. Place 1 tortilla in the base of an 8-inch round springform cake pan. Layer the torta as shown below. Bake about 25 minutes or until heated through. Serve wedges with a spoonful of sour cream.

*Tomatoes baked with a sprinkling of herbs make a delicious accompaniment for **Layered Mexican Torta**.*

PER SERVING
Calories **576**, Saturated Fat **5g**, Total Fat **14g**, Sodium **434mg**, Cholesterol **53mg**, Protein **36g**, Carbohydrate **86g**, Fiber **20g**.

MAKING A LAYERED TORTA

1 *Spoon half of the spicy bean mixture over the first tortilla, then top with another tortilla.*

2 *Spoon half of the beef mixture over the tortilla and top with another tortilla. Repeat the layers, ending with the remaining beef mixture.*

3 *Top the beef mixture with the sliced scallions and bake the torta about 25 minutes or until heated through.*

4 *Carefully remove the torta from the pan by releasing the spring and lifting off the ring. Cut into wedges.*

Lentil and Chicken Cassoulet

Cooking technique ■ *Lentils don't need soaking – just simmer until tender. For a low-fat cassoulet, bake them with chicken. Or team them with mushrooms for a meatless main dish. Add ground beef for a healthy shepherd's pie.*

● Serves **8** ● Preparation Time **30 minutes** ● Cooking Time **1 hour**

PER SERVING
Calories **337**, Saturated Fat **1g**, Total Fat **6g**, Sodium **185mg**, Cholesterol **43mg**, Protein **30g**, Carbohydrate **4g**, Fiber **10g**.

2 cups brown, red, or green lentils

2 sprigs fresh rosemary or 1 teaspoon dried

2 tablespoons olive or canola oil

1 chicken (3¹/₂–4 pounds), cut into 8 pieces and skinned

2 onions, coarsely chopped

2 each large carrots and turnips, peeled and coarsely chopped

2 cloves garlic, finely chopped

1 can (14 ounces) crushed tomatoes

2 cups chicken stock, page 18

2 tablespoons red wine vinegar

¹/₈ teaspoon each salt and pepper

1 Rinse the lentils in a sieve under running water. Transfer to a saucepan, cover with 2 to 3 quarts water, and add rosemary. Bring to a boil and simmer, partially covered, 15 to 20 minutes or until almost tender.

2 Drain well and discard the rosemary sprigs. Heat the oil in a Dutch oven. Add the chicken and cook about 8 minutes or until well browned on all sides. Using tongs, transfer to a plate and keep warm.

A robust casserole gently spiced with garlic and rosemary –
Lentil and Chicken Cassoulet.

3 Add the onions, carrots, turnips, and garlic to the Dutch oven and sauté, stirring, about 7 minutes or until browned and softened. Return the chicken to the Dutch oven with the tomatoes, stock, and lentils.

4 Bring to a boil, cover, and simmer 20 to 25 minutes or until the chicken and lentils are tender. Stir in the vinegar and season with the salt and pepper. Simmer, uncovered, about 5 minutes longer.

> **COOKING TIP**
> *Beans double in volume once cooked, so if a recipe calls for 1¹/₂ cups cooked beans, use ³/₄ cup dried.*

Mediterranean Lentils with Mushrooms

For a delicious meatless meal, serve over rice with yogurt or low-fat sour cream.

- Serves **8**
- Preparation Time **20 minutes plus marinating time**
- Cooking Time **30 minutes**

¹/₄ cup olive or canola oil
Finely grated zest and juice of 1 lemon
1 teaspoon each dried thyme and oregano
¹/₈ teaspoon each salt and pepper
1 pound mushrooms, halved
2 cups brown, red, or green lentils
1 can (14 ounces) crushed tomatoes
¹/₂ cup chicken stock, page 18
¹/₂ cup sliced pitted black olives

1 In a large bowl, make the marinade: Combine the oil with the lemon zest and juice, thyme, oregano, salt, and pepper.

2 Add the mushrooms to the marinade and toss to coat well. Allow to marinate at room temperature about 1 hour.

3 Meanwhile, rinse the lentils in a sieve under running water. Transfer to a saucepan and cover with 2 to 3 quarts water. Bring to a boil and simmer, partially covered, 15 to 20 minutes or until almost tender. Drain well.

4 Heat a large nonstick skillet over moderate heat. Add the mushrooms with the marinade and sauté, stirring constantly, until softened and browned.

5 Add the lentils, tomatoes, stock, and olives to the skillet. Bring the mixture to a boil and simmer, partially covered, 10 to 15 minutes or until the lentils and mushrooms are very tender.

PER SERVING
Calories **265**, Saturated Fat **1g**, Total Fat **8g**, Sodium **159mg**, Cholesterol **0mg**, Protein **16g**, Carbohydrate **36g**, Fiber **8g**.

Hearty Lentil Shepherd's Pie

- Serves **6**
- Preparation Time **25 minutes**
- Cooking Time **1 hour 10 minutes**

2 cups brown, red, or green lentils
8 ounces lean ground beef
2 large onions, coarsely chopped
2 cloves garlic, finely chopped
1 teaspoon each dried thyme and rosemary
1 can (14 ounces) crushed tomatoes
¹/₂–1 cup beef or vegetable stock, page 18
Pinch of salt and pepper
1¹/₂ pounds all-purpose potatoes, cut into pieces
1 tablespoon olive oil
3 tablespoons low-fat sour cream

1 Rinse the lentils in a sieve under running water. Transfer to a saucepan and cover with 2 to 3 quarts water. Bring to a boil, then simmer, partially covered, about 20 minutes or until almost tender. Drain well.

2 Heat a large deep nonstick skillet over moderate heat. Add the beef and sauté, stirring, until browned. Using a slotted spoon, transfer to a strainer to drain. Add the onions, garlic, thyme, and rosemary to the skillet and sauté about 5 minutes or until softened.

3 Stir in the tomatoes, stock, and lentils, and season with the salt and pepper. Partially cover the pan and simmer about 10 minutes or until tender.

4 With potatotes, olive oil, and sour cream, prepare Creamy Low-Fat Mashed Potatoes, page 185.

5 Preheat the oven to 350°F. Spoon the lentil mixture into a 13" x 9" x 2" baking dish in an even layer. Spoon the mashed potatoes on top and spread out to an even layer. Bake 35 to 40 minutes or until piping hot and bubbling.

PER SERVING
Calories **446**, Saturated Fat **2g**, Total Fat **7g**, Sodium **140mg**, Cholesterol **30mg**, Protein **31g**, Carbohydrate **67g**, Fiber **12g**.

PASTA & PIZZA

From hearty casseroles to delicate angel hair, this chapter shows pasta in all its variety. But the best news is that these mouth-watering dishes are good for you. The body requires complex carbohydrates for a slow but steady supply of energy, and pasta supplies them. And it is versatile: You can serve pasta with cream or tomato sauce, fish or meat; you can stuff, layer, and bake it. On the pages that follow you'll find new ideas and old favorites — pasta casseroles that can be made in advance and sauces that can be whipped up at the last minute. And take a tip from the Italians: serve your pasta with a little less sauce — you'll save on fat and calories. So keep pasta in your cupboard, and rustle up a quick Mediterranean-style meal anytime you want.

Ziti with Tuna, Tomatoes, and Olives, page 253

At one time pasta was thought of as a fattening food, but this myth has been dispelled and it is now considered healthful and nutritious, providing protein, fiber, and B vitamins. Because it's full of energy-giving complex carbohydrates, it is also very satisfying.

Buying pasta

Most supermarkets carry two basic types of pasta.

Dried pasta: Made from durum wheat with just enough egg to bind it together, dried pasta is sold in many different shapes, from long, thin spaghetti to short, tubular macaroni. Dried pasta has a firm texture when cooked.

Fresh pasta: Easy to make at home, fresh pasta has a slightly softer texture and is preferred by many gourmets because it has a fresher taste and is quicker to cook. Fresh pasta is available in many supermarkets but is more expensive.

Flavored pasta

You can buy pasta in a variety of flavors that add color and visual appeal as well. Spinach pasta is one of the most readily available and has the advantage of being higher in dietary fiber than plain pasta. It can be served with any sauce but looks particularly pretty with cream sauces.

PASTA YIELDS

3 ounces dry	Cooked
Elbow (short)	1½ cups
Fresh pasta	1 cup
Orzo	1½ cups
Spaghetti	1½ cups
Wheels	1¼ cups
Fusilli	1½ cups

Red tomato pasta is strongly flavored and is best served in combination with white or green pasta and never with a tomato sauce.

Storing pasta

Dried pasta will keep for up to a year if stored in a covered container in a cool, dry place. Fresh pasta should be stored in an airtight container. It will keep for up to 5 days in the refrigerator, about 6 months in the freezer.

Cooking and serving

Plan about 3 ounces of dried or 4 ounces fresh pasta per person for a main-course serving. Use ³/₄ pound dried or 1 pound fresh pasta to serve four. Cooking in plenty of water prevents sticking. Bring to a rolling boil before adding pasta. Add a squeeze of fresh lemon juice for extra flavor. Different manufacturers use varying combinations of flour and egg, which means that the cooking time will differ, even with the same shape pasta. So always cook pasta according to the instructions on the package. Start checking for

doneness a few minutes before the cooking time is up so that you're sure not to overcook it. When done, pasta should be al dente, which means tender but still firm to the bite, with no hard white center. Do not let pasta get mushy. Be especially careful not to overcook pasta that is to be used in baked dishes. After cooking, drain and toss immediately in the sauce. If the pasta is to be served cold, rinse in cold water. You should also rinse any pasta that is to be handled, such as lasagne noodles or shells.

USING LEFTOVER PASTA

Here are some easy ways to use up cooked pasta.

◆ Plunge in boiling water for 1 minute, then drain. Serve with leftover sauce.

◆ Toss any leftover pasta with a little olive oil in a pan until heated through, then place the pasta in an ovenproof dish and top with reduced-sodium tomato sauce and a little grated Parmesan or low-fat Cheddar. Bake at 350°F until bubbling and golden.

◆ Add leftover pasta to a salad or simply toss with low-fat dressing.

Which pasta?

Although there is no fixed rule, the shape of the pasta helps determine the cooking method and what kind of sauce to serve. Long strands, such as spaghetti, vermicelli, fettuccine, linguine, and tagliatelle, which are all smooth and fine, need a light dressing or thin tomato sauce. Thicker sauces are better served with ridged or hollow pasta shapes, such as penne and rigatoni. Spiral shapes, such as fusilli, are good with most meat, or vegetable-based sauces because chunky bits of food cling to the ridges. Large pasta like manicotti, conchiglie (shells), and cannelloni are suitable for baking and stuffing, while large, flat pasta such as lasagne noodles are ideal for layering with sauce and cheese. If you don't have the particular pasta called for in a recipe, just substitute a similar shape.

Bow-ties/Farfalle: *Butterfly shape. Small, medium, or large in yellow, red, or green. Goes well with fresh tomato sauce. Often made with egg.*

Penne: *"Quill pens" – tubular pasta with ends cut off diagonally like a quill. Good with chunky meat sauces or well-flavored tomato sauce.*

Vermicelli: *"Little worms", slightly finer than spaghetti. Best with light tomato sauces and seafood.*

Fettuccine: *Thin, ribbon-like strips sold in bunches. Good with any meat sauce.*

Cannelloni: *Large tubes. Fill with mixture of choice. Available in oven-ready and precooked versions.*

Manicotti: *"Sleeves" – large tubes that can be ridged or smooth. Usually stuffed and baked with a sauce.*

Macaroni: *Fat tubular shape. Good with rich meat- or cheese-based sauces.*

Conchiglie: *Jumbo shells – best stuffed. Smaller shells – good with meat, tomato, cheese, or creamy sauces.*

Tagliatelle: *Flat noodle-like pasta good with meaty sauces.*

Rigatoni: *Tubular pasta with ridged surface. Good with rich chunky sauces.*

Wheels: *Shaped like cartwheels. Absorb sauce very well because of their shape.*

Spaghetti: *Means "little strands" and comes in many thicknesses. Goes well with tomato and meat sauces.*

Fusilli: *Long hollow spaghetti shaped like a spring. Good with garlic- and oil-based sauces, particularly those with seafood or tomatoes.*

Capellini: *Fine spaghetti. The name means "fine hair".*

Creamy Pasta Primavera

Cooking technique ■ *For a thick, luscious sauce that's low in fat, make a cream base using low-fat milk. Add part-skim ricotta cheese and blend until smooth.*

Add nutrients ■ *Stir in vegetables for extra vitamins. Add meat or fish for protein.*

● Serves **6** ● Preparation Time **5 minutes** ● Cooking Time **20–25 minutes**

PER SERVING
Calories **450**, Saturated Fat **4g**,
Total Fat **11g**, Sodium **243mg**,
Cholesterol **104mg**, Protein **21g**,
Carbohydrate **70g**, Fiber **6g**.

1 tablespoon olive oil
4 teaspoons all-purpose flour
1½ cups 1% low-fat milk
1 sweet red pepper, diced
1 cup low-fat ricotta cheese
⅛ teaspoon each salt and pepper

1 package (10 ounces) frozen peas and carrots, thawed and drained
3 tablespoons grated Parmesan cheese
1 pound fettuccine or tagliatelle

1 In a nonstick saucepan, heat oil over moderate heat. Add flour and cook, stirring, about 1 minute or until a paste is formed. Remove the pan from the heat.

2 Stir in the milk a little at a time, so that no lumps form. Return the pan to the heat, slowly bring to a boil, and simmer, stirring frequently, until thickened.

3 Add sweet pepper and simmer about 3 minutes or until slightly softened. Add ricotta cheese, salt, and pepper to the mixture and stir to blend well.

*Only the taste is rich – **Creamy Pasta Primavera** accompanied by a sweet pepper salad.*

4 Stir in peas and carrots and 2 tablespoons of the Parmesan cheese. Simmer a few minutes longer, until cheese melts and vegetables are tender.

5 Meanwhile, in a pot of boiling water, cook fettuccine according to package directions or until barely tender. Drain thoroughly.

6 Transfer to a bowl. Pour sauce over pasta and toss. Return to pan and stir just until heated through. Serve sprinkled with the remaining cheese.

Angel Hair Carbonara

- Serves **6**
- Preparation Time **15 minutes**
- Cooking Time **20 minutes**

4 strips reduced-sodium turkey bacon, coarsely chopped

1 large onion, coarsely chopped

2 cloves garlic, finely chopped

2 tablespoons all-purpose flour

2 cups 1% low-fat milk

1 cup low-fat ricotta cheese

$^{1}/_{4}$ cup chopped parsley

3 tablespoons grated Parmesan cheese

$^{1}/_{8}$ teaspoon each salt and pepper

1 pound capellini (angel hair pasta)

1 In a nonstick saucepan, cook the bacon, stirring, about 5 minutes or until fat is rendered. Using a slotted spoon, transfer to a plate. Sauté onion and garlic about 3 minutes. Add flour and cook, stirring, until browned. Remove pan from the heat.

2 Stir in milk as in Step 2 of the master recipe.

3 Blend in ricotta cheese, then add reserved bacon, parsley, 2 tablespoons of Parmesan cheese, salt, and pepper. Simmer a few minutes longer. Keep sauce warm.

4 Cook and serve pasta as in Steps 5 and 6 of master recipe, sprinkling with remaining cheese.

PER SERVING
Calories **431**, Saturated Fat **3g**, Total Fat **8g**, Sodium **350mg**, Cholesterol **28mg**, Protein **20g**, Carbohydrate **67g**, Fiber **4g**.

Linguine with Creamy Shrimp

- Serves **6**
- Preparation Time **15 minutes**
- Cooking Time **20 minutes**

2 tablespoons olive oil

2 tablespoons flour

1 cup 1% low-fat milk

$^{3}/_{4}$ cup fish stock, page 18

2 tablespoons tomato paste

8 ounces small shrimp, peeled and deveined

1 cup frozen peas, thawed

2 scallions, thinly sliced

Dash of hot red pepper sauce

2 tablespoons chopped fresh basil or 2 teaspoons dried

$^{1}/_{8}$ teaspoon each salt and pepper

1 pound linguine or spaghetti

1 Heat oil and add flour as in Step 1 of the master recipe. Gradually stir in milk, fish stock, and tomato paste until smooth.

2 Return pan to the heat and bring to a boil, stirring. Boil for about 1 minute or until thickened.

3 Reduce heat; add shrimp and peas and simmer 2 to 3 minutes or until shrimp turn pink. Stir in scallions, hot red pepper sauce, basil, salt, and pepper. Keep the sauce warm.

4 Cook and serve the pasta as in Steps 5 and 6 of the master recipe.

PER SERVING
Calories **405**, Saturated Fat **1g**, Total Fat **7g**, Sodium **192mg**, Cholesterol **45mg**, Protein **19g**, Carbohydrate **64g**, Fiber **5g**.

Pasta with Creamy Chicken

- Serves **8**
- Preparation Time **20 minutes**
- Cooking Time **30 minutes**

1 tablespoon olive oil

1 large onion, coarsely chopped

2 cloves garlic, finely chopped

8 ounces mushrooms, sliced

12 ounces boneless, skinless chicken breast halves, sliced

$^{1}/_{4}$ cup all-purpose flour

2 cups chicken stock, page 18

1 cup low-fat sour cream

2 tablespoons chopped chives

$^{1}/_{8}$ teaspoon each salt and pepper

1 pound fusilli or medium shells

1 In a nonstick skillet, heat the oil. Sauté onion and garlic 5 minutes. Add mushrooms; sauté 3 minutes. Add chicken; sauté 5 minutes.

2 Stir in flour and cook until chicken and vegetables are coated. Remove from the heat; add stock and stir until smooth. Place sour cream in a bowl.

3 Return skillet to heat and simmer a few minutes, stirring. Remove from heat and stir a few tablespoons of skillet liquid into sour cream. Stir sour cream mixture into skillet. Add chives, salt, and pepper. Keep sauce warm.

4 Cook and serve pasta as in Steps 5 and 6 of master recipe.

PER SERVING
Calories **468**, Saturated Fat **2g**, Total Fat **7g**, Sodium **158mg**, Cholesterol **40mg**, Protein **28g**, Carbohydrate **71g**, Fiber **4g**.

Pasta, Chicken, and Sage Casserole

Cooking technique ▪ *Replace the cream sauce found in most pasta casseroles with an herbed tomato sauce and low-fat cheese. Add chicken, ham, or lean ground meat for protein. Top off the dish with part-skim mozzarella and serve piping hot.*

Save time ▪ *Prepare the day before, cover, and refrigerate. Then bake and serve.*

● Serves 6 ● Preparation Time **25 minutes** ● Cooking Time **50 minutes**

PER SERVING
Calories **460**, Saturated Fat **2g**,
Total Fat **6g**, Sodium **179mg**,
Cholesterol **38mg**, Protein **28g**,
Carbohydrate **73g**, Fiber **7g**.

1 tablespoon olive oil

3 stalks celery, coarsely chopped

2 large onions, coarsely chopped

2 cloves garlic, finely chopped

2 boneless, skinless chicken
  breast halves (about
  12 ounces), coarsely chopped

4 ounces mushrooms, sliced

3 cups reduced-sodium
  tomato sauce

2 tablespoons chopped fresh
  sage or 1 tablespoon dried

1/8 teaspoon each salt and pepper

1 pound penne or fusilli

1/2 cup shredded part-skim
  mozzarella cheese

1 In a large nonstick skillet, heat the oil over moderate heat. Add the celery, onions, and garlic and sauté about 5 minutes or until softened.

2 Add the chicken and sauté, stirring, about 5 minutes. Stir in the mushrooms and cook 2 to 3 minutes longer or until softened.

3 Stir in the tomato sauce, sage, salt, and pepper and simmer, stirring occasionally, about 5 minutes or until all the vegetables are tender.

COOKING TIP
Freezing tends to concentrate certain flavors, so if you decide to freeze this dish, omit the sage and seasonings until you are ready to reheat.

4 Meanwhile, preheat the oven to 350°F. Bring a large pot of water to a boil. Add the penne and cook according to package directions or until just tender. Remove from the heat and drain well.

5 Add the penne to the skillet with the chicken and vegetables and stir gently to mix well.

6 Spoon the mixture into a 13" x 9" x 2" baking dish or individual baking dishes. Sprinkle cheese over pasta and sauce mixture. Bake 20 to 25 minutes or until the cheese is melted and browned and the sauce is bubbling hot.

Hot, hearty, and healthy – that's **Pasta, Chicken, and Sage Casserole.**
Serve with broiled yellow peppers, tomatoes, and zucchini.

Ziti, Ham, and Mushroom Casserole

Look for low-fat, reduced-sodium ham steaks near the bacon in your supermarket. Freeze what you don't use.

- Serves **6**
- Preparation Time **15 minutes**
- Cooking Time **40 minutes**

1 tablespoon olive oil

1 large onion, coarsely chopped

2 cloves garlic, finely chopped

2 cups sliced mushrooms

1 can (28 ounces) crushed tomatoes

8 ounces reduced-sodium, reduced-fat baked ham, chopped

4 ounces frozen peas, thawed

$^1/_2$ cup part-skim ricotta cheese

$^1/_8$ teaspoon pepper

1 pound ziti

2 ounces part-skim mozzarella cheese, shredded

1 In a large nonstick skillet, heat the oil over moderate heat. Add the onion and garlic and sauté about 5 minutes or until soft.

2 Stir in the mushrooms and tomatoes and simmer about 5 minutes or until the sauce thickens slightly. Stir in ham, peas, ricotta cheese, and pepper and simmer a few minutes longer.

3 Meanwhile, preheat the oven to 375°F. Cook and drain the pasta as in Step 4 of the master recipe. Place the pasta in a 13" x 9" x 2" baking dish and mix with half of the sauce. Spoon the remaining sauce over the pasta. Sprinkle with the mozzarella and bake about 20 minutes or until bubbling and very hot.

PER SERVING
Calories **462**, Saturated Fat **3g**, Total Fat **9g**, Sodium **573mg**, Cholesterol **32mg**, Protein **25g**, Carbohydrate **70g**, Fiber **2g**.

CHOPPING AND CRUSHING GARLIC

To chop garlic, use a heavy kitchen knife and chop the cloves as finely as possible. Then, with the flat of the knife blade, press down firmly and crush the chopped garlic.

Alternatively, peel the garlic cloves and place them, one at a time, in a garlic press. Squeeze the handles firmly together, then scrape off the crushed garlic with the tip of a knife.

Macaroni, Beef, and Sweet Pepper Casserole

It is important to drain the beef fat from the pan and replace it with olive oil before cooking the onions and peppers. This helps to reduce the saturated fat.

- Serves **6**
- Preparation Time **20 minutes**
- Cooking Time **45 minutes**

8 ounces lean ground beef

1 tablespoon olive oil

2 large onions, coarsely chopped

2 cloves garlic, finely chopped

3 sweet red, yellow, or green peppers, sliced

1 cup reduced-sodium tomato sauce

2 tablespoons chopped fresh basil or 1 tablespoon dried

$^1/_8$ teaspoon each salt and pepper

1 pound elbow macaroni

$^1/_2$ cup shredded part-skim mozzarella cheese

1 Heat a large nonstick skillet over moderate heat. Add the ground beef and cook, stirring, until all the fat is rendered and the meat is browned. Using a slotted spoon, transfer the beef to a plate. Drain off all the fat from the pan.

2 Add the oil to the skillet and heat. Add the onions and garlic and sauté about 5 minutes or until softened. Add the peppers and sauté about 8 minutes longer or until softened.

3 Return the beef to the pan, stir in the tomato sauce, basil, salt, and pepper, and simmer, stirring occasionally, about 5 minutes or until all the vegetables are tender.

4 Meanwhile, preheat the oven to 350°F. Cook and drain the pasta as in Step 4 of the master recipe. Add the macaroni to the skillet with the meat and pepper sauce and gently stir together to mix well.

6 Spoon the mixture into a 3-quart baking dish. Sprinkle the cheese over the top. Bake about 25 minutes or until the cheese is melted and browned and the sauce is bubbling hot.

PER SERVING
Calories **451**, Saturated Fat **3g**, Total Fat **8g**, Sodium **172mg**, Cholesterol **32mg**, Protein **25g**, Carbohydrate **69g**, Fiber **2g**.

It is worth searching for fresh basil because its pungent flavor cannot be equaled by the dried herb.

Pasta, Sausage, and Tomato Casserole

Italian sausage in a low-fat diet? It's possible if you blanch the sausage as shown below. You can also use this method of reducing fat for sausage links.

- Serves **6**
- Preparation Time **20 minutes**
- Cooking Time **50 minutes**

---

8 ounces spicy Italian sausages or a combination of sweet and spicy sausages, casings pricked with a fork

2 large onions, coarsely chopped

2 cloves garlic, finely chopped

1 cup sliced mushrooms

3 cups reduced-sodium tomato sauce

2 tablespoons chopped fresh basil or 1 tablespoon dried

¹/₈ teaspoon pepper

1 pound large pasta shells

¹/₂ cup shredded part-skim mozzarella cheese

1 Bring a deep nonstick skillet filled with water to a boil. Add the sausages and blanch peel, and slice them (see box, right).

2 Drain the skillet and return to the heat. Add the sliced sausages to the skillet and cook 5 to 6 minutes. Add the onions and garlic and cook about 3 minutes or until softened. Add the mushrooms and cook about 2 minutes longer or until softened.

3 Stir in tomato sauce, basil, and pepper and simmer, stirring occasionally, about 5 minutes or until all the vegetables are tender.

4 Meanwhile, preheat oven to 350°F. Cook and drain pasta as in Step 4 of master recipe. Spoon one-third of the sausage sauce into a 13" x 9" x 2" baking dish and spread into an even layer. Top with half of the pasta shells.

5 Repeat layering the sauce mixture and pasta, finishing with the sauce. Sprinkle the cheese over the top. Bake about 25 minutes or until the cheese is melted and browned and the sauce is bubbling hot.

Pasta, Sausage, and Tomato Casserole contains blanched sausages, so you can enjoy the flavor with less fat.

PER SERVING
Calories **518**, Saturated Fat **5g**, Total Fat **14g**, Sodium **618mg**, Cholesterol **42mg**, Protein **25g**, Carbohydrate **73g**, Fiber **3g**.

BLANCHING, PEELING, AND SLICING SAUSAGES

1 *Prick the sausages. In order to remove some of the fat, place the sausages in a saucepan filled with water and bring to a boil. Simmer for about 2 minutes or until the casings are pale.*

2 *Drain the sausages and allow to cool enough to handle. On a chopping board, slit the casings with a sharp knife and peel the sausages carefully with your fingers.*

3 *With a sharp knife, cut the peeled sausages across into thick slices.*

Fettuccine with Tomato Sauce and Ricotta Dumplings

Reduce fat ▪ *Replace meatballs with low-fat cheese dumplings, tuna, or eggplant.*

● Serves **6** ● Preparation Time **15 minutes** ● Cooking Time **35–40 minutes**

PER SERVING
Calories **431**, Saturated Fat **2g**, Total Fat **7g**, Sodium **322mg**, Cholesterol **96mg**, Protein **19g**, Carbohydrate **78g**, Fiber **8g**.

2 large onions, coarsely chopped
2 cloves garlic, finely chopped
$^1/_4$ cup chicken stock, page 18
1 can (28 ounces) crushed tomatoes
$^1/_8$ teaspoon each salt and pepper
Pinch of hot red pepper flakes

$^1/_2$ cup part-skim ricotta cheese
$^1/_4$ cup grated Parmesan cheese
1 egg white
2 tablespoons all-purpose flour
1 tablespoon chopped fresh basil or 1 teaspoon dried
1 pound fettuccine or spaghetti

1 In a nonstick skillet, simmer onions and garlic in stock, stirring, 8 minutes. Add tomatoes and cook 4 minutes. Add salt, pepper, and hot red pepper flakes.

2 In a bowl, mix both cheeses, egg white, flour, and basil. Form into small balls and drop into a saucepan of boiling water.

3 Simmer the dumplings gently until firm. Meanwhile, cook fettuccine according to package directions or until just tender. Drain and serve with the tomato sauce and dumplings.

Fettuccine with Tomato Sauce and Ricotta Dumplings is served with Cauliflower Provençal, page 172.

Pasta with Basil Tomato Sauce

- Serves **6**
- Preparation Time **30 minutes**
- Cooking Time **1 hour**

3 large onions, coarsely chopped

3 cloves garlic, finely chopped

1/4 cup chicken stock, page 18

5 pounds fresh ripe plum tomatoes, coarsely chopped

2 tablespoons tomato paste

2 tablespoons chopped parsley

2 teaspoons dried basil

1/8 teaspoon each salt and pepper

Pinch of hot red pepper flakes

1 pound linguine or spaghetti

1/4 cup grated Parmesan cheese

1 This recipe makes about 8 cups of sauce, so freeze the extra for future use. In a large nonstick saucepan, simmer onions and garlic in stock about 10 minutes.

2 Add tomatoes and tomato paste, cover, and cook, stirring, about 20 minutes.

3 Uncover and add herbs. Cook, stirring, 30 minutes or until a rich sauce forms. Add salt, pepper, and hot red pepper flakes.

4 Meanwhile, cook pasta according to package directions or until just tender. Drain and serve in individual bowls. Pour 1/2 cup of sauce over each serving and sprinkle with the cheese.

PER SERVING
Calories **348**, Saturated Fat **1g**,
Total Fat **3g**, Sodium **130mg**,
Cholesterol **3mg**, Protein **13g**,
Carbohydrate **66g**, Fiber **6g**.

Ziti with Tuna, Tomatoes, and Olives

- Serves **6**
- Preparation Time **10 minutes**
- Cooking Time **20 minutes**

1 1/2 tablespoons olive oil

2 cloves garlic, finely chopped

1 can (14 ounces) crushed tomatoes

2 tablespoons chopped fresh basil or 2 teaspoons dried

1/8 teaspoon each salt and pepper

Pinch of hot red pepper flakes

2 cans (7 ounces each) chunk light tuna in water, drained

1 pound ziti or elbow macaroni

1/4 cup sliced black olives

1 In a large nonstick saucepan, heat oil. Sauté garlic, stirring, 1 to 2 minutes or until very soft.

2 Add tomatoes and cook, stirring, about 10 minutes or until they cook down to a rich sauce.

3 Stir in the basil and simmer about 3 minutes longer. Add salt, pepper, and hot red pepper flakes. Add the tuna fish and stir gently to combine.

4 Meanwhile, cook pasta according to package directions or until just tender. Drain and transfer to a serving dish. Pour tuna sauce over the pasta and top with the sliced olives.

PER SERVING
Calories **415**, Saturated Fat **1g**,
Total Fat **6g**, Sodium **365mg**,
Cholesterol **10mg**, Protein **27g**,
Carbohydrate **63g**, Fiber **5g**.

Tagliatelle with Roasted Tomatoes and Eggplant

- Serves **6**
- Preparation Time **20 minutes**
- Cooking Time **1 hour 5 minutes**

2 tablespoons olive oil

2 large onions, coarsely chopped

1 eggplant, coarsely chopped

2 pounds fresh ripe plum tomatoes, coarsely chopped

2 tablespoons tomato paste

2 tablespoons chopped parsley

2 teaspoons dried basil

1/8 teaspoon each salt and pepper

Pinch of hot red pepper flakes

1 pound tagliatelle or fettuccine

1/4 cup grated Parmesan cheese

1 Preheat the oven to 350°F. Pour the oil into a nonstick roasting pan. Add the onions and eggplant and roast, stirring occasionally, about 25 minutes or until very soft and golden brown.

2 Add the chopped tomatoes, cover, and cook, stirring occasionally, about 20 minutes longer or until the tomatoes have cooked down to a pulp.

3 Stir in the tomato paste, herbs, salt, pepper, and hot red pepper flakes. Return to the oven and cook 10 to 15 minutes longer.

4 Meanwhile, cook the tagliatelle according to package directions or until just tender. Drain and place in a serving bowl. Pour the tomato sauce over the pasta. Sprinkle with the cheese.

PER SERVING
Calories **439**, Saturated Fat **2g**,
Total Fat **11g**, Sodium **205mg**,
Cholesterol **90mg**, Protein **16g**,
Carbohydrate **76g**, Fiber **9g**.

Tagliatelle with Roasted Tomatoes and Eggplant can be served with chicken, as shown, or on its own.

No-Cook Sweet Pepper Sauce

Cooking technique ▪ *Marinate fresh vegetables in oil, vinegar, and spices. Serve over pasta.*
Add vitamins ▪ *The vegetables retain more nutrients because they aren't cooked.*

• Serves **6** • Preparation Time **30 minutes plus marinating time** • Cooking Time **15 minutes**

PER SERVING
Calories **400**, Saturated Fat **1g**, Total Fat **7g**, Sodium **139mg**, Cholesterol **2mg**, Protein **13g**, Carbohydrate **70g**, Fiber **7g**.

2 cloves garlic, finely chopped

2 large onions, chopped

2 sweet red, yellow, or green peppers, diced

1 large zucchini, diced

3 celery stalks, diced

2 carrots, diced

2 tablespoons olive oil

2 tablespoons balsamic or red wine vinegar

1/8 teaspoon each salt and pepper

2 tablespoons each chopped fresh basil and parsley

1 pound spaghetti

3 tablespoons grated Parmesan cheese

1 In a bowl, combine garlic and all the vegetables. Add oil, vinegar, salt, and pepper and toss to coat well. Cover and marinate for 2 hours in the refrigerator.

2 Remove mixture from refrigerator and stir in herbs. Allow to come to room temperature. Cook spaghetti according to package directions or until it is tender.

3 Drain and transfer to a bowl. Sprinkle with cheese and toss well. Divide the pasta into individual servings and spoon the sauce over each. Serve at once.

Perfect for a hot summer night – No-Cook Sweet Pepper Sauce served with spaghetti.

No-Cook Tomato Olive Sauce

- Serves **6**
- Preparation Time **18 minutes** plus marinating time
- Cooking Time **15 minutes**

---

1 pound fresh ripe tomatoes, coarsely chopped

1 package (9 ounces) frozen artichoke hearts or asparagus, thawed

6 ounces sliced black olives

2 tablespoons olive oil

2 tablespoons balsamic or red wine vinegar

1/8 teaspoon each salt and pepper

1/4 cup chopped parsley

1 pound penne or bow-tie pasta

1 In a bowl, combine tomatoes, artichoke hearts, and olives. Add oil, vinegar, salt, and pepper and toss to coat well. Cover and marinate for 2 hours in the refrigerator.

2 Remove mixture from refrigerator and stir in parsley. Let come to room temperature.

3 Cook the penne according to package directions or until tender. Drain the pasta and transfer to individual serving bowls.

4 Spoon some of the vegetable sauce over each portion and serve at once.

PER SERVING
Calories **390**, Saturated Fat **1g**, Total Fat **9g**, Sodium **327mg**, Cholesterol **0mg**, Protein **12g**, Carbohydrate **66g**, Fiber **8g**.

No-Cook Spinach Sauce

- Serves **6**
- Preparation Time **15 minutes** plus marinating time
- Cooking Time **15 minutes**

---

1 package (10 ounces) frozen spinach, thawed and drained

1/2 cup chopped fresh basil or 2 teaspoons dried

2 zucchini, diced

1 yellow squash, diced

1 sweet red or green pepper, thinly sliced

2 tablespoons olive oil

2 tablespoons red wine vinegar

1/8 teaspoon each salt and pepper

1 pound tagliatelle or fettuccine

2 tablespoons grated Parmesan cheese

1 Place spinach and basil in a food processor and finely chop or, using a sharp knife, finely chop by hand. Transfer to a bowl.

2 Add fresh vegetables, oil, vinegar, salt, and pepper and toss to coat well. Cover and marinate for 2 hours in the refrigerator.

3 Remove mixture from the refrigerator and allow to come to room temperature.

4 Cook pasta according to package directions. Drain and transfer to a serving bowl. Add cheese and mix. Pour sauce over and toss to coat. Serve at once.

PER SERVING
Calories **387**, Saturated Fat **2g**, Total Fat **10g**, Sodium **148mg**, Cholesterol **88mg**, Protein **75g**, Carbohydrate **66g**, Fiber **7g**.

No-Cook Tex-Mex Sauce

- Serves **6**
- Preparation Time **15 minutes** plus marinating time
- Cooking Time **15 minutes**

---

1 can (14 ounces) crushed tomatoes

1 large red onion, finely chopped

1 can (15–16 ounces) red kidney beans, rinsed and drained

2 tablespoons olive oil

1 tablespoon chili powder

1/8 teaspoon each salt and pepper

1 pound wagon-wheel pasta or farfalle

1/4 cup shredded reduced-fat Cheddar cheese

1 ripe avocado, peeled, pitted, and cubed (optional)

1 In a large bowl, combine the crushed tomatoes, chopped onion, red kidney beans, oil, and chili powder and mix well; season with the salt and pepper. Cover and marinate for 2 hours in the refrigerator.

2 Remove the vegetables and beans from the refrigerator and allow the mixture to come to room temperature.

3 Bring a large pot of water to a boil. Cook the pasta according to package directions or until tender. Drain the pasta and transfer to a large serving bowl. Add the cheese and toss until mixed well and the cheese melts slightly.

4 Pour the marinated vegetable and bean mixture over the pasta. Add the avocado cubes, if using, and toss to coat the pasta. Serve at once.

PER SERVING
Calories **471**, Saturated Fat **2g**, Total Fat **12g**, Sodium **260mg**, Cholesterol **3mg**, Protein **17g**, Carbohydrate **76g**, Fiber **9g**.

No-Cook Tex-Mex Sauce finds the ideal partner in wagon-wheel pasta.

Mediterranean Stuffed Shells

Cooking technique ■ *To slim down manicotti and other stuffed pastas, fill them with shrimp or chicken instead of sausage. Use more vegetables in the sauce for fiber and vitamins.*

Reduce fat ■ *Use part-skim mozzarella and ricotta cheese.*

Reduce sodium ■ *Soak the anchovies in milk to extract salt. Omit them altogether if on a salt-restricted diet.*

● Serves **6** ● Preparation Time **20 minutes plus soaking time** ● Cooking Time **50 minutes**

PER SERVING
Calories **441**, Saturated Fat **2g**,
Total Fat **6g**, Sodium **462mg**,
Cholesterol **8mg**, Protein **18g**,
Carbohydrate **80g**, Fiber **9g**.

---

1 can (2 ounces) anchovy fillets in oil, drained

¹/₂ cup 1% low-fat milk

1 pound jumbo pasta shells

1 tablespoon olive oil

1 large onion, chopped

2 cloves garlic, finely chopped

2 large sweet green peppers, diced

2 stalks celery, chopped

10 ounces mushrooms, sliced

2 cans (14 ounces) crushed tomatoes

¹/₄ cup chopped black olives

¹/₈ teaspoon each black pepper and crushed red pepper flakes

3 tablespoons chopped fresh basil or 1 tablespoon dried

¹/₄ cup grated Parmesan cheese

1 In a small bowl, place the anchovies and cover with the milk. Allow to stand at least 1 hour, then drain and discard the milk. Chop the anchovy fillets.

2 Bring a large pot of water to a boil. Add the pasta and cook according to package directions or until just tender. Remove from the heat and drain well. Let cool.

3 Meanwhile, in a large non-stick skillet, heat the oil over moderate heat. Sauté onion and garlic about 5 minutes or until soft. Add sweet peppers and celery and cook about 2 minutes longer. Add mushrooms and cook about 3 minutes longer.

4 In a small saucepan, place the crushed tomatoes, olives, anchovies, and both peppers. Simmer about 5 minutes or until the sauce has thickened slightly. Stir in the chopped basil.

5 Preheat the oven to 375°F. Spoon a layer of sauce on the bottom of a 13" x 9" x 2" baking dish. Using a spoon, fill the shells with the vegetable mixture.

6 Place the filled shells in the baking dish, cover with the remaining sauce, and sprinkle with the Parmesan cheese. Bake about 30 minutes or until bubbling and very hot.

*Anchovies and red pepper add zest to **Mediterranean Stuffed Shells**.*
Serve them with a Greek salad on the side.

Lasagne Spirals with Shrimp and Broccoli

This lasagne is made by wrapping individual noodles around the filling. Cannelloni can be substituted for the lasagne noodles.

- Serves **8**
- Preparation Time **35 minutes**
- Cooking Time **1 hour**

16 lasagne noodles
2 cups 1% low-fat milk
1 cup fish stock, page 18
3 tablespoons cornstarch
2 ounces low-fat, low-sodium Swiss cheese, grated
2 tablespoons olive oil
16 large shrimp, peeled and deveined
1 large onion, coarsely chopped
2 cloves garlic, finely chopped
2 packages (10 ounces) frozen chopped broccoli, thawed
1 cup part-skim ricotta cheese
¹/₈ teaspoon each salt and pepper

1 Cook and drain the lasagne noodles as in Step 2 of the master recipe. Separate the noodles and lay flat on wax paper to cool.

2 Meanwhile, in a large saucepan, heat the milk over moderate heat until it simmers. In a small bowl, combine stock and cornstarch until smooth. Stir into the milk and simmer until mixture thickens, about 5 minutes. Add Swiss cheese and stir until melted. Remove pan from the heat and set aside.

3 In a large nonstick skillet, heat the oil over moderate heat. Add the shrimp and cook, stirring, about 2 minutes or until just pink. Using a slotted spoon, transfer shrimp to a plate.

4 In the same skillet, sauté onion and garlic about 4 minutes until browned. Add broccoli and sauté 2 minutes longer. Remove the skillet from the heat. Stir in ricotta cheese, salt, and pepper.

5 Preheat the oven to 375°F. Spoon a layer of sauce on the bottom of a 13" x 9" x 2" baking dish. Place a shrimp and about ¹/₄ cup broccoli mixture on each lasagne noodle, leaving about 1¹/₂ inch uncovered at each end. Fold noodle over the shrimp and the broccoli mixture and roll up. Place rolls in baking dish and cover with remaining sauce. Bake about 30 minutes or until bubbling and very hot.

COOKING TIP

Make sure there is not too much filling. Then roll the lasagne noodles up carefully to avoid splitting the pasta.

PER SERVING
Calories **340**, Saturated Fat **3g**,
Total Fat **9g**, Sodium **169mg**,
Cholesterol **39mg**, Protein **19g**,
Carbohydrate **46g**, Fiber **4g**.

Chicken- and Mushroom-Stuffed Shells

- Serves **6**
- Preparation Time **30 minutes**
- Cooking Time **1 hour 25 minutes**

1 pound jumbo pasta shells
2 tablespoons olive oil
2 cloves garlic, finely chopped
8 ounces mushrooms, sliced
4 boneless, skinless chicken breast halves (about 1¹/₂ pounds), diced
1 can (28 ounces) crushed tomatoes
1 cup chicken stock, page 18
¹/₃ cup chopped parsley or 1 tablespoon dried
¹/₈ teaspoon each salt and pepper
¹/₄ cup grated Parmesan cheese

1 Bring a large pot of water to a boil. Add the jumbo shells and cook according to package directions or until barely tender. Remove from the heat. Rinse under running water to remove the excess starch. Drain well.

COOKING TIP
Rinsing pasta stops it from overcooking and makes it less likely to stick together.

---

2 Meanwhile, in a large non-stick skillet, heat the oil over moderate heat. Add the garlic and sauté about 1 minute or until browned. Add the mushrooms and cook about 2 minutes or until soft. Transfer to a bowl. Add the chicken to the skillet and sauté about 15 minutes or until golden. Remove and add to the mushroom mixture.

Pasta shells are called conchiglie *in Italian.*

3 In the same skillet, combine the crushed tomatoes and chicken stock. Bring to a boil and simmer about 5 minutes or until the sauce has thickened slightly.

4 Stir the parsley into the sauce and add the salt and pepper. Simmer the sauce about 10 minutes longer or until it has thickened more.

5 Preheat the oven to 375°F. Spoon a layer of sauce on the bottom of a 13" x 9" x 2" baking dish. Using a spoon, fill the shells with the chicken mixture. Place in the baking dish, cover with the remaining sauce, and sprinkle with the Parmesan cheese. Bake about 35 minutes or until bubbling and very hot.

PER SERVING
Calories **526**, Saturated Fat **2g**,
Total Fat **9g**, Sodium **354mg**,
Cholesterol **69mg**, Protein **4g**,
Carbohydrate **70g**, Fiber **7g**.

Cheese and Vegetable Manicotti

A pastry bag makes it easier to stuff the manicotti, but you can also do it with a spoon. You can also stuff jumbo shells with this filling.

- Serves **4**
- Preparation Time **30 minutes**
- Cooking Time **1¼ hours**

1 tablespoon olive or canola oil

1 onion, finely chopped

2 cloves garlic, finely chopped

2 zucchini, diced

1 small eggplant, diced

1 cup chopped mushrooms

2 tablespoons chopped fresh basil or 2 teaspoons dried

⅛ teaspoon each salt and pepper

1 cup part-skim ricotta cheese

1 can (28–29 ounces) reduced-sodium tomato sauce

16 manicotti or cannelloni

1 package (10 ounces) frozen chopped spinach, thawed and drained

½ cup shredded part-skim mozzarella cheese

1 Preheat the oven to 350°F. In a large nonstick skillet, heat the oil over moderate heat. Add onion and garlic and sauté 4 to 5 minutes, until just softened.

2 Stir in zucchini and eggplant and sauté 5 minutes longer. Add the mushrooms and cook for 3 minutes or until all the vegetables are tender.

3 Remove the skillet from the heat and stir in the basil, salt, and pepper. Transfer the vegetable mixture to a large bowl and stir in the ricotta cheese until blended.

4 Spoon one-third of the tomato sauce into a 13" x 9" x 2" baking dish. Using a spoon or pastry bag (see box, right), generously fill each manicotti with the vegetable stuffing.

5 Place half of the stuffed manicotti in the baking dish and spoon on half of the remaining sauce. Place the remaining stuffed manicotti on top and cover with the remaining sauce.

6 Spread the spinach evenly on top, sprinkle with the mozzarella, and cover the dish tightly with aluminum foil. Bake for 55 to 60 minutes or until the manicotti are fork-tender.

PER SERVING
Calories **519**, Saturated Fat **5g**, Total Fat **13g**, Sodium **328mg**, Cholesterol **27mg**, Protein **26g**, Carbohydrate **81g**, Fiber **12g**.

*A fresh-tasting cucumber and dill salad goes well with **Cheese and Vegetable Manicotti**.*

STUFFING MANICOTTI OR CANNELLONI

1 *Using a spoon, fill a pastry bag fitted with a plain ½-inch nozzle with the stuffing mixture.*

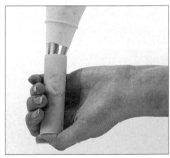

2 *Squeeze the stuffing into the pasta tube, making sure that the bottom end is blocked.*

3 *Pour the sauce into the baking dish and carefully arrange the filled pasta tubes on top.*

Spaghetti with Clam Sauce

Cooking technique ▪ *For a succulent low-fat meal, sauté shellfish in olive oil and garlic. Add vegetables and simmer to blend the flavors. Serve over hot pasta.*

● Serves **6** ● Preparation Time **15 minutes** ● Cooking Time **20 minutes**

PER SERVING
Calories **383**, Saturated Fat **1g**, Total Fat **5g**, Sodium **157mg**, Cholesterol **19mg**, Protein **20g**, Carbohydrate **64g**, Fiber **5g**.

1 tablespoon olive oil

2 large shallots, finely chopped

2 cloves garlic, finely chopped

2 cans (6½ ounces each) clams, drained and rinsed

1 package (10 ounces) frozen chopped spinach, thawed and drained

3 cups fish stock, page 18

1 tablespoon cornstarch

Finely grated zest and juice of 1 lemon

¼ cup chopped parsley

⅛ teaspoon each salt and pepper

1 pound spaghetti

1 In a large nonstick skillet, heat the oil over moderate heat. Add the shallots and garlic and sauté about 2 minutes or until softened but not browned.

2 Stir in the clams and chopped spinach and cook about 1 minute longer to combine. Pour in the stock and bring to a boil. Simmer the mixture about 7 minutes or until the flavors have blended.

Spaghetti with Clam Sauce tastes even better when made with spinach. It is served here with Green Beans with Tomatoes and Herbs, page 166.

3 In a small bowl, combine the cornstarch, lemon zest, and juice. Stir mixture into simmering clam sauce. Return sauce to a boil and simmer, stirring, about 1 minute or until slightly thickened. Stir in parsley, salt, and pepper. Keep the sauce warm.

4 Meanwhile, bring a large pot of water to a boil. Add the dried pasta and return to a boil. Cook the pasta according to package directions, stirring occasionally, or until just tender. Remove from the heat, drain the pasta thoroughly, and place in a large bowl. Pour the sauce over the pasta and toss to coat well. Transfer the tossed pasta to a serving bowl.

Capellini with Red Clam Sauce

- Serves **6**
- Preparation Time **16 minutes**
- Cooking Time **20 minutes**

2 tablespoons olive oil
2 large onions, coarsely chopped
2 cloves garlic, finely chopped
2 cans (6¹/₂ ounces each) clams, drained and rinsed
1 cup dry white wine or fish stock, page 18
1 can (14 ounces) reduced-sodium tomato sauce
Finely grated zest and juice of 1 lemon
¹/₄ cup chopped parsley
¹/₈ teaspoon each salt and pepper
1 pound capellini

1 In a large nonstick skillet, heat the oil over moderate heat. Sauté onions and garlic about 5 minutes or until softened

2 Stir in the clams and wine and bring to a boil. Simmer the mixture about 5 minutes or until the flavors have blended.

3 Stir in the tomato sauce and the lemon zest and juice. Return the sauce to a boil and simmer, stirring, about 5 minutes or until slightly thickened. Stir in the parsley, salt, and pepper. Keep the sauce warm.

4 Cook and serve the pasta as in Step 4 of the master recipe.

PER SERVING
Calories **441**, Saturated Fat **1g**, Total Fat **7g**, Sodium **103mg**, Cholesterol **19mg**, Protein **18g**, Carbohydrate **69g**, Fiber **6g**.

Fusilli with Shrimp Sauce

- Serves **6**
- Preparation Time **25 minutes**
- Cooking Time **20 minutes**

2 tablespoons olive oil
2 large onions, finely chopped
2 cloves garlic, finely chopped
¹/₄ cup sun-dried tomatoes, soaked, then chopped (optional)
1 can (28 ounces) crushed tomatoes
1 cup vegetable stock, page 18
8 ounces shrimp, peeled and deveined
¹/₄ cup chopped fresh basil or parsley
¹/₄ cup sliced black olives
¹/₈ teaspoon pepper
1 pound fusilli or penne

1 In a large nonstick skillet, heat the oil over moderate heat. Sauté onions and garlic about 5 minutes.

2 Stir in the sun-dried tomatoes, if using, and cook a few minutes longer. Add the crushed tomatoes and stock and simmer 5 minutes.

3 Stir in shrimp, basil, and olives and simmer about 4 minutes or until shrimp are cooked. Add pepper. Keep sauce warm.

4 Cook and serve the pasta as in Step 4 of master recipe, using individual serving bowls.

PER SERVING
Calories **455**, Saturated Fat **1g**, Total Fat **7g**, Sodium **266mg**, Cholesterol **56mg**, Protein **22g**, Carbohydrate **77g**, Fiber **9g**.

Vermicelli with Mussel Sauce

- Serves **6**
- Preparation Time **35 minutes**
- Cooking Time **30 minutes**

2 tablespoons olive oil
2 large onions, finely chopped
1 cup fish stock, page 18
2 pounds fresh mussels, shells scrubbed, beards removed
1 cup crushed tomatoes
2 tablespoons tomato paste
Finely grated zest and juice of 1 lemon
¹/₄ cup chopped parsley
¹/₈ teaspoon each salt and pepper
1 pound vermicelli or linguine

1 In a large saucepan, heat the oil over moderate heat. Sauté onions about 5 minutes. Pour in stock and bring to a boil.

2 *Tap mussels and discard any that do not close.* Add mussels, cover, and steam 5 to 10 minutes or until shells have opened. Remove from the heat and, using a slotted spoon, transfer mussels to a bowl. *Discard any unopened.*

3 Add tomatoes, tomato paste, lemon zest, and juice to pan. Simmer about 5 minutes. Remove mussels from their shells and stir into sauce. Stir in parsley, salt, and pepper. Keep sauce warm.

4 Cook and serve the pasta as in Step 4 of the master recipe.

PER SERVING
Calories **395**, Saturated Fat **1g**, Total Fat **7g**, Sodium **199mg**, Cholesterol **8mg**, Protein **15g**, Carbohydrate **68g**, Fiber **6g**.

Quick Tortilla Pizzas

Cooking technique ▪ *It's easy to enjoy homemade pizza without spending a lot of time. The trick is to use already prepared breads, rather than pizza dough, as the crust. Serve as a snack or light meal.*

Add nutrients ▪ *Top with tomato sauce, fresh vegetables, and low-fat cheese.*

● Serves **4** ● Preparation Time **20 minutes** ● Cooking Time **25 minutes**

PER SERVING
Calories **215**, Saturated Fat **2g**, Total Fat **7g**, Sodium **371mg**, Cholesterol **10mg**, Protein **9g**, Carbohydrate **34g**, Fiber **2g**.

8 flour tortillas (6" diameter)	2 cloves garlic, finely chopped
$\frac{1}{2}$ cup reduced-sodium tomato sauce	2 tablespoons chopped parsley
	$\frac{1}{8}$ teaspoon pepper
1 can (3–4 ounces) jalapeño or green chili peppers, drained	$\frac{1}{2}$ cup shredded low-fat Cheddar cheese

1 Preheat oven to 300°F. Wrap the pile of tortillas in foil and warm in the oven about 10 minutes. Increase the oven temperature to 375°F .

2 Unwrap the tortillas and arrange them in a single layer on 2 nonstick baking sheets. Spread a thin layer of the tomato sauce over each tortilla.

3 Coarsely chop the jalapeño peppers. Sprinkle garlic, jalapeños, parsley, and pepper over the sauce. Sprinkle cheese on top. Bake 10 to 15 minutes.

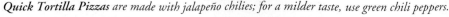

Quick Tortilla Pizzas *are made with jalapeño chilies; for a milder taste, use green chili peppers.*

English Muffin Pizzas

- Serves **6**
- Preparation Time **20 minutes**
- Cooking Time **35 minutes**

6 English muffins

8 ounces sweet Italian or turkey sausage, sliced

1 large onion, coarsely chopped

1 sweet red or green pepper, coarsely chopped

2 cloves garlic, finely chopped

1 cup reduced-sodium tomato sauce

2 teaspoons dried rosemary, crumbled

³/₄ cup shredded part-skim mozzarella cheese

1 Preheat oven to 375°F. Slice muffins in half, arrange them in a single layer on a baking sheet, and bake 8 to 10 minutes.

2 Heat a nonstick skillet and add sausage. Cook, stirring, 6 minutes or until fat is rendered. Using a slotted spoon, transfer to a plate. Drain off most of fat from skillet.

3 Add onion, sweet pepper, and garlic to skillet and sauté about 5 minutes. Stir in tomato sauce and rosemary. Return sausage to skillet and simmer, stirring occasionally, 3 to 4 minutes.

4 Spoon a little sausage mixture onto each muffin half; top with cheese. Bake 4 to 5 minutes.

PER SERVING
Calories **343**, Saturated Fat **6g**, Total Fat **16g**, Sodium **731mg**, Cholesterol **37mg**, Protein **15g**, Carbohydrate **35g**, Fiber **3g**.

Pita Pizzas

- Serves **4**
- Preparation Time **15 minutes**
- Cooking Time **25 minutes**

4 pita rounds (6" diameter)

8 ounces lean ground lamb

2 cloves garlic, finely chopped

1 large onion, coarsely chopped

1 cup reduced-sodium tomato sauce

¹/₄ teaspoon ground nutmeg

¹/₈ teaspoon pepper

¹/₄ cup chopped walnuts, toasted

¹/₂ cup crumbled feta cheese

1 Preheat the oven to 375°F. Warm pita rounds about 5 minutes then split in half. Place halves in a single layer on a baking sheet.

2 Heat a nonstick skillet over moderate heat. Add lamb and sauté about 5 minutes or until the fat is rendered and meat is browned. Using a slotted spoon, transfer lamb to a plate lined with paper towels. Drain off most of the fat from skillet. Add garlic and onion and sauté about 5 minutes.

3 Return the lamb to the skillet with the tomato sauce, nutmeg, and pepper and simmer 2 minutes. Stir in the walnuts.

4 Spoon some of the lamb mixture onto each pita bread half and sprinkle each with a little crumbled cheese. Bake pizzas until the cheese has melted.

PER SERVING
Calories **354**, Saturated Fat **6g**, Total Fat **15g**, Sodium **589mg**, Cholesterol **62mg**, Protein **22g**, Carbohydrate **33g**, Fiber **3g**.

French Bread Pizzas

- Serves **4**
- Preparation Time **15 minutes**
- Cooking Time **45 minutes**

1 loaf French or Italian bread

2 tablespoons olive oil

8 ounces lean turkey sausage

2 large onions, thinly sliced

6 ounces mushrooms, sliced

¹/₂ teaspoon dried sage

¹/₂ cup sliced black olives

2 tablespoons grated Parmesan cheese

1 Preheat the oven to 375°F. Cut the French bread lengthwise in half, and cut each half into two pieces crosswise. Place the pieces, cut side up, on a baking sheet and brush with half of the oil. Bake about 4 minutes.

2 Heat a nonstick skillet over moderate heat. Add the turkey sausage and sauté, stirring, until all the fat is rendered and the sausage is browned. Using a slotted spoon, transfer the sausage to a plate and drain off nearly all the fat from the pan.

3 Heat the remaining olive oil in the skillet, add the onions, and sauté about 5 minutes or until very soft and browned. Add the mushrooms and cook about 5 minutes longer or until soft and browned. Return the sausage to the skillet with the sage and cook a few minutes longer.

4 Spoon the sausage mixture over the bread pieces and top with the sliced olives. Sprinkle with the cheese and bake 10 to 15 minutes or until the cheese is heated through. Place under a preheated broiler for 5 minutes, until cheese is melted and golden brown.

PER SERVING
Calories **578**, Saturated Fat **2g**, Total Fat **23g**, Sodium **745mg**, Cholesterol **2mg**, Protein **23g**, Carbohydrate **69g**, Fiber **5g**.

*Pizza goes international —
(left to right)* **Pita Pizza,
English Muffin Pizza,
and French Bread Pizza.**

Mexican Whole-Wheat Pizza

Cooking technique ▪ *Make your own herbed crust with whole-wheat flour.*
Reduce cholesterol ▪ *Instead of pepperoni, use low-fat cheese, turkey sausage, and vegetables.*

● Serves **4** ● Preparation Time **1 hour 50 minutes** ● Cooking Time **20–30 minutes**

PER SERVING
Calories **524**, Saturated Fat **5g**,
Total Fat **18g**, Sodium **691mg**,
Cholesterol **42mg**, Protein **25g**,
Carbohydrate **71g**, Fiber **8g**.

COOKING TIP
*If you prefer, you can use
1 package (10 ounces) refrigerated pizza crust dough.*

For the dough
1 cup water (105°–115°F)

1 package (¼ ounce) active
dry yeast

1 teaspoon sugar

1½–2 cups all-purpose flour

1 cup whole-wheat flour

2 tablespoons olive oil

⅛ teaspoon each salt and pepper

½–1 teaspoon chili powder

For the topping
½ cup reduced-sodium salsa

1 cup fresh or frozen corn kernels

1 can (4 ounces) chopped green
chilies, drained

4 ounces turkey sausage, cooked

4 ounces reduced-fat Monterey
Jack cheese, shredded

1 In a small bowl, combine the warm water with the yeast and the sugar. Allow the yeast to rest 5 minutes or until it becomes foamy.

2 In a bowl, combine flours. Make a well in the center and pour in yeast mixture with oil, salt, and pepper. Gradually stir until dough comes together into a ball.

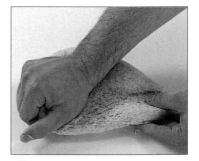

3 On a lightly floured surface, knead dough about 8 minutes. Place in a lightly oiled bowl, cover, and let rise 30 to 60 minutes or until doubled in volume.

*Add spice to your life – **Mexican Whole-Wheat Pizza** topped with green chilies and turkey sausage.*

4 Punch air out of dough and place on a floured surface. Cover and let rest for 15 minutes. Roll out to 15 by 10 inches; place on a lightly oiled baking sheet.

5 Press chili powder lightly on edge of dough. Preheat oven to 425°F. Spread a layer of salsa over dough, then scatter corn, chilies, and turkey sausage on top.

6 Sprinkle with the shredded cheese. Bake 10 to 20 minutes or until the pizza crust is brown and the cheese is melted and golden.

Plum Tomato, Mushroom, and Basil Pizza

- Serves **4**
- Preparation Time **20** minutes or **1** hour **40** minutes
- Cooking Time **10–20** minutes

Dough as in master recipe or 1 package (10 ounces) refrigerated pizza crust dough

¹/₄ cup grated Parmesan cheese

For the topping

¹/₂ cup reduced-sodium tomato sauce

8 basil leaves or 1 teaspoon dried

4 ounces mushrooms, sliced

2 fresh plum tomatoes, chopped

1¹/₂ cups small broccoli florets (optional)

³/₄ cup shredded part-skim mozzarella cheese

¹/₄ cup sliced black olives

Pinch of pepper

1 Make dough as in Steps 1 to 4 of master recipe, adding Parmesan to flours in Step 2. (If using store-bought, press Parmesan into dough.)

2 Preheat the oven to 425°F. Spread tomato sauce over dough. Arrange basil, mushrooms, tomatoes, and broccoli on top.

3 Sprinkle with mozzarella cheese, olives, and pepper. Bake 10 to 20 minutes or until crust is brown and cheese is golden.

PER SERVING
Calories **469**, Saturated Fat **5g**, Total Fat **14g**, Sodium **382mg**, Cholesterol **17mg**, Protein **20g**, Carbohydrate **68g**, Fiber **8g**.

Tuna and Tomato Pizza

- Serves **4**
- Preparation Time **20** minutes or **1** hour **40** minutes
- Cooking Time **35** minutes

Dough as in master recipe or 1 package (10 ounces) refrigerated pizza crust dough

1 tablespoon tomato paste

For the topping

2 tablespoons olive or canola oil

2 large onions, sliced ¹/₈–¹/₄ inch thick

1 large sweet red or green pepper, sliced

1 can (6–7 ounces) solid white tuna in water, drained and flaked

³/₄ cup shredded part-skim mozzarella cheese

¹/₂ cup sliced black olives

1 Make dough as in Steps 1 to 4 of master recipe, adding tomato paste to the mixture. (If using store-bought, spread center of dough with tomato paste.)

2 Preheat the oven to 425°F. Heat oil in a nonstick skillet, add onions and sweet pepper; cook 15 minutes or until caramelized.

3 Arrange tuna and the onion and sweet pepper mixture on top of dough. Sprinkle with cheese and olives. Bake for 10 to 20 minutes or until crust is brown and the cheese is melted and golden.

PER SERVING
Calories **594**, Saturated Fat **4g**, Total Fat **20g**, Sodium **502mg**, Cholesterol **20mg**, Protein **29g**, Carbohydrate **76g**, Fiber **9g**.

Goat Cheese Pizza with Herb Crust

- Serves **4**
- Preparation Time **10** minutes or **1** hour **50** minutes
- Cooking Time **10–20** minutes

Dough as in master recipe or 1 package (10 ounces) refrigerated pizza crust dough

3 tablespoons mixed dried herbs

For the topping

2 tablespoons olive oil

¹/₄ cup chopped walnuts

2 tablespoons chopped fresh basil

¹/₈ teaspoon each salt and pepper

4 ounces goat cheese, crumbled, or mozzarella cheese, shredded

1 Make dough as in Steps 1 to 4 of the master recipe, adding the dried herbs to the flours before mixing. (If using store-bought, press dried herbs into the dough.)

2 Preheat the oven to 425°F. Brush the dough with the olive oil. Sprinkle the walnuts and basil over the dough, then season with the salt and pepper.

3 Sprinkle with the crumbled cheese. Bake 10 to 20 minutes or until the pizza crust is brown and the cheese is melted and golden.

PER SERVING
Calories **489**, Saturated Fat **5g**, Total Fat **23g**, Sodium **281mg**, Cholesterol **19mg**, Protein **13g**, Carbohydrate **58g**, Fiber **6g**.

EGGS & CHEESE

Ever since cholesterol was linked with heart disease,
health-conscious eaters have been cutting down
on eggs and cheese. But if you still long for a slice of
quiche, don't despair. **The How-To Book of Healthy**
Cooking *will show you how to enjoy your favorite dishes*
while keeping fat and cholesterol under control. The
trick is to use low-fat cheeses and fat-free egg whites
whenever possible. Then add fresh vegetables and herbs,
and you have a nutritious low-fat meal. Try our quiches,
stratas, and Italian-style frittatas. And don't forget, these
dishes contain all the health benefits of eggs and cheese,
like protein, iron, calcium, and other minerals. Now
let **The How-To Book of Healthy Cooking** *help*
you put eggs and cheese back on the menu.

Chicken and Asparagus Quiche, page 274

Eggs not only are delicious but have many nutritional benefits. One egg provides 6 grams of high-quality protein, 25% of the daily requirement for vitamin B12, and moderate amounts of folic acid and minerals. The major drawback is cholesterol. One egg contains 200 mg – about two-thirds of your suggested daily intake.

The cholesterol question

Recent research, however, has shown that saturated fat is more likely to elevate blood cholesterol than dietary cholesterol. As a result, medical experts are more lenient about egg consumption.

The American Heart Association still restricts anyone with heart disease to just 1 egg per week plus a few whites but now says healthy adults can eat up to 4 whole eggs per week.

There's good news for the cook too. All of the cholesterol resides in the yolk, while most of the protein is in the whites. This means that you can substitute egg whites for whole eggs and eliminate the cholesterol while still adding protein to your diet. Or you can use a combination of whole eggs and egg whites so that you get the flavor and nutrients of the yolk while keeping the cholesterol down.

YOLKS VERSUS WHITES

Here's where the nutrients are.

Per Egg	White	Yolk	Whole
Calories	17	58	75
Protein g	4	2	6
Saturated Fat g	0	1.5	1.5
Cholesterol mg	0	213	213
Vitamin A IU	0	318	318
Vitamin B12 mcg	0.1	0.4	0.5
Folic acid mcg	0	24	24

Beating eggs

When beating egg whites, always make sure they're at room temperature and that the bowl is clean and grease-free. Using either a balloon whisk or hand-held electric whisk, whip until they hold stiff, moist peaks. If whipped until dry, they will be difficult to fold into a mixture. Once they are whipped, don't delay. Carefully fold a small portion of beaten egg white into a mixture to lighten it before folding in the rest.

TESTING EGGS FOR FRESHNESS

1 *A fresh egg will sink to the bottom of a bowl of water.*

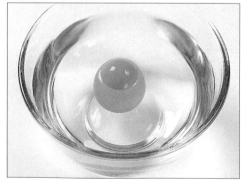

2 *An egg that floats is stale and should not be used.*

SELECTING LOW-FAT CHEESES

It pays healthwise to buy low-fat cheeses. In addition to being lower in fat, they are often higher in calcium.

3½-ounce serving	Calories	Fat g	Saturated Fat g	Cholesterol mg	Calcium mg	Sodium mg
Cheddar	403	33	21	105	721	621
Reduced-fat Cheddar	280	18	11	17	875	770
Cream cheese	349	35	22	110	80	269
Low-fat cream cheese	259	23	15	77	73	395
Feta	264	21	15	89	493	1,116
Monterey Jack	373	30	19	89	746	536
Low-fat Monterey Jack	280	21	10	70	742	532
Mozzarella	318	25	16	89	575	415
Part-skim mozzarella	280	17	11	54	731	528
Neufchâtel	260	23	15	76	75	349
Parmesan	392	26	16	68	1,184	1,602
Ricotta	174	13	8	51	207	84
Part-skim ricotta	138	8	5	31	272	125
Swiss	376	28	18	92	961	260
Low-fat Swiss	339	24	14	66	952	259

Cheese and your health

Versatile cheese is an excellent source of calcium and protein and a delicious addition to many dishes. However, it is also high in saturated fat and cholesterol. Health experts recommend that you limit your intake to only one or two servings daily of low-fat cheese. The savings in fat can be substantial (see chart above), but there are drawbacks. Some of the aged reduced-fat cheeses, such as Cheddar and Swiss, don't taste quite as good. So you may prefer to eat the full-fat cheese occasionally as a snack and use low-fat cheeses for cooking, where other ingredients boost the flavor.

Read labels carefully

Manufacturers sometimes add extra salt to low-fat cheeses to make them taste better. So you should always check the labeling carefully. Terms like "light" can refer to either the sodium or the fat content.

Your poorest choice nutritionally is processed cheeses, which have been blended or pasteurized. They are generally higher in sodium and slightly low in protein, calcium, and iron.

Storing cheese

Wrap cheeses individually in plastic wrap and store stronger-tasting cheeses separately. The harder the cheese, the longer it will keep: Cheddar keeps in the refrigerator for up to 5 weeks if well wrapped. Ricotta and soft cheeses can be kept up to 5 days and discarded if mold develops.

Cooking with cheese

Many low-fat cheeses, particularly part-skim milk ricotta and mozzarella cheeses, work well in recipes, and low-fat cream cheese can usually be substituted for cream cheese. However, some of the aged reduced-fat cheeses take about 25% longer to melt than regular cheese and tend to toughen if direct heat is used, so use low temperatures and short cooking times. Add reduced-fat cheese, shredded or grated, to a recipe at the last minute, so that it melts quickly and blends into sauces.

Mozzarella

Parmesan

Low-fat Swiss

Monterey Jack

Neufchâtel

Cheddar

Ricotta

Herbed Cheese Strata

Cooking technique ■ *For this simple, low-fat verion of a soufflé, just stir together bread cubes, egg whites, low-fat cheese, and milk. Bake until puffed and golden. Vary the flavor by adding herbs, fruit, or vegetables.*

● Serves **4** ● Preparation Time **10 minutes plus standing time** ● Cooking Time **40–50 minutes**

PER SERVING
Calories **316**, Saturated Fat **5g**, Total Fat **11g**, Sodium **653mg**, Cholesterol **131mg**, Protein **24g**, Carbohydrate **32g**, Fiber **2g**.

Vegetable oil cooking spray

8 slices day-old oatmeal bread or white bread, in ¹/₂-inch cubes

4 ounces reduced-fat Cheddar cheese, shredded, or goat cheese, sliced

2 cups 1% low-fat milk

4 egg whites

2 whole eggs

¹/₂ teaspoon baking powder

1 tablespoon chopped parsley or 2 teaspoons dried

¹/₈ teaspoon pepper

1 Preheat oven to 375°F. Coat an 8" x 8" x 2" baking dish with cooking spray. Add three-quarters of the bread, all the cheese, then remaining bread.

2 In a medium bowl, whisk together milk, egg whites, whole eggs, baking powder, parsley, and pepper until well combined.

3 Ladle the egg mixture into the baking dish. Bake 40 to 50 minutes or until it is puffed and golden. Let stand 5 minutes before cutting.

Herbed Cheese Strata has the creamy good taste of a soufflé but is much easier to make.

Tomato and Onion Strata

- Serves **4**
- Preparation Time **12 minutes** plus standing time
- Cooking Time **45–55 minutes**

Vegetable oil cooking spray

8 slices day-old oatmeal bread or white bread, in ¹/₂-inch cubes

1 large ripe tomato, sliced

1 teaspoon olive or canola oil

1 small onion, chopped

2 cups 1% low-fat milk

4 egg whites

2 whole eggs

¹/₂ teaspoon baking powder

1 teaspoon dried dill weed

¹/₄ teaspoon pepper

2 tablespoons grated Parmesan cheese

1 Preheat oven to 375°F. Coat an 8" x 8" x 2" baking dish with cooking spray. Place three-quarters of the bread cubes in dish; top with tomato.

2 In a nonstick skillet, heat oil and sauté onion 3 to 4 minutes. Spread onion on top of tomato. Top with remaining bread cubes.

3 In a medium bowl, whisk together milk, egg whites, eggs, baking powder, dill, and pepper.

4 Pour mixture into baking dish, sprinkle with cheese, and bake as in Step 3 of master recipe.

PER SERVING
Calories **282**, Saturated Fat **3g**, Total Fat **8g**, Sodium **497mg**, Cholesterol **113mg**, Protein **17g**, Carbohydrate **36g**, Fiber **3g**.

Apple and Cheddar Strata

- Serves **4**
- Preparation Time **12 minutes** plus standing time
- Cooking Time **40–50 minutes**

Vegetable oil cooking spray

8 slices day-old raisin, oatmeal, or white bread, in ¹/₂-inch cubes

1 tablespoon olive or canola oil

2 apples, cored and diced

¹/₂ cup shredded reduced-fat Cheddar cheese

2 teaspoons brown sugar

2 cups 1% low-fat milk

4 egg whites

2 whole eggs

¹/₂ teaspoon baking powder

Ground cinnamon

1 Preheat oven to 375°F. Coat an 8" x 8" x 2" baking dish with cooking spray. Place three-quarters of bread cubes in dish.

2 In a nonstick skillet, heat oil. Sauté apples until tender. Arrange apples and cheese on bread and sprinkle with brown sugar.

3 In a medium bowl, whisk together milk, egg whites, eggs, and baking powder. Pour egg mixture into baking dish. Sprinkle with a little ground cinnamon and bake 40 to 50 minutes or until it is puffed and golden. Allow to stand 5 minutes before cutting.

PER SERVING
Calories **377**, Saturated Fat **4g**, Total Fat **12g**, Sodium **477mg**, Cholesterol **122mg**, Protein **19g**, Carbohydrate **52g**, Fiber **4g**.

Rarebit Strata

- Serves **4**
- Preparation Time **10 minutes**
- Cooking Time **20–25 minutes**

Vegetable oil cooking spray

1 loaf (1 pound) Italian bread, about 15 inches long

1 cup 1% low-fat milk

4 egg whites

2 whole eggs

¹/₂ teaspoon baking powder

¹/₄ teaspoon pepper

4 ounces finely grated Gruyère, Swiss, or reduced-fat Cheddar cheese

¹/₂ teaspoon dry mustard

2 tablespoons grated Parmesan cheese

1 Preheat oven to 375°F. Generously coat a nonstick baking sheet with cooking spray. Trim off ends of bread and cut into ³/₄ inch slices.

2 In a medium bowl, whisk together milk, egg whites, eggs, baking powder, pepper, Gruyère cheese, and mustard. Dip each bread slice in egg mixture until it is well soaked on both sides. Transfer it to baking sheet and repeat with remaining slices. Spoon any remaining cheese-egg mixture over slices.

3 Sprinkle the slices with the Parmesan cheese and bake 20 to 25 minutes or until they are puffed and golden.

PER SERVING
Calories **533**, Saturated Fat **7g**, Total Fat **13g**, Sodium **886mg**, Cholesterol **142mg**, Protein **30g**, Carbohydrate **68g**, Fiber **3g**.

You can serve **Rarebit Strata** *for breakfast, lunch, or a light supper.*

Spinach Quiche

Reduce fat ▪ *For a lean and luscious quiche, replace some of the eggs with egg whites. Use low-fat cream cheese in both filling and crust. You can also make a nutritious crust with potatoes (see page 275).*
Add nutrients ▪ *Add spinach, onions, and other vitamin-rich vegetables to the filling.*
Save time ▪ *Use a prepared pastry shell or pie crust mix.*

● Serves **6** ● Preparation Time **15 minutes plus chilling and standing time** ● Cooking Time **1 hour 10 minutes**

PER SERVING
Calories **304**, Saturated Fat **6g**,
Total Fat **17g**, Sodium **241mg**,
Cholesterol **91mg**, Protein **12g**,
Carbohydrate **27g**, Fiber **3g**.

For the pastry

³/₄–1 cup all-purpose flour

¹/₂–³/₄ cup whole-wheat flour

Pinch of salt

3 tablespoons olive oil

2 tablespoons low-fat cream cheese

4 tablespoons ice water

For the filling

1 tablespoon olive oil

1 onion, finely chopped

1 clove garlic, finely chopped

1 package (10 ounces) frozen chopped spinach, thawed and drained

1 cup 1% low-fat milk

¹/₂ cup low-fat cream cheese

1 tablespoon all-purpose flour

2 whole eggs

2 egg whites

2 tablespoons chopped fresh herbs, such as parsley, basil, or chives

¹/₈ teaspoon each salt and pepper

1 Make the pastry: In a large bowl, combine both flours with salt. Add oil and cream cheese and, using a pastry blender or 2 table knives, cut them into the flours until the mixture resembles coarse crumbs.

2 Add the water gradually and cut into the mixture until the dough comes together to form a solid mass. Turn out onto a floured surface and very lightly knead together into a smooth dough. Cover with plastic wrap and refrigerate at least 1 hour.

3 Preheat oven to 425°F. Make the filling: In a non-stick skillet, heat oil over moderate heat. Sauté onion and garlic 5 minutes. Add spinach and cook, stirring, until liquid has evaporated. Remove from the heat.

4 In another bowl, combine the milk, cream cheese, flour, eggs, egg whites, herbs, salt, and pepper. Whisk together until smooth.

5 On a lightly floured surface, roll out dough to about an 11-inch circle. Carefully wrap dough over rolling pin and transfer to a 9-inch loose-bottomed tart pan or quiche dish. Trim dough even with rim.

6 Spread filling evenly in pastry shell. Ladle egg mixture over. Bake 15 minutes; reduce temperature to 325°F and bake 35 to 45 minutes longer or until set. Let stand 30 minutes before slicing.

Spinach Quiche *is ideal for entertaining because you can make it ahead
and serve later. Just add bread and a salad.*

Chicken and Asparagus Quiche

For a change of pace, you can substitute turkey for the chicken, and thawed frozen peas for the asparagus.

- Serves **6**
- Preparation Time **15 minutes** plus chilling and standing time
- Cooking Time **1 hour 20 minutes**

For the pastry

3/4–1 cup all-purpose flour

1/2–3/4 cup whole-wheat flour

Pinch of salt

3 tablespoons olive oil

2 tablespoons low-fat cream cheese

4 tablespoons ice water

For the filling

2 cups chicken stock, page 18

2 boneless, skinless chicken breast halves (about 3/4 pound)

1 pound fresh asparagus, cut into 1-inch lengths

1 cup 1% low-fat milk

1/2 cup low-fat cream cheese

1 tablespoon all-purpose flour

2 whole eggs

2 egg whites

1/4 teaspoon dry mustard

1/8 teaspoon each salt and pepper

1 In a large bowl, make the pastry as in Steps 1 and 2 of the master recipe.

2 Meanwhile, make the filling: In a skillet, bring the stock to a boil. Add the chicken breasts, reduce heat, cover, and simmer 10 to 15 minutes or until tender. Using a slotted spoon, transfer to a plate and allow to cool.

3 Add the asparagus to the stock and simmer about 8 minutes or until almost tender. Drain and allow to cool. Coarsely chop the chicken.

4 Preheat the oven to 425°F. In another bowl, combine the milk, cream cheese, flour, eggs, egg whites, dry mustard, salt, and pepper. Whisk together until smooth.

5 On a lightly floured surface, roll out pastry dough to about an 11-inch circle. Carefully wrap dough over rolling pin and transfer to a 9-inch pie plate or quiche dish. Trim dough even with the rim of the dish.

6 Add the chopped chicken and asparagus to pastry shell in an even layer. Pour egg and milk mixture over. Bake about 15 minutes; reduce temperature to 325°F and continue to bake for 35 to 45 minutes or until egg mixture is puffed and golden and feels almost set (mixture will continue cooking once removed from oven). Make sure center is cooked. Let stand for 30 minutes before slicing.

PER SERVING
Calories **367**, Saturated Fat **6g**, Total Fat **18g**, Sodium **289mg**, Cholesterol **124mg**, Protein **26g**, Carbohydrate **26g**, Fiber **3g**.

Sausage, Mushroom, and Rice Flan

This pie is a departure from other quiches. The rice is mixed right in with the eggs and vegetables, so there's no need for a crust.

- Serves **6**
- Preparation Time **10 minutes** plus standing time
- Cooking Time **1 hour 30 minutes**

2 cups water

1 cup chicken stock, page 18

1 cup long-grain or brown rice

Salt and pepper

1 tablespoon olive or canola oil

8 ounces Italian-style turkey sausage links

1 onion, finely chopped

8 ounces sliced mushrooms

1 cup 1% low-fat milk

1/2 cup low-fat cream cheese, softened

2 whole eggs

2 egg whites

2 tablespoons chopped fresh chives or parsley

1 In a saucepan, bring the water and stock to a boil. Add the rice and a pinch of salt and cook 20 to 25 minutes or until very tender. Drain well and allow to cool. Place in a large bowl. Preheat oven to 350°F.

2 In a nonstick skillet, heat 1 teaspoon oil over moderate heat. Add the sausage links and cook 8 to 9 minutes or until browned and cooked through. Remove pan from heat and drain links on paper towels. Slice and add to rice.

3 In the skillet, heat the remaining oil over moderate heat and sauté the onions for 2 to 3 minutes. Add the mushrooms and sauté 2 to 3 minutes longer or until onions are soft and golden. Remove from the heat and stir into the rice mixture.

4 In a bowl, combine the milk with the cream cheese, eggs, egg whites, chives, and 1/8 teaspoon each salt and pepper. Whisk together until smooth and creamy. Add to the rice mixture and stir well to combine.

5 Pour the mixture into a nonstick 10-inch pie plate. Bake 50 to 60 minutes or until the mixture is puffed and golden and feels almost set (the mixture will continue cooking once removed from the oven). Make sure the center is cooked. Let stand 30 minutes before slicing.

COOKING TIP
The cooking time for different brands of rice can vary so it is always advisable to check the package directions.

PER SERVING
Calories **310**, Saturated Fat **5g**, Total Fat **12g**, Sodium **525mg**, Cholesterol **111mg**, Protein **17g**, Carbohydrate **33g**, Fiber **1g**.

Leek Quiche with Layered Potato Crust

The "crust" for this quiche is made with sliced baked potatoes, which are placed on the bottom and top of the filling. Leave the skin on the potatoes for maximum nutritional value but avoid potatoes with green patches. You can substitute sweet potatoes for white.

- Serves **6**
- Preparation Time **15 minutes** plus standing time
- Cooking Time **1 hour 20 minutes**

---

3 large baking potatoes, thinly sliced

2 tablespoons olive oil

For the filling

1 tablespoon olive oil

8 ounces leeks, trimmed and thinly sliced

1 small onion, finely chopped

1 clove garlic, finely chopped

1 cup 1% low-fat milk

¹/₂ cup low-fat cream cheese

2 whole eggs

2 egg whites

2 tablespoons chopped fresh chives or parsley

¹/₈ teaspoon each salt and pepper

1 Preheat the oven to 400°F. Arrange the potato slices on 3 nonstick baking sheets and lightly brush with the 2 tablespoons of oil. Bake the potatoes, turning once, about 25 minutes or until tender and golden on both sides. Remove from the oven and allow to cool slightly. Reduce temperature to 350°F.

2 Arrange half of the potatoes in the bottom and sides of a 9-inch round baking dish, overlapping them slightly (see box).

3 Meanwhile, make the filling: In a non-stick skillet, heat oil over moderate heat. Add leeks, onion, and garlic and sauté 5 to 7 minutes or until softened. Remove from the heat and allow to cool slightly.

4 In another bowl, combine the milk with the cream cheese, eggs, egg whites, herbs, salt, and pepper. Whisk together until smooth. Stir in the leek mixture.

5 Pour the egg and leek mixture into the baking dish. Top with the remaining potato slices.

6 Bake 40 to 50 minutes or until the egg mixture is puffed and golden and feels almost set (the mixture will continue cooking once removed from the oven). Make sure the center is cooked. Let stand 30 minutes before slicing.

COOKING TIP
Once the potatoes are sliced, be sure to cook them at once. They will discolor if left in the air.

PER SERVING
Calories **283**, Saturated Fat **5g**, Total Fat **14g**, Sodium **193mg**, Cholesterol **87mg**, Protein **9g**, Carbohydrate **32g**, Fiber **4g**.

*For a five-star lunch, serve **Leek Quiche with Layered Potato Crust**.*

MAKING A POTATO CRUST

1 *Brush the potato slices lightly with oil and bake until tender. Using a spatula, turn them once during baking so that they are golden on both sides.*

2 *Carefully arrange the potato slices on the bottom and sides of the tart pan or quiche dish, overlapping them slightly so that they form a solid base.*

Ham and Cheese Frittata

Cooking technique ▪ *These delicious Italian-style omelets do not have to be turned. Simply pour the egg mixture into a frying pan and cook over low heat until set.*
Reduce fat ▪ *Use egg whites, low-fat dairy products, and just enough ham for accent.*

● Serves **4** ● Preparation Time **15 minutes** ● Cooking Time **25–30 minutes**

PER SERVING
Calories **372**, Saturated Fat **8g**,
Total Fat **22g**, Sodium **713mg**,
Cholesterol **263mg**, Protein **32g**,
Carbohydrate **11g**, Fiber **1g**.

$^1/_4$ cup 1% low-fat milk

$^1/_4$ cup low-fat sour cream

4 whole eggs

4 egg whites

2 tablespoons grated
  Parmesan cheese

$^1/_8$ teaspoon pepper

1 tablespoon olive or canola oil

2 onions, coarsely chopped

6 ounces reduced-sodium,
  reduced-fat ham,
  coarsely chopped

$^3/_4$ cup shredded part-skim
  mozzarella cheese

1 In a mixing bowl, combine the milk with the sour cream until blended. Add the whole eggs and then the egg whites, one at a time, whisking well after each addition. Stir in the Parmesan cheese and season with the pepper.

2 In a 10-inch nonstick skillet, heat the oil over moderate heat. Add the onions and sauté, stirring, about 7 to 9 minutes or until soft and golden brown. Add the ham to the skillet and sauté, stirring, a few minutes longer.

Roasted Pepper Potato Salad, page 301, makes a healthy accompaniment to **Ham and Cheese Frittata**.

3 Arrange the ham and onion mixture evenly in the skillet. Reduce the heat to low. Pour the egg and milk mixture into the skillet. Sprinkle the mozzarella cheese over the mixture.

4 Cover and cook the frittata for 15 to 20 minutes or until set and puffed. Transfer to a serving dish, cut into wedges, and serve at once.

COOKING TIP
Make sure that you cook the frittata over low heat so that the bottom doesn't burn.

Potato and Spinach Frittata

- Serves **4**
- Preparation Time **15 minutes**
- Cooking Time **30–35 minutes**

$^1/_4$ cup 1% low-fat milk

$^1/_4$ cup low-fat sour cream

4 whole eggs

4 egg whites

$^1/_8$ teaspoon each salt and pepper

1 tablespoon olive or canola oil

1 onion, chopped

8 ounces small potatoes, thinly sliced

1 pound fresh spinach, washed and thinly sliced

2 tablespoons chopped parsley or chives

1 Make egg and milk mixture as in Step 1 of master recipe. Season with salt and pepper.

2 In a 10-inch nonstick skillet, heat the oil over moderate heat. Sauté onion 2 to 3 minutes. Add the potatoes and sauté, stirring, about 5 minutes. Add the spinach and $^1/_4$ cup water; cover and cook 5 to 8 minutes or until the liquid has evaporated.

3 Add the egg and milk mixture to the vegetables as in Step 3 of the master recipe. Sprinkle the parsley over the mixture.

4 Cook and serve the frittata as in Step 4 of the master recipe.

PER SERVING
Calories **248**, Saturated Fat **2g**, Total Fat **12g**, Sodium **301mg**, Cholesterol **214mg**, Protein **15g**, Carbohydrate **21g**, Fiber **5g**.

Tomato, Olive, and Pepper Frittata

- Serves **4**
- Preparation Time **15 minutes**
- Cooking Time **25–30 minutes**

$^1/_4$ cup 1% low-fat milk

$^1/_4$ cup low-fat sour cream

4 whole eggs

4 egg whites

$^1/_8$ teaspoon each salt and pepper

1 tablespoon olive or canola oil

2 sweet green peppers, thinly sliced

1 large firm tomato, coarsely chopped

$^1/_3$ cup sliced black olives

2 tablespoons chopped fresh basil or parsley

1 Make egg and milk mixture as in Step 1 of master recipe. Season with salt and pepper.

2 In a 10-inch nonstick skillet, heat oil over moderate heat. Sauté peppers about 8 minutes or until soft and golden brown. Add tomato to the skillet and sauté, stirring, until quite soft.

3 Add the egg and milk mixture to the vegetables as in Step 3 of the master recipe. Sprinkle the olives and basil over the mixture.

4 Cook and serve the frittata as in Step 4 of the master recipe.

PER SERVING
Calories **183**, Saturated Fat **2g**, Total Fat **12g**, Sodium **260mg**, Cholesterol **214mg**, Protein **11g**, Carbohydrate **6g**, Fiber **1g**.

Pasta Frittata with Sausage and Mushrooms

- Serves **4**
- Preparation Time **15 minutes**
- Cooking Time **35 minutes**

$^1/_4$ cup 1% low-fat milk

$^1/_4$ cup low-fat sour cream

4 whole eggs

4 egg whites

1 teaspoon dried thyme

$^1/_8$ teaspoon salt and pepper

1 teaspoon olive or canola oil

4 ounces Italian-style turkey sausage links, casings removed

1 onion, thinly sliced

8 ounces mushrooms, sliced

1 cup cooked small pasta shells or elbow macaroni

1 Make egg and milk mixture as in Step 1 of master recipe. Season with the thyme, salt, and pepper.

2 In a 10-inch nonstick skillet, heat the oil over moderate heat. Cook sausages, stirring, about 4 minutes. Add onion and sauté about 3 minutes. Add mushrooms and sauté about 4 minutes. Add pasta shells and stir to combine.

3 Add egg and milk mixture to sausage mixture as in Step 3 of the master recipe.

4 Cook and serve the frittata as in Step 4 of the master recipe.

PER SERVING
Calories **260**, Saturated Fat **2g**, Total Fat **12g**, Sodium **450mg**, Cholesterol **232mg**, Protein **19g**, Carbohydrate **19g**, Fiber **1g**.

Swiss Cheese Pepper Soufflés

Cooking technique ▪ *Make the soft, creamy filling with egg whites, low-fat cheese, and milk. Spoon into pepper shells and bake until golden brown.*

Add nutrients ▪ *In addition to providing a handy container, peppers have the most vitamin C of any fruit or vegetable – three times your Daily Values.*

● Serves **4** ● Preparation Time **30 minutes** ● Cooking Time **25 minutes**

PER SERVING
Calories **215**, Saturated Fat **5g**, Total Fat **11g**, Sodium **300mg**, Cholesterol **75mg**, Protein **18g**, Carbohydrate **11g**, Fiber **1g**.

4 sweet green or red peppers
1 tablespoon margarine or butter
2 tablespoons all-purpose flour
³/₄ cup 1% low-fat milk
1 egg yolk
¹/₈ teaspoon each salt and pepper

1 cup shredded low-fat Swiss cheese (about 4 ounces)
4 scallions, finely chopped
4 egg whites
2 tablespoons grated Parmesan cheese

1 Preheat oven to 400°F. Cut tops off peppers and reserve. Remove core and seeds. Cut a thin slice from base of peppers so that they will stand up.

2 Bring a pan of water to a boil. Add peppers and tops, cover, and simmer for 3 minutes or until barely tender. Drain and place in a baking dish.

3 In a saucepan, melt margarine; add flour and cook, stirring, for 1 to 2 minutes. Remove from the heat and stir in milk. Simmer until thickened.

Serve them hot from the oven – Swiss Cheese Pepper Soufflés.

4 Cool slightly, then stir in the egg yolk, salt, pepper, and Swiss cheese. Mix the scallions into the sauce.

5 Whip the egg whites until stiff peaks form and carefully fold into the sauce.

6 Divide filling among the peppers and sprinkle with Parmesan. Bake for 25 minutes or until the filling is puffed and golden. Add tops to peppers.

Ricotta Pepper Soufflés

- Serves **4**
- Preparation time **30 minutes**
- Cooking time **25 minutes**

4 sweet red peppers

1 tablespoon margarine or butter

2 tablespoons all-purpose flour

³/₄ cup 1% low-fat milk

1 egg yolk

1 cup part-skim ricotta cheese

1 package (10 ounces) frozen chopped spinach, thawed and drained

¹/₂ teaspoon ground nutmeg

¹/₈ teaspoon each salt and pepper

4 egg whites

2 tablespoons grated Parmesan cheese

1 Preheat oven to 400°F. Cut peppers in half lengthwise and remove core and seeds. Blanch as in Step 2 of the master recipe.

2 Make the sauce as in Step 3 of the master recipe.

3 Cool slightly, then stir in egg yolk, ricotta cheese, spinach, nutmeg, salt, and pepper. Whip egg whites until stiff peaks form and carefully fold into sauce.

4 Divide filling among peppers and top with Parmesan cheese. Bake for 25 minutes or until peppers are tender and filling is puffed.

PER SERVING
Calories **222**, Saturated Fat **3g**, Total Fat **10g**, Sodium **291mg**, Cholesterol **215mg**, Protein **16g**, Carbohydrate **19g**, Fiber **5g**.

Feta Cheese Pepper Soufflés

- Serves **4**
- Preparation time **30 minutes**
- Cooking time **30 minutes**

4 sweet yellow peppers

1 tablespoon margarine or butter

2 tablespoons all-purpose flour

³/₄ cup 1% low-fat milk

1 egg yolk

1 cup feta cheese, crumbled

4 tomatoes, seeded and chopped

12 black olives, chopped

¹/₄ cup minced red onion

2 tablespoons chopped fresh basil

¹/₈ teaspoon pepper

4 egg whites

1 Preheat oven to 400°F. Cut the peppers in half lengthwise and remove cores and seeds. Blanch as in Step 2 of the master recipe.

2 Make the sauce as in Step 3 of the master recipe.

3 Cool slightly, then stir in egg yolk. Set aside ¹/₄ cup of feta. Mix remainder with tomatoes, olives, onion, basil, and pepper.

4 Whip the egg whites until stiff peaks form and fold into sauce.

5 Divide filling among peppers and top with remaining feta. Bake for 30 minutes or until tender and the filling is puffed.

PER SERVING
Calories **192**, Saturated Fat **3g**, Total Fat **11g**, Sodium **317mg**, Cholesterol **215mg**, Protein **13g**, Carbohydrate **12g**, Fiber **2g**.

Chiles Rellenos

- Serves **4**
- Preparation time **30 minutes**
- Cooking time **30 minutes**

8 large, fresh poblano chilies

1 tablespoon margarine or butter

2 tablespoons all-purpose flour

³/₄ cup 1% low-fat milk

1 egg yolk

5 ounces low-fat Monterey Jack cheese, shredded

1 can (28 ounces) crushed tomatoes

1 tablespoon olive or canola oil

1 small onion, chopped

1 clove garlic, crushed

¹/₂ teaspoon ground cumin

¹/₈ teaspoon pepper

1 Preheat oven to 400°F. Make a slit in each chili, remove seeds, and pat dry inside and out. Blanch as in Step 2 of master recipe.

2 Make sauce as in Step 3 of master recipe. Cool slightly; stir in egg yolk and 1 cup cheese.

3 Purée tomatoes in a blender. Heat oil and sauté onion and garlic for about 4 minutes. Add cumin and cook for 1 minute; add tomatoes and pepper.

4 Spoon cheese mixture into chilies. Pour half of tomato sauce in a baking dish; add chilies. Add remaining sauce and cheese. Bake for 30 minutes, until filling is set.

PER SERVING
Calories **273**, Saturated Fat **5g**, Total Fat **15g**, Sodium **561mg**, Cholesterol **78mg**, Protein **16g**, Carbohydrate **22g**, Fiber **3g**.

SALADS

Salad greens and vegetables come in
colors and shapes as lovely as anything in
the flower garden. They are also rich in fiber and
vitamins. And salads need never be boring — you
can serve them chilled or warm, with sweet, spicy,
or creamy dressings, as a side dish or the main event.
The How-To Book of Healthy Cooking takes
advantage of all the fresh greens and vegetables in an
exciting collection of recipes. You'll find wonderful new
ideas for tossed salads and hearty main-dish salads.
Finally, you'll find information on selecting,
storing, and preparing salad greens, plus recipes
for low-fat salad dressings. So why not toss
a healthy, colorful salad right now?

Chicken Tarragon Salad, page 297

When it comes to making a salad, there are no hard-and-fast rules. You can create a simple salad with leafy vegetables such as watercress and endive, or a substantial mixed salad with cooked meats. But the most important thing is to make sure that your salad contains plenty of vitamin-rich fresh fruits, and vegetables.

Making healthful salads

Some of the most commonly used salad ingredients, such as cucumbers, celery, and mushrooms, add crunch or flavor rather than vitamins. So make sure that your tossed salads contain some of the high-nutrition vegetables. For vitamin C, your best bets are tomatoes, sweet peppers, and radishes, as well as oranges and grapefruit.

Carrots and spinach are good sources of vitamin A. Parsley and chives not only add fresh flavor but are also excellent sources of vitamin C. Sprinkle them over salads whenever you can, and why not toss in some beans or chick-peas for fiber at the same time?

Your choice of greens is very important. Although many people like the crunchy texture of iceberg lettuce, it does not have much nutritional value. Romaine lettuce and chicory, which are both high in calcium and vitamin C, are much more nutritious. One of your best bets is arugula, also known as rocket. This slightly bitter green is a member of the cruciferous family of vegetables, so it is very rich in beta carotene as well as vitamin C. The chart below will help you make a selection, but in general, the darker the green, the more vitamins it contains.

Buying and storing greens

Select fresh, crisp, and vividly colored leaves, with no signs of browning or insect damage. Discard any wilted outer leaves and carefully wash the rest. Dry well on kitchen towels, a clean dish towel, or in a salad spinner, as any wetness dilutes the dressing and reduces crispness. Store clean leaves in the refrigerator, wrapped in a clean towel.

The only equipment needed to make a salad is a sharp knife, a chopping board, and a salad bowl. Any bowl is suitable for tossing your salad except those made from aluminum or enamel, which could react to the acid from a vinaigrette dressing.

Dressing the salad

Nothing is more important to a salad than a good dressing. It can be thick and creamy or light and tangy, but above all it should balance the taste and texture of the salad. If you are using bitter endive, match it with a honey dressing. If you're making a fish salad, use lemon juice to enhance the sweet fresh taste of the seafood. Go easy on the salt and add flavor with herbs and lemon juice or vinegar.

FREEZING HERBS

Remove stems from fresh herbs such as parsley, basil, mint, or sage before freezing. Place the leaves in plastic bags or small plastic freezer boxes, then freeze. Add the frozen herbs, without thawing first, to salad dressings or to marinades for warm salads.

WHY YOU SHOULD EAT SALAD GREENS

Low-calorie leafy greens add beta carotene, calcium, vitamin C, and iron to your diet. This chart shows your best source of each nutrient.

2-ounce/1-cup serving	Calories	Beta carotene mg	Calcium mg	Vitamin C mg	Iron mg
Arugula	11	2.0	45	154	0.5
Belgian endive	7	trace	0	9	0.5
Bibb and Boston	6	trace	4	17	1.0
Chicory	11	1.0	12	50	0.5
Iceberg	6	trace	2	9	0.5
Radicchio	3	0.9	32	8	0.0
Red leaf	9	0.5	9	34	0.5
Romaine	8	1.0	12	34	0.5
Watercress	11	1.0	21	60	0.4

Adding flavor with herbs

Herbs add wonderful flavor to salads and reduce the need for salt. You can stir them into a dressing, use them for marinating salad vegetables and meats, or just toss them in with the greens. Here's how to get the best results:

Use fresh herbs if available; they add more flavor. If fresh are not available, combine 1 tablespoon chopped flat-leaf parsley with 1 teaspoon dried herb.

Store fresh herbs, stems down, in 2 inches of water in the refrigerator. Cover the leaves loosely with a plastic bag. They will keep for about 2 weeks.

Buy small containers of any dried herbs you don't use frequently. Otherwise you may have to discard them, as they start to lose flavor after a year.

The best salad oil

When making your own dressing, the most important ingredient is the oil. Olive oil is particulary good because it has a fruity taste that goes with meat and vegetables as well as greens. More important, it is a monounsaturated oil, so it's your best choice healthwise. You will find three types in the stores:

Extra virgin olive oil is derived from the first pressing of the olives and has a maximum acidity of 1% which means that it is especially delicious. It is considered the finest of the olive oils, and this is reflected in the price. Extra virgin olive oil smokes when heated. So save it for salads, where it adds lots of flavor, and use less expensive olive oil for cooking.

Virgin olive oil comes from the second pressing and has a maximum acidity of 2%. It tastes almost as good as extra virgin olive oil and is slightly less expensive.

Olive oil (regular) comes from later pressings and is processed, so it is considered slightly less healthful. It also has a higher acidity, so it is not quite as good in salad dressings as extra virgin. However, it heats well and is excellent for cooking.

Light olive oil is produced from the last pressing and has a very mild flavor. Light does not refer to the calories or fat. All of these olive oils have roughly 120 calories per tablespoon and about 14 grams of fat.

To keep olive oil from becoming rancid, store it in a dark place. It should keep for about 6 months. If you want your oil to last longer, store it in the refrigerator, where it will last for up to a year. Olive oil solidifies when it's cold and must be allowed to warm before it is used.

A choice of vinegars

A well-flavored vinegar adds a wonderful piquancy to salad dressings and marinades, so you don't need to add too much oil. Choose from these varieties:

Balsamic vinegar is made from white grapes. It is dark, with a mellow sweet-sour flavor that comes from being aged in wooden barrels for 10 years. Balsamic is expensive, but the intense flavor makes it well worth the price.

Cider vinegar is made from fermented apple cider. It is fairly sharp and tangy and adds zest to salad dressing if you like the flavor. Use sparingly in apple salads.

Herb vinegars add extra flavor to salads. Tarragon vinegar is good in sauces, rosemary vinegar in mayonnaise, thyme or dill vinegar in salad dressings.

Wine vinegar can be made from white, red, or rosé wine. Use white or red in dressings for tossed salads; add the red to dressings for meat or fish salads.

MAKING HERB VINEGARS

1 *Choose healthy, unblemished herbs, bought at their peak of freshness. Tarragon, thyme, dill, and rosemary are particularly good. Trim the stems and remove any old leaves.*

Save bottles with unusual shapes – your herb vinegar can make an attractive gift.

2 *Insert a sprig of fresh herb into 2 cups white wine vinegar and reseal the bottle. Allow 2 weeks for the flavor to infuse. Will keep about 3 months, or 1 year if strained and rebottled.*

Making Tossed Salads

A properly made tossed salad is refreshing, healthful, and a feast for the eye as well as the palate. Here's how to ensure perfect results:

- *Select a mixture of leaves for contrasting flavors and colors. Plan about 1 cup per person.*
- *Tear rather than cut salad greens to avoid bruising.*
- *Prepare the dressing ¹/₂ hour ahead. This gives the flavors time to mellow and blend.*
- *For each cup of greens, place 1 tablespoon of dressing in the salad bowl. Just before serving, add greens and toss lightly.*
- *Add salt and pepper at the last moment; otherwise they will wilt the greens.*

ARUGULA has a bright green, irregularly-shaped leaf with a distinctive peppery taste.

BIBB is a small variety of butter-head lettuce. It has a small, round, loosely formed head with soft, buttery leaves and a succulent flavor. Boston is similar to bibb but larger.

ENDIVE comes in two types: Belgian or curly. Belgian endive is a pale, spear-shaped vegetable, while curly endive looks like a large, loose lettuce with frilly leaves that are dark green on the outside and pale yellow in the center. Both have a slightly bitter flavor.

ICEBERG is a variety of crisp-head lettuce with a round head of pale, tightly packed leaves. It keeps well, and although the flavor is rather bland, its crispness makes it a good addition to salads.

RADICCHIO has deep red leaves, making it a decorative addition to a salad. The flavor is slightly bitter, but the texture is firm.

RED LEAF is a loose-leafed, frilly lettuce with leaves on a stalk rather than in a tight head. Red leaf has a crisp texture and full flavor.

ROMAINE is a long lettuce with dark green outer leaves that are paler in the center. The crunchy leaves have a faintly bitter taste.

WATERCRESS is a member of the mustard family, which accounts for its peppery flavor. It has small, dark green leaves.

Arugula

Bibb

Radicchio

Belgian Endive

Red Leaf

Watercress

Curly Endive

Romaine

Some simple combinations

Radicchio, strips of sweet yellow pepper, and black olives.

Iceberg lettuce, spinach, scallions, and shredded carrot.

Arugula, chervil, watercress, and edible flowers.

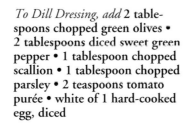

Shredded cabbage, carrot, and sweet green pepper.

Potato, celery, and red onions.

Snow peas, mushrooms, baby corn, and sweet red pepper.

Mixed leaf salad of curly endive, red leaf, and Belgian endive.

Dill Dressing

Combine 5 tablespoons plain nonfat yogurt • 2 tablespoons chopped fresh dill or 2 teaspoons dried • 1 tablespoon white wine vinegar • 1 small sweet onion, finely chopped • salt and black pepper • 1 teaspoon coarse-grained mustard

Per Tablespoon Calories 8, Saturated Fat 0g, Total Fat 0g.

Thousand Island Dressing

To Dill Dressing, add 2 tablespoons chopped green olives • 2 tablespoons diced sweet green pepper • 1 tablespoon chopped scallion • 1 tablespoon chopped parsley • 2 teaspoons tomato purée • white of 1 hard-cooked egg, diced

Per Tablespoon Calories 7, Saturated Fat 0g, Total Fat 0g.

Low-Fat Vinaigrette

Whisk together 1/4 cup vinegar or lemon juice • 1/4 cup water • 2 tablespoons olive oil • 1 teaspoon sugar • salt and pepper

Per Tablespoon Calories 25, Saturated Fat 0g, Total Fat 3g.

Salsa Dressing

Whisk together 1 cup reduced-sodium tomato sauce • 1 chili pepper, halved, seeded, and minced • 2 tablespoons chopped fresh cilantro or parsley • 1 clove garlic, crushed

Per Tablespoon Calories 5, Saturated Fat 0g, Total Fat 0g.

Yogurt Dressing

Blend or whisk together 3 tablespoons plain nonfat yogurt • 2 tablespoons chopped parsley • 1 tablespoon olive oil • 2 teaspoons Dijon mustard • 1 teaspoon lime juice

Per Tablespoon Calories 23, Saturated Fat 0g, Total Fat 2g.

Soy Dressing

Combine 1/4 cup reduced-sodium soy sauce • 1/4 cup chopped fresh cilantro or parsley • 2 tablespoons olive oil • 1 teaspoon honey • 2 cloves garlic, crushed

Per Tablespoon Calories 33, Saturated Fat 0g, Total Fat 3g.

Dill Dressing

Thousand Island Dressing

Macaroni Primavera

Reduce fat ■ *Make the dressing with nonfat yogurt and reduced-fat mayonnaise.*
Add nutrients ■ *This salad is high in protein, thanks to the yogurt and pasta. Step up the vitamin content by adding lots of crunchy fresh vegetables.*

● Serves **4** ● Preparation Time **15 minutes** ● Cooking Time **20 minutes**

PER SERVING
Calories **391**, Saturated Fat **2g**, Total Fat **9g**, Sodium **378mg**, Cholesterol **9mg**, Protein **15g**, Carbohydrate **62g**, Fiber **6g**.

1 cup small broccoli florets	1¹/₂ teaspoons Dijon mustard
¹/₂ cup frozen peas	3 tablespoons red wine vinegar
2 carrots, cut into matchsticks	¹/₈ teaspoon each salt and pepper
8 ounces elbow macaroni	2 stalks celery, coarsely chopped
1¹/₂ cups plain nonfat yogurt	1 red onion, coarsely chopped
6 tablespoons reduced-fat mayonnaise	2 tablespoons chopped fresh parsley, chives, or basil

1 Bring a pot of water to a boil. Fill a bowl with ice and water. Add broccoli to pot and simmer 1 to 2 minutes or until crisp-tender. Transfer florets to the bowl.

2 Return the pot to a boil and add the peas. Simmer about 2 minutes or until crisp-tender; remove from the heat and add to the broccoli.

3 Return pot to a boil again and add carrots. Simmer 3 to 4 minutes or until crisp-tender; remove from the heat and add to the broccoli and peas.

Macaroni Primavera, shown here with shrimp kabobs, can be served warm or chilled.

4 Again return the water to a boil. Add the pasta and cook according to package directions or until tender. Drain the pasta and rinse under cold running water.

5 Make the dressing: In a bowl, combine the plain yogurt with the mayonnaise, mustard, wine vinegar, salt, and pepper until thoroughly blended.

6 Drain vegetables and toss with pasta and dressing. Add celery and onion. Sprinkle with herbs and mix well. Serve or cover and chill until ready to serve.

Orzo Salad with Peas and Corn

- Serves **6**
- Preparation Time **10 minutes**
- Cooking Time **15 minutes**

3 large carrots, diced
2 cups frozen corn kernels
2 cups frozen baby peas
1 pound orzo
1¹/₂ cups plain nonfat yogurt
6 tablespoons reduced-fat mayonnaise
1¹/₂ teaspoons Dijon mustard
3 tablespoons lemon juice
¹/₈ teaspoon each salt and pepper
¹/₂ pint cherry tomatoes, halved
3 scallions, sliced
2 tablespoons chopped chives

1 Bring a pot of water to a boil. Add carrots and simmer for about 2 minutes. Add corn and peas and simmer 2 to 3 minutes. Drain.

2 Bring a saucepan of water to a boil. Add pasta and cook according to package directions or until tender. Drain and rinse.

3 Make the dressing: In a small bowl, combine yogurt, mayonnaise, mustard, lemon juice, salt, and pepper until blended.

4 Toss vegetables and orzo with dressing. Add tomatoes and scallions and sprinkle with chives. Serve or cover and chill until ready to serve.

PER SERVING
Calories **470**, Saturated Fat **1g**, Total Fat **7g**, Sodium **286mg**, Cholesterol **6mg**, Protein **16g**, Carbohydrate **86g**, Fiber **10g**.

Roasted Vegetable Pasta Salad

- Serves **6**
- Preparation Time **20 minutes**
- Cooking Time **20 minutes**

2 sweet red, yellow, or green peppers, chopped
2 small zucchini, sliced
2 small yellow squash, chopped
4 ounces mushrooms, sliced
6 tablespoons olive or canola oil
1 pound radiatori or pasta ruffles
3 tablespoons red wine vinegar
1¹/₂ teaspoons Dijon mustard
¹/₈ teaspoon each salt and pepper
¹/₄ cup shredded fresh basil or parsley

1 Preheat broiler, line rack with aluminum foil, and set 5 to 6 inches from the heat. Place vegetables on foil and brush with 1¹/₂ tablespoons of oil. Broil about 10 minutes. Transfer to a bowl.

2 Meanwhile, bring a pot of water to a boil. Add pasta and cook according to package directions. Drain and rinse.

3 Make the dressing: In a small bowl, combine remaining oil with vinegar, mustard, salt, and pepper. Mix pasta and vegetables, toss with dressing, and sprinkle with basil. Serve or cover and chill until ready to serve.

PER SERVING
Calories **435**, Saturated Fat **2g**, Total Fat **15g**, Sodium **62mg**, Cholesterol **0mg**, Protein **11g**, Carbohydrate **62g**, Fiber **2g**.

Eggplant Tomato Pasta Salad

- Serves **6**
- Preparation Time **20–25 minutes**
- Cooking Time **30 minutes**

1 pound bow-tie pasta or fusilli
¹/₄ cup olive or canola oil
2 large red onions, chopped
2 cloves garlic, finely chopped
1 small eggplant, diced
4 stalks celery, coarsely chopped
1 can (14 ounces) crushed tomatoes
2 tablespoons red wine vinegar
¹/₈ teaspoon each salt and pepper
¹/₄ cup chopped parsley

1 Bring a pot of water to a boil. Add pasta and cook according to package directions or until tender. Drain and rinse. Transfer to a bowl.

2 Meanwhile, in a skillet, heat 2 tablespoons of oil. Sauté onions and garlic about 9 minutes or until browned. Add eggplant and celery and cook about 5 minutes longer or until soft. Stir in tomatoes and simmer about 5 minutes.

3 Remove the skillet from the heat and stir in remaining oil, vinegar, salt, and pepper. Add eggplant-tomato mixture to pasta and sprinkle with parsley. Toss and serve or cover and chill until ready to serve.

PER SERVING
Calories **429**, Saturated Fat **1g**, Total Fat **11g**, Sodium **146mg**, Cholesterol **0mg**, Protein **12g**, Carbohydrate **71g**, Fiber **5g**.

Warm Beef and Potato Salad

Cooking technique ■ *For a scrumptious main-dish salad, marinate lean meat for flavor. Then cook until tender and toss with a low-fat dressing – serve warm.*

Add nutrients ■ *Mix in vegetables or fruit and serve on a bed of crisp greens.*

● Serves **6** ● Preparation Time **20 minutes plus marinating time** ● Cooking Time **15–20 minutes**

PER SERVING
Calories **272**, Saturated Fat **4g**,
Total Fat **13g**, Sodium **85mg**,
Cholesterol **38mg**, Protein **18g**,
Carbohydrate **21g**, Fiber **3g**.

5 tablespoons olive or canola oil

3 tablespoons red wine vinegar

1 clove garlic, finely chopped

¹/₈ teaspoon each salt and pepper

Dash of hot red pepper sauce

1 pound lean London broil or flank steak

1 pound baby new or small red potatoes, halved

1 large red onion, thinly sliced

8 ounces button mushrooms, halved

4 cups red and green leaf lettuce, torn into large pieces

1 In a bowl, combine 4 table-spoons oil, vinegar, garlic, salt, pepper, and pepper sauce. With a sharp knife, trim off fat, then thinly slice beef across the grain.

2 Transfer beef to a large bowl. Add half of the marinade and toss to coat thoroughly. Cover and refrigerate the meat at least 1 hour.

3 Meanwhile, bring a large saucepan of water to a boil. Add potatoes and simmer 10 minutes or until tender. Remove from the heat, drain, and cool slightly.

Warm Beef and Potato Salad makes a healthy and satisfying summer meal.

4 Drain meat and discard marinade. Heat a large nonstick skillet until very hot. Cook beef, turning once, 1 to 2 minutes. Transfer to a clean bowl.

5 Clean skillet with paper towels. Heat remaining oil and sauté onion and mushrooms 3 to 5 minutes. Add to the beef with the potatoes.

6 Pour remaining marinade over the beef and potato mixture and gently toss to coat well. Serve the warm salad on a bed of prepared lettuce.

Warm Pork and Orange Salad

- Serves **4**
- Preparation Time **30 minutes** plus marinating time
- Cooking Time **10 minutes**

---

5 tablespoons olive or canola oil

¹/₄ cup orange juice

2 tablespoons lemon juice

2 large oranges (zest of 1 finely grated)

¹/₈ teaspoon each salt and pepper

1 pound lean boned pork loin

1 large red onion, thinly sliced

4 cups red and green leaf lettuce, torn into large pieces

1 In a bowl, combine 4 tablespoons of oil, both juices, orange zest, salt, and pepper. Slice meat as in Step 1 of master recipe.

2 Using half of the marinade, marinate the meat as in Step 2 of the master recipe. Peel the oranges and section.

3 Drain meat and discard marinade. Heat a large nonstick skillet until very hot. Cook pork, turning once, 2 to 3 minutes or until cooked. Transfer to a clean bowl.

4 Heat remaining oil and sauté onion 3 to 5 minutes. Add oranges and cook, stirring, a few minutes longer. Add to the pork.

5 Serve on a bed of lettuce as in Step 6 of the master recipe.

PER SERVING
Calories **303**, Saturated Fat **4g**, Total Fat **18g**, Sodium **113mg**, Cholesterol **71mg**, Protein **26g**, Carbohydrate **7g**, Fiber **2g**.

Warm Goat Cheese Salad

- Serves **4**
- Preparation Time **7 minutes** plus marinating time
- Cooking Time **4–6 minutes**

---

¹/₄ cup olive or canola oil

3 tablespoons white wine vinegar

1 clove garlic, finely chopped

2 tablespoons chopped fresh herbs, such as parsley or chives

¹/₈ teaspoon pepper

Dash of hot red pepper sauce

1 log (8 ounces) goat cheese

1 baguette French bread

4 cups red and green leaf lettuce, torn into large pieces

1 In a large bowl, combine oil, vinegar, garlic, herbs, pepper, and hot red pepper sauce. Cut cheese across into 12 slices. Add to marinade mixture and toss to coat. Cover and marinate at least 1 hour.

2 Preheat broiler. Cut baguette into twelve ³/₄-inch slices and place on a broiler rack. Brown on one side about 2 to 3 minutes.

3 Drain cheese, reserving the marinade. Turn the toast over and place a slice of cheese on top of each. Broil 1 to 2 minutes longer.

4 Place toasts on the prepared lettuce leaves and spoon remaining marinade over.

PER SERVING
Calories **528**, Saturated Fat **8g**, Total Fat **25g**, Sodium **863mg**, Cholesterol **39mg**, Protein **16g**, Carbohydrate **56g**, Fiber **3g**.

Warm Cabbage and Bacon Salad

- Serves **4**
- Preparation Time **20 minutes**
- Cooking Time **20 minutes**

---

8 ounces turkey bacon strips, coarsely chopped

2 tablespoons olive or canola oil

1 clove garlic, finely chopped

¹/₈ teaspoon pepper

3 cups each finely shredded red and green cabbage

1 large red onion, thinly sliced

3 tablespoons red wine vinegar

4 cups red and green leaf lettuce, torn into large pieces

1 Heat a deep nonstick skillet. Sauté bacon 8 to 10 minutes or until fat is rendered. Using a slotted spoon, transfer to paper towels and reserve.

2 Add the oil to the skillet with the garlic and pepper and cook 2 to 3 minutes.

3 Add cabbage, onion, and vinegar to the skillet and stir well until thoroughly coated. Cover the pan and cook 2 to 3 minutes or until almost tender but still crisp to the bite.

4 Remove the lid and cook about 1 minute longer or until liquid has almost evaporated. Return the crisp bacon to the pan and stir just to combine. Serve on a bed of prepared lettuce.

PER SERVING
Calories **289**, Saturated Fat **7g**, Total Fat **23g**, Sodium **1308mg**, Cholesterol **57mg**, Protein **21g**, Carbohydrate **10g**, Fiber **3g**.

Salmon Salad Vinaigrette

Cooking technique ■ *Poach fish fillets in stock, then shred the meat and combine with crisp fresh vegetables. Add a zesty citrus vinaigrette dressing to bring out the sweet fresh flavor of the seafood.*

Save time ■ *Use canned salmon instead of fresh – it contains just as much of the omega-3 fatty acids, which have a protective effect on the heart. Just be sure to drain off the oil. Do the same with sardines.*

● Serves **4** ● Preparation Time **15 minutes** ● Cooking Time **10 minutes**

PER SERVING
Calories **402**, Saturated Fat **3g**,
Total Fat **21g**, Sodium **127mg**,
Cholesterol **63mg**, Protein **26g**,
Carbohydrate **28g**, Fiber **3g**.

1 pound skinless salmon fillet or canned salmon in water, drained

2 cups fish stock, page 18

4 cups water

1 pound baby new potatoes, halved if large

1 large cucumber, peeled, seeded, and thinly sliced

1 small red onion, finely chopped

¹/₄ cup olive or canola oil

2 tablespoons lime juice

¹/₈ teaspoon each salt and pepper

Dash of hot red pepper sauce

2 tablespoons chopped fresh basil or parsley

1 Rinse the salmon fillet under cold running water and remove any small bones. In a large skillet, combine the stock with the water and bring to a boil over moderate heat. (If using canned salmon, omit Steps 1 and 2.)

2 Add the salmon to the boiling liquid, return to a boil, and cover the skillet. Lower the heat and simmer 9 to 10 minutes.

3 Meanwhile, bring another pan of water to a boil. Add the potatoes and return to a boil. Simmer the potatoes 15 to 20 minutes or until tender. Drain the potatoes, rinse under cold water, and allow to cool.

4 Remove the salmon from the stock and drain well. Into a large bowl, coarsely shred the fish, being careful to remove any remaining bones. Add the sliced cucumber, and chopped onion.

5 Make the dressing: In a small bowl, combine the oil, lime juice, salt, pepper, hot red pepper sauce, and chopped basil.

6 Pour about three-quarters of the dressing over the fish and vegetables and gently toss. Arrange fish mixture over the potatoes and drizzle with remaining dressing. Serve or cover and refrigerate until needed.

Salmon Salad Vinaigrette *is proof that salads can be perfect for that special meal.*
Serve with lemon and lime wedges and garnish with basil leaves.

Shrimp Salad with Tomato Vinaigrette

Most supermarkets carry shelled precooked shrimp in the frozen or fresh fish section. Although they are expensive, they make this dish even quicker to prepare.

- Serves **4**
- Preparation Time **15 minutes** plus chilling time
- Cooking Time **10 minutes**

---

1 pound large shrimp

¹⁄₄ cup olive or canola oil

8 ounces mushrooms, sliced

4 scallions, sliced

3 large plum or small regular tomatoes, coarsely chopped

4 stalks celery, diced

2 tablespoons lemon juice

¹⁄₈ teaspoon each salt and pepper

Dash of hot red pepper sauce

2 tablespoons chopped parsley or cilantro

4 cups green leaf lettuce, torn into large pieces

---

1 Bring a large saucepan of water to a boil over moderate heat. Add the shrimp and simmer 3 to 5 minutes or until just tender. Remove from the heat and drain well. Peel and devein (see page 45).

2 Meanwhile, in a nonstick skillet, heat 1 tablespoon of the oil over moderate heat. Add the mushrooms and scallions and sauté 2 to 3 minutes or until just tender. Remove from the heat and transfer to a bowl. Add the tomatoes, stir to mix well, and allow to cool.

3 Reserving a few shrimp for the garnish, cut the remaining into ¹⁄₂-inch pieces. Stir into the tomato mixture with the celery.

4 Make the dressing: In a small bowl, combine the remaining oil with the lemon juice, salt, pepper, hot red pepper sauce, and parsley, and stir until thoroughly blended.

> ### COOKING TIP
> *If you buy frozen shelled cooked shrimp, thaw and drain them thoroughly before using.*

5 Pour dressing over shrimp, tomato, and celery mixture and gently toss together until well coated. Either serve at room temperature or cover and refrigerate until needed. Serve on a bed of prepared lettuce and garnish with reserved whole shrimp.

PER SERVING
Calories **299**, Saturated Fat **2g**, Total Fat **16g**, Sodium **291mg**, Cholesterol **175mg**, Protein **26g**, Carbohydrate **14g**, Fiber **4g**.

RAW AND COOKED SHRIMP

Fresh raw shrimp are soft and the flesh is blue in color, almost translucent.

Cooked shrimp are firm. The flesh is pink in color and opaque, with no trace of blue.

GETTING AHEAD

If you want to save time, you can prepare the shrimp (as in Step 1) the day before. Allow them to cool, then place them in a bowl; cover with plastic wrap and refrigerate. It is important not to keep cooked seafood too long, so be sure to use them the next day. Or you can cook and freeze them up to 3 months in a freezer bag.

Shrimp Salad with Tomato Vinaigrette makes an attractive main dish or, in smaller portions, a delicious starter.

Sardine Salad Vinaigrette

Balsamic vinegar and capers impart a deliciously tart flavor to this sardine salad. If you prefer to reduce the level of tartness, substitute chopped black olives for the capers.

- Serves **4**
- Preparation time **12 minutes**
- Cooking time **10 minutes**

---

1 pound sardine fillets, skinned, or 2 cans (4 ounces each) sardines, drained

1 large cucumber, peeled, seeded, and thinly sliced

6 scallions, thinly sliced

3 tablespoons olive oil

1 tablespoon balsamic vinegar or red wine vinegar

$1/8$ teaspoon salt and pepper

Dash of hot red pepper sauce

Finely grated zest of 1 lemon

4 cups prepared salad leaves, torn into large pieces

1 tablespoon chopped parsley

1 tablespoon capers, drained

1 tablespoon grated carrot

1 Preheat the broiler, setting the rack about 4 inches from the heat. Place the sardine fillets on a broiler rack and broil for 3 to 4 minutes on each side or until the fish flakes easily. (If using canned sardines, do not broil.) Cut sardines into $1^1/2$-inch pieces.

2 Place the cucumber in a bowl with the scallions.

3 Make the dressing: In a small bowl, combine the olive oil with the balsamic vinegar, salt, pepper, hot red pepper sauce, and lemon zest until thoroughly blended. Pour half the dressing over the cucumber mixture and toss until well coated.

4 Arrange the salad leaves on a serving dish and add the cucumber mixture and sardine fillets. Sprinkle with the remaining dressing and the parsley, capers, and grated carrot. Either serve at room temperature or cover and refrigerate until needed.

PER SERVING
Calories **205**, Saturated Fat **2g**, Total Fat **14g**, Sodium **449mg**, Cholesterol **80mg**, Protein **15g**, Carbohydrate **6g**, Fiber **2g**.

FILLETING SARDINES

1 *If you buy whole sardines, cut off the heads and open the fish out flat. If necessary, extend the cut toward the tail.*

2 *Grasp the head end of the backbone and gently pull it away from the fish. It should come out easily. Cut off the tail.*

Mixed Seafood Salad Vinaigrette

Lime juice and hot red pepper sauce create a peppy dressing that you may wish to use on other salads. It's best to use uncooked shrimp and scallops the same day you buy them.

- Serves **6**
- Preparation Time **25 minutes**
- Cooking Time **15 minutes**

---

8 ounces skinless fish fillets, such as cod or halibut

2 cups fish stock, page 18

2 cups water

4 ounces small shrimp, peeled and deveined

4 ounces bay scallops or small sea scallops

4 stalks celery, diced

1 small cucumber, peeled, seeded, and diced

1 large red onion, coarsely chopped

2 tablespoons chopped cilantro or parsley

$1/4$ cup olive or canola oil

2 tablespoons lime juice

$1/8$ teaspoon each salt and pepper

Dash of hot red pepper sauce

4 cups prepared salad leaves, torn into large pieces

6 small tomatoes, quartered

1 Rinse fish under cold running water and remove any small bones. In a deep skillet, combine stock and water; bring to a boil over moderate heat.

2 Add fish to the skillet, cover, and simmer 5 to 10 minutes or until barely tender. Using a slotted spoon, transfer the fish to a plate and cool. Return liquid to a boil and add shrimp and scallops. Simmer the shellfish 2 to 5 minutes or until cooked through. Remove from the heat and drain.

3 Coarsely shred the white fish, being careful to remove any remaining bones. Transfer the fish to a large bowl. Add the shellfish.

4 Add the celery, cucumber, onion, and cilantro to the fish.

5 Make the dressing: In a small bowl, combine the oil with the lime juice, salt, pepper, and hot red pepper sauce until thoroughly blended. Pour the dressing over the fish and vegetables and gently toss together until well coated. Either serve at room temperature or cover and refrigerate until needed. Serve on a bed of prepared salad leaves and tomato.

PER SERVING
Calories **195**, Saturated Fat **1g**, Total Fat **10g**, Sodium **160mg**, Cholesterol **52mg**, Protein **16g**, Carbohydrate **11g**, Fiber **3g**.

Fresh cilantro is exceptionally good with seafood.

Rainbow Coleslaw

Reduce fat ▪ *Make the dressing with nonfat yogurt and reduced-fat mayonnaise.*
Add nutrients ▪ *Cabbage and carrots are high in beta carotene; spinach provides iron; and all are rich in vitamin C. Add nuts or lean meat for protein.*

● Serves 12 ● Preparation Time **30 minutes plus chilling time**

PER SERVING
Calories **56**, Saturated Fat **1g**, Total Fat **4g**, Sodium **53mg**, Cholesterol **1mg**, Protein **1g**, Carbohydrate **4g**, Fiber **2g**.

¹/₄ small head (4 ounces) each white, green, and red cabbage

1 cup shredded carrot

1 cup shredded spinach

1 sweet red pepper, thinly sliced

1 red onion, thinly sliced

¹/₄ cup plain nonfat yogurt

3 tablespoons olive oil

2 tablespoons reduced-fat mayonnaise

1 tablespoon chopped fresh mint

2 teaspoons wine vinegar

¹/₈ teaspoon each salt and pepper

Pinch of curry powder

1 Trim the stem ends from the cabbages. Remove and discard any outer wilted leaves. Using a long, sharp knife, cut the cabbages lengthwise in half and then into quarters.

2 Cut out and discard the cores from the cabbage quarters. Thinly shred the cabbage leaves, cutting lengthwise or crosswise across the cabbage, depending on the size of shred desired.

*Crunchy, colorful **Rainbow Coleslaw** is low in fat and calories. It is served here with Pasta Frittata with Sausage and Mushrooms, page 277.*

3 Place the shredded cabbage in a large bowl with the shredded carrot, spinach, red pepper, and red onion.

4 Make the dressing: In a small bowl, mix the yogurt, olive oil, mayonnaise, mint, vinegar, salt, pepper, and curry powder. Pour the dressing over the cabbage mixture and toss together until well coated. Cover and refrigerate for at least 30 minutes before serving.

Fruit 'n' Nut Slaw

- Serves **10**
- Preparation Time **30 minutes** plus chilling time

1 head (1³/₄ pounds) red cabbage

2 cups halved green seedless grapes

1 cup quartered radishes

¹/₄ cup chopped hazelnuts or walnuts, toasted

¹/₃ cup plain nonfat yogurt

2 tablespoons chopped mango chutney or other chutney

2 tablespoons chopped cilantro or parsley

1 Trim stem end from cabbage. Remove and discard any outer wilted leaves. With a long, sharp knife, cut cabbage lengthwise in half and then into quarters.

2 Cut out and discard cores from cabbage quarters. Thinly shred cabbage leaves, cutting lengthwise or crosswise, depending on size of shred desired.

3 Place the shredded cabbage in a large bowl. Add the grapes, radishes, and hazelnuts.

4 Make the dressing: In a small bowl, mix the yogurt with the chutney and cilantro. Pour the dressing over the cabbage mixture and toss together until coated. Cover and refrigerate for at least 30 minutes before serving.

PER SERVING
Calories **89**, Saturated Fat **0g**, Total Fat **3g**, Sodium **17mg**, Cholesterol **0mg**, Protein **2g**, Carbohydrate **17g**, Fiber **3g**.

Chinese Chicken Coleslaw

- Serves **8**
- Preparation Time **20 minutes**
- Cooking Time **6 minutes**

1 head (1¹/₄ pounds) Chinese cabbage

4 tablespoons olive oil

2 teaspoons toasted sesame oil

2 boneless, skinless chicken breast halves, thinly sliced (about 8 ounces)

3 scallions, thinly sliced

2 tablespoons white wine vinegar

2 teaspoons reduced-sodium soy sauce

¹/₄ teaspoon ground ginger

¹/₈ teaspoon each salt and pepper

1 tablespoon toasted sesame seeds

1 Trim and shred cabbage as in Steps 1 and 2 of master recipe.

2 In a large nonstick skillet, heat 2 tablespoons of olive oil with sesame oil. Add cabbage and sauté, stirring, about 3 minutes. Transfer to a bowl to cool.

3 Reheat skillet and sauté chicken about 3 minutes or until cooked. Add to cabbage with the scallions.

4 Make the dressing: In a small bowl, whisk remaining oil with vinegar, soy sauce, ginger, salt, and pepper. Pour over cabbage mixture and toss to coat. Sprinkle with sesame seeds and serve.

PER SERVING
Calories **128**, Saturated Fat **1g**, Total Fat **9g**, Sodium **116mg**, Cholesterol **16mg**, Protein **8g**, Carbohydrate **5g**, Fiber **2g**.

Cabbage with Pork and Pears

- Serves **10**
- Preparation Time **20 minutes**
- Cooking Time **6 minutes**

1 head (1³/₄ pounds) red cabbage

4 tablespoons olive oil

8 ounces boneless lean pork loin, cubed

4 stalks celery, thinly sliced

2 cups diced pears

¹/₄ cup cider vinegar

2 tablespoons plain nonfat yogurt

1 teaspoon dry mustard

1 teaspoon brown sugar

¹/₈ teaspoon each salt and pepper

1 Trim and shred the cabbage as in Steps 1 and 2 of the master recipe.

2 In a large skillet, heat 2 tablespoons of the oil over moderate heat. Add the cabbage and sauté, stirring, about 3 minutes or until slightly soft. Transfer to a bowl and let cool.

3 Reheat skillet and sauté the pork about 3 minutes or until cooked. Add to cabbage with celery and pears.

4 Make the dressing: In a small bowl, whisk remaining oil with vinegar, yogurt, mustard, brown sugar, salt, and pepper. Pour dressing over cabbage mixture and toss to coat.

PER SERVING
Calories **131**, Saturated Fat **1g**, Total Fat **7g**, Sodium **66mg**, Cholesterol **14mg**, Protein **7g**, Carbohydrate **12g**, Fiber **3g**.

New-style Chicken Salad

Reduce fat ▪ *For a leaner salad, marinate chicken and vegetables in oil and spices. Grill and serve warm. Or poach the poultry and make a traditional creamy dressing using yogurt and lemon juice instead of mayonnaise.*

Add nutrients ▪ *Add a generous helping of fresh vegetables, fruit, or greens.*

● Serves 4 ● Preparation Time 25 minutes plus marinating time ● Cooking Time 10–15 minutes

PER SERVING
Calories **301** Saturated Fat **1g**,
Total Fat **6g**, Sodium **138mg**,
Cholesterol **99mg**, Protein **43g**,
Carbohydrate **18g**, Fiber **6g**.

4 boneless, skinless chicken breast halves (1¹/₂ pounds)	¹/₄ cup olive or canola oil
2 sweet red, yellow, or green peppers, sliced	2 tablespoons lemon juice
	1 teaspoon finely grated lemon zest
1 large red onion, thickly sliced	2 teaspoons dried basil
2 zucchini, thickly sliced	¹/₈ teaspoon each salt and pepper
¹/₂ pint cherry tomatoes, halved	4 cups mixed lettuce

1 Cut each chicken breast half into 4 slices. Place in a baking dish. Place the peppers, onion, zucchini, and cherry tomatoes in a separate dish.

2 In a small bowl, combine oil with lemon juice and zest, basil, salt, and pepper until blended. Spoon half the marinade over chicken and remaining marinade over vegetables and toss to coat. Cover both dishes with plastic wrap and marinate in the refrigerator at least 2 hours. Remove chicken from marinade; drain and discard marinade.

In the summer, why not set the table outdoors and enjoy **New-style Chicken Salad** *alfresco.*

3 Preheat the broiler or grill. Broil or grill the chicken 6 to 8 minutes or until cooked through, turning once. Transfer the chicken breasts to a platter, cover, and keep them warm.

4 Add the vegetables to the broiler or grill and cook until browned and softened, turning once and brushing twice with the marinade. Serve the chicken and vegetables on a bed of the lettuce leaves.

COOKING TIP

When grilling sliced or small vegetables, cover the rack with aluminum foil so that they don't fall through. Then pierce all over with a fork to let any juices run off.

Duck and Green Bean Salad

- Serves **4**
- Preparation Time **10 minutes**
- Cooking Time **30 minutes**

Vegetable oil cooking spray

4 boneless, skinless duck breast halves (1^1/$_2$ pounds)

8 ounces mushrooms, sliced

^{1}/$_4$ cup olive or canola oil

1 sweet green pepper, sliced

8 ounces green beans

2 cups water

2 tablespoons lime juice

1 teaspoon whole-grain mustard

^{1}/$_8$ teaspoon each salt and pepper

4 cups red leaf lettuce

2 tablespoons freeze-dried chives

1 Preheat oven to 350°F. Coat a nonstick skillet with vegetable oil spray, heat, and cook duck 6 minutes on each side or until browned. Slice on a diagonal.

2 Return skillet to the heat and sauté the mushrooms for 3 minutes; transfer to a bowl. Add 1 teaspoon of oil to skillet and sauté green pepper for 5 minutes. Add beans and water, cover, and simmer 10 minutes. Drain and toss with the mushrooms.

3 Make the dressing: Combine remaining oil, lime juice, mustard, salt, and pepper. Arrange the vegetables on lettuce; add duck and dressing. Garnish with chives.

PER SERVING
Calories **384**, Saturated Fat **4g**, Total Fat **22g**, Sodium **204mg**, Cholesterol **132mg**, Protein **37g**, Carbohydrate **11g**, Fiber **3g**.

Chicken Tarragon Salad

- Serves **4**
- Preparation Time **35 minutes** plus chilling time
- Cooking Time **15 minutes**

---

4 boneless, skinless chicken breast halves (1^1/$_2$ pounds)

2 cups chicken stock, page 18

2 cups water

3 teaspoons dried tarragon

2 apples, cored and diced

2 stalks celery, diced

1 large red onion, chopped

1 cup plain nonfat yogurt

2 tablespoons olive or canola oil

2 tablespoons lemon juice

^{1}/$_8$ teaspoon each salt and pepper

2 cups red leaf lettuce

1 Trim fat from chicken. In a skillet, combine stock, water, and 2 teaspoons tarragon. Add chicken, cover, and simmer 15 minutes, until cooked through.

2 Using a slotted spoon, transfer chicken to a plate and allow to cool. Cut chicken into bite-size pieces and place in a large bowl. Add apples, celery, and onion.

3 Make the dressing: Combine yogurt, oil, lemon juice, remaining tarragon, salt, and pepper.

4 Pour dressing over salad and toss. Cover and chill 1 hour. Serve on a bed of the lettuce.

PER SERVING
Calories **348**, Saturated Fat **2g**, Total Fat **9g**, Sodium **243mg**, Cholesterol **100mg**, Protein **44g**, Carbohydrate **22g**, Fiber **3g**.

Turkey and Grape Salad

- Serves **4**
- Preparation Time **12 minutes** plus chilling time
- Cooking Time **9 minutes**

---

2 tablespoons olive or canola oil

1 pound boneless, skinless turkey breast cutlets

^{1}/$_2$ cup pecan pieces

2 cups small red seedless grapes

6 scallions, thinly sliced

2 stalks celery, diced

1 cup plain nonfat yogurt

2 tablespoons lemon juice

1 teaspoon finely grated lemon zest

2 teaspoons Dijon mustard

^{1}/$_8$ teaspoon each salt and pepper

2 cups red leaf lettuce

1 In a nonstick skillet, heat 1 tablespoon oil. Sauté turkey for 4 minutes. Using tongs, remove to a board and pour pan juices into a small bowl. Dice turkey and place in another bowl.

2 Reheat skillet; toast pecans, stirring, 3 minutes. Add to turkey with grapes, scallions, and celery.

3 Make the dressing: Whisk the yogurt, remaining oil, lemon juice and zest, mustard, salt, and pepper into the pan juices until blended. Pour over salad and toss. Cover and chill 1 hour. Serve on a bed of the lettuce.

PER SERVING
Calories **356**, Saturated Fat **2g**, Total Fat **19g**, Sodium **266mg**, Cholesterol **69mg**, Protein **32g**, Carbohydrate **20g**, Fiber **3g**.

Confetti Rice Salad

Cooking technique ▪ *Combine cooked rice with crunchy vegetables and a zesty vinaigrette dressing. For a main dish, add beans, nuts, or shrimp for more protein.*
Add fiber ▪ *Use brown rice instead of white, cooked according to package directions.*

● Serves **8** ● Preparation Time **15 minutes plus cooling time** ● Cooking Time **15 minutes**

PER SERVING
Calories **287**, Saturated Fat **1g**,
Total Fat **7g**, Sodium **94mg**,
Cholesterol **0mg**, Protein **6g**,
Carbohydrate **49g**, Fiber **4g**.

3 cups vegetable stock, page 18

2 cups water

2 cups long-grain white rice

1 cup fresh or frozen corn kernels

1 cup frozen baby peas

2 large carrots, diced

1 large red onion, finely chopped

1 sweet red or green pepper, diced

¹/₄ cup olive or canola oil

2 tablespoons red wine vinegar

1 teaspoon Dijon mustard

¹/₈ teaspoon each salt and pepper

1 In a large saucepan, combine the stock with the 2 cups water and bring to a boil. Add the rice. Cover the pan and simmer the rice 20 to 25 minutes or until tender. Remove from the heat and refrigerate until needed.

2 Meanwhile, in a small saucepan, bring 1 inch of water to a boil. Add the corn kernels and peas and cook 4 to 6 minutes or until tender. Using a slotted spoon, transfer them to a large bowl.

Confetti Rice Salad makes a superb meatless meal served with a bean dish to complete the protein. Here it's Chick-pea and Roasted Garlic Spread on Pita, page 233.

3 Return the water to a boil and add the carrots. Cook about 8 minutes or until tender. Drain and add to the corn and peas with the onion, sweet pepper, and rice.

4 In a small bowl, combine the oil, vinegar, mustard, salt, and pepper and whisk together. Pour the dressing over the rice and vegetables and gently toss together until evenly coated with the dressing.

COOKING TIP
The salad will improve if you let it stand several hours. This allows the flavor of the dressing to permeate the rice.

Italian Rice and Bean Salad

- Serves **8**
- Preparation Time **15 minutes** plus cooling time
- Cooking Time **25 minutes**

3 cups vegetable stock, page 18

2 cups water

2 cups long-grain white rice

¹/₄ cup olive or canola oil

1 large red onion, coarsely chopped

3 small zucchini, diced

3 ripe tomatoes, coarsely chopped

1 can (16 ounces) cannellini beans, drained and rinsed

2 tablespoons finely chopped canned pimientos

2 tablespoons balsamic or red wine vinegar

¹/₈ teaspoon each salt and pepper

1 Prepare the rice as in Step 1 of the master recipe.

2 Meanwhile, in a nonstick skillet, heat half of the oil over moderate heat. Sauté the onion and zucchini about 7 minutes. Add tomatoes and cook a few minutes longer. Using a slotted spoon, transfer vegetables to a large bowl. Add rice and beans.

3 In a bowl, combine remaining oil, pimientos, vinegar, salt, and pepper. Pour dressing over rice salad and gently toss to coat well.

PER SERVING
Calories **313**, Saturated Fat **1g**, Total Fat **8g**, Sodium **201mg**, Cholesterol **0mg**, Protein **8g**, Carbohydrate **53g**, Fiber **5g**.

Wild Rice and Vegetable Salad

- Serves **8**
- Preparation Time **15 minutes** plus cooling time
- Cooking Time **15 minutes**

3 cups vegetable stock, page 18

2 cups water

¹/₂ cup wild rice

1¹/₂ cups long-grain white rice

1 small butternut squash or pumpkin, flesh cut into 1-inch cubes (4 cups)

2 large turnips, cut into 1-inch cubes

¹/₄ cup olive or canola oil

2 tablespoons red wine vinegar

¹/₈ teaspoon pepper

¹/₂ cup toasted chopped pecans or walnuts

1 Prepare the rice as in Step 1 of master recipe, cooking the wild rice for 15 minutes, then adding the white rice and simmering 20 to 25 minutes longer.

2 Meanwhile, preheat the oven to 375°F. Combine the squash and turnips in a nonstick roasting pan. Pour half of the oil over and toss to coat well. Roast about 40 minutes. Transfer to a bowl and add the rice.

3 In a small bowl, combine remaining oil, vinegar, salt, and pepper. Pour the dressing over the rice and vegetables, add pecans, and gently toss to coat well.

PER SERVING
Calories **297**, Saturated Fat **1g**, Total Fat **12g**, Sodium **82mg**, Cholesterol **0mg**, Protein **5g**, Carbohydrate **43g**, Fiber **3g**.

Shrimp and Rice Salad

- Serves **6**
- Preparation Time **12 minutes**
- Cooking Time **25 minutes**

3 cups vegetable stock, page 18

2 cups water

2 cups long-grain white rice

12 ounces medium shrimp, peeled and deveined

6 scallions, thinly sliced

1 package (9 ounces) frozen artichoke hearts, thawed and halved, or frozen peas, thawed

¹/₄ cup olive or canola oil

2 tablespoons lemon juice

1 teaspoon reduced-sodium soy sauce

¹/₈ teaspoon each salt and pepper

1 Prepare the rice as in Step 1 of the master recipe.

2 Meanwhile, bring a small saucepan of water to a boil. Add shrimp and cook about 3 minutes or until cooked through. Using a slotted spoon, transfer the shrimp to a large bowl.

3 Add the scallions, artichoke hearts, and rice to the shrimp and gently toss to coat well.

4 In a small bowl, combine the oil, lemon juice, soy sauce, salt, and pepper and whisk together. Pour the dressing over the rice, shrimp, and vegetables and gently toss to coat well.

PER SERVING
Calories **372**, Saturated Fat **2g**, Total Fat **10g**, Sodium **189mg**, Cholesterol **56mg**, Protein **14g**, Carbohydrate **55g**, Fiber **4g**.

Old-Fashioned Potato Salad

Reduce fat ▪ *Turn a caloric dish into a healthful one by replacing the mayonnaise with low-fat yogurt and sour cream. Or make it with a vinaigrette dressing.*
Add nutrients ▪ *Use sweet potatoes for more beta carotene. Add eggs or meat for protein.*

● Serves **6** ● Preparation Time **20 minutes** ● Cooking Time **15 minutes**

PER SERVING
Calories **173**, Saturated Fat **2g**, Total Fat **6g**, Sodium **228mg**, Cholesterol **76mg**, Protein **7g**, Carbohydrate **24g**, Fiber **2g**.

1½ **pounds new or small red potatoes, halved or quartered**

2 **eggs**

2 **stalks celery, diced**

1 **small cucumber, peeled, seeded, and diced**

4 **scallions, sliced**

½ **cup plain nonfat yogurt**

¼ **cup low-fat sour cream**

¼ **cup low-fat mayonnaise**

2 **tablespoons red wine vinegar**

1 **tablespoon Dijon mustard**

⅛ **teaspoon each salt and pepper**

2 **tablespoons chopped parsley**

1 Place the potatoes in a steamer basket and set in a large saucepan over about 1 inch of cold water. Cover the pan and bring the water to a boil over moderately high heat. Steam the potatoes 10 to 15 minutes or until tender. Transfer to a large bowl.

2 Meanwhile, place the eggs in a saucepan and cover with cold water. Bring to a boil over moderate heat and simmer about 8 minutes. Drain and place under cold running water. When cool, peel off the shells and coarsely chop. Add to potatoes along with the celery, cucumber, and scallions.

Old-Fashioned Potato Salad has a totally new fat and calorie count. Here it is served with turkey cutlets and Roasted Tomatoes with Herbs, page 189.

3 Make the dressing: In a small bowl, combine the yogurt with the sour cream, mayonnaise, vinegar, mustard, salt, and pepper.

4 Pour the dressing over the potatoes, eggs, and vegetables. Add the parsley and toss to coat well. Either serve at room temperature or cover and refrigerate until ready to serve.

COOKING TIP

To prevent a gray ring from forming around the yolk of hard-cooked eggs, remove them from the pan and crack to let steam escape. Plunge them into cold water and let sit for several minutes.

Deviled Potato Salad

- Serves **6**
- Preparation Time **15 minutes**
- Cooking Time **20 minutes**

1¹/₂ **pounds new or small red potatoes, halved or quartered**

2 **stalks celery, diced**

4 **scallions, sliced**

2 **tablespoons chopped canned green chilies**

2 **cloves garlic, finely chopped**

¹/₄ **cup low-fat sour cream**

¹/₄ **cup low-fat mayonnaise**

¹/₄ **cup olive or canola oil**

2 **tablespoons red wine vinegar**

1 **tablespoon Dijon mustard**

¹/₄ **teaspoon hot red pepper sauce**

¹/₈ **teaspoon each salt and pepper**

1 Steam the potatoes and transfer to a large bowl as in Step 1 of the master recipe.

2 Add the celery, scallions, green chilies, and garlic.

3 Make the dressing: In a small bowl, combine the sour cream with the mayonnaise, oil, vinegar, mustard, hot red pepper sauce, salt, and pepper.

4 Pour the dressing over the potatoes and vegetables and toss to coat well. Either serve at room temperature or cover and refrigerate until ready to serve.

PER SERVING
Calories **218**, Saturated Fat **2g**, Total Fat **13g**, Sodium **205mg**, Cholesterol **5mg**, Protein **3g**, Carbohydrate **22g**, Fiber **2g**.

Minty Ham and Sweet Potato Salad

- Serves **8**
- Preparation Time **12 minutes**
- Cooking Time **15 minutes**

2 **pounds sweet potatoes, peeled and cut into 1-inch pieces**

4 **sprigs mint**

2 **cups frozen baby peas**

8 **ounces reduced-sodium, reduced-fat ham, diced**

1 **large red onion, chopped**

¹/₂ **cup plain nonfat yogurt**

¹/₄ **cup low-fat sour cream**

2 **tablespoons cider vinegar**

2 **tablespoons coarse-grained mustard**

¹/₈ **teaspoon each salt and pepper**

1 Steam the sweet potatoes and half of the mint about 12 minutes as in Step 1 of master recipe. Add the peas and cook about 3 minutes longer. Drain and transfer to a large bowl. Discard the mint; add ham and onion.

2 Make the dressing: In a small bowl, combine the yogurt, sour cream, vinegar, mustard, salt, and pepper. Finely chop remaining mint leaves.

3 Pour dressing over potatoes, ham, and vegetables. Add chopped mint and toss. Serve at room temperature or cover and refrigerate until ready to serve.

PER SERVING
Calories **227**, Saturated Fat **1g**, Total Fat **4g**, Sodium **403mg**, Cholesterol **15mg**, Protein **11g**, Carbohydrate **37g**, Fiber **5g**.

Roasted Pepper Potato Salad

- Serves **6**
- Preparation Time **20 minutes**
- Cooking Time **20 minutes**

1¹/₂ **pounds red potatoes, cut into 1-inch pieces**

3 **large sweet red, yellow, or green peppers, sliced**

1 **clove garlic, thinly sliced**

¹/₄ **cup olive or canola oil**

2 **cups shredded romaine lettuce**

1 **large red onion, finely chopped**

2 **tablespoons lemon juice**

1 **tablespoon coarse-grained mustard**

¹/₈ **teaspoon each salt and pepper**

¹/₄ **cup chopped basil leaves**

1 Preheat oven to 400°F. Steam potatoes and transfer to a bowl as in Step 1 of the master recipe.

2 Meanwhile, place peppers and garlic in a shallow roasting pan. Add 1¹/₂ tablespoons of oil; toss to coat. Roast vegetables about 20 minutes. Add to potatoes with lettuce and onion.

3 Make the dressing: In a small bowl, combine the remaining oil with the lemon juice, mustard, salt, and pepper.

4 Pour dressing over the potatoes and vegetables. Add the basil and toss to coat well. Either serve at room temperature or cover and refrigerate until ready to serve.

PER SERVING
Calories **200**, Saturated Fat **1g**, Total Fat **9g**, Sodium **72mg**, Cholesterol **0mg**, Protein **4g**, Carbohydrate **27g**, Fiber **4g**.

BREADS

Freshly baked bread is always delicious, and the pleasure's doubled when you've made it yourself. **The How-To Book of Healthy Cooking** *dispels the myth that bread-making is difficult and takes you through the whole process step-by-step. Techniques are explained, and there are lots of hints and tips to make it easy. On these pages you'll find a wonderful variety of whole-grain and sweet breads designed with health in mind. To increase fiber, nutritious whole-wheat flour, wheat germ, and oatmeal are used as much as possible. Molasses takes the place of sugar; yogurt and buttermilk replace whole milk. Once you've mastered the basics, you can have fun with different glazes and toppings, varied shapes and flours. So why not start baking!*

Strawberry Bran Waffles, page 321

One of the most comforting smells in the world is the tantalizing aroma of baking bread. Better yet, baking your own bread allows you to make breads that are exceptionally healthful – high in protein, fiber, B vitamins, calcium, and iron; low in fat and sugar.

Quick and yeast breads

This chapter shows you how to make a wide variety of quick and yeast breads. Quick breads, which include pancakes, waffles, and corn bread, are so called because they are quicker and easier to make than yeast breads. They use baking powder, baking soda, or steam to make them rise, and they do not have to be kneaded. Yeast breads, which include dinner rolls and sandwich breads, are made with yeast, which creates carbon dioxide bubbles that forces the bread to rise. Most yeast breads are kneaded to make the dough more elastic and create a higher bread with a finer texture.

Flour power

Selecting the right flour is very important, as it affects the taste, texture, and nutritional content of bread. Whole-grain flours are more nutritious than white because they have been processed less and thus retain more B vitamins and fiber. However, they are also heavier, and if you make bread with whole-wheat flour alone, it can be too dense to be palatable. Therefore most of the recipes in this book use a combination of all-purpose and whole-wheat flours for better taste and texture as well as good nutrition.

All-purpose flour is regular white flour. Made from the starchy heart of the wheat after the bran and germ have been removed, it is often enriched with vitamins and minerals. White flour comes in two varieties, bleached and unbleached. The unbleached is preferable for bread making because it is sturdier, slightly more nutritious, and creates a finer-textured bread. You will also find variation in the protein content of all-purpose flours because they are made with a blend of soft and hard wheats. Hard wheat contains more protein, while soft wheat has less protein but creates lighter, flakier baked goods. For bread making, look for an all-purpose flour that

The most frequently used flour products are all-purpose, whole-wheat, wheat germ, and cornmeal (shown left to right).

has 11 grams or more of protein per cup. Not only is it more nutritious, but the extra protein will make the dough stronger and more elastic and create better volume.

Whole-wheat flour is made by grinding the whole grain, including the germ and bran. As a result, it contains more fiber and B vitamins. Because it contains all of the natural oils, it can become rancid; check the sell-by date and make sure it is fresh. Keep at room temperature for up to a month or in a tightly covered container in the freezer up to a year.

Wheat germ is the heart of the wheat and a rich source of protein, iron, B vitamins, and E. It is added to bread and other baked goods for extra nutrition as well as its lightly nutty taste.

Cornmeal is ground from whole white or yellow corn kernels and contains both the bran and the heart. It is more granular and less refined than corn flour. Cornmeal is a good source of protein. However, it has no gluten, which is needed to make an elastic dough that will rise. So it must be combined with wheat flour to make corn bread or muffins.

THE FINISHED LOAF

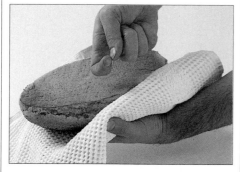

To test if the loaf is fully baked, tap on the base. If it is done, it will sound hollow.

The perfectly baked loaf should have a crisp crust, a moist crumb, and even texture.

Reducing sugar

Yeast needs some sugar to become activated. Therefore yeast breads must have some sweetener if they are to rise properly. However, you can cut down on the amount of sweetener in both yeast and quick breads, and you don't have to use refined sugar. Honey and molasses, which have slightly more nutrients, work just as well, and they each have a distinctive flavor. In fact, many cooks feel that they work better in heartier, whole-grain breads.

When using yeast, always check that the yeast is dissolved in liquid at the temperature recommended in the recipe.

Reducing fat

Bread also needs fat to give it a light, smooth texture. However, in most cases you can substitute low-fat milk, yogurt, or buttermilk for whole milk or cream. Buttermilk works particularly well in baked goods, adding a slightly tart flavor and making a finer, more tender crumb. Buttermilk is made commercially by adding special bacterial cultures to milk. It can also be purchased as a dry buttermilk powder, or you can make your own (see box).

To reduce cholesterol, egg whites can be substituted for whole eggs, although an occasional yolk is needed for color, flavor, and nutrients.

Storing and freezing

Once the bread is cool, wrap in plastic wrap and store in a cool place or bread box. Never leave unwrapped, or the bread will dry out quickly.

To freeze, wrap the loaf in foil or plastic wrap and then put it in a plastic bag. Press out any air and seal. Wrapped like this, it should keep for 3 months.

Finishing touches

For extra taste and nutrition, sprinkle seeds or grains over the bread before baking.

Poppyseeds add a nutty flavor when heated.

Rosemary adds a distinctive flavor.

Sesame seeds are high in iron, potassium, and phosphorus.

Sunflower seeds are rich in calcium, thiamine, vitamin B6, and folic acid.

Cornmeal adds texture and taste.

Wheat berries are a good source of fiber and vitamin E.

WHAT WENT WRONG

. . . with my yeast bread?

◆ Very close texture can be due to stale or insufficient yeast or the addition of too much salt or sugar.

◆ If your bread collapses when put into the oven, the dough was left to rise for too long; that is, it was overproofed.

◆ An uneven texture with large holes means the dough was not punched down sufficiently. Or it was left uncovered during its rising.

. . . with my quick bread?

◆ Uneven rising means the pan was not in the center of the oven, or the oven was at the wrong temperature.

◆ Close texture means the dough was overmixed, it was too wet or too dry, the oven was too hot, or there was insufficient baking.

Whole-Wheat Bread

Add nutrients ■ *Bake a more healthful loaf with fiber-rich whole-wheat flour, low-fat milk, and molasses instead of sugar.*

- Makes **18 slices** ● Preparation Time **15 minutes plus rising time**
  ● Cooking Time **30 minutes**

PER SLICE
Calories **105,** Saturated Fat **1g,**
Total Fat **2g,** Sodium **90mg,**
Cholesterol **1mg,** Protein **3g,**
Carbohydrate **19g,** Fiber **2g.**

---

2 cups whole-wheat flour

1 cup all-purpose flour

1 package (¹/₄ ounce) active dry yeast

1 tablespoon sugar

¹/₂ teaspoon salt

1 cup 1% low-fat milk plus extra for glazing

3 tablespoons molasses

3 tablespoons margarine or butter

Vegetable oil cooking spray

1 tablespoon wheat germ

KNEADING THE DOUGH

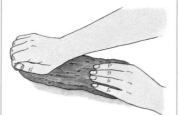

1 *Lightly flour a work surface. With one hand, hold one end of the dough firmly then pull the other end away from you until the dough is stretched out but not breaking.*

2 *Fold the far end of the dough back toward you, so that it doubles back onto itself. Continue the stretching and folding process for as long as directed in recipe.*

1 In a large bowl, combine the whole-wheat flour, all-purpose flour, yeast, sugar, and salt.

2 In a saucepan, heat 1 cup of milk with the molasses and margarine over low heat until very warm (120°–130°F).

3 Add the liquid gradually to the dry ingredients and mix until a soft dough forms.

4 Turn dough onto a lightly floured surface. Knead 10 minutes; shape into a ball. Lightly grease a bowl with vegetable oil spray and place dough in it.

5 Turn the dough to coat lightly with oil and prevent drying out. Cover with a towel and let rise in a warm place (80°–85°F) for 2 hours, until doubled in size.

6 Punch dough down, then transfer to a lightly floured surface. Roll out into a 12- by 8-inch rectangle, then roll up tightly from the shortest end.

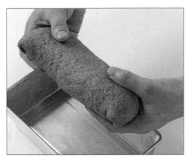

7 Pinch ends together and tuck underneath. Place in a lightly greased 9- by 5-inch loaf pan with the seam underneath.

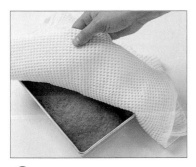

8 Cover the loaf pan with a towel and let rise in a warm place for about 1 hour or until doubled in size. Preheat the oven to 400°F.

9 Brush loaf with milk and sprinkle with wheat germ. Bake for 30 minutes, until golden and there is a hollow sound when tapped. Cool on a wire rack.

*Not only is home-baked **Whole-Wheat Bread** more nutritious than store-bought — it tastes better too.*

Raisin and Walnut Whole-Wheat Rolls

Molasses, with its strong, distinctive flavor, adds interest to these rolls. It is also rich in iron. Have fun experimenting with different ways to shape dough – it's simpler than you think!

- Makes **12 rolls**
- Preparation time **15 minutes** plus rising time
- Cooking time **15 minutes**

---

2 cups whole-wheat flour

1 cup all-purpose flour

1 package ($1/4$ ounce) active dry yeast

1 tablespoon sugar

$1/2$ teaspoon salt

$1/2$ cup chopped walnuts

$1/3$ cup seedless raisins

$11/4$ cup 1% low-fat milk plus 1 tablespoon for glazing

3 tablespoons molasses

3 tablespoons margarine or butter

Vegetable oil cooking spray

1 egg

1 Prepare the dough as in Steps 1 to 5 of the master recipe, adding the walnuts and raisins to the dried ingredients.

2 Punch down the dough and transfer to a lightly floured work surface. Cut dough into 12 pieces and shape into rolls according to your preference (see box, below, for a choice of alternative shapes).

3 Lightly grease a baking sheet with cooking spray and place rolls on it. Flatten them very slightly and cover with a towel. Let rise in a warm place about 30 minutes or until dough has doubled in size.

4 Preheat the oven to 400°F. Beat the egg and remaining milk together and brush over the tops of the rolls. Bake for 10 to 15 minutes or until they sound hollow when tapped on the bottom with the fingertips. Cool on a wire rack.

Raisin and Walnut Whole-Wheat Rolls are high in fiber, low in saturated fat.

PER ROLL
Calories **208**, Saturated Fat **1g**, Total Fat **7g**, Sodium **142mg**, Cholesterol **19mg**, Protein **6g**, Carbohydrate **32g**, Fiber **3g**.

FOUR WAYS TO SHAPE ROLLS

For a bow shape, roll the dough into a long rope. Gently tie a single knot, pulling the ends through without breaking the dough.

For a twist, roll the dough into a long rope and fold it in half. Gently twist halves over each other. On a baking tray, press the ends gently so that they stay closed.

For a snail shape, roll the dough into a long rope and wind it round into a spiral. Tuck the outer end of the dough underneath the spiral.

For a Parker House roll, shape the dough piece into a ball. Pat it into a round $1/4$ inch thick, brush with milk, and fold in half, pressing down firmly.

Multi-Grain Seeded Bread

As well as adding flavor to this loaf, the seeds are a good source of potassium, vitamin E, protein, and iron.

- Makes **18 slices**
- Preparation time **15 minutes** plus rising time
- Cooking time **30 minutes**

1¹/₂ cups whole-wheat flour

³/₄ cup all-purpose flour

1 package (¹/₄ ounce) active dry yeast

¹/₂ teaspoon salt

3 tablespoons each sunflower, sesame, and pumpkin seeds

¹/₃ cup rolled oats

1 cup water

2 tablespoons molasses

1 egg white

1% low-fat milk for glazing

---

1 In a large bowl, combine whole-wheat flour, all-purpose flour, yeast, and salt. In another bowl, mix the sunflower seeds, sesame seeds, pumpkin seeds, and oats.

2 In a saucepan, heat the water and molasses over low heat, until very warm (120°–130°F).

Sunflower, sesame, and pumpkin seeds add taste and texture.

3 Add the liquid to the flour mixture with the egg white and make the dough as in Steps 3 to 5 of the master recipe. Punch down dough and work in the seed mixture, reserving 2 tablespoons of the seeds. Shape and place in pan as in Steps 6 and 7 of the master recipe.

4 Cover the loaf pan with a towel and let rise in a warm place for about 1 hour or until doubled in size. Preheat oven to 350°F.

5 Brush the top of the loaf with milk and sprinkle with the reserved seed mixture. Bake for 30 minutes or until loaf sounds hollow when lightly tapped with the fingertips. Cool on a wire rack.

PER SLICE
Calories **95**, Saturated Fat **0g**, Total Fat **3g**, Sodium **67mg**, Cholesterol **0mg**, Protein **4g**, Carbohydrate **14g**, Fiber **2g**.

Poppyseed Loaf

- Makes **20 slices**
- Preparation time **15 minutes** plus rising time
- Cooking time **30 minutes**

---

2 cups all-purpose flour

1 cup whole-wheat flour

1 package (¹/₄ ounce) active dry yeast

1 teaspoon sugar

¹/₂ teaspoon salt

1 cup 1% low-fat milk

2 tablespoons margarine or butter

1 egg white

Vegetable oil cooking spray for greasing

1% low-fat milk for glazing

1 tablespoon poppy seeds

---

1 In a large bowl, combine the all-purpose flour, whole-wheat flour, yeast, sugar, and salt.

> **COOKING TIP**
> *Make sure you use your dry yeast by the expiration date on the package; otherwise it won't work well. Also, mix it with liquid that is only warm. If it is too hot, it will kill the yeast.*

2 In a saucepan, heat the milk and margarine over low heat until warm.

3 Add the milk gradually to the dry ingredients and mix until a dough begins to form. Add the egg white and mix to form a fairly firm dough.

4 Knead the dough and let rise as in Steps 4 and 5 of the master recipe.

5 Preheat oven to 400°F. Punch the dough down and shape into a large oval, tapering the ends. Place on a lightly greased baking sheet. With a sharp knife, cut 4 to 6 diagonal slashes on top of the loaf, brush with the milk, and sprinkle with the poppy seeds. Bake for 30 minutes or until loaf sounds hollow when tapped with the fingertips. Cool on a wire rack.

PER SLICE
Calories **85**, Saturated Fat **0g**, Total Fat **1g**, Sodium **74mg**, Cholesterol **1mg**, Protein **3g**, Carbohydrate **15g**, Fiber **1g**.

SHAPING AND SLASHING THE LOAF

1 *Shape the dough into a large oval, tapering the ends with your hands.*

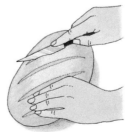

2 *Using a sharp knife, cut 4 to 6 diagonal slashes on the top of the loaf.*

Home-style Corn Bread

Reduce fat ▪ *Use low-fat milk and olive oil instead of butter. Grease the pan with vegetable oil cooking spray.*
Add fiber ▪ *Mix in fresh corn – it adds more vitamins.*

● Makes **16 pieces** ● Preparation Time **10 minutes** ● Cooking Time **20 minutes**

PER SQUARE
Calories **101**, Saturated Fat **1g**, Total Fat **4g**, Sodium **131mg**, Cholesterol **14mg**, Protein **2g**, Carbohydrate **14g**, Fiber **1g**.

Vegetable oil cooking spray
1 ear corn or $^2/_3$ cup frozen corn, thawed
1 cup all-purpose flour
$^3/_4$ cup cornmeal
1 tablespoon baking powder
$^1/_2$ teaspoon salt
$^2/_3$ cup 1% low-fat milk
$^1/_4$ cup olive or canola oil
1 egg
1 tablespoon honey

1 Preheat oven to 425°F. Lightly grease an 8" x 8" x 2" baking pan with vegetable oil spray. Using a sharp knife, remove corn kernels (page 174). Set aside.

2 In a medium bowl, thoroughly mix the all-purpose flour, cornmeal, baking powder, and salt.

3 In a small bowl, combine the corn, milk, oil, egg, and honey, and beat well to mix.

*Bursting with the flavor of sweet fresh corn – **Home-style Corn Bread**.*

4 Pour the egg mixture into the bowl with the flour and cornmeal. Quickly and thoroughly mix together.

5 Pour the batter into the prepared baking pan, scraping any batter off sides of bowl into the pan. Spread the batter evenly with a spatula.

6 Bake for 20 to 25 minutes or until lightly browned and a knife inserted in the center comes out clean. Cut into 1³/₄-inch squares and serve at once.

Two-Cheese Corn Bread

- Makes **16 pieces**
- Preparation time **15 minutes**
- Cooking time **20 minutes**

Vegetable oil cooking spray
1 cup all-purpose flour
³/₄ cup cornmeal
¹/₄ cup grated Parmesan cheese
¹/₄ cup shredded low-fat Cheddar or Monterey Jack cheese
1 tablespoon baking powder
¹/₂ teaspoon salt
²/₃ cup 1% low-fat milk
¹/₄ cup olive or canola oil
1 egg
1 tablespoon honey

1 Preheat oven to 425°F. Lightly grease an 8" x 8" x 2" baking pan with vegetable oil spray.

2 In a medium bowl, thoroughly mix the all-purpose flour, cornmeal, Parmesan cheese, Cheddar cheese, baking powder, and salt.

3 In a small bowl, combine the milk, oil, egg, and honey and beat well to mix.

4 Pour the egg mixture into the bowl with the flour and cornmeal. Quickly and thoroughly mix together.

5 Pour the batter into the prepared baking pan, scraping any batter off the sides of the bowl into the pan. Spread the batter evenly with a spatula.

6 Bake for 20 to 25 minutes or until lightly browned and a knife inserted in the center comes out clean. Cut into 1³/₄-inch squares and serve at once.

PER SQUARE
Calories **108**, Saturated Fat **1g**, Total Fat **5g**, Sodium **173mg**, Cholesterol **16mg**, Protein **3g**, Carbohydrate **13g**, Fiber **1g**.

Ham and Tomato Corn Bread

- Makes **16 pieces**
- Preparation time **15 minutes**
- Cooking time **20 minutes**

Vegetable oil cooking spray
1 cup all-purpose flour
³/₄ cup cornmeal
1 tablespoon baking powder
¹/₂ teaspoon salt
4 ounces reduced-sodium, reduced-fat ham, chopped
¹/₃ cup sun-dried tomatoes in oil, drained and chopped, or 1 plum tomato, seeded and chopped
2 tablespoons chopped fresh chives
²/₃ cup 1% low-fat milk
¹/₄ cup olive or canola oil
1 egg
1 tablespoon honey

1 Preheat the oven to 425°F. Lightly grease an 8" x 8" x 2" baking pan with vegetable oil spray.

2 In a medium bowl, thoroughly mix the all-purpose flour, cornmeal, baking powder, salt, ham, sun-dried tomatoes, and chives.

3 In a small bowl, combine the milk, oil, egg, and honey and beat well to mix.

4 Pour the egg mixture into the bowl with the flour and cornmeal. Quickly and thoroughly mix together.

5 Pour the batter into the prepared baking pan. Spread the batter evenly with a spatula.

6 Bake for 20 to 25 minutes or until lightly browned and a knife inserted in the center comes out clean. Cut into 1³/₄-inch squares and serve at once.

PER SQUARE
Calories **109**, Saturated Fat **1g**, Total Fat **4g**, Sodium **192mg**, Cholesterol **17mg**, Protein **4g**, Carbohydrate **14g**, Fiber **1g**.

Golden Light Biscuits

Reduce fat ▪ *For tender, flaky biscuits, use buttermilk or nonfat yogurt instead of shortening. In addition to cutting down on the fat, you will increase the protein to 3 grams per biscuit.*

Add fiber ▪ *Mix in wheat germ and whole-wheat flour.*

● Makes **16 biscuits** ● Preparation Time **15 minutes** ● Cooking Time **12 minutes**

PER BISCUIT
Calories **67**, Saturated Fat **0g**, Total Fat **0g**, Sodium **127mg**, Cholesterol **0mg**, Protein **3g**, Carbohydrate **13g**, Fiber **1g**.

1½ cups all-purpose flour
½ cup whole-wheat flour
2 tablespoons wheat germ
2 teaspoons baking powder
½ teaspoon salt

¼ teaspoon baking soda
1 cup plain nonfat yogurt or
   ¾ cup buttermilk
1% low-fat milk for glazing

1 Preheat oven to 450°F. In a large bowl, mix together the all-purpose flour, whole-wheat flour, wheat germ, baking powder, salt, and baking soda.

2 Add the yogurt to the bowl and mix with a fork until the mixture holds together and forms a soft dough that leaves the sides of the bowl.

Golden Light Biscuits can be served with ham, as at left, topped with fruit preserves, or as an accompaniment to soups, stews, meat, and poultry.

3 On a lightly floured work surface, knead the dough 4 to 6 times. Roll out the dough to ¹/₂-inch thickness. Flour a 2-inch round cutter and cut out biscuits from the dough, using a firm downward action, without twisting the cutter.

4 Place the biscuits 1 inch apart on a lightly greased baking sheet. Press the dough trimmings together without kneading, then roll and cut out biscuits until all the dough is used. Brush the tops of the biscuits with low-fat milk and bake for 10 to 12 minutes or until golden.

Tomato Basil Biscuits

- Makes **22 biscuits**
- Preparation time **20 minutes**
- Cooking time **12 minutes**

1¹/₂ cups all-purpose flour

¹/₂ cup whole-wheat flour

2 tablespoons wheat germ

4 teaspoons baking powder

¹/₂ teaspoon salt

¹/₈ teaspoon black pepper

1 plum tomato, seeded and finely chopped

2 tablespoons chopped fresh basil

2 teaspoons tomato paste

1 cup plain nonfat yogurt or ³/₄ cup buttermilk

1% low-fat milk for glazing

1 Preheat the oven to 450°F. In a large bowl, mix together the all-purpose flour, whole-wheat flour, wheat germ, baking powder, salt, and pepper.

2 In a bowl, mix the tomato, basil, and tomato paste with the yogurt, then add to the flour mixture. Mix with a fork until the mixture holds together and forms a soft dough that leaves the sides of the bowl.

3 Roll out the dough as in Step 3 of the master recipe.

4 Glaze and bake the biscuits as in Step 4 of the master recipe.

PER BISCUIT
Calories **51**, Saturated Fat **0g**, Total Fat **0g**, Sodium **114mg**, Cholesterol **0mg**, Protein **2g**, Carbohydrate **10g**, Fiber **1g**.

Oatmeal and Raisin Biscuits

- Makes **20 biscuits**
- Preparation time **15 minutes**
- Cooking time **12 minutes**

1¹/₂ cups all-purpose flour

¹/₂ cup rolled oats plus 2 teaspoons for sprinkling

¹/₃ cup raisins

2 teaspoons baking powder

¹/₂ teaspoon baking soda

¹/₄ teaspoon salt

1 cup plain nonfat yogurt or ³/₄ cup buttermilk

1 Preheat the oven to 450°F. In a large bowl, mix together the all-purpose flour, ¹/₂ cup oats, raisins, baking powder, baking soda, and salt.

2 Add the yogurt to the bowl and mix with a fork until the mixture holds together and forms a soft dough that leaves the sides of the bowl.

3 Roll out the dough as in Step 3 of the master recipe.

4 Bake the biscuits as in Step 4 of the master recipe, sprinkling the tops of the biscuits with the remaining oats.

PER BISCUIT
Calories **57**, Saturated Fat **0g**, Total Fat **0g**, Sodium **85mg**, Cholesterol **0mg**, Protein **2g**, Carbohydrate **12g**, Fiber **1g**.

Herb and Cheese Biscuits

- Makes **20 biscuits**
- Preparation time **20 minutes**
- Cooking time **12 minutes**

1¹/₂ cups all-purpose flour

¹/₂ cup whole-wheat flour

¹/₂ cup shredded low-fat Cheddar cheese plus 1 tablespoon for sprinkling

1 tablespoon each chopped fresh chives and parsley

2 teaspoons baking powder

¹/₂ teaspoon salt

¹/₄ teaspoon baking soda

1 cup plain nonfat yogurt or ³/₄ cup buttermilk

1 Preheat the oven to 450°F. In a large bowl, mix together the all-purpose flour, whole-wheat flour, ¹/₂ cup cheese, herbs, baking powder, salt, and baking soda .

2 Add the yogurt to the bowl and mix with a fork until the mixture holds together and forms a soft dough that leaves the sides of the bowl.

3 Roll out the dough as in Step 3 of the master recipe.

4 Sprinkle the biscuits with remaining cheese and bake as in Step 4 of the master recipe.

PER BISCUIT
Calories **69**, Saturated Fat **0g**, Total Fat **1g**, Sodium **126mg**, Cholesterol **2mg**, Protein **3g**, Carbohydrate **10g**, Fiber **3g**.

Carrot and Zucchini Bread

Reduce fat ▪ *Low-fat yogurt makes an excellent substitute for butter, and it keeps the bread moist. Egg whites can replace one of the whole eggs.*

Add fiber ▪ *Whole-wheat flour, carrot, and nuts are all good sources of fiber. The carrot adds sweetness, so you need less sugar.*

• Serves **8** • Preparation Time **15 minutes** • Cooking Time **40 minutes**

PER SLICE
Calories **151**, Saturated Fat **0g**,
Total Fat **3g**, Sodium **173mg**,
Cholesterol **24mg**, Protein **6g**,
Carbohydrate **26g**, Fiber **2g**.

Vegetable oil cooking spray

1 cup all-purpose flour

¹/₂ cup whole-wheat flour

2 tablespoons brown sugar

2 teaspoons baking powder

¹/₄ teaspoon salt

1 teaspoon vanilla extract

1 egg

2 egg whites

¹/₂ cup each shredded carrot
and zucchini

¹/₃ cup plain nonfat yogurt

¹/₄ cup walnuts, chopped

1 tablespoon honey

2 teaspoons finely grated
lemon zest

1 Preheat oven to 350°F. Lightly grease an 8¹/₂- by 4¹/₂-inch loaf pan with vegetable oil cooking spray.

2 In a large bowl, mix the all-purpose flour, whole-wheat flour, brown sugar, baking powder, and salt.

3 In a medium bowl, lightly beat the vanilla extract with the egg and egg whites. Stir in the carrot, zucchini, yogurt, walnuts, honey, and lemon zest.

4 Add the egg and zucchini mixture to the flour mixture and beat quickly until just mixed.

5 Transfer the batter to the prepared loaf pan and spread evenly with a spatula.

6 Bake the bread for 35 to 40 minutes or until a fine skewer or toothpick inserted in the center comes out clean and dry.

*It is still possible to indulge and eat a sweet bread if you choose high-fiber low-fat **Carrot and Zucchini Bread**.*
Enjoy it with a cup of coffee or tea.

Lemon-Walnut Bread

You can extract more juice from lemons if you heat them first. Place the whole lemons in the microwave and heat them on high for 30 seconds. Then squeeze the juice as usual.

- Serves **8**
- Preparation time **15 minutes**
- Cooking time **30 minutes**

Vegetable oil cooking spray

1 cup all-purpose flour

$^1/_2$ cup whole-wheat flour

2 tablespoons brown sugar

2 teaspoons baking powder

$^1/_2$ teaspoon baking soda

$^1/_2$ teaspoon salt

1 teaspoon vanilla extract

1 egg

2 egg whites

$^1/_3$ cup plain nonfat yogurt

$^1/_4$ cup coarsely chopped walnuts

2 tablespoons honey

2 teaspoons finely grated
  lemon zest

6 tablespoons lemon juice

---

1 Preheat oven to 350°F. Lightly grease an 8$^1/_2$- by 4$^1/_2$-inch loaf pan with cooking spray. In a large bowl, mix both flours, brown sugar, baking powder, baking soda, and salt.

2 In a medium bowl, lightly beat the vanilla extract with the egg and egg whites. Stir in yogurt, walnuts, 1 tablespoon honey, 1 teaspoon lemon zest, and 3 tablespoons lemon juice. Add to the flour mixture and beat quickly until just mixed.

3 Transfer the batter to the prepared loaf pan and spread evenly with a spatula.

4 Bake the bread for about 30 minutes or until a fine skewer or toothpick inserted in the center comes out clean and dry.

5 Prepare syrup: In a saucepan, heat the remaining lemon zest, juice, and honey 3 to 4 minutes, until the zest is tender and the syrup is thick.

6 Turn the bread out of the pan. While still warm, poke some holes in the top of the bread with a skewer and brush the lemon syrup over the top. Repeat until all the syrup is used.

PER SLICE
Calories **158**, Saturated Fat **0g**, Total Fat **3g**, Sodium **288mg**, Cholesterol **27mg**, Protein **5g**, Carbohydrate **28g**, Fiber **2g**.

The flavors of lemon and walnuts combine particularly well.

Blueberry Buttermilk Muffins

These also taste great made with raspberries in place of blueberries. To help raspberries keep their shape, freeze them before adding to batter.

- Makes **10**
- Preparation time **15 minutes**
- Cooking time **15 minutes**

Vegetable oil cooking spray

1 cup all-purpose flour

$^3/_4$ cup whole-wheat flour

2 tablespoons brown sugar

1 teaspoon baking powder

$^1/_4$ teaspoon baking soda

Pinch of salt

1 cup plain nonfat yogurt

2 egg whites

1 teaspoon vanilla extract

$^3/_4$ cup blueberries, fresh or
  frozen and thawed

Finely grated zest of 1 lemon

---

1 Preheat oven to 400°F. Lightly grease ten 2$^1/_2$-inch muffin cups with the vegetable oil cooking spray.

2 In a large bowl, mix the all-purpose flour, whole-wheat flour, brown sugar, baking powder, baking soda, and salt.

3 In a small bowl, beat together the yogurt, egg whites, and vanilla extract. Add to the flour mixture and beat quickly until just mixed. Gently fold the blueberries and lemon zest into the batter.

4 Spoon the batter into the prepared muffin cups. Bake for 15 minutes or until a fine skewer or toothpick inserted into the center of one of the muffins comes out clean and dry.

Cultivated blueberries are in markets most of the year.

PER MUFFIN
Calories **109** Saturated Fat **0g**, Total Fat **0g**, Sodium **93mg**, Cholesterol **0mg**, Protein **5g**, Carbohydrate **22g**, Fiber **2g**.

REHEATING MUFFINS

To recapture that just-out-of-the-oven, fresh-baked taste — wrap the muffins in foil and reheat in a 400 °F oven for 10 to 15 minutes.

Apple Oatmeal Muffins

Apples, raisins, whole-wheat flour, and oats provide all-important fiber in a delicious package. Serve a batch for breakfast, and you're sure to have a healthy start to the day.

- Makes **10**
- Preparation time **15 minutes**
- Cooking time **15 minutes**

Vegetable oil cooking spray

1 cup all-purpose flour

³/₄ cup whole-wheat flour

3 tablespoons rolled oats

3 tablespoons brown sugar

1 teaspoon baking powder

¹/₄ teaspoon baking soda

Pinch of salt

1 cup plain nonfat yogurt

2 egg whites

1 teaspoon vanilla extract

1 large apple, peeled, cored, and diced

1 teaspoon ground cinnamon

¹/₄ cup raisins

1 Preheat the oven to 400°F. Lightly grease ten 2¹/₂-inch muffin cups with the vegetable oil cooking spray.

2 In a large bowl, mix the all-purpose flour, whole-wheat flour, 2 tablespoons rolled oats, 2 tablespoons brown sugar, baking powder, baking soda, and salt.

3 In a small bowl, beat together the yogurt, egg whites, and vanilla extract. Add to the flour mixture and beat quickly until just mixed. In a small bowl, mix the remaining sugar with the apple, cinnamon, and raisins, then quickly fold into the batter.

4 Spoon the batter into the prepared muffin cups. Sprinkle with the remaining oats.

5 Bake for 15 minutes or until a fine skewer or toothpick inserted in the center of one of the muffins comes out clean and dry.

PER MUFFIN
Calories **139**, Saturated Fat **0g**, Total Fat **1g**, Sodium **94mg**, Cholesterol **0mg**, Protein **5g**, Carbohydrate **30g**, Fiber **2g**.

BAKING MUFFINS

1 *Make sure that the muffin cups are filled only about two-thirds full, as the mixture will rise during baking.*

2 *Remove the muffins immediately after they have finished baking, or they will become slightly soggy. If necessary, loosen the edges with a spatula.*

*These almost fat-free **Apple Oatmeal Muffins** make a delightful and healthy treat at any time of day.*

Cinnamon Raisin Rolls

Reduce fat ■ *To trim the calories from these delectable sweet rolls, use low-fat milk, egg whites, and less sugar. Mix in whole-wheat flour for fiber.*

● Makes **32** rolls ● Preparation Time **30** minutes plus rising time ● Cooking Time **15** minutes

PER ROLL
Calories **130**, Saturated Fat **0g**,
Total Fat **2g**, Sodium **62mg**,
Cholesterol **7mg**, Protein **4g**,
Carbohydrate **24g**, Fiber **2g**.

4¹/₂ cups all-purpose flour
2 cups whole-wheat flour
¹/₄ cup sugar
1 package (¹/₄ ounce) active dry yeast
1 teaspoon ground cinnamon
¹/₂ teaspoon salt

2 cups 1% low-fat milk, plus extra for glazing
¹/₄ cup margarine or butter
1 egg plus 2 egg whites
¹/₂ cup raisins
¹/₄ cup confectioners sugar
1 tablespoon lemon juice

1 In a bowl, combine both flours, sugar, yeast, cinnamon, and salt. In a saucepan, slowly heat the milk and margarine over low heat until very warm.

2 Remove from the heat and beat into dry ingredients until thoroughly mixed. Whisk the egg and egg whites together and stir into the dough with the raisins.

3 Continue mixing for 2 to 3 minutes or until the dough comes away from the sides of the bowl.

Cinnamon Raisin Rolls *– wholesome tea-time treats with an exciting lemon glaze.*

4 Shape dough into a ball and turn out onto a floured work surface. To knead, lift one edge and fold it toward center, pressing down with the other hand.

7 Turn out dough onto a lightly floured surface. Push your hand into center of dough, then pull edges to center and turn over. Divide evenly into 32 pieces.

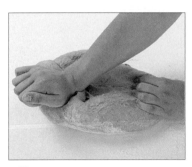

5 Give dough a quarter turn and repeat folding and pressing. Knead for 8 to 10 minutes or until dough is smooth, elastic, and does not stick to the surface.

8 Preheat oven to 350°F. To shape, roll each piece into a 6-inch rope. Tie each into a knot. Place on 3 greased baking sheets, cover, and let rise until doubled.

6 Place dough in a lightly greased bowl and turn. Cover loosely with plastic wrap and a towel. Leave in a warm place for 2 hours or until doubled in size.

9 Brush with milk. Bake 15 minutes or until rolls are golden and sound hollow when tapped. Blend sugar and lemon juice; brush on warm rolls.

Honey Pecan Rolls

- Makes **32 rolls**
- Preparation time **30 minutes** plus rising time
- Cooking time **20 minutes**

4¹/₂ cups all-purpose flour
2 cups whole-wheat flour
¹/₄ cup brown sugar
1 package (¹/₄ ounce) active dry yeast
¹/₂ teaspoon salt
2 cups 1% low-fat milk
1 egg
2 egg whites
¹/₂ cup chopped pecans, toasted
3 tablespoons honey

1 Prepare and bake dough as in Steps 1 to 7 of the master recipe, omitting cinnamon, margarine, and raisins. Add pecans and 1 tablespoon honey to the dough in Step 2.

2 Shape dough into rounds or as desired. (For different shapes of rolls, see page 308.)

3 Preheat the oven to 375°F. Place rolls on a lightly greased baking sheet, cover, and let rise until doubled in size, about 1 hour.

4 Bake rolls for 20 minutes or until they are golden brown and sound hollow when tapped. In a saucepan, warm remaining 2 tablespoons honey and brush on rolls while they are still warm.

PER ROLL
Calories **123**, Saturated Fat **0g**, Total Fat **2g**, Sodium **48mg**, Cholesterol **7mg**, Protein **4g**, Carbohydrate **23g**, Fiber **2g**.

Sour Cream Coffee Cake

- Serves **8**
- Preparation time **30 minutes** plus rising time
- Cooking time **25 minutes**

1 cup all-purpose flour
¹/₄ cup whole-wheat flour
1 tablespoon sugar
2 teaspoons active dry yeast
¹/₄ teaspoon salt
¹/₄ cup 1% low-fat milk
1 tablespoon margarine or butter
1 egg
1 egg white
¹/₄ cup low-fat sour cream
1 tablespoon brown sugar
1 tablespoon finely chopped walnuts

1 Make the dough as in Steps 1 to 5 of the master recipe, omitting cinnamon and raisins. Add low-fat sour cream to the dough in Step 2.

2 Press the dough into a lightly greased 9-inch cake pan. Leave to rise for 2¹/₂ hours or until nearly tripled in size.

3 While the dough is rising, preheat the oven to 375°F. Press the dough down lightly and sprinkle the top with the sugar and walnuts. Bake for 25 minutes or until golden brown. If the nuts brown too quickly, cover top of cake with aluminum foil.

PER SERVING
Calories **125**, Saturated Fat **1g**, Total Fat **3g**, Sodium **109mg**, Cholesterol **28mg**, Protein **4g**, Carbohydrate **20g**, Fiber **1g**.

Whole-Grain Pancakes

Add nutrients ▪ *For delicious high-fiber pancakes, mix in rolled oats, wheat germ, and whole-wheat flour. To lower the fat, use yogurt and buttermilk.*

● Makes **12** pancakes ● Preparation Time **10** minutes ● Cooking Time **15** minutes

PER PANCAKE
Calories **86**, Saturated Fat **0g**,
Total Fat **1g**, Sodium **131mg**,
Cholesterol **1mg**, Protein **5g**,
Carbohydrate **16g**, Fiber **3g**.

1 cup whole-wheat flour	1 cup 1% low-fat milk
¼ cup rolled oats	1¼ cups plain nonfat yogurt
1 tablespoon toasted wheat germ	2 egg whites
2 tablespoons brown sugar	Vegetable oil cooking spray
2 teaspoons baking powder	2 cups raspberries or blueberries
¼ teaspoon salt	

1 In a large bowl, mix the flour, oats, wheat germ, sugar, baking powder, and salt.

2 In another bowl, beat milk and ½ cup yogurt with the egg whites until mixed. Add to flour mixture and beat quickly just to moisten dry ingredients.

3 Spray a nonstick skillet with cooking spray and heat until hot. *Do not use cooking spray near flame.*

Fresh raspberries and nonfat yogurt make a glorious topping for **Whole-Grain Pancakes.**

4 Measure ¹/₄ cup of batter for each pancake and pour into the hot skillet, making 4 pancakes at the same time.

5 When bubbles show on the top, lift the pancakes with a spatula. If browned underneath, turn over and cook until the other side is golden brown.

6 Transfer the pancakes to a heated platter and serve with raspberries and remaining yogurt. If not serving at once, cover and keep warm in a low oven.

Buttermilk Blueberry Pancakes

- Makes **12 pancakes**
- Preparation time **10 minutes**
- Cooking time **15 minutes**

1 cup whole-wheat flour
¹/₄ cup rolled oats
1 tablespoon toasted wheat germ
2 tablespoons brown sugar
2 teaspoons baking powder
¹/₄ teaspoon salt
1 cup buttermilk
1¹/₄ cup plain nonfat yogurt
2 egg whites
1 cup blueberries, fresh or frozen and thawed
1 teaspoon honey

1 In a large bowl, mix all the dry ingredients together as in Step 1 of the master recipe.

2 In another bowl, beat buttermilk, ¹/₂ cup yogurt, and egg whites until mixed. Add to flour mixture and beat quickly just to moisten. Stir in blueberries.

3 Cook the pancakes as in Steps 3, 4, and 5 of the master recipe.

4 Serve on a heated platter. Mix honey with remaining yogurt and serve with pancakes. If not serving at once, cover pancakes and keep warm in a low oven.

PER PANCAKE
Calories **84**, Saturated Fat **0g**, Total Fat **1g**, Sodium **143mg**, Cholesterol **1mg**, Protein **5g**, Carbohydrate **16g**, Fiber **2g**.

Strawberry Bran Waffles

- Makes **12 waffles**
- Preparation time **15 minutes**
- Cooking time **15 minutes**

1 cup whole-wheat flour
¹/₂ cup bran cereal flakes
1 teaspoon baking powder
¹/₄ teaspoon salt
1 cup 1% low-fat milk
¹/₂ cup low-fat sour cream
Honey
2 egg whites
2 cups sliced strawberries

1 Prepare waffle maker according to the manufacturer's directions. In a large bowl, combine flour, cereal, baking powder, and salt.

2 Make a hole in center of dry ingredients and pour in milk, sour cream, and 1 teaspoon honey. Beat a few times to mix well.

3 Whip the egg whites until stiff peaks form and fold them into the batter until just blended.

4 Pour enough batter into center of waffle maker to cover two-thirds of grid. Close lid and bake 9 minutes or until lid lifts easily.

5 Remove baked waffles with a fork and serve with sliced strawberries and honey to taste.

PER WAFFLE
Calories **75**, Saturated Fat **1g**, Total Fat **1g**, Sodium **119mg**, Cholesterol **2mg**, Protein **4g**, Carbohydrate **14g**, Fiber **3g**.

Date and Pecan Waffles

- Makes **12 waffles**
- Preparation time **15 minutes**
- Cooking time **15 minutes**

1 cup whole-wheat flour
¹/₄ cup rolled oats
1 tablespoon toasted wheat germ
2 tablespoons brown sugar
2 teaspoons baking powder
¹/₄ teaspoon salt
1 cup 1% low-fat milk
¹/₂ cup plain nonfat yogurt
¹/₄ cup chopped dates
¹/₄ cup chopped pecans
2 egg whites
Maple syrup, warmed

1 Prepare waffle maker according to the manufacturer's directions. In a large bowl, combine flour, oats, wheat germ, sugar, baking powder, and salt.

2 Make a hole in the center of the dry ingredients and pour in milk and yogurt. Beat to mix thoroughly. Stir in dates and pecans.

3 Whip egg whites until stiff peaks form and gently fold into batter. Pour enough batter into center of waffle maker to cover two-thirds of grid. Close lid; bake 5 minutes or until lid lifts easily.

4 Remove baked waffles with a fork and serve with maple syrup.

PER WAFFLE
Calories **93**, Saturated Fat **0g**, Total Fat **2g**, Sodium **121mg**, Cholesterol **1mg**, Protein **4g**, Carbohydrate **16g**, Fiber **2g**.

DESSERTS

A meal just isn't the same without dessert. And anyone who grew up on old-fashioned pies and puddings finds it difficult to give them up. The good news is that you don't have to. Eat smaller servings, use the recipes in **The How-To Book of Healthy Cooking,** *and you can continue to enjoy desserts. These recipes emphasise wholesome ingredients such as fruit, yogurt, and even vegetables, so you're getting more protein and vitamins — and less sugar. Where possible, whole-wheat flour is used to add fiber. You'll find a delicious dessert for every occasion — hot summer nights, cold winter evenings, or when company's coming. Best of all, you'll know that these desserts are healthful as well as delicious.*

Cranberry Maple Sauce with Apples, page 341

B aking is a science as much as an art, so making a more healthful dessert can be tricky. Pastry needs butter if it is to be light and flaky, while custards require eggs if they are to set properly. However, if you begin with wholesome fresh ingredients and aim at simply reducing fat and sugar – as opposed to cutting them out completely – you can make desserts that deliver nutritional value and still satisfy your sweet tooth.

A healthful start

The best way to create a nutritious dessert is to begin with fresh fruit. Just one apple provides 17% of your daily requirement for fiber; cantaloupe is a superb source of beta carotene; and strawberries deliver as much vitamin C as citrus fruits.

Unbleached flour is used in most recipes because it contains a little more protein, fiber, and vitamins than bleached and it combines nicely with whole-wheat flour. Wheat germ can be added for vitamins B and E, rolled oats for soluble fiber, and cornmeal for protein and fiber. These whole-grain products also give a slightly nuttier flavor and more texture. However, some of the tart crusts require the softer all-purpose flour, which yields a lighter flakier crust.

Reducing sugar

Refined sugar consists of empty calories and has no nutritional benefit. Therefore you really do need to cut back on the total amount of sweetener. The recipes that follow show you how to add flavor instead of sweetness with nuts, spices, vanilla, and fruit extracts. In addition, there are sugar substitutes that add richer shadings of flavor and, in some cases, more nutritional value.

Apple juice works well in fruit desserts, such as pies and cobblers. For the best nutritional value, buy a juice that has been fortified with vitamin C.

Maple syrup has a light, caramel flavor that marries well with fruit and even some vegetables like acorn squash. Buy pure maple syrup rather than imitation, which is a blend of corn syrup and artificial flavors.

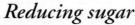

Brown sugar is refined white sugar colored with molasses. It adds a rounder, fuller, slightly burned flavor that is quite delicious. Use it in moderation.

Honey has a few trace minerals; otherwise it is nutritionally almost equivalent to refined sugar. However, it is a bit sweeter, so you get more sweetness with fewer calories. Honey also holds moisture well, so baked products keep longer.

Molasses is an excellent source of iron and has a dark, rich flavor that works particularly well in hearty desserts like steamed puddings.

Orange juice adds a citrus flavor to fruit desserts, as well as sweetness. It is an excellent source of vitamin C and folic acid.

WHY YOU SHOULD EAT FRESH FRUIT

Delicious fruit is an excellent source of vitamin C, fiber, and beta carotene (see the chart on page 11 for the health benefits of each). It is also an excellent source of potassium, which helps keep blood pressure low.

3½-ounce serving	Calories	Carbohydrate g	Fiber g	Vitamin A IU	Vitamin C mg	Potassium mg
Apple	56	14	1.0	90	7	110
Apricot	51	13	0.6	2,700	10	281
Blueberries	62	15	1.5	100	14	81
Cherries, sweet	70	17.5	0.5	110	10	191
Cranberries	46	11	1.5	40	11	82
Grapes	69	16	0.6	100	4	158
Mango	66	17	1.0	4,800	35	189
Melon, cantaloupe	30	7.5	0.3	3,400	33	251
Orange	49	12	0.5	200	50	200
Peach	38	10	0.6	1,330	7	202
Pear	61	15	1.5	20	4	130
Pineapple	52	14	0.5	70	17	146
Raisins	289	77	1.0	20	1	763
Raspberries	57	14	3.0	130	25	168
Strawberries	37	8.5	1.0	60	59	164

Reducing fat

Many desserts, puddings in particular, require milk or cream; however, low-fat milk, buttermilk, sour cream, and yogurt work just as well with considerably less saturated fat. Evaporated skim milk makes an especially good substitute for cream because it has a thick, creamy consistency. And don't forget – all of these milk products add protein and calcium too. You can substitute egg whites for whole eggs in most dessert recipes; custards and some sauces may need a yolk or two for thickening. Finally, instead of topping desserts with ice cream, use frozen yogurt, sherbet, or a creamy low-fat custard sauce (see box below).

Margarine versus butter

Pie crusts need shortening to make them tender and flaky, while cakes need a little fat if they are to rise. In some recipes, you can use low-fat cream cheese, yogurt, or olive oil with good results. However, the lighter pie crusts just don't taste right without a little margarine or butter. Butter in particular adds an exquisite sweet, light flavor to pastries. So a few of these recipes call for several tablespoons of margarine or butter to ensure pleasing texture and taste.

Whether you use margarine or butter is a matter of choice. The disadvantage of using margarine is that it contains trans-fatty acids, which act like saturated fats in the body. However, butter is higher in saturated fat than margarine, so it's a toss-up.

If you prefer to use reduced-fat margarines, make sure they have at least 70% fat. The very low reduced-fat margarines don't work well in baking or cooking, and they don't taste as good as butter or margarine. If in doubt, check the label. Expert bakers usually recommend sweet butter for pastries because it has no salt, which means it has a shorter shelf life and should be fresher.

LOW-FAT CUSTARD SAUCE

Serve this luscious topping over fresh berries, pound cake, fruit compotes, cakes, pies, and cobblers instead of ice cream.

In a saucepan, combine 2 cups 1% low-fat milk, 2 tablespoons sugar, 1 egg yolk, and 1 tablespoon cornstarch. Whisk over moderately low heat about 10 minutes, until smooth and thickened. Stir in 1 tablespoon vanilla extract. Serves 4.

PER ¹/₂ CUP SERVING
Calories **96**, Saturated Fat **1g**, Total Fat **3g**, Sodium **63mg**, Cholesterol **58mg**, Protein **5g**, Carbohydrate **14g**, Fiber **0g**.

PERFECT BAKING EVERY TIME

Pie-making tips

◆ Use very cold water to make pastry dough – ice water is even better. Just pour the water into a glass over ice cubes and measure from there.

◆ For extra-light pastry, add a little lemon juice to the cold water.

◆ Chill the rolling pin and board.

◆ Chill pastry in the refrigerator before rolling.

◆ Use a marble slab or an acrylic board for rolling out pastry.

◆ Use as little flour as possible when rolling dough – too much toughens it.

◆ Handle dough as little as possible.

◆ Nonstick, dark metal, and ovenproof glass pans are better for baking pastry because they absorb heat; bright pans reflect it. Crusts will brown faster and more evenly.

Cake-making tips

◆ Make sure your oven temperature is accurate – check with an oven thermometer.

◆ Preheat the oven for 15 minutes before baking.

◆ To blend better and create a higher, lighter cake, make sure your ingredients are at room temperature.

◆ For a light cake, beat the butter or shortening thoroughly.

◆ Beat egg whites to high peaks – see illustration on page 335.

◆ Line pans with wax paper to prevent sticking.

◆ Place cakes in the center of the oven – they will bake more evenly.

◆ To tell when a cake is cooked, press the top lightly – if done, the cake will spring back and the sides will have shrunk away from the pan.

Walnut-Raisin Pudding

Cooking technique ■ *Puddings need eggs to help them set. However, you can limit the yolks to one and use more high-protein whites. Bake the pudding in a water bath, or "bain-marie," to keep it from cooking too fast and curdling.*

Add fiber ■ *Mix in rice, fruit, nuts, or bread – you'll increase flavor and vitamins.*

● Serves 4 ● Preparation Time **12 minutes** ● Cooking Time **30–35 minutes**

PER SERVING
Calories **162**, Saturated Fat **1g**, Total Fat **5g**, Sodium **46mg**, Cholesterol **53mg**, Protein **6g**, Carbohydrate **24g**, Fiber **1g**.

¹/₂ cup orange juice	¹/₄ cup raisins
1 egg yolk	¹/₄ cup chopped walnuts, toasted
1 teaspoon honey	
1 teaspoon vanilla extract	3 egg whites
²/₃ cup cooked rice	Vegetable oil cooking spray

1 Preheat oven to 325°F. In a large mixing bowl, mix the orange juice with the egg yolk, honey, and vanilla extract.

2 Stir in the cooked rice, raisins, and toasted walnuts. In another bowl, whip the egg whites until soft peaks form, then carefully fold into the mixture with a large metal spoon.

Warm and soothing, ***Walnut-Raisin Pudding*** *is perfect on a cold winter night.*

3 Pour into 4 custard dishes that have been lightly coated with vegetable oil spray or lightly greased with vegetable oil.

4 Place custard dishes in a 13" x 9" x 2" baking pan and carefully add boiling water to the baking pan to a depth of 1 inch. Bake, uncovered, for 30 to 35 minutes or until just set.

COOKING TIP
Check the water in the bain-marie during cooking and fill up as necessary to prevent it from boiling away.

Chocolate and Orange Bread Pudding

- Serves **4**
- Preparation Time **12 minutes**
- Cooking Time **35–40 minutes**

$^1/_2$ cup orange juice

1 egg yolk

1 teaspoon honey

1 teaspoon vanilla extract

1 tablespoon finely grated orange zest

2 teaspoons unsweetened cocoa powder

3 egg whites

Vegetable oil cooking spray

4 slices oatmeal bread, crusts removed, then cubed

1 Preheat oven to 325°F. In a large mixing bowl, mix the orange juice, egg yolk, honey, vanilla extract, and orange zest.

2 Sieve the cocoa through a fine sieve and fold into the egg yolk mixture. Whip egg whites until stiff peaks form and, using a large metal spoon, carefully fold in.

3 Lightly coat a 1-quart casserole with vegetable oil spray and add bread cubes. Pour egg mixture into casserole.

4 Stand casserole in a baking pan as in Step 4 of the master recipe and bake 35 to 40 minutes or until golden brown. Serve hot.

PER SERVING
Calories **128**, Saturated Fat **1g**, Total Fat **3g**, Sodium **199mg**, Cholesterol **53mg**, Protein **6g**, Carbohydrate **20g**, Fiber **2g**.

Steamed Apple Pudding

- Serves **4**
- Preparation Time **10 minutes**
- Cooking Time **1 hour 10 minutes**

$^1/_4$ cup molasses or honey

1 cup peeled, chopped apples

$^1/_4$ cup orange juice

1 tablespoon butter, melted

1 tablespoon grated orange zest

1 egg yolk

1 teaspoon vanilla extract

1 cup all-purpose flour

$^1/_2$ teaspoon baking powder

$^1/_4$ teaspoon baking soda

Vegetable oil cooking spray

1 In a saucepan, gently warm 2 tablespoons molasses. Add the apples and cook about 10 minutes.

2 In a bowl, mix remaining molasses, orange juice, butter, orange zest, egg yolk, and vanilla extract. In a large bowl, mix the flour, baking powder, and soda.

3 Add the egg and apple mixtures to the flour mixture.

4 Coat 4 custard dishes with vegetable oil spray and spoon in the batter. Cover the dishes with wax paper.

5 Place dishes on a trivet in a heavy saucepan over 1 inch of boiling water. Cover and steam over low heat for 1 hour.

PER SERVING
Calories **227**, Saturated Fat **2g**, Total Fat **5g**, Sodium **127mg**, Cholesterol **61mg**, Protein **4g**, Carbohydrate **43g**, Fiber **2g**.

Sweet Potato Pudding

- Serves **6**
- Preparation Time **15 minutes**
- Cooking Time **40–45 minutes**

2 eggs

2 cups mashed sweet potatoes, canned or fresh

$^3/_4$ cup evaporated skim milk

$^1/_2$ cup packed light brown sugar

2 tablespoons margarine or butter, melted

2 tablespoons rum or lemon juice

$^1/_8$ teaspoon each ground nutmeg, cinnamon, and ginger

4 egg whites

Vegetable oil cooking spray

Low-Fat Custard Sauce, page 325 (optional)

1 Preheat oven to 350°F. In a large mixing bowl, beat the eggs with the mashed sweet potatoes, evaporated skim milk, brown sugar, margarine, rum, and spices.

2 Whip egg whites until stiff peaks form and, using a large metal spoon, carefully fold into the sweet potato mixture.

3 Lightly coat a 1-quart casserole or soufflé dish with vegetable oil spray or vegetable oil. Transfer mixture to the casserole and bake for 40 to 45 minutes or until golden. Serve with custard sauce or low-fat ice cream if you like.

PER SERVING
Calories **260**, Saturated Fat **3g**, Total Fat **6g**, Sodium **203mg**, Cholesterol **82mg**, Protein **9g**, Carbohydrate **42g**, Fiber **2g**.

Apricot and Pear Compote

Cooking technique ■ *Simmering a combination of fruits together creates especially rich flavor. Add nuts or raisins for texture. Serve warm or at room temperature with cookies, low-fat ice cream, or frozen yogurt.*

Add nutrients ■ *Simmer the fruit in orange juice to add vitamins and reduce sugar.*

● Serves **4** ● Preparation Time **5 minutes plus cooling time** ● Cooking Time **15 minutes**

PER SERVING
Calories **171**, Saturated Fat **0g**,
Total Fat **1g**, Sodium **3mg**,
Cholesterol **0mg**, Protein **2g**,
Carbohydrate **43g**, Fiber **4g**.

1¹/₃ **cups orange juice**	**1 clove**
Finely grated zest and juice of 1 lemon	**8 fresh apricots, halved**
2 tablespoons honey	**2 firm but ripe pears, quartered**
2 teaspoons vanilla extract	**2 tablespoons raisins**

1 In a saucepan, combine orange juice, lemon zest and juice, honey, vanilla extract, and clove. Bring to a boil, then reduce heat and simmer for 5 minutes.

2 Add the apricots and pears and bring to a boil. Reduce the heat, cover, and simmer for 5 to 8 minutes or until the fruit is just tender.

3 Add the raisins, then remove the pan from the heat and allow to cool to room temperature in the syrup. Remove the clove before serving.

*Fruity, fiber-rich **Apricot and Pear Compote** is perfect for a light dessert.*

Tropical Fruit Compote

- Serves **4**
- Preparation Time **25 minutes** plus cooling time
- Cooking Time **6 minutes**

1¹/₃ cups pineapple or orange juice

Finely grated zest and juice of 1 lemon

2 tablespoons honey

2 tablespoons light rum or orange liqueur (optional)

¹/₂ teaspoon freshly grated ginger or ¹/₄ teaspoon ground

1 mango, peeled and pitted

1 papaya, peeled and seeded

2 kiwi fruit, peeled

3 cups cubed pineapple

1 In a medium saucepan, combine the pineapple juice, lemon zest and juice, honey, rum, and ginger, and bring to a boil over moderate heat. Boil for 1 minute.

2 Cut the mango and papaya into cubes. Slice the kiwi fruit.

3 Combine all the prepared fruit in a bowl, pour the syrup over the fruit and allow to cool to room temperature with the fruit.

PER SERVING
Calories **242**, Saturated Fat **0g**, Total Fat **1g**, Sodium **8mg**, Cholesterol **0mg**, Protein **2g**, Carbohydrate **58g**, Fiber **6g**.

Peach and Almond Compote

- Serves **4**
- Preparation Time **10 minutes** plus cooling time
- Cooking Time **25–30 minutes**

---

2 cups apple or orange juice

¹/₄ cup honey

1 tablespoon lemon juice

2 teaspoons finely grated orange zest

1 teaspoon almond extract

8 ounces dried peaches, halved

¹/₄ cup slivered almonds, toasted

1 tablespoon chopped fresh mint

1 In a medium saucepan, combine the apple juice, honey, lemon juice, orange zest, and almond extract. Bring to a boil over moderate heat, then reduce the heat and simmer for 5 minutes.

2 Add the peaches to the syrup, partially cover, and simmer 20 to 25 minutes.

3 Transfer to a serving bowl and allow the fruit to cool to room temperature in the syrup. Add the almonds and sprinkle with the mint before serving.

PER SERVING
Calories **311**, Saturated Fat **0g**, Total Fat **5g**, Sodium **12mg**, Cholesterol **0mg**, Protein **4g**, Carbohydrate **69g**, Fiber **6g**.

Dried Fruit Compote

- Serves **4**
- Preparation Time **10 minutes** plus cooling time
- Cooking Time **25–30 minutes**

---

2 cups orange juice

¹/₄ cup honey

1 teaspoon finely grated orange zest

1 teaspoon finely grated lemon zest

1 tablespoon lemon juice

Pinch each ground cloves and nutmeg

8 ounces mixed dried fruit such as prunes, apricots, apples, peaches

¹/₄ cup currants or raisins

Dried Fruit Compote contains plenty of fiber to aid digestion.

1 In a medium saucepan, combine orange juice, honey, orange and lemon zest, lemon juice, cloves, and nutmeg. Bring to a boil over moderate heat, then reduce the heat and simmer for 5 minutes.

2 Add the dried fruit and currants to the pan. Bring to a boil, then reduce the heat, cover, and simmer for 15 to 20 minutes or until fruit is very soft.

3 Transfer to a serving bowl and allow the fruit to cool to room temperature in the syrup.

PER SERVING
Calories **282**, Saturated Fat **0g**, Total Fat **1g**, Sodium **19mg**, Cholesterol **0mg**, Protein **3g**, Carbohydrate **76g**, Fiber **7g**.

Peach Cobbler

Reduce calories ■ *Sweeten the filling with fruit juice and preserves instead of sugar.*
Add nutrients ■ *Make the topping with whole-wheat flour and rolled oats.*

● Serves **6** ● Preparation Time **15 minutes** ● Cooking Time **25–30 minutes**

PER SERVING
Calories **190**, Saturated Fat **0g**,
Total Fat **1g**, Sodium **71mg**,
Cholesterol **36mg**, Protein **4g**,
Carbohydrate **42g**, Fiber **3g**.

¹/₄ cup peach nectar or water

¹/₄ cup peach or apricot preserves

1 tablespoon cornstarch

1 teaspoon lemon juice

2 cups frozen peaches, thawed and cubed

For the topping

¹/₃ cup whole-wheat flour

¹/₃ cup all-purpose flour

¹/₄ cup rolled oats

2 tablespoons brown sugar

1 teaspoon baking powder

¹/₄ teaspoon ground cinnamon

1 egg

¹/₄ cup 1% low-fat milk

1 Lightly grease an 8" x 8" x 2" baking dish. In a medium saucepan, combine the peach nectar, preserves, cornstarch, and lemon juice and stir until blended.

2 Stir in the peaches and cook over moderate heat for about 5 minutes, stirring constantly, until the mixture boils and thickens. Boil for 1 minute, stirring constantly. Remove from the heat and cover to keep warm.

*This golden brown **Peach Cobbler** is a more healthful version of the one Grandma used to make — but it tastes just as good.*

3 Preheat oven to 400°F. Make topping: In a medium mixing bowl, combine the flours, oats, brown sugar, baking powder, and cinnamon. Mix the egg and milk together in a cup and add to the flour mixture. Mix to form a soft, spoonable dough. Transfer the peach mixture to the baking dish.

4 Using a spoon, drop small portions of the dough over the peaches to make a "cobbled" effect. Bake 20 to 30 minutes or until bubbling, crisp, and golden.

COOKING TIP
If fresh peaches are in season, use 4 cups cubed ripe peaches, peeled and pitted, in this recipe.

Blueberry Oat Crumble

- Serves **6**
- Preparation time **15 minutes**
- Cooking time **25–30 minutes**

1/4 cup blueberry preserves or grape jelly

1 tablespoon cornstarch

1 teaspoon lemon juice

1/8 teaspoon ground nutmeg

4 cups blueberries, fresh or frozen and thawed

For the topping

1/3 cup whole-wheat flour

1/3 cup all-purpose flour

1/4 cup rolled oats

2 tablespoons brown sugar

1 teaspoon baking powder

1/4 teaspoon ground cinnamon

1 egg

1/4 cup 1% low-fat milk

1 Lightly grease an 8" x 8" x 2" baking dish. In a saucepan, combine preserves, cornstarch, lemon juice, and nutmeg. Stir until blended.

2 Stir in the blueberries and cook as in Step 2 of the master recipe.

3 Preheat oven to 400°F. Make the topping as in Step 3 of master recipe. Spoon filling into baking dish and top with dough as in Step 4 of master recipe.

4 Bake for 20 to 25 minutes or until bubbling and crisp.

PER SERVING
Calories **189**, Saturated Fat **0g**, Total Fat **2g**, Sodium **78mg**, Cholesterol **36mg**, Protein **4g**, Carbohydrate **41g**, Fiber **4g**.

Apple Raspberry Brown Betty

- Serves **4**
- Preparation time **30 minutes**
- Cooking time **30–35 minutes**

1/4 cup unsweetened apple juice

1/4 cup apple or currant jelly

1 tablespoon cornstarch

20 ounces apples, peeled, cored, and thinly sliced

1/3 cup currants

1 cup frozen raspberries, thawed

For the topping

1/4 cup rolled oats

3 tablespoons fresh bread crumbs

2 tablespoons brown sugar

1 tablespoon margarine or butter, melted

1/2 teaspoon ground cinnamon

1 Lightly grease an 8" x 8" x 2" baking dish. In a saucepan, combine apple juice, apple jelly, and cornstarch. Stir until blended.

2 Stir in apples and cook as in Step 2 of the master recipe for about 2 minutes. Boil for 1 minute, stirring constantly. Allow to cool. Spoon into baking dish.

3 Gently fold currants into mixture and layer raspberries on top.

4 Preheat oven to 400°F. In a bowl, combine the topping ingredients and mix well. Sprinkle over the fruit and bake for 25 to 30 minutes or until crisp.

PER SERVING
Calories **279**, Saturated Fat **1g**, Total Fat **4g**, Sodium **51mg**, Cholesterol **0mg**, Protein **2g**, Carbohydrate **63g**, Fiber **5g**.

Pear and Coconut Crisp

- Serves **6**
- Preparation time **30 minutes**
- Cooking time **30–35 minutes**

1/4 cup pineapple juice or water

1/4 cup pineapple or apricot preserves

1 tablespoon cornstarch

1 teaspoon rum extract

4 cups firm Bosc pears, cored and thinly sliced

For the topping

1/4 cup rolled oats

2 tablespoons brown sugar

2 tablespoons flaked coconut

2 tablespoons chopped walnuts or almonds

1 tablespoon margarine or butter, melted

1 Lightly grease an 8" x 8" x 2" baking dish. In a saucepan, combine pineapple juice, preserves, cornstarch, and rum extract.

2 Stir in pears and cook as in Step 2 of the master recipe for about 2 minutes. Boil for 1 minute, stirring constantly. Allow to cool. Spoon into baking dish.

3 Preheat oven to 400°F. Make the topping: In a bowl, combine all the topping ingredients and mix well. Sprinkle evenly over the fruit in the baking dish. Bake for 25 to 30 minutes or until bubbling and crisp.

PER SERVING
Calories **178**, Saturated Fat **1g**, Total Fat **5g**, Sodium **31mg**, Cholesterol **0mg**, Protein **1g**, Carbohydrate **34g**, Fiber **3g**.

Fresh Fruit Tart

Cooking technique ▪ _For a flaky crust, some shortening is necessary, but it has been reduced._

Add nutrients ▪ _Add oatmeal for fiber, then fill the shell with vitamin-rich fresh fruit._

- Serves **8** ● Preparation Time **25 minutes plus chilling time**
- Cooking Time **25–35 minutes**

PER SERVING

Calories **244**, Saturated Fat **3g**, Total Fat **10g**, Sodium **76mg**, Cholesterol **28mg**, Protein **5g**, Carbohydrate **35g**, Fiber **3g**.

For the dough

³/₄ cup all-purpose flour

2 tablespoons whole-wheat flour

¹/₄ cup rolled oats

¹/₂ teaspoon ground cinnamon

¹/₄ teaspoon ground nutmeg

3 tablespoons margarine or butter

3 tablespoons solid vegetable shortening

3–4 tablespoons 1% low-fat milk, ice cold

For the filling

1 egg

¹/₃ cup sugar

3 tablespoons cornstarch

1¹/₄ cups 1% low-fat milk

1¹/₄ teaspoons lemon juice

1 teaspoon vanilla extract

4–6 strawberries, sliced

³/₄ cup raspberries

³/₄ cup blueberries

1–2 kiwi fruit, peeled, quartered, and thinly sliced

2 tablespoons apple jelly

DECORATING THE EDGE OF A TART SHELL

Using a sharp knife or small cookie cutter, cut out leaf shapes from the pastry. Moisten edge of tart shell and press on leaves, overlapping slightly.

Roll out dough ¹/₈ inch thick and cut into strips ¹/₄-inch wide. Braid 3 strips and press lightly onto the moistened tart shell edge to cover.

1 In a bowl, mix the flours, oats, and spices. Add the margarine and vegetable shortening and cut in with a pastry blender or 2 knives until coarse crumbs form.

2 Add milk so that mixture forms a soft dough. Gently knead dough and shape into a ball; wrap in wax paper and refrigerate for 30 to 60 minutes.

3 Preheat oven to 425°F. On a lightly floured work surface, roll out dough to ¹/₈-inch thickness. Transfer to a 9-inch tart pan, press to line pan, and trim excess.

4 Cover bottom of shell with foil and fill with dried beans. Bake for 10 minutes or until pastry is set. Remove foil and beans and bake until golden. Allow to cool.

5 Remove shell from pan and place on a serving plate. In a bowl, lightly beat egg. In a small saucepan, blend sugar and cornstarch with a little milk.

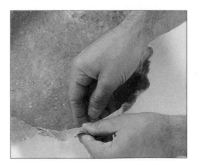

6 Stir in remaining milk and cook gently for 1 minute. Remove from the heat and slowly stir into egg. Return to pan and cook, stirring, for 2 to 3 minutes.

7 Remove from heat and stir in the lemon juice and vanilla extract. Let filling cool about 20 minutes, then pour into tart shell.

8 Divide the tart into eight sections and arrange the four fruits in sequence in the sections or, if preferred, scatter the fruit evenly over the whole tart.

9 Melt the apple jelly and brush over the fruit. Cut the tart into 8 wedges and serve.

*This beautiful **Fresh Fruit Tart** captures the best of summer's flavors. Serve it with a little nonfat yogurt if you like.*

Down-Home Cherry Pie

- Serves **10**
- Preparation Time **20 minutes** plus chilling time
- Cooking Time **50–60 minutes**

For the dough

1¹/₂ cups all-purpose flour

¹/₂ cup rolled oats

¹/₄ cup whole-wheat pastry flour or whole-wheat flour

2 tablespoons brown sugar

1 teaspoon ground cinnamon

¹/₂ teaspoon ground nutmeg

6 tablespoons margarine or butter

6 tablespoons solid vegetable shortening

4–5 tablespoons 1% low-fat milk, ice cold

For the filling

³/₄ cup sugar

¹/₄ cup cornstarch

2 cans (1 pound each) cherries, drained, 1 cup juice reserved

1 teaspoon cherry or almond extract

1 Using the dough ingredients, prepare the crust as in Steps 1 and 2 of the master recipe. Divide dough into 2 pieces, one slightly larger than the other. Wrap in wax paper and refrigerate for 30 to 60 minutes.

2 In a saucepan, combine the sugar, cornstarch, reserved juice, and cherry extract. Add the cherries and heat over low heat, stirring constantly, until the mixture boils and thickens. Boil for 3 minutes, then remove from the heat. Allow to cool slightly.

3 Preheat the oven to 425°F. On a lightly floured work surface, roll out the larger piece of dough to ¹/₈-inch thickness. Line a 9-inch pie pan, leaving the edge untrimmed. Transfer the cherry filling to the pie shell.

4 For top crust, roll out the remaining dough to ¹/₈-inch thickness. Cut a few slashes in the dough, then center it over the filling. Trim both edges with a sharp knife, then pinch top and bottom crusts together. Bake the pie for 40 to 50 minutes or until the pastry is golden brown.

PER SERVING
Calories **334**, Saturated Fat **3g**,
Total Fat **14g**, Sodium **83mg**,
Cholesterol **0mg**, Protein **3g**,
Carbohydrate **50g**, Fiber **2g**.

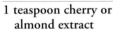
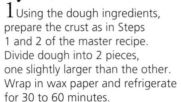

The flavor of nutmeg (top) will be better if you grind it yourself. Cinnamon sticks (below left) are the bark of the tree. They can also be ground into a powdered spice.

Cinnamon Peach Tart

- Serves **10**
- Preparation Time **30 minutes** plus chilling time
- Cooking Time **40–50 minutes**

For the dough

1¹/₂ cups all-purpose flour

¹/₂ cup whole-wheat pastry flour or whole-wheat flour

¹/₄ cup toasted wheat germ

2 tablespoons brown sugar

1 teaspoon ground cinnamon

¹/₂ teaspoon ground nutmeg

6 tablespoons margarine or butter

6 tablespoons solid vegetable shortening

4–5 tablespoons 1% low-fat milk, ice cold

For the filling

¹/₄ cup sugar plus 2 teaspoons for sprinkling

¹/₄ cup brown sugar

¹/₄ cup all-purpose flour

³/₄ teaspoon ground ginger

6 medium peaches, peeled, pitted, and sliced, or 3¹/₂ cups sliced peaches, frozen and thawed

1 teaspoon lemon juice

1 tablespoon 1% low-fat milk

1 Using the dough ingredients, prepare the crust as in Steps 1 and 2 of the master recipe and divide into 2 equal pieces. On a lightly floured work surface, roll out one piece of dough to ¹/₈-inch thickness. Line a 9-inch pie pan, leaving the edge untrimmed.

2 In a bowl, mix the sugars, flour, and ginger. Arrange peach halves in pie shell and sprinkle with lemon juice and flour-sugar mixture.

3 Preheat the oven to 425°F. Roll out the remaining dough into a circle 11 inches in diameter and cut into 9 strips of equal width. Arrange the strips over the tart in a lattice pattern.

4 Trim the edges and pinch to make a decorative edge. Brush dough with the milk. Bake for 50 minutes, until the crust is golden. Sprinkle with 2 teaspoons sugar and serve warm or cold.

PER SERVING
Calories **300**, Saturated Fat **3g**,
Total Fat **14g**, Sodium **73mg**,
Cholesterol **0mg**, Protein **4g**,
Carbohydrate **34g**, Fiber **4g**.

MAKING A LATTICE

Roll out the dough into a circle about 2 inches larger than your pie pan and cut into strips of equal width. Place half of the strips of dough ³/₄ inch apart over the filling, and press each end of the strip to seal. Place the remaining strips across the first, at an angle, to form a lattice design, then seal the ends as before.

Lemon-Coconut Meringue Pie

*Tart and summery lemon pie is naturally low in fat —
this one is also very low in calories. Use freshly squeezed
lemon juice for the best flavor.*

- Serves **8**
- Preparation Time **20 minutes plus chilling time**
- Cooking Time **40 minutes**

For the dough

³/₄ **cup all-purpose flour**

¹/₄ **cup whole-wheat pastry flour
or whole-wheat flour**

¹/₄ **cup sweetened flaked
coconut**

3 tablespoons canola oil

**1 tablespoon margarine or
butter, melted**

**2 tablespoons 1% low-fat milk,
ice cold**

For the filling

1 egg yolk

1¹/₂ cups water

1 cup sugar

6 tablespoons cornstarch

¹/₃ **cup lemon juice**

**1 tablespoon finely grated
lemon zest**

**1 tablespoon margarine or
butter**

For the topping

3 egg whites

2 tablespoons sugar

1 Using dough ingredients, prepare crust as in Steps 1 and 2 of master recipe. Preheat oven to 425°F. On a lightly floured work surface, roll out dough and line a 9-inch tart pan. Cover bottom of shell with aluminium foil and fill with dried beans or rice and bake for 10 minutes. Remove foil and beans and continue to bake until golden. Cool for 10 minutes.

2 Meanwhile make the filling: In a bowl, beat the egg yolk and the 1¹/₂ cups water together. In a small pan, blend the sugar and cornstarch. Slowly whisk the egg mixture into the cornstarch.

3 Cook over moderate heat, stirring constantly, until boiling. Cook, stirring, for 1 minute; the mixture will be very thick. Add the lemon juice and zest; mix until smooth. Add butter and stir until it melts. Cool for about 5 minutes.

4 Lower oven temperature to 350°F. Make topping: Using a hand-held mixer, whip egg whites until foamy; gradually add sugar and whip until stiff peaks form.

5 Carefully remove the pie shell from the pan and place on a baking sheet. Fill the shell with the lemon filling. Spoon the whipped egg whites on top to cover the filling. Spread the egg whites out to the edges of the shell, taking care not to flatten them (see box, below).

6 Bake for 15 to 20 minutes or until light golden brown. Cool on a rack and serve chilled.

*The whole
family will love
Lemon-Coconut
Meringue Pie.*

PER SERVING
Calories **270**, Saturated Fat **2g**,
Total Fat **9g**, Sodium **54mg**,
Cholesterol **27mg**, Protein **3g**,
Carbohydrate **45g**, Fiber **1g**.

WHISKING EGG WHITES AND COVERING THE PIE

1 *Whip the egg whites until
soft peaks form.*

2 *Add the sugar. Continue
whipping the egg whites
until stiff peaks form.*

3 *Spoon the whipped egg
whites over the top of the
lemon filling, spreading out
gently so that the peaks
do not become flattened.*

Fruit Upside-Down Cake

Reduce fat ■ *Apple juice and nonfat yogurt replace the butter in these moist cakes.*

● Serves **8** ● Preparation Time **25 minutes** ● Cooking Time **40–50 minutes**

PER SERVING
Calories **313**, Saturated Fat **1g**, Total Fat **8g**, Sodium **194mg**, Cholesterol **27mg**, Protein **7g**, Carbohydrate **55g**, Fiber **2g**.

For the topping

2 tablespoons brown sugar

8 ounces plums, sliced

8 ounces cherries, pitted

For the batter

2 cups all-purpose flour

1 teaspoon each baking powder and baking soda

1¹/₂ teaspoons ground ginger

3 egg whites

1 egg yolk

¹/₂ cup frozen apple juice concentrate, thawed

¹/₄ cup canola oil

¹/₄ cup honey

1 teaspoon vanilla extract

1 cup plain nonfat yogurt

1 For the topping, lightly grease a 9-inch round nonstick cake pan. Sprinkle brown sugar over the bottom of the pan. Line the pan with the plums and cherries.

2 Preheat the oven to 350°F. Make the batter: In a medium bowl, combine flour, baking powder, baking soda, and ginger.

3 In another bowl, using an electric mixer or whisk, beat egg whites until soft peaks form. Gently stir in egg yolk, juice concentrate, oil, honey, and vanilla.

*For special occasions, serve **Fruit Upside-Down Cake** with Low-Fat Custard Sauce, page 325.*

4 Gently fold in approximately one-third of flour mixture, followed by one-third of yogurt. Repeat until all the flour and yogurt are incorporated.

5 Pour the batter over the fruit and bake for 40 to 50 minutes or until well risen.

6 Allow the cake to rest in the pan for 10 minutes. Then carefully turn out upside down onto a serving plate. Serve warm.

Apricot and Almond Upside-Down Cake

- Serves **8**
- Preparation Time **20 minutes**
- Cooking Time **40–50 minutes**

For the topping

2 tablespoons brown sugar

1 pound fresh apricots, halved and pitted, or 8 ounces dried apricots, soaked for 8 hours

¹/₃ cup blanched whole almonds

Finely grated zest of 1 lemon

For the batter

2 cups all-purpose flour

1 teaspoon each baking powder and baking soda

1 teaspoon each ground ginger and cinnamon

3 egg whites

1 egg yolk

¹/₂ cup frozen apple juice concentrate, thawed

¹/₄ cup canola oil

¹/₄ cup honey

1 teaspoon vanilla extract

1 cup plain nonfat yogurt

1 Preheat the oven to 350°F. Prepare the cake pan and line with apricots as in Step 1 of the master recipe. If using dried apricots, drain and pat dry before using. Sprinkle the apricots with the blanched almonds and lemon zest.

2 Using the batter ingredients, make the batter as in Steps 2 to 4 of the master recipe.

3 Pour the batter over the apricots and bake for 45 to 50 minutes or until well risen. Let rest in the pan for 10 minutes, then carefully turn out upside down onto a serving plate. Serve warm.

PER SERVING
Calories **354**, Saturated Fat **1g**, Total Fat **11g**, Sodium **189mg**, Cholesterol **27mg**, Protein **9g**, Carbohydrate **54g**, Fiber **3g**.

French Apple Cake

- Serves **8**
- Preparation Time **20 minutes**
- Cooking Time **50–60 minutes**

For the topping

2 tablespoons margarine or butter

1 tablespoon honey

1 tablespoon brown sugar

4 apples, peeled, cored, and cut into 8 wedges

1 teaspoon solid vegetable shortening

¹/₃ cup currants or raisins

For the batter

2 cups all-purpose flour

1 teaspoon each baking powder and baking soda

1 teaspoon each ground ginger and cinnamon

3 egg whites

1 egg yolk

¹/₂ cup frozen apple juice concentrate, thawed

¹/₄ cup canola oil

¹/₄ cup honey

1 teaspoon vanilla extract

1 cup plain nonfat yogurt

1 Preheat the oven to 350°F. In a large nonstick skillet, melt the margarine over moderate heat. Stir in the honey and brown sugar and cook until sugar is dissolved. Add apples and cook, stirring frequently, about 10 minutes or until just tender. With the shortening, lightly grease a 9-inch cake pan. Spoon apples into pan and sprinkle currants on top.

2 Using the batter ingredients, make the batter as in Steps 2 to 4 of the master recipe. Pour the batter over the apples and bake for 40 to 50 minutes or until well risen.

3 Cool in the pan for 10 minutes, then turn out upside down onto a serving plate. Take care when turning out because the tart will be very juicy. Serve warm or cold.

PER SERVING
Calories **358**, Saturated Fat **1g**, Total Fat **11g**, Sodium **216mg**, Cholesterol **27mg**, Protein **7g**, Carbohydrate **60g**, Fiber **3g**.

Italian Biscotti

Cooking technique ■ *These crisp cookies are baked twice. First you make a log and bake until firm. Then slice the log into individual cookies and bake again.*

Reduce fat ■ *Biscotti are made with just 2 eggs and no shortening, so there's virtually no saturated fat.*

● Makes **20** ● Preparation Time **15 minutes** ● Cooking Time **45–50 minutes**

PER BISCUIT
Calories **120**, Saturated Fat **0g**, Total Fat **1g**, Sodium **12mg**, Cholesterol **21mg**, Protein **3g**, Carbohydrate **25g**, Fiber **0g**.

Vegetable oil cooking spray	2 egg whites
2¹/₂ cups all-purpose flour	1 tablespoon canola oil
1¹/₄ cups sugar	2 teaspoons anise or vanilla extract
2 large eggs	

1 Preheat oven to 350°F. Lightly coat a 15¹/₂- by 10¹/₂-inch jelly roll pan with vegetable oil cooking spray and dust with flour.

2 In a medium bowl, combine flour and sugar. In a small bowl, lightly beat the eggs, egg whites, oil, and anise extract. Using a rubber spatula, stir the egg mixture into the dry ingredients until a dough is formed.

Italian Biscotti are perfect for dipping into dessert wine or coffee.

3 Using the rubber spatula, transfer the dough onto the pan. Wet the spatula with water and shape the dough into a log about 15 by 3 inches.

4 Bake for 30 to 35 minutes, after which time the log will have flattened considerably. Remove from oven and cut crosswise into ³/₄-inch slices. Place the slices on a clean baking sheet and continue to bake for 15 minutes or until lightly crisp. Remove from oven and place biscotti on a wire rack to cool.

Chocolate Biscotti

- Makes **20**
- Preparation Time **30 minutes**
- Cooking Time **50–55 minutes**

Vegetable oil cooking spray

2 cups all-purpose flour

1¹/₄ cups sugar

¹/₄ cup cocoa powder

2 large eggs

2 egg whites

1 tablespoon canola oil

2 teaspoons finely grated orange zest

1 teaspoon each orange and vanilla extract

¹/₂ cup semisweet chocolate chips

1 Preheat oven and prepare jelly roll pan as in Step 1 of the master recipe.

2 In a bowl, combine flour, sugar, and cocoa. In a small bowl, lightly beat eggs, egg whites, oil, orange zest, and both extracts. Stir egg mixture into dry ingredients to form a dough.

3 Shape and bake the dough as in Steps 3 and 4 of master recipe.

4 Using a double boiler or in the microwave oven, melt the chocolate chips. Spread chocolate on each biscotti. Return them to the rack and allow chocolate to harden before serving, or cool in the refrigerator.

PER BISCUIT
Calories **145**, Saturated Fat **1g**,
Total Fat **3g**, Sodium **20mg**,
Cholesterol **21mg**, Protein **3g**,
Carbohydrate **28g**, Fiber **1g**.

Cappuccino Biscotti

- Makes **20**
- Preparation Time **25 minutes**
- Cooking Time **45–50 minutes**

Vegetable oil cooking spray

2¹/₂ cups all-purpose flour

1¹/₄ cups sugar

¹/₄ cup freeze-dried instant coffee

2 large eggs

2 egg whites

1 tablespoon canola oil

2 teaspoons vanilla extract

²/₃ cup confectioners sugar

2 tablespoons 1% low-fat milk

³/₄ teaspoon ground cinnamon

³/₄ teaspoon brown sugar

1 Preheat oven and prepare jelly roll pan as in Step 1 of the master recipe.

2 In a bowl, combine flour, sugar, and coffee. In a small bowl, lightly beat eggs, egg whites, oil, and vanilla extract. Stir egg mixture into dry ingredients to form a dough.

3 Shape and bake dough as in Steps 3 and 4 of master recipe, placing wire rack on wax paper.

4 In a bowl, blend confectioners sugar and milk. Drizzle icing on each biscotti. Mix cinnamon and brown sugar and sprinkle on each biscotti. Allow icing to dry.

PER BISCUIT
Calories **139**, Saturated Fat **0g**,
Total Fat **1g**, Sodium **13mg**,
Cholesterol **21mg**, Protein **3g**,
Carbohydrate **29g**, Fiber **0g**.

Nut and Spice Biscotti

- Makes **20**
- Preparation Time **25 minutes**
- Cooking Time **45–50 minutes**

Vegetable oil cooking spray

2¹/₂ cups all-purpose flour

²/₃ cup sugar

²/₃ cup packed dark brown sugar

¹/₂ cup chopped walnuts, toasted

¹/₄ cup dried currants

1¹/₂ teaspoons apple-pie spice

2 large eggs

2 egg whites

1 tablespoon canola oil

2 teaspoons vanilla extract

²/₃ cup confectioners sugar

1¹/₂ tablespoons 1% low-fat milk

1 teaspoon maple extract

1 Preheat oven and prepare jelly roll pan as in Step 1 of the master recipe.

2 In a bowl, combine flour, sugar, brown sugar, walnuts, currants, and apple-pie spice. In a small bowl, lightly beat eggs, egg whites, oil, and vanilla extract. Stir egg mixture into dry ingredients to form a dough.

3 Shape and bake dough as in Steps 3 and 4 of master recipe, placing wire rack on wax paper.

4 Blend confectioners sugar, milk, and maple extract. Drizzle on each biscotti; allow to dry.

PER BISCUIT
Calories **166**, Saturated Fat **0g**,
Total Fat **3g**, Sodium **15mg**,
Cholesterol **21mg**, Protein **3g**,
Carbohydrate **32g**, Fiber **1g**.

Raspberry Dessert Sauce with Cantaloupe

Cooking technique ▪ *Purée fresh fruit and flavorings. For a creamy sauce, blend in a low-fat cheese such as ricotta. Serve over fruit, yogurt, or angel cake.*

● Serves **4** ● Preparation Time **20 minutes**

PER SERVING
Calories **135**, Saturated Fat **0g**, Total Fat **1g**, Sodium **16mg**, Cholesterol **0mg**, Protein **2g**, Carbohydrate **33g**, Fiber **7g**.

1 package (12 ounces) frozen raspberries	**2 tablespoons honey**
1 teaspoon lemon juice	**1 medium cantaloupe**
	Fresh mint leaves

1 Reserve a few raspberries for garnish and keep them frozen. In a food processor or blender, purée the remaining raspberries until smooth. Strain the purée through a medium-fine sieve.

2 Add fresh lemon juice and honey to the raspberry purée and stir to mix well. Set aside.

Raspberry Dessert Sauce with Cantaloupe has all the color and goodness of fresh fruit. And it takes just minutes to prepare.

3 Cut the cantaloupe into quarters and remove the seeds and rind. Using a sharp knife, slice each quarter lengthwise without cutting completely through. Open out each quarter into a fan shape.

COOKING TIP

To check a melon for ripeness, push the stalk end in slightly, using light pressure. There will be a fragrant aroma if ripe.

4 Spread a quarter of the raspberry purée on the center of four 10-inch plates. Place a cantaloupe fan on each plate and decorate with fresh mint leaves and the reserved raspberries.

Ginger Cream Sauce with Grapes

This lightly spiced sauce also works well over fresh raspberries or pears.

- Serves **4**
- Preparation Time **20 minutes**

---

2 ounces Neufchâtel cheese, softened

$1/4$ cup plain nonfat yogurt

$1/4$ cup frozen apple juice concentrate, thawed

$1/8$ teaspoon ground ginger

2 cups green grapes

2 cups red grapes or blueberries

COOKING TIP

To vary the flavor of this sauce, substitute grape juice and ground cinnamon for the apple juice and ginger.

---

1 In a food processor or blender, process the Neufchâtel cheese, yogurt, apple juice concentrate, and ginger until smooth.

2 Divide the grapes among 4 parfait glasses and spoon equal amounts of the sauce over each.

PER SERVING
Calories **144**, Saturated Fat **2g**, Total Fat **4g**, Sodium **77mg**, Cholesterol **11mg**, Protein **3g**, Carbohydrate **27g**, Fiber **2g**.

Berry Cheese Sauce with Nectarines

For an exceptionally delicious sauce, make this recipe with a combination of berries.

- Serves **4**
- Preparation Time **20 minutes**

$3/4$ cup part-skim ricotta cheese

2 tablespoons confectioners sugar

$3/4$ cup ripe strawberries, raspberries, or pitted cherries or a combination

$1/4$ teaspoon vanilla extract

4 nectarines or peaches, peeled, halved, and pitted

4 large strawberries, sliced, for decoration

---

1 In a food processor or blender, process the part-skim ricotta cheese with the confectioners sugar until smooth.

2 Add the strawberries, raspberries, or cherries with the vanilla extract and purée until a smooth sauce is formed.

3 Place nectarine halves, cut side down, on a plate. Spoon the sauce over the fruit and decorate with the sliced strawberries. Either chill or serve immediately.

PER SERVING
Calories **160**, Saturated Fat **2g**, Total Fat **4g**, Sodium **58mg**, Cholesterol **14mg**, Protein **7g**, Carbohydrate **25g**, Fiber **3g**.

Cranberry Maple Sauce with Apples

- Serves **4**
- Preparation Time **5 minutes**
- Cooking Time **20 minutes**

---

4 large apples

2 cups frozen cranberries, thawed

1 cup orange juice

Finely grated zest of 1 lemon

$1/4$ cup chopped nuts

2 tablespoons maple syrup

COOKING TIP

To serve with pears, peel, halve, and core 4 pears. Place in $1/2$ inch of boiling water in a large skillet. Cook 20 minutes or until tender.

---

1 Core the apples and, using a sharp knife, make a cut through the skin around the center of each. Place in a microwave-safe baking dish, add 1 cup of water, and cook in the microwave on high for 7 to 9 minutes or until tender.

2 In a saucepan, combine the cranberries, orange juice, and lemon zest. Bring to a boil and simmer gently for 3 to 4 minutes or until the cranberries pop.

3 Remove the pan from the heat and stir in the chopped nuts and maple syrup. Pour the sauce over the apples and serve.

PER SERVING
Calories **235**, Saturated Fat **1g**, Total Fat **5g**, Sodium **10mg**, Cholesterol **0mg**, Protein **2g**, Carbohydrate **49g**, Fiber **7g**.

Lemon-Walnut Frozen Yogurt

Cooking technique ■ *This scrumptious collection of frozen yogurts requires an ice cream maker. Follow the manufacturer's instructions for proper freezing. Serve them on their own or as a low-fat topping for cakes and pies.*

Add nutrients ■ *Frozen yogurt adds protein to your meal — 4 to 7 grams per serving.*

● Serves **6** ● Preparation Time **20 minutes plus freezing time** ● Cooking Time **2 minutes**

PER SERVING
Calories **174**, Saturated Fat **1g**, Total Fat **7g**, Sodium **54mg**, Cholesterol **2mg**, Protein **6g**, Carbohydrate **25g**, Fiber **1g**.

1 envelope unflavored gelatin
³⁄₄ cup 1% low-fat milk
¹⁄₂ cup sugar
1¹⁄₄ cups plain nonfat yogurt

¹⁄₄ cup lemon juice
Finely grated zest of 1 lemon
¹⁄₂ cup coarsely chopped walnuts or pistachios

1 In a saucepan, sprinkle gelatin over milk and let stand for 1 minute. Stir in sugar and set over moderately low heat, stirring, about 2 minutes, until dissolved.

2 Allow to cool until thickened, stirring occasionally. Transfer mixture to a large bowl and whisk in yogurt, lemon juice, and zest.

3 Stir in the walnuts and freeze the mixture in an ice cream maker.

Lemon-Walnut Frozen Yogurt — the most refreshing dessert you can imagine.

Strawberry Frozen Yogurt

Try adding a little kirsch liqueur to this recipe. It will impart a subtle cherry flavor.

- Serves **8**
- Preparation time **20 minutes** plus freezing time
- Cooking time **2 minutes**

---

1 envelope unflavored gelatin

1 cup 1% low-fat milk

¹/₃ cup sugar

1¹/₄ cups plain nonfat yogurt

1 cup sliced strawberries, fresh or frozen and thawed

1 tablespoon kirsch (optional)

> ### COOKING TIP
> *Sprinkle gelatin onto liquid, never the other way round. Always give gelatin a few minutes to swell before heating.*

1 Dissolve the gelatin as in Step 1 of the master recipe.

2 Transfer the mixture to a large bowl and whisk in the yogurt. Fold in the strawberries and kirsch, if using.

3 Freeze in an ice cream maker.

PER SERVING
Calories **76**, Saturated Fat **0g**, Total Fat **0g**, Sodium **44mg**, Cholesterol **2mg**, Protein **4g**, Carbohydrate **14g**, Fiber **1g**.

Chocolate Buttermilk Frozen Yogurt

- Serves **8**
- Preparation Time **20 minutes** plus freezing time
- Cooking Time **2 minutes**

---

1 envelope unflavored gelatin

³/₄ cup buttermilk

¹/₂ cup light brown sugar

1¹/₄ cups nonfat plain yogurt

¹/₂ cup evaporated skim milk, chilled

1¹/₂ tablespoons unsweetened cocoa powder

¹/₄ teaspoon ground cinnamon

> ### COOKING TIP
> *Evaporated skim milk must always be chilled before it can be whipped.*

1 Dissolve gelatin as in Step 1 of the master recipe, using buttermilk in place of low-fat milk.

2 Transfer gelatin mixture to a bowl. Whisk in yogurt. Whip evaporated skim milk until soft peaks form, then fold into yogurt mixture. Sift cocoa powder and cinnamon. Add to yogurt mixture.

3 Freeze in an ice cream maker.

PER SERVING
Calories **99**, Saturated Fat **0g**, Total Fat **0g**, Sodium **75mg**, Cholesterol **2mg**, Protein **5g**, Carbohydrate **19g**, Fiber **0g**.

Apple-Pumpkin Frozen Yogurt

Here's a tasty twist on pumpkin pie, and a nutritious one. Pumpkin is rich in vitamin A, beta carotene, and potassium.

- Serves **8**
- Preparation Time **20 minutes** plus freezing time
- Cooking Time **2 minutes**

---

1 envelope unflavored gelatin

¹/₂ cup frozen apple juice concentrate, thawed

¹/₃ cup light brown sugar

¹/₂ cup evaporated skim milk, chilled

1¹/₄ cups nonfat plain yogurt

1¹/₄ cups canned pumpkin

¹/₂ teaspoon apple-pie spice

---

1 Dissolve gelatin as in Step 1 of the master recipe, substituting apple juice concentrate for the low-fat milk.

2 While the gelatin mixture is cooling, whip the evaporated skim milk until soft peaks form.

3 Stir yogurt, pumpkin, and apple-pie spice into cooled gelatin mixture. Add yogurt mixture to whipped evaporated skim milk and beat for 1 minute.

4 Freeze in an ice cream maker.

PER SERVING
Calories **111**, Saturated Fat **0g**, Total Fat **0g**, Sodium **55mg**, Cholesterol **1mg**, Protein **4g**, Carbohydrate **24g**, Fiber **1g**.

The clean, fresh taste of **Apple-Pumpkin Frozen Yogurt** *is perfect after a hearty meal.*

Index